IT and Accounting

The Chapman & Hall Series in Accounting and Finance

Consulting editors
John Perrin, Emeritus Professor of the University of Warwick and Price Waterhouse Fellow in Public Sector Accounting at the University of Exeter; Richard M. S. Wilson, Professor of Management Control in the School of Finance and Information at the Queen's University of Belfast and L. C. L. Skerratt, Professor of Financial Accounting at the University of Manchester.

H. M. Coombs and D. E. Jenkins
Public Sector Financial Management

J. C. Drury
Management and Cost Accounting (2nd edn)
(Also available: **Students' Manual, Teachers' Manual**)

C. R. Emmanuel, D. T. Otley and K. Merchant
Accounting for Management Control (2nd edn)
(Also available: **Teachers' Manual**)

C. R. Emmanuel, D. T. Otley and K. Merchant (editors)
Readings in Accounting for Management Control

D. Henley, C. Holtham, A. Likierman and J. Perrin
Public Sector Accounting and Financial Control (3rd edn)

R. C. Laughlin and R. H. Gray
Financial Accounting: method and meaning
(Also available: **Teachers' Guide**)

G. A. Lee
Modern Financial Accounting (4th edn)
(Also available: **Solutions Manual**)

T. A. Lee
Income and Value Measurement (3rd edn)

T. A. Lee
Company Financial Reporting (2nd edn)

T. A. Lee
Cash Flow Accounting

S. P. Lumby
Investment Appraisal and Financing Decisions (4th edn)
(Also available: **Students' Manual**)

A. G. Puxty and J. C. Dodds
Financial Management: method and meaning (2nd edn)
(Also available: **Teachers' Guide**)

J. M. Samuels, F. M. Wilkes and R. E. Brayshaw
Management of Company Finance (5th edn)
(Also available: **Students' Manual**)

B. C. Williams and B. J. Spaul
IT and Accounting: The impact of information technology

R. M. S. Wilson and Wai Fong Chua
Managerial Accounting: method and meaning
(Also available: **Teachers' Guide**)

IT AND ACCOUNTING
The impact of information technology

Edited by Bernard C. Williams,

School of Information Systems,
University of East Anglia

and

Barry J. Spaul,

Department of Economics,
Exeter University

CHAPMAN & HALL
University and Professional Division
London · New York · Tokyo · Melbourne · Madras

Published by Chapman & Hall, 2-6 Boundary Row, London SE1 8HN, UK

Chapman & Hall, 2-6 Boundary Row, London SE1 8HN, UK

Blackie Academic & Professional, Wester Cleddens Road, Bishopbriggs, Glasgow G64 2NZ, UK

Chapman & Hall Inc., One Penn Plaza, 41st Floor, New York, NY10119, USA

Chapman & Hall Japan, Thomson Publishing Japan, Hirakawacho Nemoto Building, 6F, 1-7-11 Hirakawa-cho, Chiyoda-ku, Tokyo 102, Japan

Chapman & Hall Australia, Thomas Nelson Australia, 102 Dodds Street, South Melbourne, Victoria 3205, Australia

Chapman & Hall India, R. Seshadri, 32 Second Main Road, CIT East, Madras 600 035, India

First edition 1991
Reprinted 1994

© 1991 Chapman & Hall

Typeset in 10/12 pt Times by J&L Composition Ltd, Filey, North Yorkshire
Printed in Great Britain by Antony Rowe Ltd

ISBN   0 412 39210 0

A Catalogue record for this book is available from the British Library

Library of Congress Cataloging-in-Publication Data available

Contents

Acknowledgements   xiii
List of contributors   xiv
Preface   xvii

**1 The impact of IT on basic accounting concepts and accountancy
education: an overview**   1
Bernard C. Williams
Introduction   1
Using computers in accounting education: a context-free approach   2
Using computers in accounting education: an in-context approach   5
The implications of a contextual approach to the use of computers
in accounting education   13
Concluding remarks   14
References   14

PART ONE ECONOMICS

2 The impact of IT on the economy   21
Peter Monk
Introduction – what is IT?   21
Production and productivity   22
Automation and the labour market   25
IT innovation and economic change   27
Towards the information economy   28
Discussion questions   31
References   31

3 The information economics approach to financial reporting   32
Martin Walker
Introduction   32
The analytical method   32
Basic principles of neoclassical information economics   33
Single person decision analysis   35
The value of public information in a social context   38

Some unresolved issues   48
Concluding remarks   52
Supplement – notes on information economics and organizational
design   53
References   55

4 **Economic theories of information: a critique**   60
  Shaun Hargreaves Heap and Yanis Varoufakis
  Introduction   60
  Search theory and Bayes' rule   61
  Rational expectations and game theory   65
  Desires and belief   72
  Summary   73
  Notes   74
  Further reading   75
  Discussion questions   76

PART TWO FINANCE

5 **The behaviour of the stock market under the influence of IT**   79
  David Ayling
  Introduction   79
  Background developments   80
  Dealing and settlements – what the system must cope with   82
  How the system has coped since Big Bang   87
  Paperless settlement   88
  A Euro-Bourse?   89
  The stock exchange of the future   89
  Further reading   90
  Discussion questions   90

6 **What is the payoff from end-user computing – evidence accumulating
  from the USA and UK**   91
  Richard Price
  Discussion questions   98

7 **Computerization at the Trustee Savings Bank**   99
  Paul Willman and Mark Holding
  Introduction   99
  Information technology in banking   100
  The history of the TSB   101
  The move to on-line, real-time   103

System developments in the 1980s   111
Conclusion   117
Acknowledgement   119
Notes   119
Appendix: chronology   121

PART THREE FINANCIAL ACCOUNTING

8 The development of matrix-based accounting   127
Stewart A. Leech and Michael J. Mepham
Introduction   127
Problems with matrix accounting   132
An integrated matrix-based accounting system   133
Relational database systems and the matrix model   140
The canonical accounting model   142
Conclusion   143
Notes   144
Further reading   144
Discussion questions   145
References   145

9 An 'events' approach to basic accounting theory   149
George H. Sorter
Two views – value and events   150
Some consequences of an events approach   153
A Statement of Basic Accounting Theory and the events theory   155
Conclusion   157
Notes   158

10 Database accounting systems   159
Guido Geerts and William E. McCarthy
An alternative view of accounting representation   160
Conceptual schemas of business enterprises   161
Ingredients of a NIAM conceptual schema   162
The book-keeping approach to accounting vs an REA semantic
model   169
An extended REA example   175
Conclusions and discussion   179
Discussion questions and exercises   181
Acknowledgement   181
References   182

PART FOUR MANAGEMENT ACCOUNTING

11 Management accounting and information technology 187
Alan Gregory
Introduction 187
Information technology changes 188
The likely impact of information technology changes on
management accounting 190
A brief review of the empirical evidence to date 197
Conclusions 199
Notes 200
References 201

12 The spreadsheet revolution and its impact on the budgeting process 203
Joan Ballantine
Introduction 203
Popularization of the concept 205
Budgetary applications of spreadsheets 205
Organizational and behavioural impacts 208
Some advantages in using spreadsheets 209
Some pitfalls or dangers of spreadsheets 210
Recent enhancements 212
Concluding remarks 213
Further reading 214
Discussion questions 214

13 Using computers as management tools 216
Paul Collier
Introduction 216
Historical perspective 217
Management activities 218
Electronic data processing 218
Management information system 219
Decision support systems 220
Executive support systems 223
Office information systems 224
Expert systems 226
A taxonomy of computers as management tools 227
Conclusion 230
Further reading 230
Discussion questions 230
References 231

PART FIVE TAX AND LAW

14 The evidential status of computer output and communications   235
  Robert Bradgate
  Introduction   235
  The legal status of computer evidence   236
  The conditions for admissibility   242
  What is special about computer evidence?   246
  The approach in other jurisdictions   248
  Conclusion   249
  Notes   250
  References   250

15 Professional negligence and the reasonableness defence in
financial-legal expert systems: a developers' perspective   252
  Vijay Mital and Les Johnson
  Introduction   253
  Liability for errors of reasoning in financial-legal ES   254
  The reasonableness test   256
  Testing a financial-legal knowledge base for reasonableness   258
  Conceptual structures significant to reasonableness   262
  Implications of not modelling significant conceptual structures   264
  Conclusions   265
  Notes   265
  Discussion questions   266
  References   267

16 Building competencies: the computerization of PAYE   270
  Romano Dyerson and Michael Roper
  Introduction   270
  Background   271
  COP and its objectives   274
  Project management   283
  Strategy issues   288
  Conclusion   292
  Notes   294
  References   297

PART SIX QUANTITATIVE METHODS

17 Operational research and information technology – impacts and
interactions   301
  Valerie Belton
  Introduction – the changing face of OR   301

OR and computers   302
The impact of IT on OR   303
OR contributions to decision support   304
Reflections on the impact of IT on OR – out of the backroom?   311
The future   312
Summary   313
Note   314
Discussion questions   314
References   314

18 Financial modelling – use or abuse   317
Robert H. Berry and Alyson J. McLintock
Introduction   317
The financial modelling process   318
Financial modelling and the computer   321
Modelling and the micro   322
The accountant as model builder   325
An appropriate modelling process   328
Discussion questions   330
References   330

19 Technology in qualitative research: an overview   332
Bryan Pfaffenberger
Introduction   332
The need for a critical perspective   334
Why microcomputers?   340
References   343

PART SEVEN BUSINESS ORGANIZATION AND POLICY

20 New technology and developments in management organization   351
John Child
Introduction   351
Relevance of changes at the operational level   353
Management structure   358
Discussion   360
Discussion questions   363
References   364

21 The networked firm   366
John Taylor and Howard Williams
Introduction   366

Background 367
The networked firm 368
The adoption of computer networks 371
Computer networks: case study examples 375
Conclusions 379
Note 380
Further reading 380
References 380

22 The impact of information technology on small businesses and entrepreneurs 382
Nigel Bryant and Robert Lambert
The changing contribution of IT to small businesses 382
Typical applications in a small business 384
A systematic approach to identifying potential applications in a small business 388
Successfully incorporating information technology into a small business's operations 391
Conclusion 394
Further reading 395
Discussion questions 395

PART EIGHT SPECIAL TOPICS

23 Artificial intelligence and accounting 401
Nigel A. D. Connell
Introduction 401
What is artificial intelligence? 402
The influence of the Japanese Fifth Generation project 403
Expert systems 404
The professional accountant and expert systems 406
Expert systems research in accountancy 408
Future developments in expert systems for the accounting profession 411
Conclusions 413
Discussion questions 414
References 415

24 Computer crime 418
Barry J. Spaul
Introduction 418
Police or privacy? 419
The techniques 420

Computers – what are the extra worries?   421
The latest trends in fraud   422
Strategies to fight computer crime   423
Conclusions   426
Discussion questions   427
References   427

25 Auditing and computers   429
John M. Court and Nicki J. Muggridge
Introduction   429
Hardware-based developments   432
The effects of hardware-based developments on the auditor   435
Intelligent knowledge-based systems   436
The effects of knowledge-based systems on the auditor   437
Communications and networking   438
The effects of improved networks and EDI on the auditor   440
Conclusions   441
Further reading   443
Discussion questions   443

**26 Computers in accounting and education: how the changing role of
accountants could be reflected in courses**   445
Edwin M. Wildey
Introduction   445
Historical development   446
The business and technological environment   448
Implications for accounting education   450
A proposed course outline   455
An integrated software suite   457
Conclusion   461
References   462

Index   466

Acknowledgements

We would like to thank all the authors who have contributed to this volume, many of whom may not know each other as they work in the various and diverse subject areas that comprise modern accountancy.

In addition, we would like to thank Pam Sinclair, Margaret Hill and Mary Guttridge for performing secretarial and administrative duties on our behalf as well as the many secretaries who undertook similar duties for our contributors.

Finally, we are indebted to both our editor Alan Nelson for helpful comment and encouragement and for maintaining confidence in us, and Malcolm Cooper (formerly of ICAEW) for his refreshing and stimulating approach to enquiry.

List of contributors

David Ayling
School of Accounting, Banking and Economics
University College of North Wales
Bangor

Joan Ballantine
Department of Finance and Information
The Queen's University
Belfast

Valerie Belton
Department of Management Science
University of Strathclyde

Robert H. Berry
School of Information Systems
University of East Anglia

Robert Bradgate
Department of Law
University of Sheffield

Nigel Bryant
Independent consultant

John Child
Sociology and Psychology Group
Aston University Management Centre

Paul Collier
Department of Economics
University of Exeter

Nigel A. D. Connell
Department of Accounting and Management Science
University of Southampton

John Court
Information Technology Group
Institute of Chartered Accountants in England and Wales

Romano Dyerson
Centre for Business Strategy
London Business School

Guido Geerts
Assistant Professor and IBM Scholar
Centre for Business Informatics
Free University
Brussels

Alan Gregory	Department of Economics
	University of Exeter
Shaun Hargreaves Heap	School of Economics and Social Studies
	University of East Anglia
	Department of Economics
	University of Sydney
	Sydney
Mark Holding	Centre of Business Strategy
	London Business School
Les Johnson	Knowledge Based Systems Group
	Department of Computer Science
	Brunel University
Robert Lambert	Department of Management Information Systems
	Cranfield School of Management
Stewart A. Leech	Department of Accountancy
	University of Tasmania
William E. McCarthy	Arthur Andersen & Co. Alumni Professor
	Department of Accounting
	University of Michigan
Alyson J. McLintock	School of Information Systems
	University of East Anglia
Michael J. Mepham	Department of Accountancy
	Heriot-Watt University
Vijay Mital	Knowledge Based Systems Group
	Department of Computer Science
	Brunel University
Peter Monk	Strathclyde Business School
	University of Strathclyde
Nicki J. Muggridge	Information Technology Group
	Institute of Chartered Accountants in England and Wales
Bryan Pfaffenberger	School of Engineering and Applied Science
	University of Virginia
Richard Price	KPMG Peat Marwick McLintock, London
Michael Roper	Centre for Business Strategy
	London Business School
George Sorter	Leonard Stern School of Business
	New York University
Barry J. Spaul	Department of Economics
	University of Exeter
John Taylor	Strathclyde Business School
	University of Strathclyde

Yanis Varoufakis	Department of Economics
	University of Sydney
	Sydney
Martin Walker	Department of Accountancy
	University of Manchester
Edwin M. Wildey	Computers in Teaching Initiative: Centre for
	Accountancy
	University of East Anglia
Bernard C. Williams	School of Information Systems
	University of East Anglia
Howard Williams	Strathclyde Business School
	University of Strathclyde
Paul Willman	Department of Organisational Behaviour
	London Business School

Preface

In the rather humble surroundings of a wooden portakabin, the first computer-based accountancy degree programme bootstrapped into life just over ten years ago. Far from being a showpiece, the facilities were located away from the main campus of the University of East Anglia in Norwich, on a sub-campus (now demolished) across the road and out of sight in the School of Computer Studies and Accountancy (now the School of Information Systems).

In the intervening period virtually all accountancy programmes have acquired elements of computing but few have gone as far as to emulate the integrated UEA approach. In most institutions, there is still a tendency to treat computers only as an adjunct to mainstream accountancy despite the following major advances in information systems and technology during the same period:

1. Network communications
2. Sophisticated human computer/interfaces
3. Software tools and methods for systems analysis and design
4. Distributed processing facilities
5. End-user computing
6. Knowledge-based tools.

Traditionally many academic accountants have little technical knowledge of any of the above or the impact that they might have on subject material appearing in their accountancy programmes. Most computing activity in accountancy courses tends to be confined to simple transaction processing or simulation modelling, more in keeping with the way in which computers were used in practice in the mid-1970s.

It is this concern that provides us with the motivation for putting together this book of readings. We wish to demonstrate not only how computers are interwoven in the modern practice of accountancy, but also how they impact on the intellectual pursuit of the main subject areas that comprise this discipline.

Recent studies in artificial intelligence such as the Alvey, Esprit and Japanese Fifth Generation initiatives have produced some unexpected results. Attempts to produce 'thinking' machines have once again forced researchers to reflect on the received wisdom about the nature of mind and matter, often challenging philosophical concepts dating back to the seventeenth century. It has also had implications for the true nature of knowledge, information and data which is crucial for the successful implementation of information systems in their particular contexts.

Similarly, we believe that advances in information systems and technology offer accounting academics a new and exciting opportunity to review previously unquestioned basic assumptions that govern those subjects that comprise accountancy. Amongst these, economics provides a good example where its inherent assumption of rational human behaviour gives rise to the notion that the provision of sufficient quantities of data will be a guarantor of arrival at a 'truth state'. The availability of modern information technology allows the possibility of testing these sorts of assumptions in a practical context and thereby enriching intellectual study.

Attempts to lead accountancy out of the positivist closet have tended to direct it towards other equally esoteric closets that often have little grounding or relevance in real-world contexts. In the last decade or so, the study of information systems, initially rooted in the closed rational system model of computer science, provides a good example of what is possible. Current information systems theory has been heavily influenced by organizational theory giving rise to the development of socio-technical models and concepts like soft systems methodology. These approaches generally make no necessary assumptions that underlying reality is ordered, but concentrate on making sense of the world in a disciplined and logical fashion.

Like information systems, accountancy has very strong practical traditions and a history of theory based on closed rational systems. We hope that this volume will help to demonstrate the similarity and closeness of information systems and accountancy and raise axiomatic questions amongst our accountancy colleagues.

Editing a collection of readings is quite different from writing a book. Naturally the choice of material and its organization is important. In this case, the breadth of material covered makes it virtually impossible for any single author to cope with it adequately. Accordingly we have gratefully delegated most of this task to leading authors in the relevant fields. Readers will notice that some of the material is contradictory – this is a deliberate policy to allow the book to be used as a seminar reader. We believe that conflict and confusion in the minds of readers are necessary prerequisites for learning as they promote discussion and corresponding internalization.

Certainly, we have found the process of discourse involved in constructing the book highly instructive. Receiving and reading the contributions has also proved extremely interesting and very stimulating. We hope that you, the reader, may share in at least part of that experience.

Bernard C. Williams
Barry J. Spaul

1 The impact of IT on basic accounting concepts and accountancy education: an overview
Bernard C. Williams

INTRODUCTION

Recent discussion in the literature (Er and Ng, 1989; Collier *et al.*, 1990), a resurgency of interest in the use of computers in accountancy education (the establishment in 1989 of a CTI Centre for Accountancy at the University of East Anglia funded jointly by the Computer Board and the accountancy profession) and the development of increasingly sophisticated computer-based integrated information systems in organizations (Hirschheim, 1985, p. 13; Sprague and McNurlin, 1986, p. 6) suggest the need to re-evaluate the role of computers in accounting and the way in which they are portrayed in accountancy education.

The first major interest in the use of computers in education arose in the 1970s probably coinciding with suitable technological developments like the increasingly widespread availability of on-line computer systems. (It is worth noting, however, that even in the 1960s, computers were in use in tertiary education. Engineering undergraduates at Imperial College were, for example, regular and constant users of off-line batch processing sytems for design purposes.) Evidence of this interest can be found in the NDPCAL initiative in the UK (Hopper, 1977) and the PLATO project in the USA (Alpert and Bitzer, 1970). In turn it would be fair to argue that

Specially commissioned for *IT and Accounting: The impact of information technology.*
Edited by Bernard C. Williams and Barry J. Spaul.
Published in 1991 by Chapman & Hall, London ISBN 0 412 39210 0.

these ideas and methods have led to developments in accountancy education resulting in work by McKeown (1976) and Bhaskar (1982, 1983). Since then, there has been a series of publications which have, in effect, argued the case for a greater degree of involvement of computers in accounting education, both as a pedagogic or teaching aid and to reflect the increasing role of computers in the practice of accountancy.

For instance, Romney (1984), Kaye (1985) and Armitage and Boritz (1986) argue the general case for the introduction of computers into the accounting curriculum. Vasarhelyi and Lin (1985) outline the use of general audit software in computer auditing classes, Ryan and Simpson (1988) discuss the use of computer-aided learning packages in financial accounting, Dickens and Harper (1986) explore the use of computer-assisted learning approaches for the calculation of earnings per share and, finally, Seddon (1987) and Engle and Joseph (1986) are strong advocates of teaching computer-based accounting information sytems. Attempts have also been made to assess the use of computers in accounting curricula by Borthick and Clark (1986) and Fetters *et al.* (1986), whilst Helmi (1986) has taken the opportunity to reflect on the issues surrounding the integration of computers into accounting education.

With the exception of Kaye (1985), the above authors have tended to portray this activity in a piecemeal fashion and as an adjunct to 'conventional' accounting and auditing. As Baldwin and Williams (1990) report, in the technological context of the 1960s and 1970s such decoupling was probably sustainable given the available technology and its use within an organizational context (e.g. off-line batch processing used principally for tabulation purposes). The outlook for the 1990s suggests the development of integrated computer-based information systems with accounting systems fully blended into an organization's information system. Already this process has begun with the development of the concept of the end-user and end-user computing.

USING COMPUTERS IN ACCOUNTING EDUCATION: A CONTEXT-FREE APPROACH

Perhaps one remarkable attribute of the accounting literature is the relative absence of a data processing dimension. This, despite the fact that the first commercial electronic digital computer (LEO) was built for a data processing application nearly 40 years ago.

Taking the leading US and UK accounting journals (Nobes, 1986) over the same period where possible, the number of articles relating to computer-based aspects of accountancy are remarkably low. For example, in the *Journal of Accountancy* between 1950–88 over 2000 articles were published with less than 60 relating to computer-based aspects. Similarly in *Accounting and Business Research*, for the period 1970 (its inception) to 1988, over 600 articles were published with nine being attributable to computer-based aspects of accounting and auditing. Closer examination of the literature reveals that over the same period (1950 onwards), it was clearly dominated by economics. It seemed that accounting was seen as a practical or metric expression of economics, the true intellectual pursuit concerned with:

(1) the allocation of a society's resources among alternative uses and the distribution of society's output among individuals and groups;
(2) the ways in which production and distribution change in time; and
(3) the efficiencies and inefficiencies of economic systems.

(Lipsey, 1983, p. 58)

Further evidence of this perception can be seen by the initial establishment of many accountancy faculties within economics departments. In recent years these ties have weakened and accountancy faculties now exist in separate departments, as part of multidisciplinary enterprises such as business schools or in select groupings such as law or computing. Accountancy has also developed a rich intellectual tradition which is reflected by the establishment of many new and diverse journals. *Accounting, Organisations and Society* represents an organizational perspective; *Journal of Information Systems* and *Accounting, Management and Information Technologies* represent computer-based perspectives; *Critical Perspectives on Accounting* represents philosophical perspectives and so on. Accounting has developed within a relatively short time to become a full member of the social sciences. It has evolved a wide range of philosophical bases (e.g. Tomkins and Groves, 1983) and draws on traditions from other social sciences such as organizational behaviour, cognitive psychology and politics, sciences such as information technology, and quasi-sciences such as economics and operational research.

Despite this pluralism, there are many who still view information technology as supplementary to the discipline, and their use of computers in accounting education is correspondingly atomistic and remote. Romney's (1984) paper provides a good example of this. In the introduction (p. 145), he identifies 'accounting, cost accounting etc.' as properly definable subjects and accounting information systems (AIS) as rather peripheral, comprising one or more of the following 'Introduction to Computers, Management Information Systems, Analysis and Design of Accounting Systems, Computer Auditing or Programming'. Although he reports the successful development of a case study approach to the teaching of AIS, the language of his paper suggests that computing in the accounting curriculum is confined to these areas.

Seddon (1987) exhibits a similar tendency. In a paper about computing in the undergraduate accounting curriculum he claims (p. 267) significant integration in Australia (compared with the UK). Disappointingly, however, the paper focuses exclusively on AIS.

Two fairly recent papers attempt to address the issue of integrating computers into accounting education (Helmi, 1986 and Armitage and Boritz, 1986). Helmi's paper is a relatively general comment which seems in the main to be concerned that students will perceive accountancy as a 'mechanical, definitive and precise process' (p. 107) analogous to the use of calculators. However, unless instructors fall into the trap outlined by Forrester (1981):

> Computers are often being used for what the computer does poorly and the human mind does well. At the same time the human mind is being used for what the human does poorly and the computer does well . . . (p. 271).

and by Vickers (1983):

> Nor are new techniques merely an addition to a workman's bag of tools. They cannot help influencing his perceptions. They help to determine what he notices, as well as what he does about it. They limit as well as enable (p. 161).

this should not be a serious problem. Armitage and Boritz present a more detailed analysis, reminiscent of a systems development life cycle (see Davis and Olson, 1985, p. 570), of how to integrate computers into the accounting curriculum. Their comprehensive approach highlights many significant and useful general issues. Their scope is, however, disappointingly narrow being only marginally wider than other authors (i.e. in addition to AIS only aspects of auditing and taxation are included).

Current developments in IT such as the cheap and widely available standardized decentralized computing power with powerful and labour-saving software tools combined with cheap network facilities linked to large data sources suggests the need to reassess radically the way in which computers are integrated into accounting curricula. The purpose of this book is to show that it should be done through the metaphor of the end-user, a term used by information systems practitioners to reflect the fully integrated role of computer-based resources in the modern business environment. End-user computing is characterized by the democratization and integration of computer power largely owing to its cheapness and wide availability. In other words, the focus of the design process for computer systems is increasingly based on the needs of the user, technology fitting itself around people rather than vice versa. Major problems for the end-user computing perspective and recurring themes in the succeeding chapters are: how to balance employee freedom or trust against control in order to maximize employee creativity for the benefit of the organization; and the requirement to consider or include social, behavioural or non-instrumental factors in the conceptualization of information sytems.

USING COMPUTERS IN ACCOUNTING EDUCATION: AN IN-CONTEXT APPROACH

Implied in the end-user perspective is a notion consistent with Forrester's comments (see above) which in turn imply a concern for a realistic allocation of activities between humans and their technology. The underlying theme is that technology should be viewed as a support or facilitator in each continuing and uniquely human problem situation. This would include its particular context (social, organizational, political factors, etc.). Whilst such a dichotomy is idealistic – for example, it may be argued that technology itself is socially constructed – it serves to signify the dangers of technocracy alone. In other words where human problem situations may be reduced to mechanistic issues dominated and led by technology without adequate space for reflection and strategies to foster and encourage change. A technocratic approach draws the barriers of enquiry too tightly giving a premature problem definition and militates against full exploration to uncover some of the many unpredictable dimensions that will always be present in any human endeavour.

Enquiry, reflection and problem definition figure prominently in modern social science (see, for example, Checkland, 1981; Schön, 1983; Morgan, 1986; and many others). This development has also been reflected in changes to the approaches of research in information systems (Mumford *et al.*, 1985) and is consistent with the philosophy underpinning end-user computing.

Accounting systems represent a significant part of any organizational information system and apart from, for example, church and social club accounts, virtually all are computer based. Increasing integration seems inevitable particularly to satisfy the demands of the end-user. It seems logical therefore that initiatives for using computers in accountancy education should not be limited to AIS (transaction processing of un-problematic data) or even to the use of spreadsheets (transaction processing or modelling of similarly unproblematic data). Rather, the implications of computing as an integral agent of change to all aspects of accounting should be addressed.

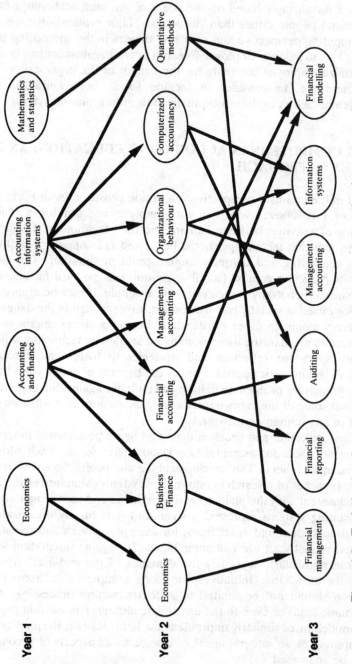

Figure 1.1   Typical units of a three-year honours accounting programme showing some possible links.

Typical components of an accounting course are given in Fig. 1.1. Two components are obviously absent: these are taxation and law. Both of them interact mainly with elements on the left-hand side of the figure, but have been omitted here for the sake of clarity and because they are often subsumed with other subject modules such as financial accounting/reporting. Taking this and Fig. 1.1 into account, the major subject streams can be reduced to eight, representing the structure of this book as follows:

1. Economics
2. Finance
3. Financial accounting
4. Management accounting
5. Tax and law
6. Quantitative methods
7. Business organization and policy
8. Other themes.

ECONOMICS

It is clear that the presence or provision of large-scale computational power facilitates the development of economic models and is particularly useful in econometrics. However, it is more difficult to imagine how IT has an impact on economics as a subject rather than its application which may be considered in the domain of quantitative methods. Two clear issues do arise. One is the general impact of IT on the 'economy' and the other is the question of the role and value of information in economics given that IT is expected to generate more of it more cheaply. These issues are discussed in Part One.

FINANCE

Finance is normally considered in two connected contexts: external finance, such as share and loan capital, and internal finance, such as working capital and project finance.

In the last few years, many of the world's major stock markets have become computerized with activities and dealings taking place at an impersonal level through the medium of computer-based systems. Whilst this has probably had an impact on the functional informational aspects of market efficiency, it is clear that this has not necessarily reduced some of the behavioural issues. For example, over-reliance on computer-controlled investment systems is often cited as one of the major contributory factors of the 1987 New York crash.

For internal finance decisions, it is particularly relevant to reflect on the benefits produced from IT investment. With increasing integration of computers and the development of the end-user concept, problems are arising from ensuring that local gains in productivity are translated into organizational gains. Some of these difficulties arise from the necessity of measuring intangible benefits in addition to the traditional financial measures of return on capital etc. This is normally further complicated by local managers not having sufficient access to the organization's overall business strategy and therefore being unable to articulate suitable performance measures.

Investment choice, both at the internal and external levels, is greatly facilitated by IT which allows the application of simulation modelling and many OR techniques such as AI and risk analysis. These issues are discussed in Part Two.

FINANCIAL ACCOUNTING

Deficiencies in financial accounting are well known. Current systems record only a very narrow aspect of exchange activities. The focus is on the economic aspects of the exchange and its dual nature, i.e. in the case of a credit sale, the exchange of goods for a future financial obligation to pay is recorded in monetary units of the day. This abstracted, transitory and relative data is used as input for a process that creates reports of a supposed absolute or authoritative nature. Inevitably, these reports fail to match the real contextual value of an organization's assets and liabilities.

In consequence, there have been attempts to improve the quality of recorded data through the use of cash flow accounting, matrix accounting, multi-entry accounting and events accounting. These approaches, often impractical in a manual system because of the need to record and process vast amounts of data, are facilitated with the development of IT. Although so far the practical implementations are limited, the opportunities for development are now available. These issues are discussed in Part Three.

MANAGEMENT ACCOUNTING

Much of management accounting is concerned with modelling and planning for decisions about cost allocation, product manufacture and sale of goods and services in the most profitable proportions. There is also a strong behavioural dimension which is considered under business organization and policy below.

Of particular interest are questions of budgeting for internal planning and cost estimation to help with decisions about whether to provide particular goods and services to customers. Traditional methods relied on manual worksheets which were normally complex, cumbersome and inflexible. Computer-based spreadsheets and other modelling systems have evolved which greatly facilitate this process, providing flexible, rapid, what-if solutions. In effect accountants and managers now have systems which allow, subject to modelling limitations, inputs to be varied to produce desired outcomes. Although iteration is possible in manual systems, the time and effort required make it virtually impossible in practice, except under very simple conditions.

Modelling possibilities on computers have also facilitated the development of various types of decision support systems which include management information systems, executive information systems and expert systems. These take advantage of computer-based data to support management decisions through the use of, for example, risk analysis, fuzzy logic and so on. The ability to make *ad hoc* enquiries is also greatly facilitated. These issues are discussed in Part Four.

TAX AND LAW

The definition of a good law is often considered its enforceability. For tax this must translate to its collectability. Indeed, it could be argued that the implementation of the community charge would not have been considered without the existence of suitable IT.

The computerization of the Inland Revenue is nearing completion presumably with the expectation that collection costs per pound of tax levied will be reduced. IT should also facilitate the computation of tax payable through the use of improved information processing and, for example, modelling procedures, particularly in disputed cases. From the taxpayer's viewpoint, IT offers enhanced modelling methods for optimizing tax planning and provides a vision of the future where inspectors and taxpayers do battle armed with computers!

Modern developments in IT such as the growing use of electronic data interchange (EDI) supported by networks and combined with new management techniques such as 'just-in-time', will have far reaching effects on contract law. One of the many questions that arises is the implication for the ownership of assets and when this is transferred from one organization to another. A related issue is the status of financial instruments that exist in and are transferred through computer systems – in other words data (electronic signals) with intrinsic value. Unlike tangible assets, their value is often much more dependent on mutual trust and belief backed up with a fragile symbol such as a computer date stamp. These issues are discussed in Part Five.

QUANTITATIVE METHODS

Unlike other subject disciplines in accountancy, operational research (or management science or quantitative methods) has had a symbiotic relationship with IT. OR was originally a background activity in many organizations but is now fully integrated mainly in the field of decision support systems where it has made many important contributions. Similarly without OR applications it could be argued that today IT would be confined to a simple role of tabulation and transaction processing. In short IT has facilitated OR and OR has developed uses for IT.

Model building, a major OR application, presents problems in the world of the end-user. When powerful financial model building software is available to users (often accountants and managers) who lack the expertise normally associated with OR specialists residing in the background, the problem of model validation can arise. This is because there is a tendency for naïve model builders to focus on data rather than empirically testable logic. The digital presentation employed by many modelling packages also discourages critical reflection of the underlying model when compared with the analogue presentation of manual models.

The overall successful development of computer-based quantitative methods often provides an enticement to ignore or exclude qualitative methods of enquiry. Although much accounting research requires the use of quantitative methods for peer validation, there is a growing recognition of the legitimacy of qualitative research methods. Qualitative data is mainly text based and there is always the temptation to avoid its richness and the tedium involved in analysing it by converting it to quantitative data. Developments in IT, particularly microcomputers, have allowed portability, confidentiality and the use of sophisticated software to process text and support analysis. These issues are discussed in Part Six.

BUSINESS ORGANIZATION AND POLICY

Introducing information technology into organizations was sometimes thought to be a non-problematic and technical activity comprising computerization of existing procedures, structures and so on. Again, to some extent this was understandable given the early role of computers in organizations as off-line batch processing tabulation sytems. The reality is a little different. The introduction of IT into an organization amounts to reorganization. It affects the way in which members of an organization have access to and process information and in consequence can have an impact on the distribution of power and relationships. Indeed, the advantages of IT can be lost to those organizations that fail to recognize this and to capitalize on it. A good deal of reflection and enquiry into existing practices and procedures and the impact of computing are necessary to gain the full benefits, both tangible and intangible, of competitive advantage.

For larger organizations, the development of extensive computer-based networks provides the opportunity for the exciting development of geographically separate modules and the creation of the 'virtual firm'.

In small firms, there is a possibility that growth can be maintained beyond traditional limiting factors by preserving some of them that contribute to success. The key characteristics of small firms are the domination and involvement of owner-managers and the consequent ability to make rapid and flexible decisions. This arises from a small span of control and the availability of all organizational information to one or two people. The growth of small firms is often limited as information generated grows and its assimilation becomes too much for a small number of people. IT can help prevent information channels from becoming clogged and maintain the flexibility, dynamism and vigour which characterize smaller organizations. These issues are discussed in Part Seven.

OTHER THEMES

The seven previous sections have outlined ways in which IT impacts on the major subject disciplines in accountancy. There are, however, areas in accountancy where it is appropriate to focus on IT itself.

The quest for artificial intelligence has a relatively long history, predating electronic computers. In recent years many attempts have been made to automate the work of professionals using AI techniques with limited success. Generally, however, the concept of stand-alone systems is disappearing in favour of the notion of AI as an interface technology in decision support systems.

The other major interest in IT, for accounting, arises from problems of computer auditing, security and fraud. With the growth of computer networks and integration of computers in organizations, the potential for computer-assisted fraud grows. Fighting fraud is a fact of life as criminals will always outwit the best controls. However, although audit and fraud are not necessarily linked, in the technological context of the 1990s, it may be appropriate to reflect on or reassess the current basic audit model and its concept of control which was developed in the 1950s in the context of very large-scale paper-based systems. These issues are discussed in Part Eight.

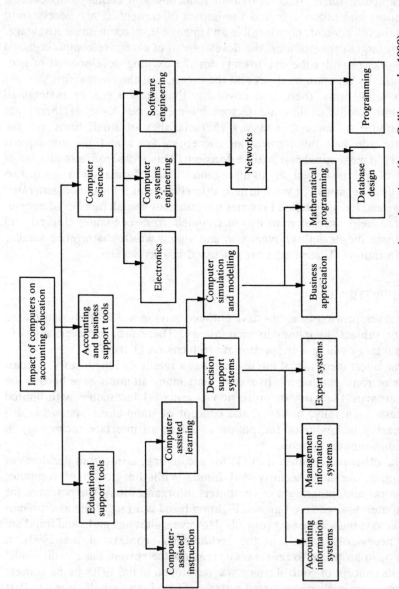

Fig. 1.2 Revised classification of the impact of computers on accounting education (from Collier *et al.*, 1990).

THE IMPLICATIONS OF A CONTEXTUAL APPROACH TO THE USE OF COMPUTERS IN ACCOUNTING EDUCATION

The previously accepted framework for computers in accountancy education proposed by Bhaskar (1982, 1983) and modified by Collier *et al.* (1990) (see Fig. 1.2) becomes less significant as the argument for an integrated approach is advanced.

Taking each of the main categories in turn, the case for educational support tools (CAI/CAL) as they are currently configured remains weak. This is effectively confirmed by the findings of Fetters *et al.* (1986), Dickens and Harper (1986) and Ryan and Simpson (1988). Unless a real alternative to textbooks can be found (Collins, 1983), such as, for example, the use of pure electronic documents (i.e. non-sequential, navigational systems where the user influences content) similar to those found on genuine hypertext/hypermedia systems (Nielsen, 1990, pp. 1–14), the case is likely to remain weak.

At the other end of the scale, the case for a detailed knowledge of computer science becomes less compelling. This is because the world of the computer practitioner is increasingly dominated by tools and methods. An obvious analogy lies with transport system designers. They do not need a detailed mechanic's knowledge of the workings of an aero engine, an electric locomotive engine or even an internal combustion engine. However, an understanding of the principles of operation and the relationship of these principles to the operation of a transport system is essential. So it is with computer hardware and software, tools and methods and organizational systems.

Returning to the end-user computing metaphor and the central element of Fig. 1.2, the growing integration becomes clearer. Modern business systems are increasingly characterized by support tools under end-user control. These take many forms with current initiatives aimed at integrating them at an organizational level (CEC, 1990). These tools, however, or their generic variants are capable of being used across the range of components in Fig. 1.2. For example, hypermedia has educational (Friedlander, 1988), pedagogic (Leggett *et al.*, 1989), commercial (Baird and Percival, 1989), audit (DeYoung, 1989), systems design (CEC, 1990) and many other applications. (A similar range of applications exists for other tools such as spreadsheets, AI shells, file management systems and so on.)

It is suggested therefore, that the focus of the use of computers in accounting education should be on integration and remain in tune with end-user tool and method developments in practice. In other words, preoccupation solely with mechanical issues (transaction processing –

AIS), book substitution (current CAI/CAL) or programming languages (interpreters/compilers are in any case tools in their own right) misses an educational opportunity.

Like the transport analogy above, the focus of accounting education can be on accounting and business systems with an understanding of the principles of operation of computer systems, tools and methods and perhaps most importantly an understanding of how these relate and impact on accounting and business subject disciplines. If computers are fully integrated into accounting education in this way, accounting education will remain in step with the integration that is taking place in the business world and it will benefit from a cross-fertilization of ideas, concepts, tools and methods.

CONCLUDING REMARKS

This introductory chapter has outlined the impact that IT has had, to varying degrees, on the main subject areas of accountancy. Succeeding chapters in the book together with suggestions for further reading provide greater detail and teaching material particularly for seminar discussions. The book demonstrates how computers are fully blended in modern accountancy and should help to counter the peripheral nature of computing that many accounting and business studies students receive through a limited exposure to AIS or other computer technique oriented activities. This does not necessarily mean that all subjects should acquire a physical computing dimension in the curricula. Rather they should be taught on the basis that modern accounting sits comfortably within a framework that contains a large integrated computing component.

REFERENCES

Alpert, D. A. and Bitzer, D. L. (1970). 'Advances in computer-based education' *Science* 167 (20 March 1970), pp. 1582–1590.

Armitage, H. E. and Boritz, J. E. (1986). 'Integrating computers into the accounting curriculum', *Issues in Accounting Education*, vol. 1, pp. 86–101.

Baird, P. and Percival, M. (1989). 'Glasgow online: database development using Apple's Hypercard', in McAleese, R. (ed.), *Hypertext: Theory into Practice*. Ablex, pp. 75–92.

Baldwin, T. J. L. and Williams, B. C. (1990). 'IT and the auditor – the next ten years', *Accountancy*, October, pp. 128–30.

Bhaskar, K. N. (1982). 'Use of computers in accountancy courses', *Accounting and Business Research*, No. 49, Winter, pp. 3–10.

Bhaskar, K. N. (1983). 'Computers and the choice for accountancy syllabuses', *Accounting and Business Research*, No. 50, Spring, pp. 83–94.

Borthick, A. F. and Clark, R. L. (1986). 'The role of productive thinking in affecting student learning with microcomputers in accounting education', *Accounting Review*, vol. LXI, no. 1, January, pp. 143–157.

CEC (Commission of the European Communities) (1990). *HECTOR Project Report*, Esprit 2 Project No. 2082, DG XIII CEC.

Checkland, P. (1981). *Systems Thinking, Systems Practice*. Wiley, Chichester.

Collier, P. A., Kaye, G. R., Spaul, B. J. and Williams, B. C. (1990) 'The use of computers in accounting courses: A new perspective: A comment', *Accounting and Business Research*, vol. 20, no. 80, Autumn, pp. 353–4.

Collins, R. (1983). 'Computers and accountancy courses: A comment', *Accounting and Business Research*, No. 52, pp. 313–315.

Davis, G. B. and Olson, M. H. (1985). *Management Information Systems*. McGraw-Hill, Singapore.

DeYoung, L. (1989). 'Hypertext challenges in the auditing domain', *Proc. ACM Hypertext 1989 Conference* (Pittsburgh, PA, 5–8 November 1989), pp. 169–180.

Dickens, T. L. and Harper, R. M. (1986). 'The use of microcomputers in intermediate accounting: Effects on student achievement and attitudes', *Journal of Accounting Education*, vol. 4, no. 1, Spring, pp. 127–46.

Engle, T. J. and Joseph, G. W. (1986). 'A successful approach to integrating computer assignments into accounting information systems courses in a manner that complements theoretical readings and classroom discussions', *Journal of Accounting Education*, vol. 4, no. 2, Fall, pp. 141–146.

Er, M. C. and Ng, A. C. (1989). 'The use of computers in accountancy courses: A new perspective. *Accountancy and Business Research*, **19** (76), 319–26.

Fetters, M., McKenzie, J. and Callaghan, D. (1986). 'Does the computer hinder accounting education? An analysis of some empirical data', *Issues in Accounting Education*, vol. 1, no. 1, pp. 76–85.

Forrester, J. W. (1981). 'Understanding the counterintuitive behaviour of social systems', in Open Systems Group' (ed.), *Systems Behaviour*, 3rd edition. Harper and Row, London, in association with Open University Press, pp. 270–287.

Friedlander, L. (1988). 'The Shakespeare Project', in Ambron, S. and Hooper, K. (eds), *Interactive Multimedia: Visions of Multimedia for Developers, Educators & Information Providers*. Microsoft Press, pp. 115–141.

Helmi, M. A. (1986). 'Integrating the microcomputer into accounting education – approaches and pitfalls', *Issues in Accounting Education*, vol. 1, no. 1, pp. 102–11.

Hirschheim, R. A. (1985). *Office Automation: A Social and Organisational Perspective*. Wiley, Chichester.

Hopper, R. (1977). *National Development Programme in Computer Assisted Learning – Final Report of the Director*. Council for Educational Technology, London.

Kaye, G. R. (1985). 'Teaching strategies in computers and accounting', *British Accounting Review*, vol. 17, no. 1, pp. 22–36.

Leggett, J., Schnase, J. L. and Kacmar, C. J. (1989). 'A short course on Hypertext', *Technical Report TAMU 89–004*. Computer Science Department, Texas A&M University College Station, TX 77843–3112, January, 1989.

Lipsey, R. G. (1983). *An Introduction to Positive Economics*, 6th edn, Weidenfeld & Nicolson, London.

McKeown, J. C. (1976). 'Computer-assisted instruction for elementary accounting,' *Accounting Review*, January, no. 1, pp. 123–130.

Morgan, G. (1986). *Images of Organisation*. Sage, Newbury Park, CA.

Mumford, E., Hirschheim, R., Fitzgerald, G. and Wood-Harper, T. (1985) *Research Methods in Information Systems*. Amsterdam, North Holland.

Nielsen, J. (1990). *Hypertext & Hypermedia*. Academic Press, New York.

Nobes, C. W. (1986). 'Academic perceptions of accounting journals in the English speaking world', *British Accounting Review*, vol. 18, no. 1, pp. 7–16.

Ryan, R. J. and Simpson, S. M. (1988). 'Computer aided instruction for *ab initio* teaching in accounting', *British Accounting Review*, vol. 20, no. 2, pp. 111–130.

Romney, M. B. (1984). 'Teaching accounting information systems using a case study approach', *Journal of Accounting Education*, vol. 2, no. 1, Spring, pp. 145–54.

Schön, D. (1983). *The Reflective Practitioner: How Professionals Think In Action*. Temple Smith, London.

Seddon, P. (1987). 'Computing in the undergraduate accounting curriculum: three distinct goals', *British Accounting Review*, vol. 19, no. 3, pp. 267–276.

Sprague, R. H. and McNurlin, B. C. (eds) (1986). *Information Systems Management in Practice*. Prentice-Hall International, Englewood Cliffs, NJ.

Tomkins, C. and Groves, R. (1983). 'The everyday accountant and researching his reality', *Accounting, Organisations and Society*, vol. 8, no. 4, pp. 361–374.

Vasarhelyi, M. A. and Lin, W. T. (1985). 'EDP auditing instruction using an interactive generalized audit software', *Journal of Accounting Education*, vol. 3, no. 2, Fall, pp. 79–89.

Vickers, G. (1983). *Human Systems are Different*. Harper & Row, London.

PART

1 Economics

The popular image of economics is that of a thoroughbred compared with accountancy – remote, theoretical and unsullied by everyday affairs. In a similar way, the image of technology seems to lie uneasily in the context of such a pure intellectual pursuit. Nevertheless, in econometrics, the last few decades have seen the development of sophisticated computer-based statistical modelling approaches. The pure economists are, of course, free to distance themselves from these 'technicians' and maintain their purity and that of their subject theory – or are they? Does IT have an impact on economics and does it cause a reflection of fundamental assumptions in the subject discipline?

The three chapters in this part can only manage to touch on these questions and raise further ones to stimulate enquiry. The first by Peter Monk is a general paper which explores the role of information and information technology in 'the economy'. In particular, it raises some important questions regarding IT which are addressed in general in the chapter, in more detail in the other chapters in this part and in further parts throughout the book. The general questions are as follows:

1. Does IT bring economic benefits for users?
2. What are the effects on activities of users and organizational structures?
3. What are the effects on employment?
4. Does information processed and communicated via IT have any economic value?
5. How can these effects and values be measured?

Throughout his discussion, Monk proposes two significant points: these are that IT not only affects the economy, it **is** the economy. Information production, comprising the construction of the necessary technology and its communication through products such as directories, catalogues, technical and academic literature, etc., accounts for a quarter to a half of national incomes. It is of the same order as government expenditure. Despite this fascinating insight, very little is known about how to value information and assess its productivity.

The second chapter by Martin Walker addresses, at a more theoretical level, the role and value of information. He provides a non-technical overview of the literature in a branch of economics known as information economics. He illustrates the utility of the information economics approach in a financial reporting application highlighting some unresolved issues, and attempts to reaffirm the often forgotten links between policy-makers and economic theory.

Information economics provides a good vehicle to examine the interrelationship between economic theory and IT. This is because information economics hinges around the notion of 'rational belief' with an implied assumption that the plentiful supply of cheap information provided by IT will assist better rational decision-making. Shaun Hargreaves Heap and Yanis Varofakis provide the last chapter in this part which is a critical review of the assumptions underlying information economics. Their conclusion that it is not sufficient to view information solely as a resource for instrumental calculation, and that processing information necessarily requires a non-instrumental component, suggests exciting possibilities for economics such as the development of a socio-instrumental (or socio-technical?) dimension to mainstream economic theory.

2 The impact of IT on 'the economy'

Peter Monk

INTRODUCTION – WHAT IS IT?

Information technology (IT) is the outcome of the recent convergence of two older technologies: computers and telecommunications. IT is the technology of automated information processing and communication. It appears in many familiar products and services – personal computers, telephones, fax machines and photocopiers – as well as in more exotic forms such as satellite and data communication systems, digital audio recording and video mixing systems. This same technology is used to run automated equipment in offices, factories, chemical plants and power stations, to aid the flight and navigation of aircraft, and to control air and rail traffic. Even common domestic appliances now contain IT components for control functions.

The list of applications of IT is practically endless yet so is the list of difficult questions raised by this technology. How does IT provide economic benefits for its users? What effects does IT have on the activities of users and on the structure of organizations in which they work? How does IT affect employment? Does the information processed and communicated via IT have any economic value? How can these effects and values be measured?

This chapter serves two main purposes. The first is to provide the reader with an outline of the ways in which IT affects the economy, through its use in commerce and industry. The second is to demonstrate that the word 'impact' – used in the title – is misleading. Here, the purpose is to show that

Specially commissioned for *IT and Accounting: The impact of information technology*.
Edited by Bernard C. Williams and Barry J. Spaul.
Published in 1991 by Chapman & Hall, London ISBN 0 412 39210 0.

IT does not so much have an 'impact' on the economy as become part of the economic environment. IT must be seen as native to the domestic economy rather than as a visitor from outside. In more formal terms, IT is endogenous rather than exogenous to the economy.

Following textbook tradition, this account of IT in the economy starts with microeconomic topics: production, investment, productivity and the employment of labour and capital. Consideration of the labour market reveals broader patterns of change linked to the use of new technology. This topic leads on to macroeconomic issues such as overall patterns of technological change and the role of technological innovation in economic development. The final part of this chapter is concerned with the present transition of Western economies from an era dominated by industrial production to one dominated by information. Despite the seemingly abstract nature of these macroeconomic processes, it is important to note that both micro and macro aspects of IT in the economy raise significant practical problems for accounting. The key to dealing with these problems is understanding the nature of information and the role of technology in economic processes.

PRODUCTION AND PRODUCTIVITY

The production of all types of goods and services is, necessarily, a highly organized process whether undertaken by individuals, small firms or the largest corporations. The way in which production is organized is intimately related to the technology employed and the rate of productivity that may be achieved. For present purposes, 'productivity' may be considered as the ratio of outputs to inputs; the more output that is produced per unit of inputs, the higher the rate of productivity. If productivity is to be increased, one or both of two changes must be implemented. The efficiency of an existing production process might be increased and the way in which production is organized might be improved through innovation (i.e. technological change). In either case, increases in productivity will depend on improvements in the information that is used in production.

The development of IT has enabled producers to improve significantly the information systems that are necessary for production. These systems provide a direct link between the technology of information processing and communication and the performance of firms across every sector of the economy. For this reason, the role of information in the production of goods and services demands closer scrutiny.

It is useful to distinguish between three categories of information used in production: design, operational and strategic information. Despite some overlaps, each type of information is used for different purposes and each is associated with different applications of IT.

Design information is the product of research and development (R&D) activity and it appears in three principal forms:

1. product designs – e.g. blueprints, drawings and technical specifications of manufactured goods, specifications of service products;
2. process designs – e.g. technical specifications of manufacturing processes, specification of systems for production of services;
3. production arrangement designs – e.g. factory layout plans, inventory control specifications for goods, organization of service delivery methods.

Design information is typically generated at considerable cost. The creation of new or amended designs requires investment of time, effort and money irrespective of how successful or valuable that information may prove to be in practice. IT in the form of computer-aided design (CAD) systems is increasingly used by firms for design activities (Kaplinsky, 1984, Chapter 3). There are two main reasons for this. The first is to reduce the cost of design information, which is a major consideration in technological innovation. The second reason is to allow designers to develop products, processes and production arrangements that are more complex than could be developed without the aid of automated information systems. Civil and military aircraft are examples of such products, as are all IT components and systems.

Although designs for products, processes and the organization of production are refined and improved over time, they do form a relatively stable constituent of the technological information used in the production of both goods and services (Monk, 1989, Chapter 7). Design outputs from R&D essentially provide the firm with the structural, technological information required for production.

Operational information, by contrast, is typically generated as a byproduct of the activity of production. This category includes both economic data for accounting (book-keeping) functions and technical data for engineering functions. For example, on receipt of components and raw materials from suppliers, a firm must record the quantities and costs of 'goods inward' for accounting purposes. Equally, technical information about the quantity and quality of those supplies will be required by production managers, stock controllers and so on. This information is commonly derived from 'goods inward inspection' by the firm or from agreed quality tests undertaken by the supplier. In manufacturing industry, even the most basic operational information necessary for production may consist of thousands of different items of data, each of which may change daily and some more frequently. Clearly, the firm's requirement for recording and processing this information will not be trivial; indeed, it often accounts for a significant proportion of production costs.

The information systems required for short-term (day-to-day) managerial control represent a major application of IT. 'Management information systems' (MIS) take a variety of forms in industry. They range from simple software packages run on personal computers, through 'office automation', to advanced integrated systems for stock control, production scheduling and accounting run on networks of computers that span a firm's entire operations (see, for example, McNurlin and Sprague, 1989). The key characteristic of MIS is that appropriate use of IT allows managers and other staff to keep informed about – and on that basis to control – each stage of the production process. Operational information that is accurate and up to date is crucial for the enhancement of efficiency in all types of production.

Strategic information provides the basis for medium- and long-term economic decisions taken by firms. These decisions concern the types of products the firm is to produce, the methods by which they are to be produced, the manner in which they are to be marketed, distributed and sold, the firm's R&D policy, and so on. The information used for this type of decision-making is normally gathered from a variety of sources, including the firm's own design and operational activities as well as external sources of economic, commercial and technical information. Once again, IT may offer efficient and effective means of processing and communication, such that variously sourced information can be integrated to provide decision-makers with new information of strategic value (Earl, 1988). The systems employed for this purpose range from sophisticated types of MIS to 'decision support systems' (DSS) and 'executive information systems' (EIS) (McNurlin and Sprague, 1989, Chapter 13).

Technical jargon makes applications of IT systems appear complex – as indeed they are, in technical terms. Yet the principle behind their widespread use in the economy is very simple. The purpose of IT is to reduce the net cost of information to users. To the extent that IT systems have this result in practice, users' investments in IT will be worthwhile. If those systems fail to reduce information costs – or to increase the value of information to users – investment in IT will be uneconomic.

However, in practice, evaluation of IT investments is not so straightforward, either before or after their implementation. The central problem is how to account for the information that is to be processed and/or communicated in order to provide economic benefits to the investor. The true cost of information is notoriously difficult to measure (Strassman, 1985). The value of information is even more problematic; it is difficult to define and essentially impossible to measure as an independent variable (see, for example, Machlup, 1962, p. 44).

Information measurement problems are just part of a broader challenge to established accounting practices represented by the increasing use of IT in commerce, industry and the public sector. One result of the availability of powerful systems for processing and communicating information – of all the types outlined above – has been to allow firms greater flexibility both in their production activities and in their chosen forms of corporate organization. The literature on flexibility in production addresses a large number of economic, political, geographical and technical issues (see Hepworth, 1989, Chapters 5 and 6 for a recent review). A consistent theme in this literature is the complex relation between technological innovation – notably in IT – and changes in the dynamics of production, both within and between firms, industries and sectors. Such changes in the economy are necessarily based on firms' development and exploitation of new design, operational and strategic information. Accounting for flexible production will mean accounting for the creation, use and effects of economically valuable information.

AUTOMATION AND THE LABOUR MARKET

One of the strongest links between technology and the economy is that involving automated production and firms' demands for labour. Widespread adoption of increasingly automated production equipment must, inevitably, lead to reductions in firms' demands for specific types of labour. Indeed, there are in general only two reasons for firms to invest in automation: first, to undertake production tasks that cannot be accomplished manually; second, to reduce production costs by displacing labour from the production process. However, in the case of automation based on IT, the relationship between production techniques and levels of employment (and unemployment) involves broader issues than just 'machines versus jobs'. The central point here concerns the nature of automation itself.

What, then, is automation? Is it qualitatively different from mechanization, as typified by the development of capital equipment during the nineteenth and early twentieth centuries? Opinion amongst economists and industry analysts has varied widely on these questions, partly as a reflection of historical changes in prevailing industrial 'high' technology (Kaplinsky, 1984, Chapter 2). Following that historical perspective, a usable definition of automation must acknowledge the dominant role of IT in present-day production technology, right across the spectrum of activities in all sectors of industry.

The common element in all forms of contemporary automation is information processing. In manufacturing and process production activities, automation requires sensor technology – to collect information about the current state of physical machines and materials – and control technology to provide mechanisms by which the state of machines (plant and equipment) can be altered. Design activities – as well as managerial, administrative and other office work – are essentially concerned with information production, as an end in itself.

In both areas of activity – physical and information production – IT provides the means to automate tasks and processes that previously required manual intervention. While it would be misleading to suggest that IT is a technology for automating 'intellectual work', it is certainly true that any task or process which is definable in terms of information processing represents a potential application for IT. It is the ubiquitous role of information in all forms and aspects of production that leads to the great generality of IT-based automation. Information processing via IT distinguishes modern automation technology as qualitatively different from the earlier means of mechanizing production.

This qualitative change in the technology of automation has been reflected in a significant change in economic debates about 'technological unemployment'. Briefly, the traditional debate concerned whether or not mechanization of capital equipment in industry would lead to a net reduction in the quantity of labour required to produce given levels of output. An important argument in this regard continues to be that industrial activities and employment practices during periods of technological change are dynamic; that technological development and economic activity are mutually related.

Consider, for example, the predictions of technological unemployment due to the 'microchip revolution' that were made in the late 1970s (e.g. Barron and Curnow, 1979; Jenkins and Sherman, 1979). The chronic mass unemployment which has persisted in the UK since that time may have been due in part to industry's adoption of IT-based automation. However, other explanations for it are equally plausible; the 'restructuring' (wholesale destruction?) of manufacturing industry, changes in public expenditure policy and economic recession all coincided with the rise of IT. The difficulty of resolving questions about the extent of technological unemployment has resulted in the traditional debate being replaced by a new approach to automation and the labour market.

The new debate concerns the relative rates of change in labour markets and in the use of IT (and other new technologies such as biotechnology) for production. Briefly, the problem is as follows. The use of new technologies requires new labour skills; continual technological change implies continual change in the types and distribution of skills and knowledge demanded of the labour force by employers. Can the labour market keep up with the rate of industrial innovation made possible by IT? Yet this question assumes naively that such innovation can occur independently of changes in the skills supplied by labour. It may be more realistic to enquire whether innovation can proceed at the rate desired by industrialists, in view of the educational and training factors which constrain changes in the skill distribution of labour.

For example, according to many commentators in industry, innovation is being restricted by a 'shortage' of people with IT skills – particularly in electronic engineering. Industry's demand for such people is practically limitless yet the potential supply of that labour – even in the long term – is restricted by the aptitudes and interests of pupils and students, and by the time required for education and training. Perhaps the present 'IT skills shortage', bemoaned by industry and government alike, is simply an expression of frustrated wishful thinking by employers and policy-makers who entertain unrealistic notions about feasible rates of change in labour markets.

IT INNOVATION AND ECONOMIC CHANGE

IT-based automation is one part of a broader set of relationships between IT and changes in the economy. Just as information processing is a common element in all forms of automation, so technological information is a common element in all forms of economic production. In both cases, IT provides a new means of gaining economic benefits from all categories of information used in production. The significance of IT in the economy is most easily judged by considering how and why new information (of any type) is produced. Where does new information come from?

It is evident that people generate new information – in the form of knowledge – during the course of paid employment both as a result of training and as a by-product of their everyday activities (i.e. 'learning by doing'). It is equally evident that information in other forms is generated as a result of organized, deliberate production activity. Examples of the latter include most design information, other written and recorded information – such as literary works, directories, catalogues, reference works and transactional accounting records – TV programmes, video and audio recordings, and computer software.

Information production is a vast and diverse activity in the economy. Most importantly, information production is just as much part of the economy as the production of agricultural commodities or manufactured goods. Accountable quantities of capital and labour – together with appropriate technology – are required as inputs to the process of producing information outputs. The technology in question is – increasingly – IT, the means to automate some processing and communication aspects of information production.

The crux of the matter is that IT is itself essentially information. Indeed, all technologies can be considered essentially as sets of information, some parts of which happen to be implemented in the form of physical machines (Monk, 1989). The implication of that view is that all forms of technological innovation – the development of new product and process designs, new techniques and methods of organization – in any sector of the economy require the production of new information.

This is the reason why IT is endogenous to the economy, not external to it. The creation of new IT systems, services and products, their production and use in all sectors of industry are all part of the domestic economy (irrespective of details such as the financial valuation of IT imports from other economies). Thus the word 'impact' in the title of this chapter is misleading: it makes no more sense to talk of the 'impact' of IT on the economy than of, say, the 'impact' of the wage mechanism. Clearly, IT plays a very major role in the operation of the economy but it does so as an integral part of the economic system.

TOWARDS THE INFORMATION ECONOMY

The development and application of IT over the past three decades has coincided with an observed change in the structure of the major Western economies. Noted first by Machlup (1962) with reference to the United States, the dominant sector of these economies is now concerned not with the production of goods but with the production of information. Machlup, followed by Porat (1977) and others, sought to estimate the contribution made to the economy by activities related to information (including knowledge). While these studies varied in method and detail, a common result emerged: that the production, distribution and use of information accounted for between a quarter and over half of national income. The information sector was thus discovered to be of the same order of magnitude as macroeconomic variables such as aggregate consumption or total government expenditure. Since economic theorists had generally assumed away information production, something was clearly wrong.

Part of the answer to this problem can be found by reconsidering the role information plays in any economy. Two roles are immediately evident. First, all forms of technology ultimately consist in sets of information, without which the organization and execution of economic production simply would not be possible. Secondly, all transactions – whether financial or technical – ultimately consist in the communication of information between economic agents. In addition, information-related activities such as education, the arts, journalism, the law and much entertainment are essential to any assumption of knowledgeable labour, entrepreneurs or consumers, and to any assumption of an economy operating within an identifiable society.

In the course of an economy's development through an industrial phase, the proportion of activities devoted to technology, transactions and knowledge will typically increase. Productivity increases in primary (extractive) and secondary (manufacturing) sectors, brought about by technological innovation, in turn release capital and labour for further development of information-related activities. The situation identified by Machlup, Porat and others may be thought of as a new, post-industrial phase of economic development. Here, the economy is characterized by the dominance of information over physical resources. In an 'Information Economy', information processing is the dominant activity; information or knowledge is the dominant resource; IT is the dominant technology.

One of the most significant characteristics of the Information Economy is that IT – including telecommunications – plays a wider role than simply being the most widely used production technology. Specifically, IT is increasingly the medium through which economic transactions take place. Modern banks now rely on large, complex IT systems both for the delivery of services to customers and for the maintenance of the national and international banking system itself. Stock market transactions provide a similar example.

The point is that IT provides the means for the operation of basic economic mechanisms, including the majority of transactions in all capital, labour and product markets. Without IT, the operation of the Information Economy would simply not be possible. In a very practical sense, the efficiency and effectiveness of the IT systems used for transactions in large part determine the efficiency of mechanisms in the economy – most notably, the relative efficiency of 'markets' as a method of organizing economic activities.

This is the major reason why, for example, the European Commission has devoted such detailed attention to the telecommunications industry during preparations for the post-1992 Single Market (CEC, 1987). It is also the major reason why the availability of IT products and services, the provision of IT skills training in education at all levels and the modernization of information-related legislation (especially on copyrights and patents) have all become important public policy issues in the USA, Japan and the European Community member states.

These macroeconomic and public policy issues may seem far removed from the day-to-day work of accountants, yet they will have a profound and direct effect on accounting practices in the 1990s and beyond. The root cause of these effects – at both the macroeconomic and microeconomic levels – is the changing role of information in production, together with the continuing development of IT as the technological means of processing and communicating that information. So far, no adequate methods exist for measuring information – let alone valuing it – within firms or within industries, sectors, national or international economies. As a consequence, productivity cannot be measured in either the dominant activity within firms or the dominant sector of the economy. Similarly, the value of investments in IT – either as production technology or as the transactional infrastructure of the economy – cannot yet be assessed with any quantitative accuracy.

In brief, IT and the Information Economy present a challenge to the accounting profession: to catch up with the reality of economic activity in the final years of the twentieth century; the simple counting and book-keeping concepts familiar to Bob Cratchett in Dickens' *A Christmas Carol* are no longer adequate for the accounting task.

FURTHER READING

IT has profound implications for the economic geography of industrialized nations, particularly the form and function of cities. These issues are treated in:

Hepworth, M. (1989). *Geography of the Information Economy*. Pinter Publishers, London.

The best guide to the economic and social aspects of the use of IT for automation in manufacturing industry is still:

Kaplinsky, R. (1984). *Automation: The Technology and Society*. Longman, Harlow.

Contemporary technological change is closely bound up with the economics of information and the role of IT in the economy. These questions are considered in:

Monk, P. J. (1989). *Technological Change in the Information Economy*. Pinter Publishers, London.

DISCUSSION QUESTIONS

1. IT systems are frequently used for a number of different applications at the same time. How might investments in IT be appraised? Are existing accounting techniques adequate for this purpose?
2. How would you account for the values of design, operational and strategic information used by firms in production? Do your answers make commercial sense?
3. 'Cost-reducing IT innovations always create unemployment.' Discuss.
4. What factors determine the distribution of IT skills amongst people in the economy? How quickly might that skill distribution change?
5. What is the 'Information Economy'? Should the IT industry be considered as a special case in such an economy? If so, on what basis and with what consequences?

REFERENCES

Barron, I. and Curnow, R. (1979) *The Future with Microelectronics: Forecasting the effects of information technology*. Open University Press, Milton Keynes.

CEC (Commission of the European Communities) (1987) *Towards a dynamic European economy: Green Paper on the development of the Common Market for telecommunications services and equipment*, COM (87) 290, CEC, ʄussels.

Earl, M. (ed.) (1988). *Information Management: The Strategic Dimension*. Oxford University Press, Oxford.

Hepworth, M. (1989). *Geography of the Information Economy*. Pinter Publishers, London.

Jenkins, C. and Sherman, B. (1979) *The Collapse of Work*. Eyre Methuen, London.

Kaplinsky, R. (1984). *Automation: The Technology and Society*. Longman, Harlow.

Machlup, F. (1962). *The Production and Distribution of Knowledge in the United States*. Princeton University Press, Princeton (USA).

McNurlin, B. C. and Sprague, R. H. (1989). *Information Systems Management in Practice*, 2nd edition. Prentice-Hall International, Englewood Cliffs, New Jersey.

Monk, P. J. (1989). *Technological Change in the Information Economy*. Pinter Publishers, London.

Porat, M. (1977) *The Information Economy*. US Department of Commerce, Office of Telecommunications, Washington DC.

Strassman, P. (1985). *Information Payoff*. Free Press, New York/Collier Macmillan, London.

3 The information economics approach to financial reporting

Martin Walker

INTRODUCTION

Since the late sixties, researchers in information economics have made a number of important contributions towards our understanding of the role and value of information in capitalist economies. This literature is of considerable potential importance for accounting policy decisions which influence the timing, quality and quantity of public financial information. Unfortunately the information economics literature is mathematically forbidding and, to outsiders at least, gives the appearance of being somewhat fragmented. The purpose of the paper is to provide a non-technical overview of the economics literature as it relates to financial reporting.

THE ANALYTICAL METHOD

Research in the information economics area to date has been primarily analytical, concerning itself with the value of information in hypothetical decision contexts. The analytical approach studies the behaviour of model economies under alternative information scenarios. For example, one might compare the behaviour of the economy in the absence of an information system with the behaviour of the economy in the presence of an information system. This kind of work is analogous to the modelling work of, say, engineers. For example, to test the wind resistance of a new car shape they construct a computer model designed to predict the likely

Source: *Accounting and Business Research*, **18** (70), pp. 170–82.
Published by the Institute of Chartered Accountants in England and Wales.

resistance factors under alternative body shapes. Of course such models cannot capture all the relevant features of reality. At best they can only take into account the main factors likely to affect the final outcome. Nevertheless such models are useful because they help to structure the thinking of the design effort and because they often produce a working 'prototype' to which minor modifications can be made to reflect the influence of the factors not taken into account by the model.

The key difference between engineering modelling and information systems modelling is the human element. The behaviour of inanimate objects like cars can be predicted on the basis of natural laws of wide validity. Unfortunately, from the modeller's point of view, the same cannot be said of the behaviour of human agents. Because of the human element the predictive success of economic models tends to be somewhat patchy, at least when judged by the standards used to assess the validity of the models of natural science. Nevertheless, when used properly, economic theory can provide a useful tool. In particular, analytical economic models are useful conceptual devices which help one to organize one's thinking about a problem. Moreover, even though the predictive ability of economic models is poor, this does not imply that society would be better off without them.

BASIC PRINCIPLES OF NEOCLASSICAL INFORMATION ECONOMICS

The information economics approach to accounting is based on the view that the demand for and supply of accounting information can and should be explained in terms of the choice behaviour of individuals. It is a scientific approach to accounting in the sense that its prime objective is to understand accounting practices and procedures.

The information economics approach is essentially neoclassical in the following sense (Hahn, 1984):

1. First, it is individualist in that it attempts to locate explanations in the actions of individual agents.
2. Second, it imposes strong assumptions with regard to the rationality of individuals. In particular almost all the information economics litera-ture assumes that individuals choose as if to maximize their own expected utility.
3. Third, to the extent that it is concerned with the results of bargaining behaviour between individuals the approach focuses entirely on equili-brium positions, i.e. positions in which the intended action choices of individuals are mutually consistent and can be implemented.

Some social scientists (e.g. Marxists) reject individualism. Most economists believe it to be the approach most likely to lead to fruitful results. Ultimately acceptance of individualism is a matter of personal conviction.

The assumption of expected utility maximization is more difficult to justify. Its main advantage is that it provides a mathematically convenient characterization of individual choice behaviour that is often consistent with observed choice behaviour. Its main limitation, for present purposes, stems from the fact that it rules out a priori any possibility of information overload. It simply assumes that individuals make full and correct use of all information available to them.

With regard to the rationality assumption it should also be stressed that the assumption of rationality is an assumption about individual behaviour. It says nothing about the rationality of society as a whole or of the rationality of collective actions such as the actions of a firm.

At first sight the restriction of focus to equilibrium positions seems somewhat limiting. Certainly this would be so if by 'equilibrium' was meant 'competitive equilibrium under market clearing conditions'. In fact there is a whole variety of equilibrium concepts which can be fruitfully applied to the analysis of bargaining under uncertainty. Most of these equilibrium concepts are derived from the theory of games rather than the somewhat narrow field of competitive equilibrium theory (see, for example, Harsanyi, 1977; Shubik, 1982; Stiglitz and Weiss, 1983).

From a policy point of view there are two possible arguments against the information economics approach: that the perfect rationality assumption renders the approach useless because it is unrealistic; and that the approach is of no practical value because it focuses only on equilibrium positions.

Against the first of these criticisms it is important to note that even though particular individuals may exhibit irrational behaviour, neverthe-less the information economics approach may yield the best predictions on average if the deviations from rationality are unsystematic and unpredict-able. Furthermore, the rationality assumption offers considerable advantages from a modelling point of view. As a practical matter, models based on rationality assumptions tend to be more tractable than models based on alternative behavioural assumptions. Against the second criticism one can argue that corporate reporting policy changes very slowly. Thus even though the predictions of information economics are valid only in the long run, this is not a practical weakness of the approach since the long-run predictions of the theory are the ones most relevant for policy-making.

Finally, we should note one other common feature of the information economics models reviewed below. All these models assume that most individuals exhibit a degree of risk aversion. This assumption motivates a demand for insurance and other forms of risk-sharing contracts.

SINGLE PERSON DECISION ANALYSIS

There are two novel features of the information economics approach which set it apart from earlier schools of thought. The first is that uncertainty is explicitly treated as a central feature of economic reality. This is in contrast to the more traditional schools of accounting thought which, at best, only treat uncertainty implicitly (namely the prudence concept, extraordinary items, lower of cost or market value, etc.). The second is that information economics attempts to analyse the demand for and supply of information in a multi-person environment where conflicts of interest are prominent. Thus most recent information economics models are concerned with multi-person economies in an uncertain environment.

However, before examining these models, it will be helpful to begin by considering a simpler model involving just one individual in an uncertain environment. In this model uncertainty is represented by assuming that, at any point in time, the economy can be in one of several possible states of the world. Information is then represented as any device which helps one either to detect the current state of the world or to forecast its future state. For example, consider the following decision problem of a farmer.

At the start of the year the farmer must decide whether to plant barley or potatoes. The profit he derives from his crop depends on whether the summer is wet or dry. The figures in the table show the farmer's profit under each weather/crop scenario. There are two alternative states of the world, 'wet' or 'dry'.

	Wet summer	Dry summer
Plant barley	£10 000	£50 000
Plant potatoes	£30 000	£20 000

Suppose the farmer believes that there is an equal probability of a wet or dry summer and that he wishes to maximize his expected profit, i.e. he is risk neutral. Then he will choose to plant barley since his expected profit from planting barley is £30 000 compared with only £25 000 if he plants potatoes.

Now suppose the farmer can purchase a perfect weather forecast before making his crop decision. In this case he will plant barley if the forecast is dry yielding a profit of £50 000 and potatoes if the forecast is wet yielding a profit of £30 000. His overall expected profit will be £40 000 which is £10 000 more than his expected profit in the absence of a perfect weather forecast.

The basic single person decision problem under uncertainty generalizes the above example to allow for more than two states of the world and for forecasting systems which range between zero information and perfect information. To present this model formally, let $A = (a_1, \ldots, a_N)$ represent a set of alternative actions. Suppose the consequence of an action depends on the state of the world. Let C represent the set of possible consequences and S represent the set of possible states. Let c_{ij} stand for the consequence of action i if state j occurs. Thus, for example, the consequence of the farmer selecting the action 'plant barley' if the state is 'wet' is £10 000.

Under a plausible set of axioms with regard to the rationality of the individual's ranking of consequences and acts, it can be shown that an individual will choose his act as if to maximize his expected utility. The expected utility of an act is defined as follows:

$$EU(a_i) = \Sigma p_i U(c_{ij}) \tag{3.1}$$

where

$EU(a_i)$ = the expected utility of action i;
$U(\cdot)$ = the utility function of the individual defined over consequences;
p_j = the subjective probability assigned by the individual to state j.

In the absence of information the individual will choose the action yielding the highest value of $EU(a_i)$. Let EU (no information) stand for the expected utility of the optimum action choice.

Information is represented in the model as a mapping from the set of states to a set of possible signals $Y \equiv (y_1, \ldots, y_k)$. The signal is received by the individual before making his action choice. On receiving a particular signal the individual will first revise his prior subjective probabilities in the light of the information conveyed by the signal. Let p_{jk} stand for the revised probability of state j given signal k. Then the expected utility of action i given signal k is simply:

$$EU(a_i|y_k) = \sum_j p_{jk} U(c_{ij}) \tag{3.2}$$

The optimum action, given signal k, is the action with the highest value of $EU(a_i|y_k)$. Let $EU(y_k)$ be the expected utility of the optimum action, given signal k, that is:

$$EU(y_k) = \underset{a_j \subset A}{\text{Max}} \ [EU(a_i|y_j)]$$

If we let p_k stand for the probability of receiving signal k, then the overall expected utility of the individual with access to information can be expressed as follows:

$$EU(\text{under information}) = \sum_k EU(y_k) \cdot p_k$$

An interesting feature of this model is that it can be used to assign a monetary value to information. In particular we can define the monetary value of information as the maximum amount of money that the individual with information would be able to pay in all states of the world and still remain as well off as he was without information. If we let EU(under information, F) stand for the expected utility under information if the individual has to pay F for the use of the information, then the individual's willingness to pay for information can be represented as the value of F such that:

$$EU(\text{under information}, F) = EU(\text{without information})$$

The model can also be used to examine how individuals rank alternative information systems. An important result in this respect is the fineness theorem which states that for any information systems (A and B) all individuals will prefer the finer of the two information systems if one system is finer than the other. On the other hand if A and B are not comparable as to fineness then the ranking of the two systems may differ from individual to individual according to the details of their preferences/prior beliefs. In particular if A and B are not comparable as to fineness then there will be some configurations of preferences and beliefs which rank A above B and some which rank B above A. Demski (1973) was the first to recognize the importance of the fineness theorem for financial reporting policy. Many financial reporting alternatives are not comparable as to fineness. For example, current cost accounts contain information which is not contained in CPP accounts and vice versa. The importance of the fineness theorem is the implication that any ranking of such non-comparable alternatives is consistent with individual rationality. Thus any attempt to prove that all rational individuals necessarily exhibit the same ranking of two or more non-comparable alternatives is doomed to failure. For example, it is impossible to prove that no rational individual would prefer CCA to CPP or vice versa.

A second general point to emerge from the single person model is recognition that the demand for information in this model relates only to a demand for state of the world forecasts. Conventional accounting statements such as balance sheets and income statements have no value in this context.

THE VALUE OF PUBLIC INFORMATION IN A SOCIAL CONTEXT

If the main purpose of corporate reporting is to provide public information to investors relevant for economic decision-making and control then it is important to understand how public information affects the decisions and welfare of individuals and society as a whole. Ideally one would like to be able to perform a cost-benefit analysis of financial reporting alternatives but at present this seems to be an unattainable goal. More realistically it seems sensible to attempt to identify the potential sources of costs and benefits, and the possible distributional consequences of financial reporting alternatives. This will provide a kind of 'conceptual framework' within which rational debate can take place.

Information economics has made a number of important advances in understanding the potential benefits of public information. The purpose of this section is to review these advances.

Before analysing the social value of information it is important to define what it means to say that a public information system has social value. By analogy with the single person case reviewed in the previous section the definition of social value employed below involves a comparison of the expected utilities of all individuals in the economy without information with the expected utilities of all individuals in the economy with information. In particular, we will say that an information system is of potential social value if, in the economy with the information system, it is possible (perhaps following some lump sum redistribution) to increase the expected utility of at least one individual without reducing the expected utility of any other individual relative to the expected utilities that the individuals would have had in the economy without the information system. This is the Pareto Criterion, an idea which can be explained by reference to Fig. 3.1 which assumes a two-person economy.

In Fig. 3.1 the horizontal axis measures the expected utility of individual 1 and the vertical axis measures the expected utility of individual 2. The curve FCG represents the Pareto frontier of the economy in the absence of information. In other words every point on the curve FCG shows the maximum level of EU_2 that can be achieved for a given level of EU_1. For example, if individual 1 achieves an expected utility of 0G the expected utility of individual 2 will be zero. The curve DABE represents the Pareto frontier of the economy in the presence of information. Here we have assumed that the introduction of information shifts the Pareto frontier of the economy outwards, i.e. information has social value.

Recent theoretical research on the economics of information has made important advances for our understanding of the social value of public

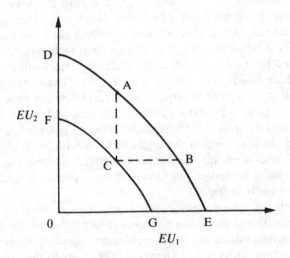

Fig. 3.1 Pareto criterion in a two-person economy.

information. The essential features of these advances can be explained by reference to a simple model economy with the following characteristics:

1. there is a given set of I consumers;
2. there is a given set of J firms;
3. there is a single commodity;
4. the life of the economy is a single period;
5. uncertainty is represented by assuming that the economy can be in one of S possible states of the world at the end of the period.

The following additional assumptions define a special case of this model which provides a useful starting point for our discussion of the social value of public information.

1. Each consumer is a risk averse expected utility maximizer.
2. The utility function of each consumer is time additive.
3. Consumers have homogeneous prior beliefs.
4. All economic agents have equal and costless access to information.
5. Each firm has an exogenously given production plan.
6. The market for firm-specific securities and claims to immediate consumption is both perfect and complete.

Implicit in assumption 6 is the idea that trade takes place only in firm-specific securities written against the end of period payoffs of the J firms.

These securities can be traded against each other or against claims to immediate consumption. The assumption of a perfect market guarantees that all economic agents behave as price takers with respect to security prices and the risk-free rate of interest. The end-of-period production of each firm is an S-dimensional vector of state contingent payoffs. The S by J matrix formed by the J firm-specific production vectors will be referred to here as the end-of-period payoff matrix. The 'completeness' part of assumption 6 is equivalent to requiring the end-of-period payoff matrix to be of full row rank. This rank condition ensures that the J firm-specific production vectors span the entire S-dimensional space of end-of-period payoff patterns. Thus, within the limits of his wealth, each consumer can achieve any end-of-period consumption pattern he desires. Moreover, given price-taking behaviour on behalf of consumers, all consumers will prefer more wealth to less.

The concept of information in this model can be represented as any device which either helps economic agents to predict which state of the world is going to occur or which helps economic agents to determine which state has occurred. Beaver and Demski (1979) refer to the former type of information as pre-decision information and the latter type as post-decision information.

It is possible to prove the following propositions (see, for example, Ohlson and Buckman, 1981):

Proposition 1
Given assumptions 1 to 6 inclusive, information has no social value in the sense that the Pareto efficient frontier of society is not affected by the introduction of information into any economy characterized by assumptions 1 to 6.

Proposition 2
In an economy for which assumptions 1 to 6 hold, if pre-decision information is introduced **after** consumers have had a preliminary opportunity to trade, no consumer will wish to retrade following the release of information and there will be no effect on the welfare of any consumer.

Proposition 3
The introduction of pre-decision information into an economy characterized by assumptions 1 to 6 before consumers have had any opportunity to trade can never result in a strict Pareto improvement and may result in every consumer being strictly worse off.

The intuition behind propositions 1 and 2 becomes clear when one recalls that the aggregate amounts of immediate consumption and state contingent end-of-period consumption are given exogenously. Thus information, at best, can only affect the distribution of claims between consumers. However, assumption 6 guarantees that a Pareto efficient allocation of claims will be achieved in the absence of information whilst assumptions 2 and 3 ensure that there will be no demand to alter the distribution of claims following the release of new information.

Proposition 3 can be understood by considering a simple example involving two consumers, two states, and two firms with the following end-of-period payoff matrix:

	State 1	State 2
Firm 1	0	100
Firm 2	100	0

The example assumes that the two consumers have identical utility functions and identical endowments of immediate consumption. In addition both consumers believe the two states are equally likely. Consumer 1 owns the whole of firm 1 and consumer 2 owns the whole of firm 2. In the absence of pre-decision information the two consumers will agree to trade 50% of firm 1 against 50% of firm 2.

Now consider the effect of a perfect pre-decision information system with the signal being released before the consumers have had an opportunity to trade. If state 1 is signalled, consumer 2 will hold on to his endowment and consumer 1 will receive nothing. Similarly consumer 2 will end up receiving nothing if state 2 is signalled. Since state 1 and state 2 are equally likely, both consumers will have a lower expected utility than they would have had in the absence of information. This deleterious effect occurs because the release of information induces a revaluation in the initial endowments of the consumers before they have had an opportunity to insure themselves by trading to a less exposed position.

So far then we have identified no source of social benefit from public information and one potential source of social cost. We will, therefore, have to relax at least one of the assumptions 1 to 6 to produce a model economy in which information has social value. In fact, by relaxing any one of assumptions 1 to 6 it is possible to construct model economies in which the provision of public information leads to a strict Pareto improvement. Assumptions 1 to 6, therefore, are both necessary and sufficient for information to have no social value.

Now if we wish to conduct our analysis within the mainstream tradition of neoclassical financial economics we must retain the first assumption. Most of the published literature on the economics of information also retains assumptions 2 and 3 (Hakansson, Ohlson and Kunkel 1982, present an analysis of an equilibrium model in which assumptions 2 and 3 are relaxed).

The remainder of this section, therefore, focuses on the implications of relaxing assumptions 4, 5 and 6 for our understanding of the social value of public information.

Within the class of models which retain assumptions 1 to 3 it is possible to show that public information has potential social value in model economies which relax any one of assumptions 4, 5 and 6. In model economies where market structures are incomplete (i.e. assumption 6 does not hold) public information may lead to improved social welfare if it facilitates the creation of new trading opportunities or new tradeable securities. We will refer to this possibility as the 'completion of markets' role of information. In model economies where production decisions are endogenous, public pre-decision information can lead to improved production investment decisions. Finally, in model economies in which assumption 4 is relaxed, social costs can arise when individuals have asymmetric access to information. The provision of public information, by removing or reducing such asymmetries, can serve to eliminate or reduce such costs. The remainder of this section examines these three possibilities in more detail.

To illustrate the 'completion of markets' role of information, consider a model economy involving just two identical individuals and three states with state contingent endowments as follows:

		S_1	S_2	S_3
Prior beliefs:		$\frac{1}{3}$	$\frac{1}{3}$	$\frac{1}{3}$
Endowments:	Individual 1	100	0	0
	Individual 2	0	100	0

Now if the state of the world is observable *ex post* by both parties they will be able to agree to share the aggregate payoff equally in state 1 and state 2. Their ability to enforce this agreement would vanish if the state of the world was not observable *ex post*. For example, if the individuals could only observe the information implicit in their own endowment no trade would be possible. Hence we can see that information relating to the state of the world may be useful in so far as it increases the set of risk-sharing opportunities.

Recent research has shown that an increase in the set of risk-sharing opportunities can be achieved in two alternative ways. One possibility is to increase the fineness of the post-decision information system and to expand the set of state contingent contracts to take advantage of the improved post-decision information. Here by 'the post-decision information system' we refer to information relating to the state of the world released at time point 1. Four points should be noted about this post-decision role of information. First, only information which is available to all parties to the contract can satisfy this role. Second, this role does not involve prediction. It simply involves **validation** of the actual state occurrence. In this sense it is probably more akin to what most lay people would regard as the proper role of accounting, i.e. the reporting of the 'facts'. Third, even though state prediction is not involved, the parties to the contract must be able to rely on the information being released *ex post* otherwise they will not be able to base a contract upon it. Fourth, the observable effect of an improvement in the post-decision information system is an increase in the variety and complexity of risk sharing contracts. Amershi (1981 and 1985) and Strong and Walker (1987, Chapters 3 and 4) contain detailed discussions on the 'completion of markets' role of post-decision information.

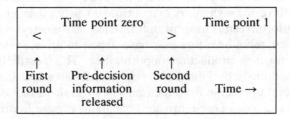

Figure 2   Time line of the iterated market regime

Ohlson and Buckman (1981) have focused on an alternative way of increasing the set of risk-sharing opportunities. This can be achieved by releasing additional pre-decision information (i.e. at time point zero) followed by an additional round of trading. Figure 3.2 illustrates the time line of the Ohlson/Buckman iterated market regime.

Under the Ohlson/Buckman approach the number of securities is held constant and the market is made more complete by allowing a further round of trading in the same set of securities following the release of pre-decision information. In comparison the post-decision information approach involves only a single round of trading but the set of tradeable securities is expanded as the fineness of the post-decision information system is increased.

Social benefits from the provision of public information may also arise where society has some control over the state contingent distribution of aggregate output, for example if society can trade output in one state against output in another, or if current output/leisure can be traded against future output/leisure. If, for example, society could forecast precisely which state was going to occur then resources could be moved into those activities which offered the greatest return in the light of the information received. (Kunkel, 1982, provides a formal demonstration of this possibility.) It is important to note that this type of benefit only arises to the extent that **real** production/investment decisions are affected by the information. To detect such influences one really needs to look at the effect of information on employment and real investment decisions. Changes in share prices and changes in the portfolios of individuals provide, at best, only indirect evidence with regard to these real effects. Finally, it should be noted that only pre-decision information is useful for this particular purpose.

The third major scenario under which public information can be of potential social value occurs when some individuals have access to private information or private information production opportunities. The economics of information has focused on two main types of information asymmetry, i.e. investor/investor asymmetry and outside investor/manager asymmetry.

The investor/investor case of information asymmetry refers to the possibility that some investors may have access to private information or private information production opportunities. This possibility was first examined rigorously by Hirshleifer (1971) and Fama and Laffer (1971). The main point to emerge from their analyses was that situations can arise when there are considerable private benefits to private information production even though the social benefits are zero. Marshall (1974) noted that this possibility provides yet another rationale for the public provision of information. If such information can be produced more cheaply than the aggregate amount spent on private information then public information will be beneficial to the extent that it leads to the attenuation of private information production. The precise details of these arguments have been criticized because they assumed that the relatively uninformed investors would simply react passively to price signals even though they would be aware that they were likely to be 'fleeced' by the informed investors. In recent years a number of models have been developed which assume a greater degree of sophistication on behalf of the uninformed investors. Relying heavily on the assumption of rational expectations, these models show that the uninformed may be able to infer some (and in some cases all) of the information available to informed investors from the behaviour of market prices (e.g. Grossman, 1976 and 1981; Grossman and Stiglitz, 1980; Hellwig, 1980; Jordan and Radner, 1982; Radner, 1968 and 1979).

The question we now need to consider is whether there would be any social benefit to public information production where all individuals form their expectations rationally and take full adantage of the information reflected in market prices. Papers by Verrecchia (1982) and Diamond

(1985) show that there will still be social benefits from the provision of public information so long as privately produced information is less than fully reflected in market prices, i.e. so long as the rational expectations equilibrium is a noisy one. As in the Marshall (1974) paper, the social benefit from public information production stems from the reduction of socially wasteful expenditure on private information production.

The case of outside investor/manager information asymmetry is an issue which has cropped up from time to time in the literature on the economic theory of the firm under the rubric of 'separation of ownership from control'. The economics of information has focused on two main issues within this context. First there is a class of models known collectively as 'agency theory' which basically deals with the issue of how to motivate managers to take decisions consistent with the interests of outside investors. In all such models the manager has a number of decision variables under his control which are not directly observable by outside investors. In some models the manager also has access to additional private information at the time he makes his decision choice. An agency problem arises where the manager's preference ranking over alternative levels of the decision variables differs from that of the shareholders. The literature often refers to such quaint decision variables as the level of expenditure on perquisites or the manager's level of effort, but there are other, possibly more important, decision variables over which conflicts of interest can arise. For example, the manager and shareholders may disagree over what kinds of project risk are acceptable. From time to time the manager may find himself in a position where he would become a social leper by adopting the decision which maximizes his shareholders' wealth (investment in South Africa for example).

The principal–agent literature has identified two major problems which arise in an agency context: the moral hazard problem and the adverse selection problem. A moral hazard problem arises when the action choice of the agent is unobservable and when the preference rankings of the principal and the agent over alternative actions diverge. An adverse selection problem arises when the agent has access to pre-decision information which is not observed by the principal. The agent uses his private information in making his action choice but the principal cannot verify whether the agent has used his information in the way that best serves the principal's interest. For example, a company manager might reject a project because of its high risk even though its acceptance would increase the market value of the firm. Outside shareholders would be unlikely to detect such a decision. Both the moral hazard problem and the adverse selection problem can be overcome by the provision of improved post-decision information. If the post-decision information system allows the principal to infer the agent's action choice then a 'forcing contract' can be used to force the agent to adopt the principal's desired action (a forcing contract is one that imposes a very high penalty on the agent if he deviates from the desired action). Similarly, if the principal can infer both the agent's choice and the agent's pre-decision information, a signal contingent forcing contract can be used to overcome the adverse selection problem. The asterisked articles (*) in the bibliography will provide a useful basis for anyone wishing to pursue the topic in greater depth. For a useful introduction to the main ideas the reader should consult Pratt and Zeckhauser (1984) and Chapter 8 of Strong and Walker (1987). Atkinson and Feltham (1982) and Watts and Zimmerman (1986) examine some of the implications of agency theory for financial accounting.

The second major class of issues that arise when managers have access to superior information is the question of whether managers will have an appropriate incentive to reveal truthfully their private information to outside investors and the related question of whether any costs will be incurred in communicating this information. The two main types of models used to examine these issues are known as 'signalling' and 'screening' models. Both types of models are game theoretic in nature and both involve two types of agents, i.e. informed insiders and uninformed outsiders. Stiglitz and Weiss (1983) have shown that the main differences between the two models stem from the fact that the informed have the first move in signalling models whilst the uninformed have the first move in screening models.

A paper by Leland and Pyle (1977) provides a useful illustrative example of a signalling model. In their model, inside owner-managers observe private information about the future prospects for an investment project (the only project available to the firm). The owner-managers decide whether or not to undertake the project and what proportion of their personal wealth to put into the project. If all owner-managers were forced to hold the same proportion of their wealth in their own project there would be no way for them to communicate credibly their information to the market, since all the managers would have an incentive to claim that the prospect for their project was good to enhance the value of the company's shares. However, when managers are free to choose what proportion of their wealth to put into their own project their choice provides a credible signal to the market about their degree of confidence in the project's success. Assuming the manager is risk-averse, holding a large proportion of his wealth in his own firm is costly because it increases his risk. Only managers who are truly confident about the firm's prospects will be willing to accept such risks. However, whilst managers are able to communicate their information credibly (via their portfolio choice decision)

there are real costs involved in signalling the information to outsiders. In particular, relative to a situation where all information is publicly
available, the inside managers lose out to the extent that their portfolios
are imperfectly diversified. These managers would, therefore, be willing to
pay for any device which would allow them to communicate their private
information credibly without a need to commit a large proportion of their
wealth to a single project.

Articles on signalling and screening frequently draw a distinction
between dissipative and non-dissipative signalling equilibrium. This distinction basically involves a comparison of the Pareto frontier of society
when all individuals have costless access to all relevant information (the
first-best frontier) with the Pareto frontier of society when there is unequal
access to information and communication is achieved via market signalling/
screening. In essence a signalling equilibrium is said to be non-dissipative if
the vector of expected utilities of all individuals in that society is a point on
the first-best frontier; otherwise the equilibrium is said to be dissipative.
Public information has social value in a signalling context if it allows the
replacement of a dissipative equilibrium by a non-dissipative equilibrium
or if it allows the replacement of one dissipative equilibrium with another
dissipative equilibrium with lower aggregate signalling costs. Again it is
important to note that public post-decision information is capable of
providing a non-dissipative solution to the signalling problem. In particular
if the public post-decision information is at least as fine as the pre-decision
information system of the insider manager, then a simple forcing contract
can be used to induce the manager to reveal his information truthfully.
More generally, provided there are no limits on the penalties one can
impose on managers, one will always be able to design a contract to induce
truth-telling behaviour provided there is a positive probability that any lie
by the manager will be detected by the post-decision information system.

Spence (1976) provides a useful introduction to the basic ideas of
signalling and screening theory. Ross (1977), in one of the earliest
applications of signalling theory to financial theory, presents a non-
dissipative signalling model of the capital structure decision. Bhattacharya
(1980) presents a non-dissipative signalling model of the dividend decision.
Miller and Rock's (1985) treatment of the dividend decision involves a
dissipative signalling equilibrium. Stiglitz and Weiss (1981) use a screening
model to explain the phenomena of credit rationing. Ross (1979) examines
the implications of signalling theory for the debate on disclosure regulation
and Bar-Yosef and Livnat (1984) use signalling theory to model the market
for auditors.

In principle, the kind of forcing contracts that can be used to eliminate
agency and signalling costs can also be used to overcome the problems

arising from investor/investor information asymmetry. If the public post-decision information system can identify the pre-decision information of traders, then the less informed can protect themselves by insisting on an insurance contract which requires the other party to the trade to pay a penalty if the post-decision information system shows that the other party traded on the basis of insider information.

In summary there seem to be five main sources of social benefit from public information:

1. To extend the range of trading opportunities with a view to improved risk sharing;
2. To improve real production/investment decisions;
3. To reduce expenditure on private information production;
4. To improve control over management decisions;
5. To reduce the costs of signalling inside information to the market.

The surprise to emerge from this survey is recognition that four out of five (the exception being item 2) of these benefits can, at least in principle, be achieved on the basis of improved post-decision information linked to a sophisticated range of public information signal contingent claims contracts. This may be good news for those who believe that accounting is essentially about the reporting of 'facts' for stewardship purposes, especially if one interprets 'stewardship' broadly as the provision of information for 'contract enforcement'.

SOME UNRESOLVED ISSUES

Three issues remain unresolved by the information economics literature.

THE NATURE OF INCOME MEASUREMENT

The models reviewed in the previous sections all represented an information system as some kind of mapping from states of the world to a set of signals. The reader may well be wondering what this has to do with accounting. Accounting provides various kinds of statements to investors, such as earnings statements and balance sheets, but it is not obvious that any of these represent an information system in the sense defined above.

A paper by Beaver and Demski (1979) attempted to apply the insights of information economics to income measurement. Their paper established the following main points:

1. In a world of perfect and complete markets all shareholders will exhibit unanimous rankings over a firm's alternative production plans. This

ranking will correspond to the ranking given by the market valuations of the alternative production plans.

2. Given the firm's production plan and a complete set of state contingent prices, one can construct an (*ex ante*) measure of economic income. The ranking of production plans induced by this income measure will be identical to the ranking given by the market valuation of the alternative production plans. Hence a fundamental income measure (in the sense that all shareholders prefer more income to less) will exist.

3. If markets are perfect and complete even though an income measure exists, its publication will be of no social value because investors have all the information they need for decision-making purposes if they know the firm's production plan and the set of state contingent prices.

4. If markets are incomplete, shareholders may differ in their rankings of alternative production plans in which case a fundamental income measure will not exist.

5. Whether or not income reporting is socially desirable depends on its ability to produce cost-effective communications between the firm and its shareholders and not on its properties as a fundamental income measure.

In concluding their paper Beaver and Demski wrote:

> ... the case for income rests on the assumption of aggregating more informative but also more costly data such that a cost-effective communication is obtained. However, this assumption is problematical and, in our view, one challenge to accounting theorists is to address the primitive question of the propriety of the accrual concept of income.

The idea that any attempt to explain financial reporting practices must be capable of demonstrating a willingness to pay on behalf of investors for financial reporting has been well received and never seriously challenged. Moreover their 'costly communications' perspective has exerted some influence on other income measurement scholars. For example, Parker *et al.* (1986) included the Beaver and Demski paper in their influential book of readings and highlighted it as a major contribution to the theory of income measurement.

For income measurement theorists the most challenging feature of the Beaver and Demski article is their claim that the propriety of accruals-based income reporting as a cost effective communications device is yet to be demonstrated. In other words a cost/benefit rationale for accruals-based income reporting has never been established and, in particular, the search for a neoclassical equilibrium model which exhibits an endogenous demand for accruals-based earnings measures has, so far, proved fruitless. The construction of a satisfactory response to this challenge stands out as a major unresolved item on the income measurement research agenda.

ON COMMERCIAL SENSITIVITY

Commercial sensitivity is often advanced by firms as a reason for resisting demands for increased financial disclosure. Given the importance of such arguments in the policy domain, it is unfortunate that commercial sensitivity has received little attention either from accounting theorists or from empirical researchers.

The limited amount of theoretical work that has been done suggests that some of the commercial sensitivity arguments are spurious, at least when viewed from the perspective of society as a whole.

Consider, for example, the case of financial disclosures to employees. Some scholars have suggested that information disclosure in a collective bargaining context may 'have adverse distributional effects from the management's point of view' (Foley and Maunders, 1977). Pope and Peel (1981) have questioned this argument. They argue that, if trade union representatives form their expectations rationally, any item of information not supplied by management will be replaced by their own unbiased estimate of that item. Sometimes the estimate will be too high and sometimes it will be too low but on average they will get it right. Hence if management does disclose the data item the only effect will be to reduce the variance of the union's forecast error. Pope and Peel argue that, in the absence of cost considerations, this reduction in variance can only be beneficial to the bargaining process.

Also from a policy point of view it is important to bear in mind that one firm's loss due to commercial sensitivity may well be ofset by gains to other firms. For example, a firm may lose out to its competitors by obeying a requirement to disclose its profit margins but it will gain from the same disclosure requirement being imposed on its competitors. Moreover, even though individual firms may suffer a net loss as a result of increased disclosure, such losses may be acceptable to its shareholders if they also hold shares in the firms which benefit from these disclosures.

Finally, it is worth noting that situations can arise when all firms in an industry would unanimously prefer increased disclosure even though this would reduce the welfare of society as a whole. This logical possibility has been demonstrated in a recent paper by Fried (1984) in the context of a duopolistic industry where each firm has access to private information about its own cost conditions. He shows that each firm will be motivated to disclose this information publicly and that the industry as a whole will be more profitable as a result of the improved coordination of the two firms' output levels. In effect the industry is able to restrict aggregate output to lower levels than it would be in the absence of disclosure. The reduced output level yields higher profits for both firms at the expense of the hapless consumer.

REGULATION

A previous section of this chapter identified the main potential sources of social benefit from the provision of public information. None of these arguments, however, in and of themselves, provide any justification for the regulation of financial reporting. The purpose of this section is to review the economic arguments for and against regulation.

There are two main lines of approach to establishing a case in favour of the regulation of financial reporting. One is to argue for regulation on equity grounds. For example, it might be argued that enhanced financial disclosure protects small investors (see, for example, the AICPA (1973) report on the objectives of financial statements). There is some scope for further research on such equity arguments. On the one hand it would be of interest to find out whether equity judgements have played a significant role in the determination of any accounting standards and, if so, to articulate the ethical judgements of standard setters. There may also be scope for normative research in this area. Rawl's Theory of Justice, Harsanyi's Utilitarian Theory of Ethics, and economic theories of fairness/superfairness, all offer interesting perspectives on the ethical issues faced by standard setters. However, at the end of the day one must always bear in mind that the government has plenty of other tools at its disposal for influencing the distribution of wealth. It may therefore be sensible for policy-makers to focus on technical and efficiency arguments in their deliberations over financial disclosure alternatives under the assumption that the distributional effects can be taken care of by other policy instruments.

Several recent papers and monographs discuss the market failure arguments for regulation (see, for example, Gonedes and Dopuch, 1974; Leftwich, 1980; Beaver, 1981; Benston, 1983; Bromwich, 1985; Taylor and Turley, 1986). The argument most frequently advanced by this literature in favour of regulation is that information appears to exhibit the classic properties of a public good in the sense that it is costly to exclude non-purchasers from its use and the use of information by one user does not exclude its use by another. This argument has been questioned by Bird and Locke (1981) who noted that it may be possible to overcome the public good problem by divorcing the rights to receive information about a firm from the other ownership rights of its shareholders. Groups of investors would be allowed to form 'clubs' to purchase exclusive information from the firm. Similar arguments have been advanced by Gonedes and Dopuch (1974). The Bird and Locke argument, however, seems to ignore the possibility that individual club members will have an incentive to resell their information to non-members.

Another frequently cited rationale for regulation is that the public provision of information reduces the level of socially wasteful private information production. This has been demonstrated in the models of Diamond and Verrecchia mentioned above. However, the demonstration that public disclosure leads to the attenuation of private information production does not provide sufficient grounds for regulation. In the Diamond model, for example, investors unanimously agree on the optimum amount of public information production without the need for any form of regulation. In a recent review of this literature Watts and Zimmerman (1986) argue that all the currently published market failure arguments in favour of regulation reduce ultimately to unsubstantiated claims that government contracting costs are lower than private contracting costs. Watts and Zimmerman conclude that, in the absence of empirical evidence on the relative costs of private and government contracting, there is no clear justification for the regulation of financial reporting.

The ideas discussed in the previous section may ultimately lead to more sophisticated analyses of the regulation issue than those criticized by Watts and Zimmerman. In particular, recognition of the importance of reliable post-decision information as a pre-condition for the existence of sophisticated risk-sharing arrangements and incentive structures leads to a different conception of the purpose and effect of regulation in relation to market forces. Often advocates of regulation are portrayed as being unsympathetic to the market economy. The very word 'regulation' carries connotations of bureaucratic bumbling. The ideas discussed in the previous section, however, lead to an alternative conception of regulation oriented towards the creation of markets which otherwise would not exist. Thus, far from operating as a drag on the workings of the free market, regulation can serve to release the market's full potential.

CONCLUDING REMARKS

The economics of information has proved useful in refining our understanding of the social benefits of information and in highlighting the distinction between the private and social benefits of information. Furthermore, the possibility that many of the social benefits of information can be achieved by using post-decision information as a basis for improved risk-sharing is an important contribution which goes some way to narrowing the divide between information economists and accountants of the 'steward-ship' school.

There are, however, a number of areas where the approach is, at best, inadequate. First, we have no satisfactory theory of commercially sensitive information. Further research on this topic is urgently required. Second, the theoretical arguments for (and against) regulation are woefully under-developed. Finally, and most worrying of all, the conceptual framework of information economics does not interface well with the accounting frame-work. As yet we have no rigorous model of an economic equilibrium in which rational individuals would be willing to pay for accruals-based earnings.

SUPPLEMENT – NOTES ON INFORMATION ECONOMICS AND ORGANIZATIONAL DESIGN

The foregoing chapter has focused on the implications of information economics for external financial reporting. However, the basic methods and concepts of information economics are applicable well beyond the narrow confines of financial reporting. In particular there have been a number of attempts to apply information economics to problems of organizational design. Agency theory is currently the best known, not to say most notorious, of these attempts but there is in fact a broader and potentially richer information economics theory of organizations which encompasses agency theory as a special case.

The basic approach of this general theory is to represent an organization as a game between self-interested players. In general the outcome of the organizational game depends on the decision and information sets of the active players, the possibilities for communication between the players, the objectives ascribed to the active players, and the extent to which the active players can make binding agreements.

The theory functions both as a positive and a normative theory of organizations. As a positive theory it can be used to predict how an organization will behave given a description of the relevant features of the organization game, i.e. who are the key players? what decisions do the key players control? what information is available to the key players? The theory can also be used to predict how the behaviour of the organization will change given a change in the organization. For example, what will happen if communication is allowed between the key players?

The theory can be used normatively to compare the expected utility payoffs to organizational participants of alternative organizational designs. In particular the theory can be used to identify the set of Pareto undominated organizational designs (an organizational design is Pareto dominated if there is another design with a Pareto efficient frontier lying to the north-west of its own Pareto efficient frontier).

From a theoretical point of view there are three major problems with the theory. First it entirely ignores the array of complex ethical and social factors which are known to influence individual behaviour within organizations. Second it imposes very strong assumptions of individual rationality – in effect it assumes unlimited calculating ability on the part of individuals. Third by focusing exclusively on the equilibrium outcomes arrived at by rational players the theory has nothing to say about the process by which the outcomes are achieved. Thus the focus is entirely on substantive rationality and issues of procedural rationality are excluded by theoretical fiat.

From a practical standpoint the theory is strictly limited by the size of game which is computationally tractable. Most of the literature focuses on games with no more than three active players.

My own view is that, in spite of the limitations outlined above, information economics does add to our ability to think constructively about organizational design issues. It is certainly no universal panacea but it does at least provide another perspective on the issues of organizational design which can be best thought of as complementary to the alternative perspectives discussed in the remainder of this book.

FURTHER READING

The further reading for this supplement has been chosen to provide the reader with an introduction to the information economics of organizational design and to provide guidance on the game theoretical background necessary for further study in the area.

Binmore, K. and Dasgupta, P. (1986). 'Game theory: A survey'. Introduction to Binmore, K. and Dasgupta, P. (eds), *Economic Organisations as Games*. Basil Blackwell, Oxford.

Hess, J. D. (1983). *The Economics of Organisation*. North-Holland, Amsterdam.

Radnes, R. and McGuire, C. B. (eds) (1972). *Decision and Organisation*. North Holland, Amsterdam, Chapters 1, 8 and 9.

Myerson, R. B. (1985). 'Bayesian equilibrium and incentive-compatibility: An introduction'. Chapter 8 in Hurwicy, L., Schmeidler, D. and Sonnenschein, H. (eds), *Social Goals and Social Organisation*. Cambridge University Press.

REFERENCES

AICPA (1973). *Report of the Study Group on the Objectives of Financial Statements.*

Amershi, A. H. (1981). *Social value of information, spot-trading and rational expectations equilibria in informationally incomplete exchange markets*, Working Paper, Graduate School of Business, Stanford University.

Amershi, A. H. (1985). 'A complete analysis of full Pareto efficiency in financial markets for arbitrary preferences', *Journal of Finance*, pp. 1235–43.

* Atkinson, A. A. and Feltham, G. (1982). 'Agency theory research and financial accounting standards', chapter in Basu, S. and Milburn, J. A. (eds), *Research to Support Standard Setting in Financial Accounting: A Canadian Perspective.* Clarkson Gordon Foundation.

* Baiman, S. (1982). 'Agency research in managerial accounting: A survey', *Journal of Accounting Literature*, vol. 1, pp. 154–213.

* Baiman, S. and Demski, J. (1980a). 'Variance analysis procedures as motivation devices', *Management Science*, August, pp. 840–8.

* Baiman, S. and Demski, J. (1980b). 'Economically optimal performance evaluation and control systems', *Journal of Accounting Research* (supplement), pp. 184–220.

* Baiman, S. and Evans, J. H. (1983). 'Decentralization and pre-decision information', *Journal of Accounting Research*, pp. 371–95.

Bar-Yosef, S. and Livnat, J. (1984). 'Auditor selection: an incentive signalling approach', *Accounting and Business Research*, pp. 301–9.

Beaver, W. H. (1981). *Financial Reporting: An Accounting Revolution.* Prentice-Hall.

Beaver, W. H. and Demski, J. (1979) 'The nature of income measurement', *Accounting Review*, vol. LIV, no. 1, pp. 38–46.

Benston, G. J. (1983). 'An analysis of the role of accounting standards for enhancing corporate governance and social responsibility', in Bromwich, M. and Hopwood, A. (eds), *Accounting Standards Setting: An International Perspective.* Pitman Books.

Bhattacharya, S. (1979). 'Imperfect information, dividend policy and the "bird in the hand" fallacy', *Bell Journal of Economics and Management Science*, pp. 259–70.

Bhattacharya, S. (1980). 'Nondissipative signalling structures and dividend policy', *Quarterly Journal of Economics*, pp. 1–24.

Bird, R. G. and Locke, S. M. (1981). 'Financial accounting reports: a market model of disclosure', *Journal of Business Finance and Accounting*, vol. 8, no. 1, pp. 27–44.

Bromwich, M. (1985). *The Economics of Accounting Standard Setting.* Prentice-Hall.

* Christensen, J. (1981). 'Communication in agencies', *Bell Journal of Economics and Management Science*, pp. 661–74.

* Christensen, J. (1982). 'The determination of performance standards and participation', *Journal of Accounting Research*, pp. 589–603.

Demski, J. S. (1973). 'The general impossibility of normative accounting standards', *Accounting Review*, pp. 718–23.

* Demski, J. S. and Feltham, G. (1978). 'Economic incentives and budgetary control systems', *Accounting Review*, pp. 336–59.

* Demski, J. S. and Sappington, D. (1984). 'Optimal incentives with multiple agents', *Journal of Economic Theory*, pp. 152–71.

Diamond, D. W. (1985). 'Optimal release of information by firms', *Journal of Finance, vol. 40, no. 4, pp. 1071–95.*

* Dye, R. A. (1983). 'Communication and post-decision information', *Journal of Accounting Research*, pp. 514–33.

* Fama, E. F. (1980). 'Agency problems and the theory of the firm', *Journal of Political Economy*, pp. 288–307.

* Fama, E. F. and Jensen, M. C. (1983a). 'Separation of ownership and control', *Journal of Law and Economics*, pp. 301–26.

* Fama, E. F. and Jensen, M. C. (1983b). 'Agency problems and residual claims', *Journal of Law and Economics*, pp. 327–50.

* Fama, E. F. and Jensen, M. C. (1985). 'Organizational forms and investment decisions', *Journal of Financial Economics*, pp. 101–20.

Fama, E. F. and Laffer, A. (1971). 'Information and capital markets', *Journal of Business*, pp. 289–98.

* Fellingham, J. C., Kwon, Y. K. and Newman, D. P. (1984). 'Ex ante randomization in agency models', *Rand Journal of Economics*, pp. 290–301.

* Feltham, F. A. (1984). 'Financial accounting research: Contributions of information economics and agency theory', in Mattessich, R. (ed.), *Modern Accounting Research: Survey and Guide.*

Foley, B. R. and Maunders, K. T. (1977). *Accounting Information Disclosure and Collective Bargaining.* Macmillan.

Fried, D. (1984). 'Incentives for information production and disclosure in a duopolistic environment', *Quarterly Journal of Economics*, pp. 367–81.

* Gjesdal, F. (1981). 'Accounting for stewardship', *Journal of Accounting Research*, pp. 208–31.

* Gjesdal, F. (1982). 'Information and incentives: the agency information problem', *Review of Economic Studies*, pp. 373–90.

Gonedes, N. and Dopuch, N. (1974). 'Capital market equilibrium, information production and selecting accounting techniques', *Journal of Accounting Research* (supplement), pp. 48–169.

* Green, J. R. and Stokey, N. (1983) 'A comparison of tournaments and contracts', *Journal of Political Economy*, pp. 349–64.

Grossman, S. J. (1976). 'On the efficiency of competitive stock markets when investors have diverse information', *Journal of Finance*, pp. 573–85.

Grossman, S. J. (1981). 'An introduction to the theory of rational expectations under asymmetric information', *Review of Economic Studies*, pp. 541–59.

* Grossman, S. J. and Hart, O. D. (1983). 'An analysis of the principal agent problem', *Econometrica*, pp. 7–45.

Grossman, S. J. and Stiglitz, J. E. (1980). 'On the impossibility of informationally efficient markets', *American Economic Review*, pp. 393–408.

Hahn, F. H. (1984). *Equilibrium and Macroeconomics*. Basil Blackwell, Oxford.

Hakansson, N. H., Ohlson, J. A. and Kunkel, G. (1982). 'Sufficient and necessary conditions for information to have social value in pure exchange', *Journal of Finance*, pp. 1169–81.

* Harris, M. and Raviv, A. (1970). 'Optimal incentive contracts with imperfect information', *Journal of Economic Theory*, pp. 231–59.

* Harris, M. and Raviv, A. (1978). 'Some results on incentive contracts with application to education and employment, health insurance and law enforcement', *American Economic Review*, pp. 20–30.

Harsanyi, J. C. (1977). *Rational Behaviour and Bargaining Behaviour in Games and Social Situations*. Cambridge University Press.

Hellwig, M. F. (1980). 'On the aggregation of information in competitive markets', *Journal of Economic Theory*, pp. 477–98.

Hirshleifer, J. (1971). 'The private and social value of information and the reward to incentive activity', *American Economic Review*, pp. 561–74.

* Holmstrom, B. (1979). 'Moral hazard and observability', *Bell Journal of Economics and Management Science*, pp. 74–91.

* Holmstrom, B. (1982). 'Moral hazard in teams', *Bell Journal of Economics and Management Science*, pp. 324–40.

* Jenson, M. C. and Meckling, W. (1976). 'Theory of the firm: managerial behavior, agency costs and ownership structure', *Journal of Financial Economics*, pp. 305–60.

* Jensen, M. C. and Smith, C. W. (1985b). 'Stockholder, manager and creditor interest: applications of agency theory', in Altman, E. I. and Subrahmanyam (eds), *Recent Advances in Corporate Finance*. Irwin.

* John, K. and Kalay, A. (1985). 'Informational content of optimal contracts', in Altman E. I. and Subrahmanyam, (eds), *Recent Advances in Corporate Finance*. Irwin.

Jordan, J. S. and Radner, R. (1982). 'Rational expectations in microeconomic models: an overview', *Journal of Economic Theory*, pp. 201–23.

Kanodia, C. (1985). 'Stochastic monitoring and moral hazard', *Journal of Accounting Research*, pp. 175–93.

Kunkel, J. G. (1982). 'Sufficient conditions for public information to have social value in a production and exchange economy', *Journal of Finance*, pp. 1005–73.

* Kunkel, J. G. and Magee, R. P. (1984). *Relative performance evaluation: an examination of theory and some empirical results*. Working paper, Kellogg Graduate School of Management.

* Lambert, R. A. (1983). 'Long term contracts and moral hazard', *Bell Journal of Economics and Management Science*, pp. 441–52.

* Lambert, R. A. (1984). 'Income smoothing as rational equilibrium behavior', *Accounting Review*, pp. 604–17.

* Lambert, R. A. (1985). 'Variance investigations in agency settings', *Journal of Accounting Research*, pp. 633–47.

* Lazear, E. P. and Rosen, S. (1981). 'Rank-order tournaments as optimum labor contracts', *Journal of Political Economy*, pp. 841–64.

Leland, H. and Pyle, D. H. (1977). 'Information asymmetries, financial structure, and fnancial intermediation', *Journal of Finance*, pp. 371–87.

Leftwich, R. (1980). 'Market failure fallacies and accounting information', *Journal of Accounting and Economics*, pp. 193–211.

Marshall, J. M. (1974). 'Private incentives and public information', *American Economic Review*, pp. 373–90.

Miller, M. H. and Rock, K. (1985). 'Dividend policy under asymmetric information', *Journal of Finance*, pp. 1031–51.

* Mirlees, J. (1975). *The Theory of Moral Hazard and Unobservable Behaviour Part 1*. Mimeo, Nuffield College, Oxford.

* Mookherjee, A. (1984). 'Optimal incentive schemes with many agents', *Review of Economic Studies*, pp. 433–46.

* Myers, S. C. (1977). 'The determinants of corporate borrowing', *Journal of Financial Economics*, pp. 147–76.

* Myerson, R. B. (1979). 'Incentive compatibility and the bargaining problem', *Econometrica*, pp. 61–73.

* Nalebluff, B. and Stiglitz, J. (1983). 'Prizes and incentives; towards a general theory of compensation and competition', *Bell Journal of Economics and Management Science*, pp. 21–43.

Ohlson, J. A. and Buckman, G. (1981). 'Towards a theory of financial accounting: welfare and public information', *Journal of Accounting Research*, pp. 399–433.

Parker, R. H., Harcourt, G. C. and Whittington, G. (1986). *Readings in the Concept and Measurement of Income*. Philip Allan.

* Penno, M. (1984). 'Asymmetry of pre-decision information and managerial accounting', *Journal of Accounting Research*, vol. 22, pp. 177–91.

Pope, D. A. and Peel, P. F. (1981). 'Information disclosures to employees and rational expectations', *Journal of Business Finance and Accounting*, pp. 139–46.

* Pratt, J. W. and Zeckhauser, J. (eds) (1984). *Principals and Agents: The Structure of Business*. Harvard Business School Press, Boston, Mass.

Radner, R. (1968). 'Competitive equilibrium under uncertainty', *Econometrica*, pp. 31–58.

Radner, R. (1979). 'Rational expectations equilibrium: generic existence and the information revealed by prices', *Econometrica*, pp. 655–78.

* Radner, R. (1980). *Does Decentralization Promote Wasteful Conflict?* Bell Laboratories Economic Discussion Paper.

* Radner, R. (1981). 'Monitoring co-operative agreements in a repeated principal–agent relationship', *Econometrica*, pp. 1127–48.

* Ramakrishnan, R. T. S. and Thakor, A. V. (1984). 'The valuation of assets under moral hazard', *Journal of Finance*, pp. 229–38.

* Rogerson, W. P. (1985). 'The first-order approach to principal–agent problems', *Econometrica*, pp. 1357–67.

* Ross, S. A. (1973). 'The economic theory of agency: the principal's problem', *American Economic Review*, pp. 134–9.

Ross, S. A. (1977). 'The determination of financial, structure: the incentive signalling approach', *Bell Journal of Economics and Management Science*, pp. 373–90.

Ross, S. A. (1979). 'Disclosure regulation in financial markets; implications of modern finance theory and signalling theory', in Edwards, F. R. (ed.), *Issues in Financial Regulation*. McGraw-Hill, New York.

* Rubinstein, A. and Yaari, M. (1983). 'Repeated insurance contracts and moral hazard', *Journal of Economic Theory*, pp. 74–97.

* Sappington, D. (1984). 'Incentive contracting with asymmetric and imperfect precontractual knowledge', *Journal of Economic Theory*, pp. 52–70.

* Shavell, S. (1979). 'Risk sharing and incentives in the principal and agency relationship', *Bell Journal of Economics and Management Science*, pp. 53–73.

Shubik, M. (1982). *Game Theory in the Social Sciences*. Cambridge MIT Press.

* Smith, C. W. and Warner, J. B. (1979). 'On financial contracting: an analysis of bond covenants', *Journal of Financial Economics*, pp. 117–61.

Spence, A. M. (1976). 'Informational aspects of market structures: an introduction', *Quarterly Journal of Economics*, pp. 591–7.

* Stiglitz, J. E. (1975). 'Incentives, risk and information: notes toward a theory of hierarchy', *Bell Journal of Economics and Management Science*, pp. 552–79.

Stiglitz, J. E. and Weiss, A. (1981). 'Credit rationing in markets with imperfect information', *American Economic Review*, pp. 393–410.

Stiglitz, J. E. and Weiss, A. (1983). *Sorting out the Differences between Screening and Signalling Models*. Princeton University Working Paper, Princeton.

Strong, N. and Walker, M. (1987). *Information and Capital Markets*. Blackwell.

Taylor, P. and Turley, S. (1986). *The Regulation of Accounting*. Blackwell.

Verrecchia, R. E. (1982). 'The use of mathematical models in financial accounting', *Journal of Accounting Research*, pp. 1–42.

* Watts, R. L. and Zimmerman, J. L. (1986). *Positive Accounting Theory*. Prentice-Hall.

4 Economic theories of information: a critique
Shaun Hargreaves Heap and Yanis Varoufakis

INTRODUCTION

How do people come to hold their beliefs about the properties of commodities, the likely behaviour of others, the future rate of inflation, and so on? These are crucial questions for economics because the behaviour of individuals depends on these and other expectations. For instance, it is the attributes of the information set which individuals go to work with that are crucial to models of adverse selection, moral hazard and signalling, to list just a few.

Neoclassical economists supply a distinctive answer to this question by focusing on the rational acquisition and processing of information. In this chapter, we provide a critical review of their analysis. In particular, we argue that the neoclassical view slides over certain difficulties in information theory which, in this context, are likely to mean that the full significance of the IT revolution is not appreciated.

The burden of the argument turns on the meaning of 'rational belief'. A belief is rational if it has been **properly** deduced from one's environment. Further, an action based on this belief is rational provided the belief has been processed **properly** and so constitutes the most appropriate response to whatever challenge the individual is facing. The snag is that specifying what we mean by **properly** in both instances is not as straightforward as neoclassical economics seems to suggest.

Neoclassical economics treats the interrelated problems of belief formation and belief processing in an 'instrumental' manner. The individual wishes

Specially commissioned for *IT and Accounting: The impact of information technology*.
Edited by Bernard C. Williams and Barry J. Spaul.
Published in 1991 by Chapman & Hall, London ISBN 0 412 39210 0.

to achieve predetermined objectives and beliefs are rational to the extent that they aid the pursuit of those ends. We will refer to this as the instrumental view of rational beliefs and, more generally, of rationality.

From this neoclassical perspective, it is natural to treat information as a resource that facilitates the maximizing calculation and to imagine that the revolution in IT will simply mean that this resource is made more plentiful, leading to ever better maximizing calculations. In short, IT simply enables us to move ever closer to what would obtain in a world of perfect information.

However, we shall argue that this vision of information and its relation to rational action is badly misleading. This argument is developed in the next three sections by a closer examination of the way information interconnects with rational decision-making in neoclassical economics. We conclude that information cannot be treated as just another commodity, the use of which can be understood in instrumental terms. Instead, the processing of information necessarily requires a non-instrumental component of decision-making; and this non-instrumental component imparts a distinctive character to outcomes. Thus, an analysis that treats information only as a resource for instrumental calculation and which focuses exclusively on how cheaper information makes it easier to satisfy preferences is likely to underplay the significance of the IT revolution. The IT revolution is also likely to impact on the non-instrumental components of decision-making, thus affecting the character of outcomes in ways which could not be predicted on instrumental grounds alone.

SEARCH THEORY AND BAYES' RULE

One neoclassical approach to information acquisition comes from search theory. Information aids instrumental calculation and its acquisition is also treated instrumentally. It is like a commodity which the rational agent will acquire up to the point where those famous first order conditions for maximization are satisfied. That is, the individual will acquire information up to the point where the marginal benefit of further information acquisition equals the marginal cost.

At first sight, this seems a straightforward application of instrumental rationality to the task of information acquisition. However, it does beg an important question. How is the individual to show the marginal benefit of further information acquisition unless he or she knows the full information set?

Suppose you are looking for a house to buy. You have already seen ten and you have chosen one out of them as the best of the bunch. Should you take time off work to view yet another one? The story goes that you should if, on average, you expect that you will gain more from having a look than the cost of looking. But how do you know in advance what the marginal benefit will be unless you know what the eleventh house looks like? The neoclassical reply has the individual holding subjective beliefs about the likely marginal benefits. But this raises a question about the rationality of those subjective beliefs. Of course, this question might be answered in turn, in a manner which keeps faith with instrumental rationality, by the individual acquiring information on these beliefs up to the point where marginal benefits equal marginal costs. This satisfies the instrumental definition of rationality, but only by pushing the question on to a higher level of beliefs: why are those subjective beliefs about beliefs rational? To reply again that information on these beliefs was acquired up to the point where marginal benefits equal marginal costs merely shifts the question on to a higher order of belief, and so on in an infinite regress.

In practice, the process does stop somewhere since we do acquire information up to some point, and what must be recognized is that the stopping rule cannot be justified with respect to instrumental rationality in the form of the equalization of marginal benefits and costs alone. There is always some non-instrumental consideration in the form of beliefs which cannot be warranted by an appeal to the instrumental acquisition of information.[1]

Setting the matter of information acquisition on one side, let us turn to the problem of how new information is to be processed and incorporated with existing beliefs. We assume some new information has been acquired and the question is what to do with it. Neoclassical theory provides us with a consistent rule for adjusting our prior beliefs in the light of this new information. The rule is usually referred to as Bayes' rule and offers the only consistent method for incorporating new information about events that are (a) independent and (b) governed by stationary probability distributions. Let us suppose that we look at the sky with the intention of updating our beliefs regarding the probability of rain. Past experience suggests that there is a 50–50 chance of rain at this time of the year. Also, we have observed that the chances of a dry day when the sky is clouded are also 50–50 (i.e. our priors are $Pr(Rain) = Pr(Rain|Cloud) = 0.5$). We look up and we see an overcast sky. How do we incorporate this new information before deciding on whether the 'costs' of carrying an umbrella should be incurred? By Bayes' rule our probability assessment of the chances of rain conditional on the observation of cloud should be:

$$Pr(Rain|Cloud) = \frac{Pr(Cloud|Rain)Pr(Rain)}{Pr(Cloud|Rain)Pr(Rain) + Pr(Cloud|No\ rain)Pr(No\ rain)}$$

or, in general:

$$Pr(A|B) = \frac{Pr(B|A)Pr(A)}{Pr(B|A)Pr(A) + Pr(B|\text{not }A)Pr(\text{not }A)}$$

Hence, in our case, the belief concerning the likelihood of rain is updated from 1/2 to 2/3 when the new information (i.e. the observation of cloud) is taken into consideration.[2]

Bayes' rule is a mathematically correct formula which, under the appropriate conditions, offers a brilliant method for utilizing new information. This is not in doubt. What gives cause for concern is that economics makes use of it when the conditions are **not** appropriate.

The problems with the wholesale application of Bayes' rule fall under two headings. First, we are confronted by difficulties with the priors of belief which appear in the formula for updating. Second, once priors are established, there is the question of whether the conditions (a) and (b) above, of independence and stationarity, are satisfied and thus whether the application of Bayes' rule is appropriate when new information surfaces. We shall briefly consider the matter of priors in this section and then we will discuss the likelihood of the conditions being satisfied in conjunction with the claims of rational expectations in the next section.

The first thing to notice about Bayes' rule is that it depends heavily on the priors of belief. When an individual entertains a poor set of priors then decision-making can go badly wrong. Suppose, for instance, you are wondering whether to be a writer or an accountant and you are uncertain (i.e. you lack information) on your talent as a writer, or the lack of it. If you knew that you had what it takes to be a writer, you would receive, say, 190 utiles from a writing career and 200 from a career in accounting. On the other hand, if you prove to be a talentless writer, you will get 80 utiles from a career in writing and 100 from a career in accounting. What should you do?

The choice of being an accountant dominates since, regardless of your talent, your utility will be greater if you choose to become an accountant. However, suppose now that you entertain a mistaken prior belief that if you actually choose to become a writer, then the chances that you are talented are 9/10; also, you think that if you choose accounting as a career, then the chances of actually being talented are lower, say, they are 50–50. The above characterizes your priors as follows:

Pr(talented|I have chosen to write) = 9/10
Pr(talented|I have chosen accounting) = 1/2

Then, the expected utility from writing becomes:

Pr(talented|writer) × 190 + Pr(not talented|writer) × 80 = 179

and the expected utility from a career in accounting is:

Pr(talented|accountant) × 200 + Pr(not talented |accountant) × 100 = 150.

Hence, you decide to become a writer and the prior belief has led you (badly!) astray. From the instrumental perspective, it is impossible to ignore the possibility of such errors and consequently, the rationality of priors must interest the instrumentally rational agent. Yet, how is the individual to judge the rationality of priors? *Ex post*, it may be obvious as in the case of the person who wrongly foresakes a career in accounting, but *ex ante* the instrumentally rational individual appears in some difficulty. To illustrate the problem, consider what priors a rational individual should assign to different events when there is extreme uncertainty. It is sometimes argued that when the individual has no good reason for assigning one probability rather than another to different events, then the rational thing to do is to assign all the events equal probabilities which sum to one. Thus, extreme uncertainty with respect to initial beliefs should not prevent a rational set of priors and the subsequent use of Bayes' rule to update these priors in the light of new information. However, this argument still presumes that we know the full range of the potential future events. Whereas, in fact, it is part of the self-conscious recognition of our ignorance that we know that some events are likely to happen in the future which we cannot even imagine today and this throws a spanner in the use of the equal probabilities assignment formula.

To appreciate this difficulty consider the options. Suppose we simply assign a probability of zero to these events which we cannot imagine, so that the equal assignment rule can go to work on those events which we can imagine. This means we know that, since we are not omniscient, there will be events in the future that will occur for which there was a prior probability assessment of zero. When those events occur, we will be unable to use Bayes' rule because it is not defined (see formula above) when the prior probability of an event is zero. So, the assignment of zero probability now to all events which we cannot imagine will knowingly lead to inconsistencies later on. Suppose alternatively, we assign some positive probability to these unimaginable events to avoid this inconsistency. We cannot escape the difficulty of not knowing what probability to assign to unimaginable events. It will always infect the assignment rule to those events which we can imagine because the probabilities must sum to one: the value assigned to these unimaginable events critically determines the residual probability which is then to be equally divided between those future events which can be imagined now.

There is no pure rational prior probability to hold in these circumstances: some degree of 'arbitrariness' cannot be avoided. Either it surfaces with some arbitrary assessment of the dimensions of one's ignorance, or the arbitrariness surfaces later when a zero probability event occurs and the individual has to use some other rule for updating beliefs at that point because Bayes' rule is not defined.

In summary, this first category of problems with Bayes' rule resembles the difficulty encountered with respect to search theory. With search theory, we could never quite get away from the problem of our initial ignorance. We could not avoid the possibility that our ignorance might affect the perception of the gains from further information acquisition. Likewise here, it is the self-conscious recognition of ignorance which can defeat the use of Bayes' rule. In both cases, the argument points to the general need to supplement the search theoretic considerations of instrumental rationality-cum-Bayes' rule with some other decision-making rule. Whether, we think of this as 'creative' or 'arbitrary' or some other species of rational belief does not matter for our purposes. The point is that if we follow the neoclassical search theoretic Bayesian route, then we have to acknowledge that something other than instrumental rationality and Bayesian statistical theory must be involved in information acquisition and processing.

RATIONAL EXPECTATIONS AND GAME THEORY

The rational expectations hypothesis promises to slice through these problems whilst keeping faith with instrumental rationality. It does this by approaching the issue of information acquisition from a different angle. The loose argument goes something like this. Instrumentally rational agents will not use an expectations generating procedure which leads to systematic errors. The reason is simple: when an individual makes systematic errors, in principle, he or she can discover the source of the systematic component and thereby remove it; and the instrumentally rational agent has every incentive to do just this because he or she will profit by the removal of such systematic errors. Hence, instrumentally rational agents will only hold expectations which suffer from random white noise errors.

In this way, the rational expectations hypothesis avoids the questions, which troubled us in the last section, of exactly how individuals acquire and process information. Instead, whatever process is used, it jumps to the outcome, which is the only outcome which rational agents will accept. At first sight, this seems an attractive solution to the issue of information collection. We may not know what and how information is collected, but these are secondary matters of interest because we know what the end result must be. However, matters are again not quite so simple upon reflection. How information is acquired and processed is only of second order significance when there is a unique resting point to which all learning schemes will eventually evolve on instrumentally rational grounds alone. But, this will not generally be the case.

There is likely to be a unique resting point, a unique set of expectations, if we falsely model the social world on the natural world and imagine that the acquisition of more information is like the fog gradually lifting to reveal the contours of the natural landscape. Returning to the earlier weather forecasting example, efficient prognosis requires that we use whatever information there is from the past in order to predict the future. The equivalent of the rational expectations hypothesis here is the assumption that an experienced forecaster may make mistakes but that they will not be systematic. On average, the prognosis will be accurate. But, the social world is not like this because the information which we hold about the world actually affects our behaviour and thereby influences the world which we observe. It is as if the weather was affected by, among other things, the mistakes we all make in predicting the weather. What a nightmare for weather forecasters! But, this is the stuff of forecasting in the social world and it contributes to the existence of multiple rational expectations equilibria (that is, more than one expectation which if widely acted upon will confirm itself but for white noise errors). In turn, this means poor information cannot simply be cast in the role of fog which obscures what we would otherwise be able to see – and to return to the discussion of the previous section, this interdependence between what we observe and our ignorance threatens to introduce non-stationarity into the probability distribution governing events and thus undermine the use of Bayes' rule.

The problem posed by the existence of multiple rational expectations equilibria can be stated simply. If instrumental rationality empowers you only to hold rational expectation, it cannot tell you which to hold when there are multiple rational expectations equilibria, since each potentially satisfies the condition of avoiding systematic errors. Again, something more must be added to the model of decision-making to explain how one equilibrium is selected.

To illustrate the problem with the rational expectations argument in more detail, we consider the following simple game where the inter-dependence between action and belief is made plain and where the beliefs now concern the actions of others. Two players, A and B, are involved in a bargaining-like situation. A can choose to drive a hard bargain by playing tough and so can B. First, we assume that there is an asymmetry: B is keener to avoid a confrontation (i.e. both playing tough) than A. Both players are instrumentally motivated, the payoffs are as Table 4.1, and a Nash equilibrium, embodying the instrumental conception of rationality, is defined as a pair of strategies where each strategy is the best reply to the other.

Table 4.1

		Player B	
		Tough	*Weak*
Player A	*Tough*	3,0	4,2*
	Weak	2,4	0,1

* Indicates a Nash equilibrium.

What is A's rational expectation concerning B's choice? Noting that this is a perfect information game,[3] it is clear that there is only one set of strategies which, if acted upon, will confirm the expectations of each player regarding the strategy of the other. Thus, there is a unique rational expectations equilibrium to which, according to equilibrium game theory, the two sides will gravitate: the Nash equilibrium. A will think: my best reply, whatever the other side does, is to play tough. B must surely see this and so must expect me to play tough. Thus, I conclude that B will choose to play weak.

In the above situation, the 'landscape' exhibits interdependence between outcomes and beliefs about those outcomes but this does not pose any special difficulty. The rational expectations hypothesis would be right to argue that the particular thought process that agents use is unimportant. What matters is that there is an equilibrium solution to which both sides will be attracted because it is unique. Consider, however, the amendment given in Table 4.2.

Table 4.2

		Player B	
		Tough	*Weak*
Player A	*Tough*	1,0	4,2*
	Weak	2,4*	0,1

* Indicates a Nash equilibrium.

We have two Nash equilibria. Strategies (tough, weak) and (weak, tough) are in equilibrium, since if A (B) plays tough it is in B's (A's) interest to play weak. It is not at all clear now what it is rational to do since there are now two potentially mutually consistent sets of beliefs, in the sense that if the individuals acted on those beliefs they would be confirmed. In short, there are two rational expectations equilibria associated with the two Nash equilibria. Interestingly, this is so although we operate in a perfect information environment. There is no 'fog' in this decision setting. The uncertainty which A and B experience is entirely due to the fact that their decisions are interdependent in a manner that can only be encountered in social science. This is where the weakness of the instrumental approach, when it is founded on the natural science paradigm, shows. For there is no way that agents can look at Table 4.2 and, by means of their instrumental rationality alone, decide what is the best course of action. The rational expectations hypothesis lends them no support.

At this stage, it is tempting to redraw our earlier conclusion. Something more must be added to the account of expectation formation if we are to explain how one expectation is selected rather than another. There must be a non-instrumental component at work. The only embellishment to this conclusion which seems to come from pursuing the rational expectations twist in the argument is that, in cases of this sort, the non-instrumental component is liable to take the form of a convention. The non-instrumental element must be shared. When there are many expectations which if widely held will confirm themselves but for white noise errors, then the trick of selecting one must involve in some degree of coordination of your choice with that of others (i.e. some mechanism for selecting one Nash equilibrium). A convention for forming expectations which is widely shared is ideally suited for the task of coordination.

However, there is a possible escape route for rational expectations theorists that we need to consider before we can legitimately draw this conclusion. It is sometimes argued that in the absence of a unique equilibrium, agents mix the available equilibria probabilistically. For instance, if you do not know whether it is best to go to the theatre or to the cinema, you effectively choose **as if** by the toss of a coin. Thus, in the game above, let A and B choose to play tough with probability q and p respectively. The suggestion is that since it can never be known which strategy (tough or weak) is best, then q and p are chosen in such a way that A and B find that their expected returns are identical whatever they choose to do. Hence, A plays tough with probability $q = 4/5$ and B with probability $p = 4/5$ and the probability that neither will dominate (i.e. that neither will play tough when the other plays weak) is greater than 1/2 (to be precise, it will be 17/25).[4] If we are to believe this story, then in the absence of a unique rational expectations equilibrium in terms of pure strategies, agents still manage to home in on a uniquely rational decision, albeit one that requires randomization.

There are two problems with this account which we will mention. First, when A plays a mixed strategy, B has no incentive to play one. When A plays tough with probability $q = 4/5$, B is indifferent between either pure strategy or any mixed strategy probabilistic combination of them. B has no reason to choose $p = 4/5$. True, $p = 4/5$ leaves A indifferent, but so what? A, confronted by $q = 4/5$, has no reason to favour $p = 4/5$ from any value between 0 and 1. Since this also works in reverse, there is no reason why rational agents should follow the above randomization. In short, there is a problem with providing an account of the motivation which supports a mixed strategy equilibrium.

Secondly there are more creative solutions to the problem of equilibrium selection than this mixed strategy one and it would be surprising if individuals who are motivated by an 'eye for the main chance' did not avail themselves of these solutions. However, these solutions only become available to the players of this game once their actions are guided by conventions, that is, shared rules for conditioning expectations which are extraneous to the game as it has been defined in terms of payoffs, common knowledge and the presumption of common instrumental rationality.

To appreciate this possibility and how it turns on a recognition that there is more to information in the real world than standard theory will allow, it must be remembered that the game in Table 4.2 is one of perfect information. That is, there is no further information to be had other than the intentions of the other side. There is no 'fog' which might be dispersed by communication. And in the absence of the ability to make binding agreements, there is no way communication between them can change the outcome. The reason is that A, for example, if given an opportunity to talk to B before the game is played, will have a strong incentive to declare that they will play tough. For if A is convincing, then B will have no option but to play weak. Thus, B knows this and will always expect A to say, beforehand, that A intends to play tough. Hence, a communication channel between the two sides is unable to provide B with any information which he did not have. In this sense, we have a game of perfect information to which IT cannot contribute anything of significance.

However, suppose there is a convention in place such that, in view of the fact that both players are expected to talk tough, if one actually declares an intention to play weak, then he or she will actually do so.[5] There is nothing in the game, its structure of payoffs, the presumption of instrumental rationality, and so on, which can explain the origin of this convention. It cannot be deduced from the game. Instead, it is extraneous to the game in this sense and we just suppose that it exists. Table 4.3 describes the payoffs from the pre-play declaration game now.

Table 4.3

| | | **Player B** | |
		Declare tough	*Declare weak*
Player A	*Declare tough*	ER	4,2*
	Declare weak	2,4*	ER

where ER denotes the set of expected returns for both players in the game of Table 4.2. It is simple to show that ER equals 8/5 for each player.

* Indicates a Nash equilibrium.

If both announce the same intention, nothing changes and their expected returns from the actual game of Table 4.2 remain unaffected. If, however, one of the two concedes while the other stands firm, then one of the two Nash equilibria of Table 4.2 will materialize without the need for randomization.

At first sight, the pre-play communication game is not dissimilar to the original one. There are two Nash equilibria in each and it is unclear what rational agents should say to each other given an opportunity to communicate. However, if we apply the standard mixed strategy solution (so as to make this observation independent of the earlier criticism of this escape route), we find that the unique rational expectations equilibrium in Table 4.3 is that each declares 'tough' with probability 6/7.[6] Remarkably, pre-play communication has changed the outcome. By exchanging information before the game proper is played, the two players have changed the outcome. Since each will concede even before the game is played with probability 1/7, the probability that neither will emerge as dominant drops from 0.68 to 0.51.[7] This means the expected returns from playing the game have increased for both players since the probability of the outcome where one dominates (i.e. with payoffs of (2, 4) or (4, 2) occurring) has risen.

In conclusion, this example illustrates how a background convention can open possibilities for fruitful communication between players. An analysis of the game without the convention does not reveal these possibilities. Yet, in the real world, it would be very surprising from an evolutionary perspective if conventions which imparted this kind of information did not arise in the playing of these games since both players can expect to profit from their employment. Accordingly, an account which ignores the role of conventions is liable to miss an important avenue through which information flows impinge on choices in the real world.

To avoid any misunderstanding on this point, it is worth making plain that this appeal to the evolutionary consequences of individuals being instrumentally motivated does not involve a flaw in the argument. To notice that individuals will profit from the existence of conventions is not the same as explaining why the particular convention exists. Any number of conventions might fulfil the task of coordinating choices in the selection of one from multiple rational expectations equilibria. Likewise, our illustration of the benefits of communication would work with any of a number of other possible background conventions. There is nothing in the game to fix the convention, the convention is extraneous to the game. Accordingly, there is no contradiction between the evolutionary argument that we expect a convention to emerge in the conduct of such games and the suggestion that the precise convention cannot itself be explained by appeals to instrumental rationality alone. Instrumental rationality merely points to the advantage of a convention, it does not indicate what convention will be used. Yet, the question of what precise convention is used is not without interest. Not only is it important in the explanation of the precise expectation which is formed, but it will also typically affect the distribution of the gains from coordination.

This last observation is important for a full appreciation both of what is at stake when the pattern of information flows is disturbed by technical change and of what is liable to be missed by orthodox theory. There is not the space to develop the point fully and so we shall make it in shorthand by considering a general game concerned with the division of the gains from cooperation where orthodox theory suggests there is a unique equilibrium. We shall demonstrate that this equilibrium solution rests on a convention. It is not embedded in what constitutes instrumentally rational behaviour. Thus we conclude from this general case that the distribution of the gains from any cooperative venture are liable to depend on conventions which cannot be derived from instrumentally rational foundations.

Take two agencies (e.g. firms, governments, a union and a firm, etc.) A and B who are involved in a division game. There is a 'pie' to be split between them and it is a matter of reaching agreement on shares that add up. If they do not, there is conflict, in which case both lose out. John Nash (1950) has produced a theory which is widely accepted within economics as the best guide to the outcome. His is an axiomatic approach and a few remarks will suffice in the present context. Nash specifies a number of axioms that should characterize his bargaining solution and proceeds to show that there is only one solution which satisfies them. The information setting is taken to be one of perfect information, in that each agency knows with certainty the objective/utility function of the other, and the Nash solution decrees that each will argue for and get a share such that the product of their utility functions is maximized.

As in the game of Table 4.2, information is not a problem. Since the payoffs/utilities are known by both, there is no piece of information that will make any difference. But, if we look closely, we will see that one of the axioms specified by Nash[8] is really a convention which could as easily be replaced by another. Nash assumes that divisions of the pie that have been shunned by the two sides cannot possibly matter. At first, this sounds reasonable. However, suppose the game is played twice in succession, the first time they freely agree to a split of, say, 60–40 for A and B respectively. Then, before the game is played again, legislation is passed which prohibits B from getting less than 40%. Nash's axiom demands that this does not affect the outcome of the second game which should also be expected to result in a 60–40 split. This may or may not be so. But, if there is a convention, which players believe to be pervasive, to the effect that each expects to get, at least, a bit more than the absolute minimum of what they can aspire to, then B may aim for a slight improvement on the 60–40 outcome, an aspiration which may be perfectly rational if he thinks that A shares the convention and thus will anticipate and accept his claim for something over 40%.

The argument here is not that Nash is wrong, only that he may or may not be. It appears to us to be no more or less reasonable for individuals to be guided by a convention which ignores or is influenced by irrelevant outcomes in this way. What matters for an agreement in the division of the pie is that both parties use the same convention and thus entertain consistent expectations about the behaviour of the other. In short, the choice of convention, and with it the division of the pie, is a matter of contingency and not instrumental rationality.

DESIRES AND BELIEF

In this section, we wish to introduce a different kind of criticism of the neoclassical treatment of information. It is born of the observation that people often complain that more information is a hindrance rather than an aid to decision-making – how often, for instance, have you felt even more bemused after reading consumer reports on a prospective consumer durable than you were before? On the model of information facilitating decision-making, this experience seems difficult to understand.

One explanation, of course, revolves around information overload. We cannot cope with more information because we do not have the time to process it. But, such prosaic considerations cannot account for some of the acute anxieties associated with additional information. By contrast, once it is acknowledged that information can have a different relationship to the ends which an individual pursues, it ceases to be so puzzling. For instance, if the information acquired gives reasons for evaluating the ends pursued rather than throwing light on how to achieve given ends, then it becomes apparent why more information sometimes causes a paralysis in decision-making. Indeed, since the individual may identify his or herself with the ends he or she pursues, it provides an obvious reason for why this sort of information can be a source of anxiety: information can threaten one's conception of oneself.

Once we relax the idea of given ends, our concept of rationality is likely to become more complicated. We might subject to Reason, not only our means,[9] but also our objectives (not to mention our prior beliefs!). Indeed, we can even be caught up in games against ourselves during the struggle rationally to accommodate simultaneous changes in information, means and ends.[10]

It serves no purpose to take this matter further here, save to remark that a contrast is sometimes drawn in these circumstances between a Humean account of motivation and a Kantian one (Hollis, 1987). In Hume, as in neoclassical economics, beliefs are the servants of desires and it is desires which motivate an individual, whereas for Kant it is beliefs which motivate the individual, and this places information in a more central role. Another view is that technological advances, such as IT, in conjunction with the evolution in social relations, have a sovereign role to play in shaping both belief and desire simultaneously. If either this or the Kantian suggestion hold, the attempt to theorize information along the lines of conventional economic theory is bound to fail. The point, then, of the observation with which we began this section is simply to provide support for the general argument of the chapter. The common experience that more information can often be a hindrance to decision-making begins to be intelligible once we switch to a more complicated model of rational action. In short, as we have argued in the earlier sections, it seems that the instrumental model just does not have all that we need if we are to make sense of the role that information plays in social life.

SUMMARY

We have argued that the instrumental conception of rationality cannot fully account for how individuals acquire and use information in economics. There are necessarily non-instrumental components of decision-making which contribute to the selection and interpretation of information. In particular, in situations where uncertainty is characterized by social interdependence, it is likely that a crucial non-instrumental source of decision-making will be the shared conventions of a society.

This failing in the instrumental account needs to be recognized because, otherwise, the full significance of the IT revolution will be missed. On the instrumental account alone, IT looks like a relatively benign intervention which should simply shift our calculations about what to do somewhat closer to what we would want to do if we inhabited a world of perfect information. IT has simply made more cheaply available a crucial resource which we use in our maximizing decisions.

However, once we acknowledge that there are non-instrumental elements in individual decision-making, the potential significance of IT grows. In so far as IT also affects the non-instrumental components of decision-making, the character of decisions may be altered dramatically. For instance, rather than moving us closer to some equilibrium which would obtain in conditions of perfect information, we may find that IT leads us to select a completely different equilibrium altogether. Conventions are an important source of non-instrumental decision-making and they also typically have a powerful influence on the way the gains of cooperation are distributed. Consequently, we conclude that a full appreciation of IT will require an analysis of whether and how IT disturbs the prevailing conventions in society.

NOTES

1. Hollis (1987) utilizes the story of Tarquinius Superbus in order to illustrate a similar point. When asked by Sibyl to pay an inordinate sum for the nine books of wisdom, Tarquinius declined. Immediately, she had three of the books burnt in front of him. When he again declined to pay the original asking price for the remaining six, she had another three destroyed. Eventually, he agreed to pay the original price for the three surviving volumes. Search theory can be used to explain why he initially declined: his expected marginal returns equalled his marginal costs at a level of purchases equal to zero. Of course, not having read the books, Tarquinius did not know what their worth was. The problem with search theory is that it can also be used to explain why he eventually changed his mind: he must have altered his subjective assessment of the prospective marginal benefits. Unfortunately, a theory that explains everything *ex post* and nothing *ex ante* carries very little weight.
2. There are two implicit assumptions here. First, there can be no rain without cloud, i.e. $\Pr(\text{Cloud}|\text{Rain}) = 1$, and, second, there is only one kind of cloud.
3. That is both sides know the payoffs and we assume that they are rational and that they know that their opponent is also rational.

4. A's expected returns are $p + (1 - p)4$ from playing tough and $2p$ from playing weak. Hence, $p = 4/5$ if both actions are to yield identical expected returns. Similarly, for q. If A's expected returns from playing tough or weak were not the same, then A would always choose one over the other. But we know that this cannot be the case, hence the equality.

5. The significance of this convention is that players are effectively committed to the weak strategy if they declare prior to the play of the game that they will play weak. But this is not too strong an assumption to make since they still have no way of committing to play tough.

6. Let p' be B's probability of declaring tough. By definition, it must be such that A is indifferent between declaring 'tough' or 'weak'. Hence, p' must

solve $\dfrac{8}{5} p + 4(1 - p) = 2p + \dfrac{8}{5} (1 - p)$. Thus, $p' = 6/7$. Similarly, for

A's optimal randomization.

7. Without communication, the probability of no dominant party is 17/25 whereas now it is $17/25(6/7 \times 6/7 + 1/7 + 1/7) = 0.513$.

8. We refer to the independence of irrelevant alternatives. We could equally have taken issue with the symmetry axiom.

9. Which is what instrumental rationality requires. Its role is to search from the appropriate means without questioning the ends.

10. Cognitive dissonance reduction is one case in point. The person who has just purchased a new Volvo may, after the event, read Volvo advertisements more avidly than before in order to justify his or her choice. Our requirements for information are not always expressible in instrumental terms.

FURTHER READING

Hargreaves Heap, S. (1989). *Rationality in Economics*. Basil Blackwell, Oxford.

Philips, L. (1988). *The Economics of Information*. Cambridge University Press.

Rasmusen, E. (1989). *Games and Information*. Basil Blackwell, Oxford.

Shaw, G. (1984). *Rational Expectations: An Elementary Exposition*. Wheatsheaf, Brighton.

REFERENCES

Hollis, M. (1987). *The Cunning of Reason*. Cambridge University Press.

Nash, J. (1950). The Bargaining Problem. *Econometrica*, **18**, 155–62.

DISCUSSION QUESTIONS

1. Suppose an eyewitness to a burglary at night identifies the robber as black. It is well known from tests that people make correct identifications of this sort in these conditions on 85% of occasions. The proportion of all robberies committed by black people is the same as the proportion of black people in the population, which is 15%. Assuming that it is reasonable for the police to issue a description of the robber as black when there is more than a 50% chance that the robber is black, is it reasonable to identify the robber as black on this occasion? (**Hint**: What would the application of Bayes' Rule suggest?)

2. Assume two players have three strategies available to each of them, 1, 2 and 3, in a game with the following payoffs:

		Player B		
		1	2	3
	1	100, 50	80, 20	1 000, 10
Player A	2	80, 10	40, 50	2 000, 80
	3	0, 0	10, 100	500, 80

(a) Find the two Nash equilibria in this game.

(b) Show that the Nash equilibria are the only strategy pairs such that the expectations of players prior to action are confirmed by the subsequent actions.

(c) Suppose p_1 is the probability that B plays strategy 1, and likewise p_2 and p_3. Find the values of p_1, p_2 and p_3 that make A hesitate over the choice of strategy. (**Hint**: Recall players never consider playing a non-Nash strategy.)

(d) Does B have a motive to do as (c) prescribes?

2 Finance

Arguably there are two aspects to finance in organizations, external and internal. Traditionally the majority of finance literature has been concerned with the abstract modelling of the logic of performance in both of these areas with little interest in the contextual attributes of the data involved. Such generic modelling processes are more appropriately addressed, for example, in Parts Four and Six that follow. This Part, however, is concerned with the way in which finance is affected by IT and this necessarily (and perhaps unconventionally) requires a consideration of some of the contextual factors of finance. Three papers have been selected, one concerned with external finance, another with internal finance and a third with a provider of finance, a member of the banking sector.

Historically stock markets were institutions where buyers and sellers of capital were brought into physical contact to ease the flow of money to projects seeking funding and provide potential investors with an overview of what investment opportunities existed. The physical proximity was originally required to enable and facilitate the flow of information between interested parties in the market-place. Information technology has had many effects on the flow of information in stock markets arising out of its ability to communicate and process data rapidly. The nature of these effects are discussed in David Ayling's paper together with the concept of the 'perfect market' in relation to its conceptual need for 'perfect information'.

The second paper by Richard Price makes a valuable contribution to a surprisingly under-researched area. While huge sums are now regularly spent on information technology by both public and private sector organizations, comparatively little research has been undertaken into the area of financial evaluation of projects after implementation. The rapidly multiplying size of information technology budgets suggests it is essential that the extent and quality of this type of evaluation match the increasingly central role of IT expenditure in many business strategies.

In the paper by Paul Willman and Mark Holding a case study approach is used to examine the role of IT in the banking sector. Their paper on the computerization of the Trustee Savings Bank discusses two periods, the early 1960s to the mid-1970s and the mid-1970s to the late 1980s. The backdrop to this technical change was the movement of the TSB into the private sector. The paper looks at the strategic role of information technology and in particular the relationship between technical change and changing competitive conditions. Some of the technical issues involved in choosing between an on-line, real-time system and a batch system which faced not only the TSB but many other banking institutions are discussed in some depth.

5 The behaviour of the stock market under the influence of IT

David Ayling

INTRODUCTION

The existence of a stock market has become a key requirement for a modern capitalist economy. Stock markets reconcile the different needs of 'suppliers' and 'users' of capital by providing facilities for raising finance for companies and public authorities (the primary market) and for dealing in securities (the secondary market). Primary and secondary market functions are interrelated in that only if a secondary market exists will subscribers to the primary market ever be able to liquidate their investments.

'Efficiency' is generally regarded as a desirable characteristic for a stock market because of its central role in the economy. Hence market participants, users and regulators are constantly concerned with the effectiveness of stock market operations which, ideally, could draw close to the concept of a 'perfect market' because of the large numbers of buyers and sellers and free access to information. Information technology (IT) should, therefore, bring stock markets closer to the concept of a perfect market by speeding up repetitive tasks, by reducing transaction costs and by supporting human decision-making with improved information systems.

Towards this end, IT can potentially improve the following aspects of stock market efficiency:

1. *Functional efficiency*. IT should improve the process of channelling resources to productive units and lower transaction costs.

Specially commissioned for *IT and Accounting: The impact of information technology*. Edited by Bernard C. Williams and Barry J. Spaul. Published in 1991 by Chapman & Hall, London ISBN 0 412 39210 0.

2. *Full insurance/complete markets efficiency.* IT should increase the number and variety of securities traded to the extent that no additional return could be earned from the introduction of a new type of security, since the return on such a new security could be reproduced by a portfolio of existing securities.
3. *Information efficiency.* The wider access to information resulting from IT should lead prices to reflect currently available information with more precision.
4. *Valuation efficiency.* Through the increased facilities for analysis from IT, prices could become more closely based on rational expectations of future payments to which stocks give title.

Whether or not IT really will bring about these improvements in stock market efficiency depends on factors such as the costs and nature of the new technology, competition between IT suppliers and users, and the willingness of market participants and users to take up the new facilities.

This chapter explains the pressures which led up to the current IT revolution, the uses to which IT can be put in the stock market, and the systems currently in operation. Motives and technology for the stock exchange of the future are then examined.

BACKGROUND DEVELOPMENTS

Until recently (1986) stock exchange procedures had changed little since the early twentieth century, when the stock exchange motto 'My word is my bond' was coined as a matter of necessity. *Uberrima fides* (utmost good faith) was an essential ingredient of a fast trading system with a slow administrative back-up. For trading purposes a 'single capacity' system operated whereby stock exchange members could be either an agent of the ultimate share purchaser (broker) or a 'stall holder' (jobber). Brokers earned a commission from their clients in return for searching out the jobber offering the best price. The jobber's 'turn' was earned by maintaining a difference between buying and selling prices (usually called a bid–ask spread). Members of the general public could not trade on the stock exchange without engaging the services of both a broker and a jobber. This system worked well for around 200 years but, by the 1980s, pressures mounted for the system to change.

In 1979 the British government abolished exchange controls as a step towards increasing the volume of international securities trade passing through the UK Stock Exchange and hence improving London's position as an important financial centre. The move brought the London Stock

Exchange into direct competition with foreign stock exchanges which were also keen to maintain or improve their international reputations. For influencing developments at the UK exchange, the USA was a particularly important competitor because transaction costs there were (potentially) lower, due to the use of a 'dual capacity' system of trading.

The advantages of the US 'dual capacity' system to investors was that they only had to pay one intermediary's fee – to a 'market-maker' who combined the roles of broker and jobber. The disadvantage of dual capacity (which was well publicized by the London Stock Exchange authorities) was that opportunities for fraud were greater since the roles of agent and principal were no longer separate and only one member firm needed to be involved in each deal.

The London Stock Exchange's response to the international competition was twofold. First of all, in 1986, an agreement between the Stock Exchange and the International Securities Regulatory Organization (ISRO) established a unified (domestic and international) London equities market called the International Stock Exchange of the United Kingdom and the Republic of Ireland (ISE). Secondly, it was decided to abandon the single capacity trading system for a dual capacity system along US lines. The method for introducing the changes was to abandon the minimum commission for brokers which had crept into the market over the years via mergers and liquidations of broking firms and enabled a certain level of monopoly power to infiltrate the market. For example, for some in-frequently traded securities, only one jobber would be making a market. Once commissions became negotiable, larger institutional clients could shop around for the lowest transaction costs. The brokers' response *would* have been to reduce the amount of business transacted via jobbers and increase 'matching' activities between buyers and sellers – thus cutting out the jobbers' turn. The jobbers response *would* most likely have been retaliation in the form of direct dealing with the general public to cut out the brokers' commission.

This potential conflict was avoided, however, by the new trading system which was in place by the time that negotiable commissions were intro-duced. The new system, which allowed stock exchange member firms to act as both principal and agent (dual capacity), was introduced in a single day (27 October 1986) and was popularly referred to as 'Big Bang'.

Since Big Bang, change has continued to characterize the London equity markets. Computer-based information systems continue to evolve, insider trading restrictions have been more narrowly defined, and the regulatory environment has generally been tightened (for example, with the establish-ment of the Securities and Investment Board). What was once a closed market has now become an open system. The trading floor has been replaced by a computerized giant screen (SEAQ – see next section) with electronic links across the globe to electronic trading systems in other countries. The improved international trading facilities have been accompanied by diversification out of domestic equity markets, and increased competition between national exchanges.

DEALING AND SETTLEMENT – WHAT THE SYSTEM MUST COPE WITH

Since Big Bang, the dealing system for equities and gilt-edged securities has been based on competing market-makers who perform similarly to the jobbers of the old system, with the important difference that they are now free to deal directly with the investing public. Registered market-makers can also offer agency broking services. The brokers of the old system have now been officially renamed broker-dealers. They continue to offer agency services to clients but, in addition, are allowed to deal as principal for their own accounts (provided that they satisfy ISE capital and liquidity requirements).

THE DEALING SYSTEM

The types of transaction undertaken by the two kinds of members with their merged roles are as follows:

1. *Intra-market transactions* where stock exchange members trade with each other for their own accounts.
2. *Customer transactions* where business is carried out for non-members (clients). Customer transactions encompass situations where a broker-dealer acts as principal, where a broker-dealer acts as agent, or where the deal is conducted directly with a market-maker.

THE ACCOUNTS SYSTEM

Fixed interest securities (gilts and public authority securities) and new issues are usually settled on the business day following the date of dealing (the 'cash settlement system'). For equities, however, the normal method for settlement is via the 'account settlement system'.

Under the account settlement system, the year is divided into 24 'accounts' which usually begin on a Monday and end eleven days later on the following Friday. (This basic timetable is adjusted to take into account bank holidays.) Actual settlement (the day that cheques change hands) occurs on the Monday, three weeks after the beginning of the account period. This system may at first seem rather long and clumsy, but is often justified by its flexibility where many trades take place within the account period. Thus an investor could buy and sell a large number of securities within an account period, but only have to pay (or receive) one cheque on Account Day to cover the net profit or loss. If an investor wishes to use them, facilities are available (at a cost) for postponing settlement until the next Account Day.

COMPUTER SYSTEMS FOR DEALING AND SETTLEMENT

TALISMAN

The Stock Exchange's computerized settlement system for equities, introduced in 1979, is called TALISMAN, an acronym for Transfer Accounting Lodgement for Investors, Stock MANagement for market-makers. It is administered by the Settlement Services Department of the Stock Exchange, and is used to settle securities registered in the UK, Eire, Australia and South Africa. For settling trades in US equities, a reciprocal arrangement called the Continuous Net Settlement Service links TALISMAN with US brokers. Another extension to TALISMAN, the Institutional Net Settlement (NIS) system, provides special facilities for financial institutions to deal with member firms.

The two basic functions served by TALISMAN are, first, transfer of documents between buyers and sellers and, secondly, cash settlement betweem member firms. The system also produces a continuous audit trail which the ISE can use to investigate illegal or unprofessional activities.

Underlying the TALISMAN system is a nominee company called SEPON (Stock Exchange POol Nominees) which holds shares in trust on behalf of the owner (first the seller and then the buyer) until the Account Day when net positions are settled.

The TALISMAN/SEPON system has undergone changes since its introduction (especially in order to take account of Big Bang) and has provided a fast, efficient, cost-effective service for its users. The volume of paperwork has been reduced because member firms can base their accounting on book-entry positions, and the responsibility for handling transfers and certification has been removed. Despite these improvements, however, the system for actually issuing share certificates following settlement is still rather slow (up to two months!) because share certification is dealt with by each company registrar rather than via a centralized system.

ARIEL

An alternative to TALISMAN for block trades, known as ARIEL, is worth mentioning here to illustrate the nature of the competition between settlement systems. ARIEL was set up in 1974, before TALISMAN, by a group of institutional investors who wished to exert pressure on the Stock Exchange to reduce transaction costs of securities trading. ARIEL was thus registered as a licensed dealer in securities to offer cheaper commissions to institutions trading in large volumes of equities. Since Big Bang, commissions for large trades have, of course, fallen on the ISE and, although around 2% of London's trading volume still passes through ARIEL, the main reason for its instigation has disappeared.

Off-board trading

The ISE does not have a monopoly on securities dealing and settlement, so if services offered are inadequate, too expensive, or geared too much towards homogeneous financial instruments, buyers and sellers of securities may go elsewhere. For example, for securities settled outside TALISMAN, a non-high-tech system links ultimate buyers and sellers. The buyer's 'ticket' is passed along until it finds the person prepared to sell the stock who then makes delivery in return for payment. Often, under this system, differences in initial buying and selling prices must be sorted out on Account Day.

INFORMATION SYSTEMS

The raw data for the Stock Exchange's information systems are supplied mainly by the market-makers who are required to make firm two-way prices (a buying or 'bid' price and a selling or 'ask' price) for at least 5000 shares in the securities for which they are registered. If no market-maker is involved in the transaction, the reporting duty falls to the broker-dealer. In return for making a market, the market-makers receive certain privileges such as access to the inter-dealer–broker (IDB) system and facilitated stock borrowing. The speed at which market-makers are required to report essential details of their transactions depends on the grade of security being bought or sold. For alpha (most actively traded) and beta (frequently traded) stocks, transaction details must be reported to the central market authority within five minutes of dealing during the 9 a.m. to 5 p.m. trading day. Details of transactions in gamma (less frequently traded) stocks need not be reported until the end of the trading day, but most market-makers report them within five minutes anyway. The permanent record of each day's trading is published in the Stock Exchange Daily Official List the following day.

COMPUTERIZED INFORMATION (SEAQ, EPIC and TOPIC)

The dealing system is linked via electronic technology to the market's main information system SEAQ (Stock Exchange Automated Quotations) which, in turn, is linked to TOPIC, the electronic price screen, and to a series of in-house systems (Fig. 5.1). The EPIC computer system links SEAQ and TOPIC to a further group of computers such as Datastream, Valueline, Reuters and Hotline, where data can be stored, analysed or transferred to a wide range of end-users.

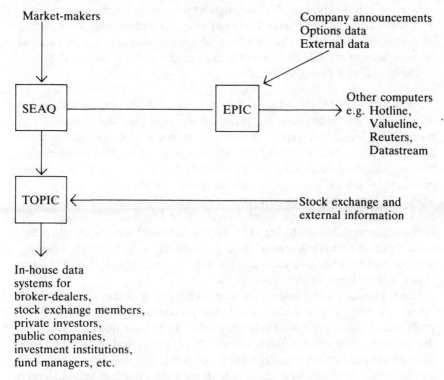

Fig. 5.1 Stock exchange data collection and dissemination.

The type of information available to end-users through SEAQ depends on how much they are willing to pay for the service, which is divided into three levels.

1. *Level 1* (the investor service) is the cheapest level and is available in the UK, Eire and the USA via international quote dealers. Details provided include the best bid and offer prices and a volume specification.
2. *Level 2* (the competing quotation, or broker-dealers' service) enables subscribers to see composite pages on the TOPIC screen. Details available include market-makers' two-way prices with size indicators. For alpha and beta stocks, the three best bid and ask prices are shown (selected on the basis of price, size and time of quotation) along with the dealing spread. For alpha stocks (only), prices for the most recent ten trades and cumulative daily trading volumes are also available. 'Indicative', rather than firm prices are available for less frequently traded gamma stocks. The Level 2 service enables investors to deal directly, by telephone, with market-makers. Investors without the service can do their trading through broker-dealers who do subscribe.
3. *Level 3* (the market-makers' service) interacts with the market's human price-setting system. This is where competing market-makers situated anywhere in the UK or Eire enter their prices and transaction details as explained in a previous section.

As with TALISMAN, an important feature of the SEAQ system is that it produces an audit trail for investigating irregular share dealing. A particularly important aspect of investor protection, know as the 'best-execution rule', can be monitored via the system. This rule requires that broker-dealers should take all reasonable steps to ensure that prices obtained by clients are at least as favourable as those displayed on the SEAQ system for a comparable size. The rule has become necessary since the changeover from single to dual capacity trading where 'Chinese walls' (i.e. insurmountable obstacles to conflicts of interest) have been erected to ensure that the broking service on the one hand, and the market making service, on the other, are carried on at arm's length. (Many member firms conduct both types of operation).

Other checks on the system include investigating delays and suspected insider dealing. For tracking fraud, the electronic system is a tool for investigators who must also rely on their 'feel for the market'. Dealings that precede price-sensitive announcements are monitored by the Exchange and sometimes further investigation is required. Bargain details available electronically are followed up by telephone calls aimed at establishing a connection between the person who dealt and anyone who would have known about a price-sensitive announcement before it was made. All information is then stored in a database (which has been under construction since Big Bang) so that patterns such as the same person dealing ahead of three or four announcements can be examined for potential future investigation.

SERVICES FOR SMALL INVESTORS

The ISE introduced a dealing service for small investors in 1988 called SAEF (SEAQ Automatic Execution Facility). The range of stocks available on the system are limited to selected alpha and beta stocks and only small deals (1000 shares initially) can be transacted. Only agency trades are permitted. Member firms enter their clients' instructions at a terminal and the transaction is then automatically executed at the most favourable price. Plans are underway to link SAEF with TALISMAN so that the settlement of small deals can become even faster and cheaper.

SAEF faces competition from alternative automated execution systems such as Barclay de Zoete Wedd's TRADE and Kleinwort Benson's BEST which hope to capture some of the smaller order market.

NON-SEAQ STOCKS

For shares that are infrequently traded (delta stocks) price details are not electronically posted. Instead TOPIC lists an electronic market-maker's index so that the market-maker dealing in any particular stock can be identified and contacted.

HOW THE SYSTEM HAS COPED SINCE BIG BANG

Big Bang and its time-zone position enabled London to rank along with New York and Tokyo as one of the main centres for securities trading. Share dealing has become generally more efficient – functionally at least – without major failure even during the world-wide stock market crash of October 1987. The fear of fraud which accompanied the changeover from single to dual capacity still exists but the situation is probably no worse than before Big Bang (although the number of actual convictions for insider dealing is still small in comparison with the number of investigations).

During the period 12 to 30 October 1987, London prices fell 27% (compared with 23% in New York). Despite some accusations that market-makers did not answer their telephones during this dramatic period, the markets remained open at all times and deals were transacted close to quoted prices apart from two hectic 15 minute intervals. Given that the crash was unanticipated, and that on 19 and 20 October the daily volume of transactions was more than double average daily transactions for 1987, the system withstood the shock well.

Particulary useful sources of information on developments at the ISE before and after the crash are the quarterly ISE-produced *Quality of*

Market Reports. Here the ISE provides information on particular aspects of the Exchange's performance. These aspects include commission rates, dealing spreads, turnover, the depth and liquidity of the market, (i.e. how quickly prices change in response to trades), development of new financial instruments, methods and techniques, and the number of market-makers in each stock. These reports show that functional efficiency (as measured by commissions, spreads and touch prices) deteriorated sharply after the 1987 crash (along with most of the world's exchanges) but has since improved.

For marketeers the period since the crash has been problematic, due to reduced investor confidence and hence a lower level of trading in equities. The order flow has steeply declined and many jobs have been lost because of the excess market-making capacity. The strongest survivors are the integrated financial firms which can exploit synergies between market-making operations and provision of other financial services.

Another problem since the crash surfaced during 1988 when a number of financial institutions began bypassing the SEAQ system to deal directly with each other. Their reason for doing this was to avoid the publicity of their actions which SEAQ automatically disseminated. Market-makers, too, claimed that publicity of large trades was not helpful because competition could guess which firms were engaging in the deals, and hence move prices against them. In an attempt to restore a central market-place the ISE introduced new rules which stated that market-makers no longer have to deal with each other at the prices posted. The question of how accurately posted prices should reflect actual prices is likely to attract increasing debate; the need to protect market-makers in vulnerable positions conflicts with the need to maintain market informational efficiency.

A further aspect of the stock exchange system which the crash threw into important relief is the slow speed of settlement during hectic trading. Even with TALISMAN, share transfers require several documents to pass between ISE firms, sellers, buyers, banks and company registrars. Some small investors have had to wait months for their documents due to the 'paper mountain' backlog. It is intended that further implementation of IT at the ISE will rectify this situation.

PAPERLESS SETTLEMENT

The ISE has plans to introduce an even more sophisticated system to increase the efficiency of settlement operations. Late 1993 is the target date for complete removal of paper from the settlement process. The planned new system, which will replace TALISMAN, is called TAURUS (Transfer and AUtomated Registration of Uncertified Stock). It will cost around £50 million to develop but, over ten years, should save the securities industry around £250 million. Clients will receive documents more like bank statements than share certificates. Company registrars will, however, continue to keep customary records in order to pay dividends and inform shareholders of meetings and so on. Linked to TAURUS will be a trade matching system to reduce the risk of error so that trade information will only have to be entered once.

The introduction of TAURUS will mark the end of the traditional stock exchange account system described earlier. It will be replaced by a 'rolling settlement' system – a continuous cycle for clearing bargains so that all trades can be settled in three working days or less. It is hoped to introduce the new system in October 1992 in line with TAURUS development.

A EURO-BOURSE?

Details of a potential international share price system, called Pipe, which could develop into Europe's largest stock market are now is a state of preparation. The envisaged system would, initially, involve collecting electronic share price information from each national market on a central computer and then transmitting it to geographically widespread buyers of the service. A potential second phase of the system would enable users to interact with the central database. This stage could, in turn, lead to a fully fledged trading system for leading European stocks.

So far, national exchanges have agreed to the first step – in principle. Whether or not the system will develop to its full potential will depend on politics rather than feasibility, since the required technology is already available.

THE STOCK EXCHANGE OF THE FUTURE

Information technology has already led to the development of inter-national markets for a vast variety of financial instruments and reduced the need for physical trading floors. It is highly likely that this trend will continue and that broker-dealers, market-makers and the investing public will be on an equal footing with regard to receipt of price information regardless of their geographical location. To put it another way, there will probably not be *a* stock exchange of the future, because the intense competition between trading systems will lead to a multitude of regional exchanges and private trading systems.

Compared with the Stock Exchange of even 20 years ago, this evolution is remarkable, representing a major improvement in the functional, full insurance and informational aspects of market efficiency. The future of valuation efficiency will depend on the quality of human information processing given the wider access to data. On the one hand, the price system could become a better reflection of the collective consciousness as applied to the matter of share valuation. On the other hand, the introduction of IT has not removed the opportunity for non-fundamental factors (such as panic) to influence share prices as they did before or after the world-wide stock market crash of 19 and 20 October 1987.

FURTHER READING

Adams, A. (1989). *Investment*. Graham and Trotman.

Ayling, D. E. (1986). *The Internationalisation of Stockmarkets*. Gower.

Cohen, K. J. *et al.* (1986). *The Microstructure of Securities Markets*. Prentice Hall.

King, P. (ed.) (1988). 'Dealing rooms of the future', *Euromoney Supplement*, April, pp. 1–24.

Madhavan, A. *et al.* (1988). *Risky business. The clearance and settlement of financial transactions*. Rodney L. White Centre for Financial Research Paper No. 40.

Neuberger, A. and Schwartz, R. A. (1989). *Current developments in the London Equity Market*. London Business School Paper, August.

Quality of Market Reports, ISE quarterly publication.

Roell, A. (1988). *Regulating information disclosure among stock exchange market makers*. LSE Financial Group Discussion Paper Series, No. 51, October.

DISCUSSION QUESTIONS

1. What is meant by stock exchange 'efficiency' and how can IT improve it?
2. In what respects is IT more important under a dual capacity trading system than under single capacity?
3. Is a two-week stock exchange account more sensible than a rolling settlement system? Why?
4. Are the prices posted on TOPIC the same as those at which trades take place?
5. What incentives could persuade investors to bypass market-makers?
6. 'The setting of stock exchange prices is an integral part of the execution of trades.' Discuss in relation to IT and other types of market.

6 What is the payoff from end-user computing – evidence accumulating from the USA and UK

Richard Price

The management consultancy of Peat Marwick and its strategic consultants Nolan Norton & Co. have been studying the growth and impact of end-user computing in both the UK and North America. This work began in 1986 when we first looked into the payoff from personal computing in the US. Over the last three years we have performed surveys, multi-company research projects and individual company studies into management practices surrounding the investment in end-user computing. This chapter summarizes the evidence we have accumulated as to the potential payoff from this growing activity in UK companies.

End-user computing can be defined as the systems and tools given directly to staff which allow them to manipulate their own or extracted data, to decide when and how to use applications and to own their own data.

Nolan Norton made a forecast in 1980 that the cost of information systems in leading companies would rise by seven times in the next ten years. They came to this forecast by looking at each segment of information systems spending: they estimated that traditional data processing would double; a further three-fold increase was forecast because of the impact of end-user computing; and the last factor was the impact of 'niche' projects – special workstations for computer-aided design, artificial intelligence, customer and supplier terminals and similar high-impact high-risk areas.

Specially commissioned for *IT and Accounting: The impact of information technology*.
Edited by Bernard C. Williams and Barry J. Spaul.
Published in 1991 by Chapman & Hall, London ISBN 0 412 39210 0

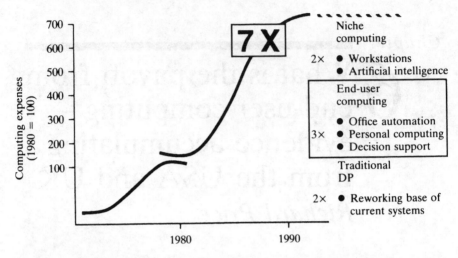

Fig. 6.1 The environment: Nolan Norton predicted seven times growth in computing investment during the 1980s – personal computing was driving much of this growth.

This forecast (illustrated in Fig. 6.1) created a considerable stir at the time. But Nolan Norton have been monitoring the growth of these companies and found that growth was stronger than expected over the first few years of the 1980s.

Now in some companies the growth appears to be tailing off. When we look into the reasons for this, we find that managements are becoming disenchanted with continually escalating spending on information systems and want to see some benefit. Actual bottom-line benefit is the demand.

The area of spending which comes under the closest scrutiny is end-user computing, the reason being that management see this as discretionary spending – they do not have to do it. Compare this to traditional data processing systems which have become institutionalized; they are difficult to remove because companies have become so dependent on them and to keep them you have to invest in reworking and maintaining them.

In a more recent study Nolan Norton have estimated that between 30 and 40% of the total information systems spend is now directed at end-user computing. This represents a large investment which in many companies has been difficult to control and for which there is little evidence of payback.

This growth is borne out by many studies in Europe. One such market research study performed by IDC (Fig. 6.2) indicates that in the period

1981 to 1987 the level of expenditure on desk-top computers has grown by over 320%.

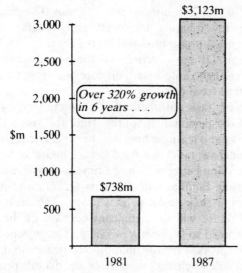

Fig. 6.2 Shipments of desk-top computers, Western Europe.

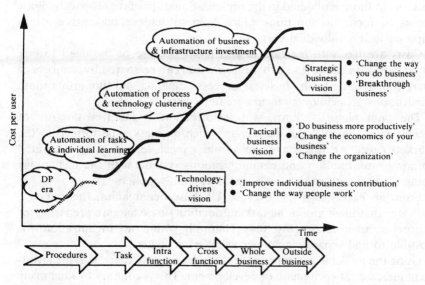

Fig. 6.3 Personal computing evolves through successive phases of application emphasis.

All the evidence suggests that investment in end-user computing has been high and for this reason we have investigated the management disciplines necessary to achieve bottom-line benefits. The framework we have developed for investigating the costs and benefits of end-user computing is based on a 4 phase model (Fig. 6.3).

The first phase – the 'DP era' – represents the period when companies invested in data processing to automate their core business procedures with little or no involvement from end-users.

The second-phase of 'task automation' is characterized by the large-scale introduction of the personal computer. Here the vision is limited to the automation of tasks and learning how best to use the technology. Users seek to be more productive; tasks that used to take hours or days now take much less and can be done better with more time to consider alternatives. When the users become familiar with the new techniques they begin to think about performing their tasks in new ways. The costs of moving through this second phase will be significant because of the volume of workstations and the need to support a novice and large user base.

The third phase of 'process transformation' recognizes that individuals rarely work in isolation. Each task is part of an overall process which supports a business function. In this phase the technology can improve the linkages between individual tasks which make up a process. This can create changes to the economics of a business and may require different work patterns to those embodied in the organizational structure. The technology begins to focus on functions which help to achieve business goals as opposed to the individual user.

Costs are likely to increase at this point because of the need to link workstations in networks so that information can be shared by numbers of users contributing to the business process. Building and supporting these applications of technology incurs greater costs.

The final phase – 'business transformation' – involves the use of technology to change the manner in which business is performed in the market-place. At this stage we would expect to see fully integrated corporate information and communications systems with the technology being applied innovatively with customers and suppliers.

From an examination of over 30 UK-based companies, the evidence indicates that most are in the task automation phase and are preparing for process transformation (Fig. 6.4). Naturally within any organization it is possible to find separate activities at different stages.

Using the model in a number of field studies we have found that the investment increases at each phase of development. This is contrary to what many managements expect. In particular, we have isolated the components of costs that all organizations can expect to incur at each phase (Fig. 6.5).

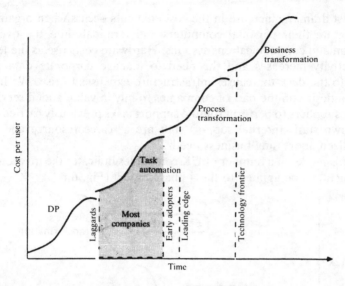

Fig. 6.4 Today most companies are migrating through the task automation phase of personal computing and some are moving to process transformation.

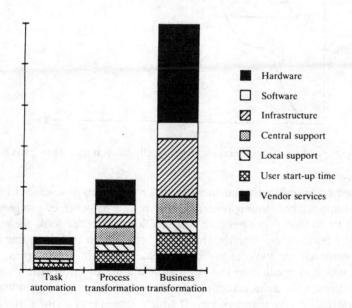

Fig. 6.5 The PC cost model.

The most dramatic increase in the cost elements occurs when organizations integrate their personal computers and terminals into the overall information and communications systems. Hardware costs rise as the level of connectivity increases and the need to manage corporate data and deliver it to the desk-top causes infrastructure expenses to rise. We have also seen a desire on the part of companies to buy in value-added services from their suppliers to perform routine support tasks previously carried out by their own staff. Internal support staff are a scarce resource and are better utilized addressing business needs.

Using this model in a number of UK companies indicates the investment values which can be applied to the 4 phase model (Fig. 6.6.).

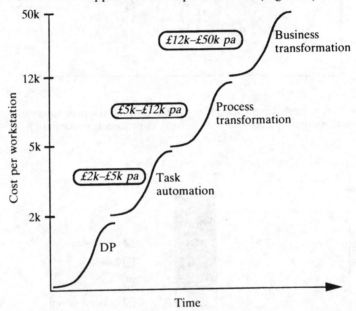

Fig. 6.6 Costs per workstation increase dramatically in each successive phase.

The need to establish the business case for this rising investment is of paramount importance. In our research there is little evidence of companies attempting to do this. Some perform cost justification but few look ahead to establish the bottom-line benefits which may accrue from such investments.

In our research we have used benefits based planning techniques, an approach which is applied to the strategic planning of information technology to support the achievement of business goals. Our findings indicate that there are different levels of payoff which correspond to the different phases of the model (Fig. 6.7.)

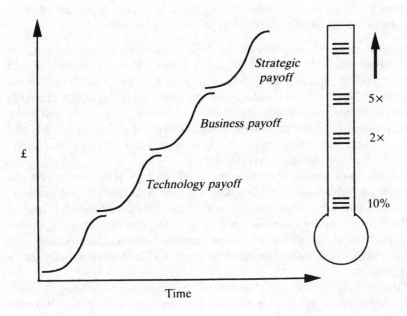

Fig. 6.7 Higher costs can yield higher payoffs.

The technical payoff comes about from individuals making productivity gains. A return of between 5 and 10% is not unrealistic. More significantly the business returns which we have evaluated at the process transformation phase can be of orders of magnitude. We have cases in the UK where investments are yielding between 2× and 5× per year. The evidence would suggest that strategic investments in IT are likely to give even higher returns by offering new ways to carry out business within a competitive market but we have found characteristics in UK companies (unlike the US) which put up hurdles to such achievements.

The main constraint we have found in the UK is that managers often cannot articulate the performance measures under their responsibility. By this we mean that they do not understand what are the key activities they are responsible for which directly impact on the organization's achievement of business goals. The cause of this in some cases has been that they do not have access to information on the overall business strategy; in other cases it has been because they have found it difficult to think in this way. Equally, the IT department is not always the best agent for this change, particularly when we have found there to be a technology driven rather than a business driven focus.

Three elements appear to be missing from the planning process of those companies which were concerned at the lack of benefits:

1. *Analyse and define the investment levels:* how much money is spent now and how much should be spent in the future? Unless management are prepared to sponsor investment it will not be possible to break successfully into the next phase; efforts would be better concentrated in cost reduction exercises to maintain the existing IT spending and make better use of existing resources, using the existing tools more widely and in a more controlled manner. This is a valid strategy and some companies will decide to go this way.

2. *Analyse and define the business goals and performance measures.* Strategic advantages are traditionally in three areas: productivity, competitive advantage, and management effectiveness. Each one of these areas can be quantified with a performance measure. Objectives in each of these will need to be identified and communicated to a specific function within the business which will take responsibility for its fulfillment.

3. *Analyse and define the benefits.* User department managers must set themselves achievable targets for improvement of the business performance measures and determine how this will result in increased profits. This will identify the activities where the investment should be targeted for greatest benefit.

The evidence suggests that where these planning elements have been applied users have been able to gain bottom-line benefits and the IT resources have been able to target their limited support capability at activities with the greatest potential for payback.

DISCUSSION QUESTIONS

1. What approaches could companies use to measure the level of investment in end-user computing?
2. What opportunities exist for companies to achieve payback from their investment in end-user computing? How should they ensure the payback reaches the bottom line?
3. Who should be the sponsor for controlling and directing this investment? What obstacles will they meet and how might they be overcome?
4. What role should end-user computing play in a company's strategic thinking? Will the 'connected workplace' have an impact on organizational effectiveness? If so, how?

7 Computerization at the Trustee Savings Bank

Paul Willman and Mark Holding

INTRODUCTION

The Trustee Savings Bank (TSB) has a very different history from many of its competitors. From 1810 to 1976 it sat in limbo between private and public sectors, not publicly owned but not operating as a profit-making concern.[1] It was a traditional thrift institution owned by Trustees, differing organizationally from both banks and building societies. Since the 1976 TSB Act, it has developed the full range of personal banking services in competition with building societies and banks.

The trajectory of technical change within the TSB is also unusual. Its on-line, real-time (OLRT) system in the 1970s focused on counter automation involving instantaneous data transmission, whereas the other clearing banks focused on batching data from branches to central processing units using back-office terminals. In part, this reflected different business priorities at TSB, but it also reflected a different attitude to the role of technology in the provision of financial services.

This case examines the TSB in the context of the UK financial services sector and attempts an assessment of the success of its technology strategy. The structure of the case is as follows. First, a brief outline of technical developments in the sector is presented. Secondly, some background features of the TSB organization are described. In the following two sections, the two main phases of technical change and their consequences are described. Finally, an assessment of the success of the TSB strategy is attempted.

This chapter was prepared as a paper within the Technology and Firm Organisation research programme conducted at the Centre for Business Strategy in association with the Institute for Organisational Research. It is part of the ESRC/DTI initiative on Technology and the Firm. The financial support of the ESRC and the DTI is gratefully acknowledged.
© 1990 Paul Willman and Mark Holding.

INFORMATION TECHNOLOGY IN BANKING[2]

Banks may currently use information technology in a variety of ways and for a variety of purposes. Cash may be dispensed and deposited, accounts debited and credited automatically. Administration may be assisted by information technology based management information systems. Inter-bank and international money transfers may be effected by use of secure utilities such as SWIFT and CHAPS. However, the central historical problem and still the central technological issue for retail banks concerns the capture and organization of account data through branches.

The large retail banks, including TSB, have thousands of branches. In each, a variety of account transactions are performed involving cash deposits and withdrawals, transfers, cheques and standing orders. Although many transactions must still be verified by signature, the main use of information technology in banking has been to generate and control a database of account information and to effect the transmission of money which transactions in the account base require.

The major UK clearing banks began to use computer technology for such data capture in the 1960s. Several phases may be distinguished. In the first, large mainframe computers, often remotely located, were employed to record account data; data were transferred by road and input manually, later using VDU screens linked directly to the central processing unit, i.e. the operation ran 'off-line'. The second stage was to put branches 'on-line' thus avoiding the need to transfer paper by road and allowing direct transmission of data; however, most banks did not operate instantaneous transmission of data, preferring 'batch' rather than 'real-time' transfer. Typically, land lines to the central unit would operate only at the end of the working day and accounts would be updated overnight.

Since land lines are expensive and business volume was growing, the third stage was a limited form of distributed processing, i.e. data were processed either in the branch or by a minicomputer covering several branches and subsequently batched to the central unit. The fourth stage involved the development of 'non-branch delivery systems' such as point-of-sale and autotellers which were linked into the central unit but avoided the branch altogether. The former could easily operate by batching, but the latter tended to be real-time for security reasons.

This is a broad brush description of the clearing bank systems, but one which captures its essential features. Three related features are of interest. The first is that such systems were designed to deliver transaction informa-tion to the centre for bank purposes rather than to the customer. The second is that they focused on cost, i.e. the reduction of labour cost in a labour-intensive sector, rather than new products or processes. The third is that, consequently, such changes were essentially process innovations rather than product innovations (or the basis for them).

The TSB is different. From an early stage, it opted for an OLRT system with counter terminals. Although systems have developed, the commitment to OLRT remains. It is necessary to understand some of the history of the organization to understand why this is the case.

THE HISTORY OF THE TSB[3]

The roots of the Trustee Savings Banks lie in the industrial revolution of the nineteenth century. Reverend Henry Duncan opened the first TSB in Dumfriesshire in 1810. His motives are worth noting since they influenced the behaviour of the organization for almost 160 years:

1. to provide a haven for the savings of the poor;
2. to encourage self-sufficiency by the promotion of thrift;
3. to alleviate the hardship caused by seasonal employment and fluctuating commodity prices.

The TSBs proved popular and spread rapidly. By the mid-nineteenth century there were over 600. Since then banks have tended to merge into larger units. But in 1973 there were still 73 banks with a total of 1549 branch offices.[4]

Prior to 1970 the TSBs were essentially vehicles for personal savings. They boasted strong local identities and close community links. Notably, their network was concentrated in Scotland and the North of England. They catered predominantly for social classes C2/D/E. In sum, they remained purely thrift organizations for the working classes.

Indeed, by statute the TSBs were never permitted to lend to their customers. Their statutory framework had been laid down by an Act of Parliament in 1817. That Act set out the rights of depositors and the duties of the banks' trustees. As a safeguard it also provided that the depositors' funds should be invested with the government or in government securities. This framework remained substantially unaltered until 1976. TSB's funds were held in a special interest bearing account at the Bank of England, and their movement was effectively controlled by the Treasury.

However, during the 1960s the savings bank market began to change in response to customers' needs and the activities of the clearing banks. Within the constraints placed upon it the TSB tried to keep pace with the changes. In 1965 the savings banks introduced cheque accounts and in 1967 the TSB Group formed its own unit trust company. The programme of computerization which the TSB embarked upon at this time was part of this modernizing trend; however, the TSB was still hampered in fully competitive operation by statutory constraints.

It was at this critical stage that the government asked the Page Committee to consider the future role and development of the National Savings Movement, the Department of National Savings, and the Trustee Savings Banks. The TSB's presented a 'shopping list' of requests to the committee. In 1973 Page reported its findings. To their surprise the TSBs got everything they asked for and more. The Page Report concluded there was a need for a banking sector catering primarly for the small saver and depositor which would provide a full range of banking services. A 'developed' TSB could fulfil this role. Such a group would have wide freedom to offer services and to invest. It would stimulate competition by offering banking services to rival effectively those of the major private sector clearing banks.

In response to the Page Report the TSBs took a major step in reducing their number by amalgamation from 73 to 19 within a year. The TSB Act followed in 1976. It revised the statutory framework accordingly, so that the TSBs could develop 'the degree of coordination and central operations necessary in order to fulfil their potential.' The TSB was given clearing bank status and was permitted to lend on its own account.

The subsequent decade (up to 1986) was an important transition period for the TSB as it set out to expand its services and compete across the board with the major clearing banks.[5] In 1976 there were approximately 750 000 cheque account holder, by 1984 there were over three and a half million. The TSBs introduced personal lending in 1977 and by November 1984 their total personal lending including mortgage lending approached £2bn. In 1978 the TSB Trustcard was launched as a member of the VISA organization. By the end of 1984 over 2 million cards were in issue representing roughly 14 per cent of the credit card market. Through its TSB Trust Company Ltd the TSB was, by 1986, the seventh largest unit trust management group and the second largest bank unit trust management company. TSB introduced commercial business in 1979.

The trend towards amalgamation proceeded. By November 1983 the number of independent TSBs had been brought down to four: TSB England and Wales, TSB Scotland, TSB Northern Ireland, TSB Channel Islands. In December 1984 the government published a White Paper and an accompanying TSB Bill. This legislation aimed to float the TSB on the stock market to allow it to move from a quasi-federal structure to that of a conventional commercial structure under the UK Companies Acts. It was hoped that this would give the TSB a more effective operating structure and also clarify its ownership and accountability. Although delayed by legal wrangles concerning the ownership of funds, the flotation eventually went ahead in September 1986.

Since flotation TSB Group Plc has continued to diversify its financial services. With £1bn of proceeds from the flotation the Group proceeded in the next 12 months to purchase the life assurance group Target for £220m, and merchant banking group Hill Samuel for £777m. The Hill Samuel takeover was an attempt to move into the corporate finance sector, and was hoped to complement TSBs existing services. However, the takeover occurred at an inopportune moment. Purchased at a price arranged before the October Crash in 1987, the Hill Samuel purchase quickly looked expensive. Overall, TSB's performance since the flotation, itself seen as a huge success, has left a lot to be desired. In June 1989 the Group reported that its yearly profits in every sector had declined over the previous 12 months. Despite this faltering, the TSB is without doubt a radically different bank from that of two decades ago. It has made a transition from a one product savings bank to a private high street bank offering a full range of financial services to its customers.

THE MOVE TO ON-LINE, REAL-TIME

This section describes and analyses in basic terms the nature of the TSB's choice of OLRT. Within the framework of the Technology Project it proceeds from a discussion of technological choice to a concern with the issues surrounding implementation.

CHOICE OF TECHNOLOGY

By the end of the 1960s, the majority of UK bank accounts were computerized and banks were moving towards on-line data transmission. By the mid-1970s, most clearing bank branches were on-line, i.e. account data were captured by branch terminals linked directly to their bank's central computer. However, the clearing banks had decided not to develop real-time technology because it was 'neither practical nor advisable from the development and operational viewpoint.'[6] They saw no advantages of real-time technology either in terms of their current operations or how they envisaged themselves developing. The clearing banks' computer systems were on-line batch systems.

In contrast, in 1971, the 35 TSBs in England and Wales, who up until then had moved in line with the general tide of bank computerization chose to implement an on-line real-time system.[7] The principle difference between real-time and batch processing systems is that with the former a central computer processes data immediately and transmits the information back to the branch terminal for the immediate use of the staff and customer, whereas the latter accounts are updated overnight and therefore any enquiry at a branch may be up to 24 hours out of date.

When considering the origins of this computer choice one needs to look at both the technology itself and the environmental factors influencing the circumstances in which the choice was made. The technology itself was sophisticated. At the time, the TSBs OLRT computer system was superior to any commercial computer system in Western Europe or North America. Savings banks are the principle international users of real-time. For instance, 94% of US savings banks were using OLRT in 1978.[8] However, TSB's choice of OLRT remains difficult to explain without reference to non-technological factors. The main environmental factors to consider were competition and history.

It has already been noted that all other major banks were computerizing in the 1960s. They did so for three reasons. First, the volume of business was growing and the expansion could not be dealt with manually. Secondly, in tight labour market conditions, clerical staff could not easily be retained or replaced. Thirdly, most branches, often in old buildings, were short of the space to process paper transactions. It was widely recognized that computerization was essential to remain competitive.[9] It was in this atmosphere that, in 1967, the TSB established a Working Party to investigate the use of OLRT computer systems in savings banking. The TSB Computer Project (now TSB Computer Services Limited) emerged from these discussions. Staffed by both computer and bank experts, the Project was responsible for design and implementation of a new system for 35 TSBs which constituted the OLRT banks. Within the Project banks formed larger groups, while maintaining their autonomous identities, to share the costs of computer installation. Four consortia were formed.[10]

Consideration of one of these consortia, the Bootle Group, highlights the pressures these consortia faced. Between 1962 and 1967 Bootle reported a 48% increase in transactions, an 87.5% increase in inter-bank withdrawals and significant increases in back-office business. By the late 1960s these factors were having their effect throughout the TSB. Transaction processing time was growing causing customer frustration, lengthening queues, and a worsening of counter relations. The working environment also deteriorated as a result, with the branch managers swamped by day-to-day administration and diverted from their job of marketing and customer servicing.[11]

In addition there were supply considerations. The only alternative to computerization to meet the demands of swelling business was to increase employment, particularly at the cashier level. Rising staff costs made that alternative unpalatable. Banking was a labour intensive industry where labour costs were rising faster than capital costs.[12]

Computerization, on the other hand, particularly OLRT, appeared to provide several answers at once. It promised to reduce the workload by displacing some functions from the branch and decreasing the number and duration of counter transactions, reallocate space in favour of the customer, increase the flexibility of interbank transactions, and to take over much of the routine work of staff (including calculation and credit of interest, debit of current account charges, completion of current account statement material, balancing of banks and banks' accounts, cash control and preparation of statistics). Crucially, OLRT offered, *ceteris paribus*, 30% staff savings because of the increase in the number of transactions possible per staff.[13]

Above these problem-solving characteristics OLRT offered more positive gains. First, it would help to improve services by reducing transaction time and making non-own branch transactions possible. What is more, it promised to release staff for non-counter work such as answering customer enquiries and problems. Second, by lessening the tedium of behind-counter work and speeding up the end-of-day balancing procedures, it promised to enhance job satisfaction. Third, OLRT was also seen to have innovating potential in a marketing sense. It would increase time available at the branch level to devote to marketing and customer servicing and would enable banks to make quicker and more informed investment decisions (if and when the TSB was permitted to provide such services and perform such tasks).

It is worth noting at this stage that many of the gains OLRT promised were, potentially at least, incompatible. For instance, if the bank wished to utilize all the potential staff savings it could not simultaneously retain released staff to perform new tasks such as responding to customer queries which were not, in themselves, income generating.

Computerization is now easy to understand, but why real-time in particular? This becomes more understandable once historical factors are considered. First, the structure of the TSB had always been branch oriented with an emphasis on personal banking and the counter services and customer relations that entailed. Hence their determination to shorten queues and transaction times. Such achievements were essential for them to maintain their traditional 'friendly and welcoming' image with customers. Real-time, by allowing up-to-date balances and facilitating inter-bank transactions, was particulary well suited to the demands of personal banking.

Secondly, their choice of OLRT was influenced by the statutory constraints the TSBs were still under. Not permitted to lend, customers accounts were not allowed to enter overdraft. Consequently up-to-the minute balances were needed. Real-time was the *only* way a computer system could provide such a facility. Of course, these restrictions were to be removed in 1976, but crucially the choice of computer system and the decisive first stages of implementation took place well before that time.

Thirdly, at least partly as a result of their historical role, TSB custom was dominated by the C2/D/E social categories. A corollary of this was the lack of any TSB corporate or international business, which could have reduced the pressure to choose real-time and increase the pressure to choose a system compatible with the international banks.

A final historical factor which influenced TSB's original choice was their regional nature. To begin with there was no coordinated national computer policy. This engendered problems which would emerge later when banks with incompatible computer systems amalgamated since not all TSBs chose real-time. Five TSBs in the south of England formed a Southern Consortium to establish a computer centre in the south-east. Their original choice was not even fully on-line and their system was never real-time. The factors influencing this particularly anomaly of TSB computerization will be looked at in more detail later.

Summing up so far, the TSB's choice of OLRT (the south excepted) arose from a combination of competitive and sociological factors. Competition made computerization necessary, while the TSB tradition of personal banking and the statutory restrictions forbidding lending made real-time the most suitable and attractive option.

THE TECHNOLOGIES CONTRASTED[14]

Reflecting the TSB's federated structure, computerization developed independently in several areas. At one stage there were seven computer centres but, by 1982, amalgamation had reduced these to four: Scotland, Northern Ireland, Wythenshawe and Crawley (both in England). Subsequently, Crawley has been closed and a second OLRT centre established at Milton Keynes. The Trustcard operation has a separate computer centre at Brighton. All the centres were on-line, but had markedly different characteristics. Only Scotland and the system which came to be based at Wythenshawe offered real-time. Crawley was a batch system. It is perhaps best to consider the histories of the OLRT and batch systems separately.

OLRT

The decision to implement OLRT was made in 1968. Initially there were four separate centres (Manchester, Kidderminster, Bootle and York), each using ICL System 4 computers. Olivetti TB49 banking terminals were used at each branch which were connected to the centres by leased PO telephone lines.

The branch terminals used by this system were simple and unintelligent with the power residing in the mainframes. They were not VDU-based, but resembled large typewriters into which passbooks for deposit accounts could be inserted and updated. There were, of course, no cheque accounts at the time and the passbook account was by far the dominant product. Nor were the terminals interactive. They could only ensure the immediate crediting and debiting of accounts and, in particular, that accounts did not become overdrawn. This was important given the statutory framework at the time. No customer enquiries could be processed.

At the end of the 1970s more aggressive marketing strategy was boosting workload and threatening to overextend the capacities of the mainframes. In addition the systems themselves were nearing the end of their term of contract and doubts about their long-term reliability were growing. Teams were set up to select a second generation system. They consisted of both computing services and seconded staff. They produced comprehensive requirements on programming systems, operations and security which were then put out to tender. The choice was in favour of a Univac mainframe and Burroughs terminals. The Wythenshawe complex was to be built to house the new, larger mainframe. This is discussed in the next section.

Batch system

In 1969, five TSBs came together to share the burdens of computerization costs. They formed a Southern Consortium to establish a computer centre in the south-east. One member, the SE TSB, had to act as a holding bank, so Crawley was *not* a free-standing computer centre but a part of the SE bank. The centre was staffed entirely by recruitment from within the TSB banking structure. This remained the case in contrast to Wythenshawe and Glasgow, both staffed almost entirely by specialist computer personnel.

By 1976 Southern Consortium encompassed 12 banks. Amalgamation had involved incorporating banks under the Surrey Row Computer Centre in London. The problems this caused were resolved in 1976 when the operations of the former London TSB Computer Centre were moved to Crawley, ending computer incompatibility which was limiting staff mobility and training. Crawley finally served the TSBs of the South-East and the Channel Islands.

The original 1970 version was not real-time. Instead it was based on an off-line philosophy, but had 'on-line data collection'. In 1980 the system went on-line to all banks. Branches then gained full access to customer information OLRT but to update accounts they still had to batch transaction work to Crawley. The results were sent back to branches by road transport the following morning.

Crawley has kept to a 'one-manufacturer' philosophy, continually updating Burroughs equipment. By 1982 a Burroughs B6800 mainframe and 828 Burroughs TD730 visual display terminals served an on-line network to 246 branches. The VDTs were connected to Crawley by leased British Telecom lines.

Glasgow system

The first choice in Scotland was for an off-line data capture batch processing system. OLRT was rejected at this early stage on a cost-effective basis. The initial system went live in September 1969. The numbers of banks on the system has steadily increased until all branches are now connected to the computerized system.

The original mainframe, a Burroughs B2500, was upgraded in 1970 to a B3500. Burroughs themselves proposed OLRT as the B3500 was perceived to be running out of capacity and would need to be replaced. A B3800 was then linked to the existing system. In contrast to the Wythenshawe system there are no concentrator sites and the terminal computers are Phillips. The Burroughs branch TCs were felt to be too large and noisy. The TCs act as support systems if the mainframe goes down, and can also be used as aid for helping the tellers balance up at the end of the day.

Unlike Crawley and Wythenshawe the Scottish system is software-based – a real-time banking package developed by Burroughs for the US Savings Banks, called 'Thrift'. The package, however, has been considerably altered as the bank's services have expanded, to offer current accounts for instance.

The English OLRT and the Scottish centres were staffed by specialist computer personnel whereas the staff at Crawley came directly from the branches and were meant to be 'bankers first and computer personnel second'.

Communications between the centres was largely informal but there were some official channels such as the Systems Services Group. Each centre, in order to remain responsive to their individual needs, maintains contact with their banks through a formal communications network. For example, in Scotland there are three levels:

1. *Steering Committee* – general managers of each bank and a trustee, meets quarterly.
2. *Management Committee* – AGMs (operations) of the banks and the data processing managers from the computer centre, meets monthly.

3. *Study Group* – systems managers and any computer personnel necessary, meets every 2–3 weeks, discusses current projects.

REASONS FOR TECHNOLOGY CHOICE

What might explain the different choices of the Northern and Southern banks? First, there were several management/decision-making differences. Northern management was more tied to the tradition of savings and therefore would have found the need for up-to-the-minute balances more pressing. Management in the South, in contrast, was closer to the TSBs high street banking rivals and saw itself as a non-traditional within the TSB. What is more, composition of the respective computerization decision-making bodies was different. That in Wythenshawe consisted heavily of computer specialists, while the body in Crawley was dominated by in-house bank experts.[15] In particular, the director of computer operations for the Northern banks was a computer specialist from outside the bank. Non-computer specialists may have been more likely to opt for proven systems. OLRT, while not completely unproven, had never before been applied in such a delicate situation, where the maintenance of the TSB's counter relations was crucial. However, support within the bank still seemed important. Indeed, there were several influential personalities in the North who acted as champions of the OLRT technology and state-of-the-art computerization.

Secondly, there were various competitive reasons for the different choices. Cheque accounts had become most important to the TSB in the South, while in the North and Scotland savings still dominated. The South wanted to follow in the footsteps of the London Clearers, while the North and Scotland were proud of the TSB's distinct tradition.

These factors have continued to influence differences in computerization. When second generation systems and terminals were being introduced the TSB South East 'chose displays rather than printing terminals for passbook updating because of its heavy involvement with cheque accounts and lending services'.[18]

IMPLEMENTATION AND PERFORMANCE

Implementation occurred at a time of radical organizational change. As a consequence of the Page Report, amalgamation became a driving force. The development of the computer consortia reflects this trend. Indeed, by offering cost-sharing incentives and through compatibility issues, computerization was a component of the amalgamation process. It is extremely difficult to separate out the effects of computerization from those of the amalgamation process, particularly where staff savings are concerned. It is also difficult to separate out the effects of computerization and of the shift in TSB strategy following legislative change when one is concerned with the development of new services.

Staff savings were made. As a consequence of a 'no redundancy' agreement with the unions, an initial staff surplus in some areas was gradually eliminated through promotion and natural wastage, although the number of staff continued to expand throughout the 1970s.[17] Queues did shorten and average transaction times fell from five minutes to one minute.[18] The TSBs good customer relationship appears to have remained intact with repeatedly favourable customer replies to how they perceive the bank.

There were two main human resource consequences of change. First, job roles changed. The new computing system took away 90% of clerical activity. Historically, the lowest, entry grade (grade 1) had focused on routine back-office clerical work; staff did not get to do counter work until after six months' training. The new system made the cashier grade the basic grade, with a training period of just a few days. The cashier's job increasingly revolved around the computer and the terminal unit, limiting their enquiry-answering role. At least to begin with, the cashier's discretion and flexibility in computer and terminal operation was limited.

It was the branch manager's role which changed most dramatically. As a consequence of computerization the branch manager was released from administration (which had previously taken up 80% of his time and now took up only 10%) to become a manager in a wider sense, able to devote energies to marketing, customer relations and the achievement and maintenance of good interpersonal relationships and the training and development of staff. One negative effect was that as the computer system took over statistical compilation and interpretation some branch managers had an initial feeling of losing control over their own branches' information system and of isolation from their customers. However, the TSB tradition of branch autonomy was a limiting factor in this respect.

Secondly, computerization affected the working environment. On the positive side it facilitated a more economic use of space. On the negative side the new terminals generated considerable heat and noise causing some staff discomfort. Ironically, these factors also made customer contact more difficult.

The TSBs service and product development during the 1970s should be seen as part of a catching-up process, which is what the Page Report, TSB Act and the TSB's own organizational and structural changes were all about. Computerization was a part of this trend. It did not act as a significant innovating force, although undeniably the range and nature of TSB's services would have been different without computerization and OLRT.

What is more, the TSB also failed to maintain its technological lead. The best example of this is the lag it suffered before energetically installing autoteller machines (ATMs). The OLRT system remained arguably the most sophisticated in the banking world and, on-line to that system, it could be claimed that TSB's ATMs did have a technological lead. However, this merely begs the question: why, then, did the TSB lag behind and not follow its competitors in this sphere?

The bank's strategy is at the heart of the matter. Bluntly, during this period the TSB was not competitively-minded, and was certainly not competitively-experienced. The origin of the new technology was a combination of factors, not least of which included the bank's tradition, ethos and statutory responsibilities. While the bank did indeed set out on a course to compete comprehensively with the major private clearing banks during this time, it was learning the competitive ropes. The whole process was a catching-up exercise. The bank faced a legacy of non-competitive strategy and objectives. What was being required was a wholesale trans-formation of the bank's ethos. This could not be expected to happen overnight. Indeed, until very recently, there were still strong forces in the bank who did not want to see the bank proceed down the course set out for it by the 'market forces' in its ranks. The legal wrangles and opposition to the flotation demonstrate this point.[19]

SYSTEM DEVELOPMENTS IN THE 1980s

HISTORY

The main development in the 1980s has been the development and move to dominance of the OLRT system. In 1980, the system was centralized at Wythenshawe and massively overhauled, dispensing with the 'dumb' terminals. Subsequently, the Crawley system was closed down and an OLRT system for the South established at Milton Keynes. In addition, new initiatives on autoteller machines and back-office automation have begun. We shall deal with each in turn.

On the Wythenshawe system after 1980, all data, new *and* old, is held on-line. To reduce the risk of total systems failure the Univac mainframe has three central processing units. The transition to Wythenshawe began in 1980 and from the Olivetti to the Burroughs terminals a year later. All banks had made the former transition by 1982 and the latter by 1984.

There are three distinct hardware components in the new system:

1. *Branch equipment.* Compared to the Olivetti terminals which were 'dumb' and unsophisticated, the Burroughs machines are complex

visual display terminals based information systems ('intelligent'). The use of intelligent terminals reflects 'social' changes, namely the need for more user facilities and massive increases in telecommunications charges making periphery work more cost-effective. They do not, however, reduce the need for a mainframe. Many bank operations (investment decisions, interest rates, clearing and other inter-bank relations) will always require a nodal point.

2. *Concentrator sites*. Groups of branches, 7–8 on average, are connected into a local regional concentrator site. Each has a minimum of three Burroughs CP9258 minicomputers. They are a new feature in the system and offer several advantages over the previous set-up. By allowing the use of a single high-speed transmission line rather than several slower-speed ones they facilitate considerable savings in line costs. They enhance the resilience of the total system by providing back-up mechanisms. And they facilitate the handling of the on-line information file, by permitting reports to be transmitted from Wythenshawe as soon as complete and then held until the branch is ready to receive them. Each concentrator site has a capacity of 30 teller positions.

3. *Mainframe*. The Sperry Univac 110/83 has three CPUs and two input/output units. The three CPUs can function independently or in combination. All items of essential equipment are at least duplicated so that if failure does occur the system can continue, although response times may lengthen.

Systems conversion and development were driven fundamentally by the same factors discussed earlier with regard to the origin of OLRT – a combination of cost increases, rapidly growing volumes of business and mounting competition. Most of these reasons still applied – indeed they were generally more pressing.

Compatibility issues, especially, had become more urgent. Most significant were the developments which culminated in the Wythenshawe and Crawley Centres, merging, as a consequence of the amalgamation of 16 TSBs into TSB England and Wales in 1984. The two systems at Wythenshawe and Crawley were, of course, incompatible. The final outcome, after a period of somewhat 'political' wrangling, was to move the South East operations to Wythenshawe and build a back-up centre in the South, at first at Crawley but eventually, due to lack of space, at Milton Keynes. The Milton Keynes building cost £7 million and the computer system itself, from Sperry, another £9 million. Since July 1985 the new centre has run the southern operations of the TSB, duplicating and working in tandem with Wythenshawe. The new system is designed to manage the instant transactions of home banking as well. The key communications between

Wythenshawe and Milton Keynes is supplied by Mercury using fibre optic cables laid alongside rail tracks.[20]

The 'triumph' of the OLRT system within TSB is worthy of discussion given that the other clearing banks have rejected OLRT and given that at least one initial reason for adoption – to prevent savings accounts becoming overdrawn – has ceased to apply. There is also some evidence that the batch system within TSB may have been performing reasonably well.

Table 7.1 gives a summary of the similarities and differences between the respective systems in 1982. OLRT may have offered the scope for staff savings *within* branches although there is no sign that this occurred in the aggregate. It may also have offered the prospect of product innovation, although this could not have been a consideration at the outset, because of legal complaints.

Table 7.1 Performance of computer centres (1982)

	Wythenshawe	Crawley	Glasgow
On-line	Yes	No	Yes
Real-time	Yes	No	No (yes later)
Personnel	336	50	106
Branches	1020	246	350
Transactions daily	1m	0.25	0.5

However, when one looks at the computer centres *themselves* it is clear that the Crawley batch system outperformed Wythenshawe in 1982 on two counts. It processed more transactions *per capita* (5050 compared with 2976) and it served more branches *per capita* (4.96 compared with 3.03). Unless advantages either in branch staff reductions or in product innovation occurred, the shedding of the batching system may have represented rejection of a technically simpler but cheaper alternative.

After the establishment of a uniform OLRT system, there were some notable developments. Office technology such as microfilming and word processing were introduced. Most significant, though, was the development and widespread installation of autoteller machines (ATMs).

Documentation on the effect, and indeed on the scale, of these changes is fairly sparse. Cowan and Willman documented staff savings which had occurred as a result of systems conversion, word processing, microfilming and ATMs.[21] They also tabulated bank estimates of future staff savings as a consequence of planned developments in those fields. Savings from the first were thought to be minimal and virtually exhausted. Those from office technology were modest and were expected to continue. The largest savings appeared in connection to ATM installations. Estimated savings of staff per ATM varied between 0.27 and 1.

Similarly, cost considerations were the driving force behind the developments in word processing and microfilming. As Cowan and Willman explain, both represent the introduction of relatively cheap, well-tried office technology into banking to deal with high-volume labour-intensive operations.[22] These developments, extended into the back-office, made up the first stages of the TSB's current back-office automation programme, discussed in detail in the post-flotation section below.

Again, with ATMs, cost considerations play a crucial but not necessarily determining role. The staff savings that Cowan and Willman report indicates that this is the case. However, the prime factor in the origin of this technological innovation was surely competition. TSB was not a leader in this field. The technology it chose was not qualitatively different to that already installed by other high street banks (except perhaps as a consequence of being attached to OLRT centrally). ATMs were and are essential to remain competitive. In 1980 the TSB lagged well behind its main competitive rivals;[23] it can now fairly legitimately claim to have clawed back much of the deficit by which it trailed.

NEW SYSTEMS AND SERVICES

ATMs

The pace of ATM installation has been maintaind since the Cowan and Willman report. By 30 June 1987, the TSB had 1787 machines, a 35% increase on the previous year, a faster growth rate than any other high street bank.[24] The TSB has also proceeded to develop its ATM services. In April 1987, TSB England and Wales announced that from the following May customers would be offered an electronic bill-payment service on its 870 machines. The service would allow customers to pay bills and juggle money between their own accounts. The service, like the TSB's cheques is free provided the account is in credit.[25] In August 1988, the TSB granted Inter Innovation a £3m contract to supply, install and service a new Cash Adapter ATM, designed to assist cashiers by dispensing cash quickly (within 10 seconds) and securely in an open-plan environment.[26].

Parallel to these technical developments, in October 1988, the TSB merged its ATM network with those of Midland and NatWest. The merged network consists of over 4000 machines. As part of that process, to enable each bank to have reciprocal access to each others ATMs, a TSB system, the CONNEX EFT package, was used to provide the TSB a gateway between the two banks' systems. While the CONNEX package is mainly used for ATM traffic it will also drive EftPos terminals, host and network interfaces, fee billing, authorization and settlement services.[27]

ATMs may be considered as a process innovation, i.e. a cheaper alternative way of dispensing cash and account information, or as a product innovation, i.e. 24 hour banking. The evidence is that ATMs located in branches do not simply displace counter transactions, but also generate further transactions, particularly enquiries. They appear to be associated with an *expansion* in branch staff numbers, but also with a shift from full-time to part-time employment.

The link between ATM operation and the growth in part-time staff appears to be as follows.[28] ATMs may displace counter transactions in at least three ways. Customers may defer cash withdrawals until after bank closing, they may use the ATM rather than the counter during opening hours, or they may use an ATM at a branch other than their own. The evidence from TSB is that throughout the day a relatively constant level of transactions is displaced, allowing part-time cashiers to cope with peak loading, but that the operation of the ATM requires maintenance, card issues, and response to leaflet requests which raises the demand for labour.

Back-office automation[29]

This project is the best evidence of the renewed thirst for new technology in the TSB. The bank is now in the last of three stages of what it terms its Back Office Project. Costing between £120m and £180m (estimates vary), this project aims ultimately to do away with paper based filing and switch to desk-top terminals and video screens which will handle all the filing and record-keeping systems and which will enable branch managers to access customer information at the touch of a button in open-plan banking halls.

The first two stages (already complete) saw the introduction of basic office functions, such as word processing. The last phase, now in progress, involves installing, across every branch in turn, 'counselling workstations' in open-plan offices. Beyond this, the final phase will extend to advanced communications, artificial intelligence and relational database technology – where different sets of records can be interrogated easily. This should be in place by the end of 1991.

Unlike other banks, which are constantly posting floppy disks to their branches to keep them up to date with technological developments the TSB software is transmitted over telephone lines from the bank's computer centres. This 'lead' is a direct result of the TSB's OLRT system which has meant that branches were always connected to the central computer systems, and that the bank always operated from a single master database of customer information.

The new system is being developed by the bank's computer specialists with Unisys, the product of merger between the Burroughs and Sperry computer groups. The TSB was already using Sperry mainframes and Burroughs counter terminals. The new system is based on Unisys's own financial systems architecture. It is designed to avoid the traditional pattern involving a branch controller using a minicomputer linked to a cluster of terminals. Such a system requires a second, expensive minicomputer in each branch as a back-up. Instead, the TSB system involves clusters of smaller minicomputers, each of which can substitute for a failed machine. The system consequently achieves resilience efficiently and cost-effectively.

On the basis of two guinea-pig trials at the Tiverton branch in Devon and the Ilford branch in Essex, the TSB claim their systems are unusually reliable despite the fact that both they and Unisys say they are operating at the limits of technology. Technological problems have arisen but the implementation timetable has not been disturbed.

The two model offices also provide useful insights into how the system is likely to be used and what are some of its likely human effects. The system has a considerable effect on the working environment of back-office staff, eliminating paper and filing cabinets and replacing them with video screens and desk top terminals. Space will be created where paper filing cabinets once stood. More crucially, though, the new technology will change the staff's jobs themselves, broadly freeing them from routine paper work to concentrate on directly serving the customer.

Martin Levett, Ilford branch manager, has described how previously his staff spent half their time engaged in paper activities and only 19% in dealing directly with the customer. During the trials of the new system that ratio was reversed. Time-savings has been a crucial issue, as Levett explains, 'I am anxious to use the system in ways that will save us time, rather than for new activities at present'.[30]

It is unclear how the time saved will be used. The TSB Central Board claims that it will be spent on new 'selling' activities. Levett's comment does not sit easily with these plans. Nevertheless, if that *is* the long-term aim then these changes in job-content require some retraining. With the emphasis on selling products to the customer, a retraining programme has been launched to teach staff this skill. The system itself ought to make the task simpler. Staff will now be able to inspect, quickly, standard reports on such matters as overdrawn accounts and loan arrears by using desk-top workstations. The bank hopes that the equipment will reduce the amount of time spent unproductively (searching records) in interviews by 50–60%. Levett further comments, 'Customers are impressed when you turn the screen to face them and they can see the figures changing before their eyes'.[31]

Most noticeable about the measures is the scale of integration into existing TSB systems. They are designed to enhance the capabilities of OLRT and will also link with Unisys financial terminals on bank counters and the ATM network. IT promises, also, to change the jobs of back-office staff as radically as OLRT transformed that of clerks and cashiers. The bank, however, projects that no redundancies will occur as a result of the automation programme. As it announced in 1987, 'Earlier this year we announced that we needed 700 extra staff because of our business growth, so we are unlikely to reduce numbers now.'[32]

Home banking[33]

Electronic home banking (customers using bank services from their own homes) is a recent development. The Bank of Scotland and Clydesdale Bank have been offering such services since 1985 and early 1987 respectively. In June 1987, the TSB moved onto the scene with a service called Speedlink, launched in England and Wales. It was the first aimed at the mass retail market. By May 1988 it had more than 50 000 subscribers (compared to an estimated 4000 on the Bank of Scotland service). Following the Bank of Scotland and the Nottingham Building Society the TSB has developed the system from a telephone link to a screen-based system. Before, Speedlink customers called a central number and identified themselves by punching their account and personal identification numbers into a special tonepad or standard push button telephone. A voice-response system then allowed them to issue instructions in a human voice. Services offered include checking an account balance, paying bills and transferring money between accounts. The service originally cost £10 a year plus the cost of phone calls. The cost of adapting the TSB's computer system to home banking was only £1m. The voice-response unit simply had to be bolted onto the Bank's mainframe.

CONCLUSION

The recent history of TSB is thus of several major episodes of technical change against a backdrop of substantial organizational change, involving merger, centralization, flotation and acquisiton. Three questions arise. The first is, how was the choice of technology made and was it due to competitive pressure? The second is, have the aims and nature of the technology changed over time? The third is, has this created a core of technological knowledge which gives the TSB a firm competitive advantage? We shall look at each in turn.

The short answer to the first question is that competitive pressures do not seem to have been important. The OLRT system does not appear to have had its origins in competitive pressures. At the time of its original adoption, such pressures could have been only dimly perceived. The TSB did not offer full banking services, and there was no immediate prospect of so doing. Those institutions which did offer full banking services used batch systems and there was some internal evidence in later years that batch systems could deliver full banking services competitively. OLRT had a strong innovation champion and the rest of the organization was not particularly technically literate. The pattern which emerged in the 1970s was one in which the North, under the influence of an innovation champion, computerized earlier than necessary, primarily for cost reasons, and chose a more sophisticated system than it needed to.

The nature of the technology has changed over time. The OLRT system has prevailed over the batch system as all regions adopted OLRT. Currently, the system is being used to support customer service improvements, such as the introduction of ATMs, as the potential of the system is being more fully exploited.

In the 1980s, organizational changes have perhaps been the principal motor for technological change. New structures and new attitudes have developed and are developing as the organization moves towards the form of a market-oriented national bank. It has already been mentioned how these trends have been reflected in the nature of recent technological change (integration of the back-office project, for instance). It may be no accident, however, that new technology coincided with the Bank's flotation.

It may also be no coincidence that at the same time as both flotation and new technology the TSB embarked on a fresh round of rationalization. An in-house team, in conjunction with consultants LEK, compiled a report reviewing the TSB's high-street banking operations. The report focused on the banks fragmented nature: 19 different computer operating centres, six different mortgage processing systems and seven direct marketing systems. Savings are hoped for as a consequence of merging departments into fewer centralized units. As the ex-TSB chairman commented as these plans were being developed in 1988:

> The new structure enables the group to maximize the value within our recent acquisitions. It will help us to focus on our key markets, to coordinate our strategies and to improve cost-effectiveness ... It will provide a clear focus on three areas, personal banking, corporate banking, and insurance and investment services – enabling the group to meet the challenges of an increasingly competitive marketplace in the 1990s.'[34]

The new chairman, Sir Nicholas Goodman, stung by the group's recent poor profit performance has already wielded the hatchet in the top echelons of the group, removing 12 main board directors and effectively sacking 103 regional directors in April 1989.[35]

Focusing on the third question, it seems clear that the OLRT system does offer competitive advantage. It offers clear advantages in the provision of customer information and information processing over batch systems. It is a flexible and high potential technology. However, this flexibility and potential has not been exploited mainly because the operation of information technology has not been integrated into banking operations; the option of importing expertise in the area rather than developing bankers into technologists has reinforced the separation of technical rather than operational concerns.

There is some evidence that, since the flotation, the concern with the development of technical advantage has been renewed. More so than other UK banks, TSB depends on the UK retail market for financial services. It has the potential to develop a technologically-based advantage in this market, over the banks if not the building societies. However, the organizational obstacles to the realization of this potential remain large.

NOTES

1. For a full description of the status of the TSB in this period see the Page Committee Report, 1973.
2. This section is based on Cockroft, J. (1984). *Microtechnology in Banking*. Economist Intelligence Unit Special Report No. 169.
3. This section is compiled from the following sources:
   'Strategic issues for Trustee Savings Bank', *Long Range Planning*, Vol. 18, No. 4, 1985, pp. 39–43.
   'Putting trust in the TSB', *Director*, December 1987, pp. 40–3.
   'TSB on tenterhooks', *Management Today*, January 1986, pp. 42–9, 96.
   'UK: ready to go public – and grow', *Euromoney*, November 1985 (Supplement), p. 106.
   'Read all about it', *Accountancy*, December 1985, pp. 10–11.
   'Hughes shouts from the hip', *Marketing*, 18 June 1987, pp. 24–5.
4. In 1974, Lloyds had 2410 branches in England, Wales and the Channel Islands, the Midland had 2600 in England and Wales, and the NatWest, in 1976, had 3300 throughout the mainland.
5. That is Barclays, Lloyds, Midland and the National Westminster Bank.

6. 'Computers in banking – the London Clearers', *The Banker*, April 1973, p. 377.
7. Wright, D. (1978). *The Management implications of on-line real-time computerization: case study of the TSB*. MPhil thesis, University of Liverpool.
8. Ibid., p. 59.
9. Willman, P. (1986). *Technological Change, Collective Bargaining, and Industrial Efficiency*. Oxford, Clarendon Press, pp. 218–20.
10. Wright, op. cit., p. 62.
11. Ibid., pp. 64–5.
12. Ibid., p. 72, n. 25.
13. Ibid., p. 72, n. 26.
14. Compiled from Cowan, R. and Willman, P. (1982). *Technical Change and Personnel Policies within the TSB*. Interim Report, Imperial College. Unless otherwise specified all data refer to 1982.
15. Ibid., p. 4.
16. *The Financial Times*, 7 February 1979.
17. Wright, op. cit., p. 92. On staff numbers, see Willman, op. cit., p. 228, Fig. 10.4.
18. Ibid., pp. 65 and 68.
19. *Glasgow Herald*, 5 November 1985, and *Guardian*, 29 August 1985.
20. *Guardian*, 16 May 1985.
21. Cowan and Willman, op. cit., pp. 220–41.
22. Ibid., p. 31.
23. Even in June 1982, when the Big Four had 2733 machines between them, TSB had only 56.
24. *Banking World*, February 1988, p. 12.
25. *The Financial Times*, 9 April 1987.
26. *Euromoney*, August 1988.
27. *The Times*, 29 October 1988, and *Euromoney*, December 1988, p. 30.
28. Willman, op. cit., p. 236.
29. Compiled from the following sources:
    The Financial Times, 5 June and 22 November 1988
    'TSB's Back Office Project: tomorrow's world today', *Euromoney*, June 1988.
30. *The Financial Times*, 22 November 1988.
31. Ibid.
32. *The Financial Times*, 5 June 1987.
33. *The Financial Times*, 15 April and 14 May 1988; *Guardian*, 23 June 1988, p. 25.
34. *Euromoney*, June 1988.
35. *Independent*, 5 June 1989, p. 25.

APPENDIX: CHRONOLOGY

1810   Reverend Duncan opens the first TSB in Dumfriesshire.
1817   Act of Parliament lays down the statutory guidelines.
1965   TSB Act permits cheque accounts.
1967   TSB Unit Trust Company formed.
       Working Party set up in Wales and Northern England to investigate OLRT.
1968   35 TSBs in Wales and Northern England decide to implement OLRT.
1969   Scottish TSBs choose off-line data capture batch processing system.
1970   Southern Consortium of five TSBs in the South East establish a computer centre at Crawley.
1973   Page Report suggests the TSB should become a 'Third Force' in banking.
1973–4 Amalgamation reduces 73 banks to 19.
1976   TSB Act paves the way to put Page suggestions into action.
1977   TSB introduces personal lending.
1978   TSB Trustcard launched.
1979   TSB introduces commercial business.
1983   Further amalgamation results in four TSBs: England and Wales, Northern Ireland, Scotland, and South East and Channel Islands.
1984   Government publishes White paper and TSB Bill outlining proposals for the bank's flotation.
1986   Flotation goes ahead in September, almost a year behind schedule.
1987   TSB purchases Target (£220m) and Hill Samuel (£777m).
1989   June: TSB announces reduced profits in every sector of its business.

3 Financial Accounting

Whilst accountants are always desperate to impress on Jenny Public and John Bull that there is more to accountancy than simple book-keeping, this section tends inevitably to focus on the data recording aspects of accountancy. In many ways the study and profession of accountancy derive from shortcomings in the data recording process. By this is meant the inability to capture complete and absolute descriptions of events, values and contexts in all dimensions. In practice, it is the professionals' role to extrapolate, compensate and guestimate. Based on their accumulated experience and intuitive (i.e. non-definable in logic) qualities, they endeavour to construct a credible reality to allow informed decisions. Accounting theorists, meanwhile, concern themselves with trying to articulate these processes, and engage in reflection and the suggestion of alternative frameworks.

The double-entry book-keeping system of recording accounting data was first documented by Pacioli and remains today a universal method. There are many reasons for this in a manual context, not least because of the self-balancing aspect. Double-entry book-keeping also represents part of the reality of the economic exchange of goods and services for financial obligations, financial obligations for cash and so on. However, it is also symbolic in the sense that only a very narrow and limited aspect of data relating to these exchanges is recorded. It is from this abstracted data that financial reports and absolute statements are prepared which purport to be authoritative. The accounting profession is well aware of the limitations of the double-entry framework and has from time to time incorporated modifications such as the inclusion of figures for revalued fixed assets, brands and even more radical approaches such as current cost accounting, not without controversy. In attempts at more 'factual' accounts, various academics have suggested cash flow accounting, events accounting and multiple-entry accounting. In a practical context, many of these alternatives seem to have made little headway, probably because the incremental cost of such recording systems does not appear to produce sufficient benefits.

This section offers three papers which discuss the possibilities of taking advantage of the ability of modern computer-based systems to store and manipulate data in a more cost-efficient manner than manual systems, the objective being the derivation of a more appropriate accounting model and more useful accounting reports. The reader is warned that they do not represent a panacea, merely a way of proceeding with enquiry.

The chapter by Stewart Leech and Mike Mepham is a general introduction to the concept of matrix accounting, first documented in 1869, which through its tabular presentation has links with present-day spreadsheets and relational databases. George Sorter's classic chapter on events accounting has been included because it so often forms the basis of many attempts that use computer-based systems to avoid the narrow constraints of the traditional value-based double-entry accounting model. The final chapter in this Part by Guido Geerts and Bill McCarthy demonstrates the use of an information systems approach through focusing on the financial system as an object, using a conceptual schema to model the accounting Universe of Discourse and incorporating it into a database accounting framework. They suggest that this results in a system which is capable of providing much richer information than would occur in the traditional charts-of-accounts debit/credit accounting model.

8 The development of matrix-based accounting

Stewart A. Leech and Michael J. Mepham

INTRODUCTION

There have been many attempts over the past three decades to represent the traditional recording and processing of accounting transactions in a new framework. Most of these attempts have involved the use of matrices in one form or another. A number of reasons were advanced for such a change. For example, it has been suggested that there would be advantages to be derived from reformulating accounting method in a more scientific or mathematical way. Another justification was the belief that computers could more easily manipulate numbers when they are stored in a matrix or table. Yet, apart from the use of matrix-based modelling software such as MULTIPLAN, LOTUS 1-2-3 and EXCEL for mainly budgeting purposes, there is little evidence that any change has been made to incorporate any of these new methods – either in the actual processing of accounting transactions by firms or in the teaching of accounting.

The earliest advocate of a matrix framework was the mathematician Augustus De Morgan who used this approach as a pedagogical device in 1869. More recent advocates include Mattessich (1957, 1958, 1964a, 1964b), Richards (1960), Kemeny, Schleifer, Snell and Thompson (1962) Charnes, Cooper and Ijiri (1963), Corcoran (1964), Ijiri (1965), Mathews (1967, 1971), Doney (1969), Johnson and Gentry (1970), Butterworth (1972), Shank (1972) and Mepham (1966, 1980). Unlike De Morgan, most of these authors suggested that matrix accounting could be a practical system. The 1960s and 1970s saw considerable advances in the use of

Specially commissioned for *IT and Accounting: The impact of information technology*. Edited by Bernard C. Williams and Barry J. Spaul. Published in 1991 by Chapman & Hall, London, ISBN 0 412 39210 0.

computer-based hardware and software for accounting applications. Since the late 1970s there have been further advances, especially in computer software, that have indicated the usefulness of matrices as structures for storing data. In addition, matrix-based financial modelling software has become a common tool in accounting. An important development at the beginning of the 1970s which emphasized the advantages of the two-dimensional table was the **relational model** for database systems. Codd (1970, 1972a and b) advocated this technique, which, in very simple terms, replaced complex data structures with two-dimensional tabular 'relations'. The emphasis is on the *user* in both financial modelling and relational database software. These developments have had a continuing effect on the design and use of accounting systems. Accountants are the major user-group of financial modelling and spreadsheet packages, and relational database management systems are now being used to develop integrated accounting applications.

Given this increasing emphasis on table structures in computer-based accounting software it seems an appropriate time to re-examine the use of a matrix framework for analysing and processing accounting transactions. Why have accountants been so reluctant to respond to these attempts at a new approach? It would seem that the development of matrix-based accounting systems would have been a logical development of financial planning models, since many of these models use the *ex post* data from transaction processing. Once in table form, the use of matrix algebra could be used to incorporate the *ex post* accounting data into the matrix-based financial planning models.

The aim of this chapter is (1) to develop an approach to incorporating a matrix into the accounting subsystems which use computer files to store detailed transactions; (2) to argue that the matrix framework can provide a more flexible and improved accounting system giving not only a natural interface to financial modelling systems, but also to enhance the use of relational database systems in accounting; and (3) to suggest that matrix notation is suitable for a new canonical model for accounting.

THE DOUBLE-ENTRY FRAMEWORK

Double-entry in manual accounting systems has a long history. Research has shown that the double-entry system dates back to somewhere in the thirteenth century. Yamey (1956, pp. 7–8) has expressed three main advantages of double-entry over earlier methods of record keeping: (1) the records are comprehensive and orderly; (2) the double entry provides a completeness check (in the ledger); and (3) summarized financial statements are easily obtained (from the ledger). Double-entry is a method that requires a dual classification of each transaction. Mattessich (1964a) and others have pointed to this 'duality principle' as the fundamental basis of accounting. The recording of double entries in T accounts is a technical process that is particularly appropriate for obtaining the necessary dual classification in manual systems. The dual property of a transaction could, however, be recorded in other forms, for example in a two-dimensional matrix, which might be more suitable for computerized systems.

THE MATRIX FRAMEWORK

The form of a matrix-based accounting system should be such as to facilitate the recording of the dual effect of each transaction, and if the system is computer-based, the form should facilitate the processing of those transactions by computer programs and the determination of desired results. In fact, at least the perceived advantages of a 'manual' double-entry system should be seen in a matrix-based system. Although alternative formulations exist, this chapter makes use of one basic matrix form[1] which will be called a **transaction matrix** (or T matrix). A two-dimensional T matrix of equal rows and columns, with row i and column i representing account number i is set up. Row i is used to hold the debits to account i and column i similarly holds the credits to that account. A transaction which is to be debited to account i and credited to account j is entered in matrix T as a *single entry* in the cell at the intersection of row i and column j. It is no longer necessary to make two entries for each transaction; a single entry into a two-dimensional matrix has the same effect as a double entry in two separate accounts.

For example, consider the following three transactions:

1. R. Lucas commenced business by depositing £2000 in the bank.
2. R. Lucas purchased furniture on credit for £500.
3. R. Lucas paid £200 on account to his creditor.

The transaction matrix (T) for R. Lucas is shown in Table 8.1 for that period.

Table 8.1 T matrix

	Credits			
Debits	*1 Cash at bank*	*2 Capital*	*3 Furniture*	*4 Creditor*
1 Cash at bank		2000		
2 Capital				
3 Furniture				500
4 Creditor	200			

In the T matrix only one entry is required for each transaction. The entries in the matrix cells are termed **elements**. Each element and each cell has two subscripts. In the T matrix the account numbers (1, 2, 3, 4) act as subscripts. By mathematical (but not spreadsheet) convention, the first subscript refers to the element's row number, the second to its column number. Here we adopt the mathematical convention. The first transation is, therefore, entered into $t_{1,2}$ the second into $t_{3,4}$ and the third into $t_{4,1}$. The row subscript (account number) indicates the account to be debited; the column subscript (account number) indicates the account to be credited.

As with a double-entry system, the T matrix is based on the accounting equation. At the end of an accounting period, the accounts can be balanced to establish whether an account has an excess of a debit amount over a credit amount, or an excess of a credit amount over a debit amount. In the example above, at the end of the three transactions, the Cash at bank account has a total of £2000 in the row (debit) entries, and a total of £200 in the column (credit) entries. When the row total is compared with the column total, the debit side is seen to be £1800 greater than the credit side. Similarly, the Capital account has a total row entry of zero, and a total column entry of £2000, leaving a credit balance of £2000. The Furniture account has a balance for £500 debit and the Creditor account a balance of £300 credit. This is illustrated in Table 8.2.

Table 8.2 T matrix with totals

		Credits			
Debits	*1 Cash at bank*	*2 Capital*	*3 Furniture*	*4 Creditor*	*Total of rows (Debits)*
1 Cash at bank		2000			2000
2 Capital					0
3 Furniture				500	500
4 Creditor	200				200
Total of columns (Credits)	200	2000	0	500	

If we adopt the convention that debits are positive (+) and credits are negative (−) and subtract column totals from corresponding row totals, an account with a debit balance (+) will be indicated by an excess of its row total over its column total, while an account with a credit balance (−) will be indicated by an excess of its column total over its row total. A listing of the account balances from the T matrix is shown in Table 8.3. In terms of the accounting equation, assets (cash £1800 and furniture £500) equal equities (creditor £300 and capital £2000). In terms of the matrix convention, total pluses (£2700) plus total minuses (£2700) equal zero.

Table 8.3 Account balances from T matrix

	Row (Debit) +	Column (Credit)−	Balance
1 Cash at bank	+2000	−200	+1800
2 Capital	+0	−2000	−2000
3 Furniture	+500	0	+500
4 Creditor	+200	−500	−300
	+2700	−2700	0

In a computer-based system, the way in which transactions are entered into a matrix can be explained as follows. If n is the number of accounts used for the accounting entity, a two-dimensional matrix of size $n \times n$ is needed. Such a matrix is established in computer memory, and programming instructions are used to enter data into the matrix, calculate the totals of rows and columns and so on.[2] The instruction required to enter data into the T matrix is an instruction to *add* data to a particular matrix entry. At the institution of an accounting entity no transactions will have been made and the matrix entries or elements are all zero. The first transaction, of any given type, that occurs replaces the appropriate zero by the amount of the transaction. For example, when R. Lucas commences business by depositing £2000 in the bank, we need to enter this amount in matrix element $t_{1,2}$ which debits cash at bank (row subscript 1) and credits capital (column subscript 2). One mode[3] of describing, in general terms, an instruction to enter the £2000 into $t_{1,2}$ is:

$$t_{1,2} \leftarrow t_{1,2} + 2000$$

The '←' sign in this statement means that the matrix element on the left-hand side ($t_{1,2}$) is *replaced by* the value of the expression on the right-hand side ($t_{1,2} + 2000$). This is equivalent to instructing the computer to evaluate the expression on the right-hand side and *move* it into the memory area ($t_{1,2}$) shown on the left-hand side. The result of the first transaction of R. Lucas is that $0 + 2000$ will be placed into $t_{1,2}$. If R. Lucas decided to deposit a further £1000 in the bank, instruction $t_{1,2} \leftarrow t_{1,2} + £1000$ would mean that $t_{1,2}$ is replaced by the £2000 already stored in $t_{1,2}$ plus another £1000. However, this means that the record of both the first transaction, £2000, and the second transaction, £1000, is lost. The amount stored in $t_{1,2}$ is now £3000, with no record of the component transactions. Further, there is no record of the date of the transactions. The only information recorded in the transaction matrix is *the effect of the transaction* on the two accounts in question. For this reason, the transaction matrix is ideal for summarizing transactions for the preparation for periodical financial statements, but not for storing the details of each transaction, such as the date and amount.

The T matrix entries for the three transactions of R. Lucas (above) are as follows:

1. $t_{1,2} \leftarrow t_{1,2} + 2000$
2. $t_{3,4} \leftarrow t_{3,4} + 500$
3. $t_{4,1} \leftarrow t_{4,1} + 200$

PROBLEMS WITH MATRIX ACCOUNTING

Advocates of matrix accounting have been interested in two distinct (yet related) uses of the framework. First, there is an interest in the use of matrix algebra to provide useful methods of manipulating accounting figures for budgeting, financial modelling, cost allocations, etc. Secondly there has been an interest in the matrix framework as a replacement for the T account framework used in manual accounting systems. It is this second use of the matrix framework which is the focus of this chapter.

In 1957 Mattessich outlined an 'Introduction to the Matrix Formulation of Accounting Systems' with the purpose '... to find with the help of matrix notation a compact and precise means of presenting accounting transactions and their systems in the most general form' (Mattessich, 1957, p. 332). In this early paper, Mattessich saw a need to establish a separate matrix for each transaction, and to provide for the addition of these transaction matrices to give a total or system matrix. A closing matrix and opening matrix are introduced to allow for the change from one accounting period to another. In his explantion of the operations required for more than one accounting period in this system, Mattessich abandons the idea of a separate matrix for each transaction: '... we present ... a transaction matrix of the second period in which all three transactions ... are recorded *(for space reasons we use only one transaction matrix)*' (p. 36, emphasis added). Mattessich does not continue this argument further. But herein lies a major problem to the operational feasibility of such a system in practice. If a separate matrix is used for each transaction, the required 'space' (in the form of computer memory) for even a moderate number of accounts would be excessive. On the other hand, if only one transaction matrix is used, the amount stored in any matrix element is the result (that is, the total) of all transactions of that type. The record of all previous transactions that affect the same two account numbers are destroyed, as shown above.

The matrix approach proposed by Mattessich, and most others, does not provide comprehensive records of transactions. Even if separate matrices were kept for different transaction types, and each matrix were expanded to *n* dimensions to allow for *n* attributes (for example, date, document, number, customer number), the same basic objection would remain – the primary memory required would be excessive. Certainly, a matrix could be partitioned and only part of it accessed at any one time. However, this reduces considerably the advantage of using a matrix in the first place – to be able to perform algebraic operations on the one set of data at the same time. This would provide little advantage over using traditional computer files and records which are normally processed iteratively one (or a few) at a time. Such a matrix, with *n* dimensions, is likely to become unwieldly and difficult to understand.

Mattessich's reply to such criticisms might be that: 'The purpose of this matrix formulation is not to introduce a new technique but to find a rational language, commonly understood among scientists, that will enable us to express all imaginable accounting systems in a concise and at the same time general and all-embracing manner' (1957, p. 337). From the theoretical viewpoint, this is an admirable objective. In database terminology, Mattessich is describing a conceptual model. However, it is unlikely to succeed unless the conceptual model can be implemented and be shown to have at least the same properties as the system that it is replacing – in this case double entry.

AN INTEGRATED MATRIX-BASED ACCOUNTING SYSTEM

In contrast to the lack of success of attempts to promote the use of a matrix framework for recording transaction data, there has been considerable acceptance of the use of matrix (or spreadsheet) methods in financial modelling. This popularity suggests that now is an appropriate time to reconsider how to overcome the problems of obtaining a matrix interface to accounting systems which typically use computer files to store detailed transactions. For example, if an accounting system can produce a matrix of *ex post* accounting data in a form compatible with financial planning models being used, the reliance on other *ad hoc* methods to extract data from accounting files for input into planning models can be minimized. At present, these other methods include manual extraction and re-entry of the *ex post* data into the models; the use of specialist programs to extract data and convert it to a matrix form suitable for entry into the models; and the use of generalized file interfaces in the modelling packages. All can be tedious tasks which might be avoided if matrix output can be obtained directly from the processing of accounting data in computer files.

The aim of this section is to integrate the maintenance and use of a T matrix with the recording, processing and reporting operations in a typical computer-based accounting system whilst avoiding the problems identified earlier. It differs from present spreadsheet applications because a matrix of *ex post* account balances is produced from the normal processing of transactions through the accounting subsystems, and, at the same time, the details of each transaction are stored on disk. The matrix holds sufficient information to produce a list of balances and financial statements, and may be used as direct input into financial modelling packages for budgeting and financial planning.

There are many different ways to design a computer-based matrix accounting system. In this section the method used is based on that devised by Doney (1969) and developed by Shank (1972). The objective is to design an accounting system which incorporates a matrix approach into accounting subsystems and which closely follows established accounting procedures.[4] In the next section the possible relevance of an alternative database approach to matrix accounting is considered.

The form that the matrix will take was described at the start of this chapter. The conventions for the matrix formulation outlined there are observed by the subsystems of a typical computer-based accounting system.

SYSTEM DESIGN

An accounting information system may be divided into subsystems to accept data which are stored in transaction files (on disk) and used to update the T matrix. Financial statments are produced directly from the T matrix. The application programs that process the data for each accounting subsystem, update the T matrix and produce financial statements may differ from one enterpise to another.[5] Most accounting systems use similar types of transaction data as input, but the organization of the data into subsystems and the output requirements (reports) may differ considerably. In order to ensure that the design is as simple as possible, the accounting system developed in this chapter will include only four subsystems:[6] sales and purchases, cash receipts and payments, general journal, and financial reporting.

The application programs underlying the first three subsystems (sales and purchases, cash receipts and payments and general journal) maintain detailed records of customers and suppliers; accept transactions as input; and produce the appropriate journals and ledger accounts report as output. The details of each transaction are stored as records in files on disk. As each transaction is entered into the system, the T matrix is updated. For updating the T matrix, the program will require the account number to be debited, the account number to be credited and the amount of the transaction. The account numbers are the subscripts of the matrix entry. The computer program would then use the instruction:

$$t_{ij} \leftarrow t_{ij} + a$$

where i = the account to be debited
j = the account to be credited
a = the amount of the transaction

to add the amount to the matrix element t_{ij}. For updating the detailed transaction files, further information will be included in the input record. For example, the account number, the transaction type (such as a sale, cash receipt, purchase, etc.), the date of the transaction, reference numbers (such as receipt number, invoice number) and amount would comprise the minimum information required. The processing undertaken by these subsystems is illustrated in Fig. 8.1.

THE TRANSACTION MATRIX

The computer files which store the detailed transactions are used to produce the journals and ledger reports. Sufficient information is stored in the T matrix to produce the trial balance and financial statements. The operations of the application programs in the financial reporting subsystem are illustrated in Fig. 8.2 and described below. Figure 8.2 is a continuation of Fig. 8.1, which together show the transaction flow through the four subsystems, the computer records held on disk, the processing of the transactions by the application programs, and the reports that are printed.

The trial balance

The extraction of a trial balance from the T matrix is a relatively simple operation undertaken by the application programs in the financial reporting subsystem. The debit (+) or credit (−) account balances must be stored in computerized form. For this purpose, a column vector (B) is established to hold the balances of the accounts. In the case of the first period's operation, the balance of each account will be the excess of the row totals over the column totals in the T matrix. This balance will be stored in the B vector and will represent the closing balance of each account for the first period's operation. This balance will then become the opening balance for the next period. When the transactions for the second period are posted to the T matrix and the net amount of debits over credits calculated for the period, the B vector (which contains the opening balance) will be updated

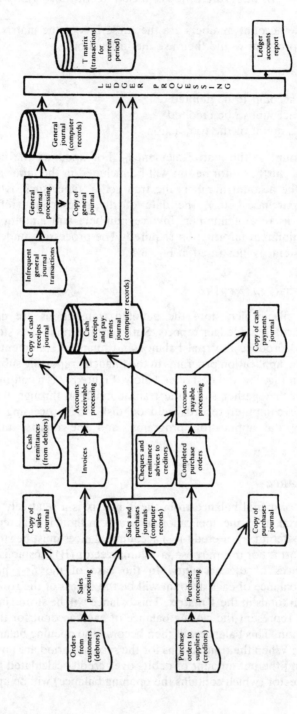

Fig. 8.1 Transaction processing subsystems for sales, purchases, cash and general journal.

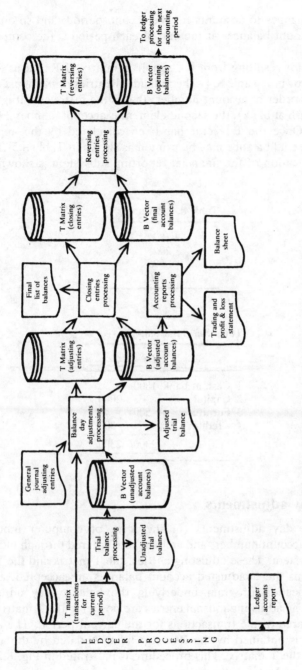

Fig. 8.2 Trial balance application for a financial reporting system.

by the net changes to accounts for the second period; and so on. The B vector of account balances at the end of each period is the computerized trial balance.

The B vector resulting from the simple T matrix of R. Lucas (see first section) is shown in Table 8.4. The individual entries or elements of the B vector are in order of account number, that is the first element is account number 1 (cash at bank), the second element is account number 2 (capital) and so on. Once the B vector has been calculated by the application program, the trial balance may be printed as shown in Table 8.5. The trial balance application of the financial reporting subsystem is shown in Fig. 8.2.

Table 8.4 B vector

+1800
−2000
+500
−300

Table 8.5 Trial balance

	Dr	Cr
1 Cash at bank	1800	
2 Capital		2000
3 Furniture	500	
4 Creditor		300
	2300	2300

Balance day adjustments

The balance day adjustments (in the form of computer input, with appropriate account numbers and amount) are entered through the general journal subsystem. These adjusting entries, the T matrix and the B vector which contains the unadjusted account balances are accepted, as input, by the application program underlying the balance day adjustments processing. The adjusting journal entries are posted to the T matrix after it has been cleared of the transactions for the current period. The adjusted trial balance is obtained by the B vector being updated by the adjusting entries from the T matrix. This procedure is illustrated in Fig. 8.2.

Preparation of accounting reports

Once the B vector (adjusted trial balance) has been updated, the preparation of accounting reports is a simple operation. A computer program uses the B vector balances as input and prints the accounting reports in the predetermined desired format.

Closing entries

The objective, once again, is to update the B vector with the closing entries so that a final list of balances may be obtained. The information required by the computer program to undertake the closing entries is: (1) the B vector (from processing of balance day adjustments) which contains the amounts needed to create the closing entries; and (2) the numbers of the revenue and expense accounts which are to be closed.

In this case, the application program can carry out the task without the need to input the closing entries through the general journal. The B vector is accepted as an input file to the closing entries program to achieve (1) above, and the revenue and expense account numbers are included in the program to achieve (2) above. As the closing entries are determined by the computer program, they are posted to the T matrix after it has been cleared of the balance day adjustments. The final list of balances is obtained by updating the B vector with the closing entries from the T matrix. This procedure is illustrated in Fig. 8.2.

Reversing entries

The B vector must be updated by reversing the appropriate balance day adjustments so that it is ready to receive transactions in the next accounting period. As the objective, once again, is to update the B vector with the reversing entries, the computer program to undertake this task requires the following information: (1) the B vector (from processing of closing entries); and (2) the account number and amounts which are to form the basis of the reversing entries.

Since it is possible for a computer to retain the amounts from the balance day adjustments subject to reversal, these entries are 'automatically' undertaken by the computer program. These amounts are posted to the T matrix after the T matrix has been cleared of closing entries. The final B vector of account balances to be used in the next accounting period is obtained by updating the B vector with the reversing entries from the T matrix. The processing of reversing entries is shown in Fig. 8.2

RELATIONAL DATABASE SYSTEMS AND THE MATRIX MODEL

The objective of the system described above was to demonstrate the viability of incorporating a matrix into typical computer-based accounting subsystems. In this section, the potential advantages of using a matrix framework in conjunction with relational database management systems are explored.

In 1969, Sorter suggested an 'events theory of accounting'. He criticized the conventional view which regards an accounting system as providing standardized inputs for the end-user's decision models, which are assumed to be known. He argued that '... it is impossible to specify input values that are optimal for the wide range of possible uses' (Sorter, 1969, p. 13). He proposed an alternative events approach which suggested that '... the purpose of accounting is to provide information about relevant economic events that might be useful in a variety of possible decision models' (p. 13). Sorter argued that this approach regards '... the function of accounting at one level removed in the decision-making process ...' allowing (or requiring) '... individual users to generate their own input values for their own individual decision models' (p.13).

Sorter did not consider the mechanics of implementing an events accounting system but his suggestions were followed up by several researchers: Colantoni, Manes and Whinston (1971), Lieberman and Whinston (1975), and Haseman and Whinston (1976). These writers proposed a database approach.

In a database events accounting system, records of events would be stored *in disaggregated form* in the database and extracted and processed as required. The change in emphasis represents a fundamental move from *account*-based procedures, which aggregate data within accounts, to a *view*-based system which allows end-users to obtain alternative views of the disaggregated data.

A relational database system (Codd, 1970) would provide considerable flexibility. The data available to a relational events accounting system would not be confined to records of past transactions and the commonly recognized (financial) attributes of such transactions. Details of (anticipated or budgeted) future events could be included and also other data such as appropriate statistics and details of orders placed and received, insurance records, plant registers, and so on. Some of this data would be recorded in associated subsystems since the accounting system would be part of a more general relational management information system. The database management system (DBMS) software would provide the means of integration, providing the means to combine such data with the more traditional accounting data.

In such a relational system there would be a need to safeguard the integrity and completeness of the (more narrowly defined) accounting data. A transaction matrix could be used for this. Consider a relational table (or file), JOURNAL, with the following attributes (or fields): Trans_No (transaction number), Date, Dr_Acc, Cr_Acc and Value (for recording the conventional details of transactions). A matrix could readily be prepared from such a relation by using the Dr_Acc and Cr_Acc attributes to identify the appropriate columns and rows of the matrix. Conversely, as Merrett (1984, pp. 351–64) proposes, such a matrix can, quite naturally, be represented by the relation. JOURNAL would be the simplest form of the traditional accounting system when this is translated to a database setting. At suitable intervals appropriate applications programs would generate the customary accounting statements (balance sheet and profit and loss account) by summing the rows and columns of this matrix as described in the previous section.

The matrix framework has other uses. When an end-user interrogates a relational database, the DBMS typically provides relevant information in the form of two-dimensional tables. In a relational events accounting system, some of the alternative views could be variations of the T matrix (described above). The system need not, however, be restricted to such 'input output' tables, it could provide a wide range of alternative views such as the following:

	Columns	*Rows*
Monthly profit and loss account	Budget, actual, variance	Types of expense and income
Expenses of cost centres for a given period	Cost centres	Types of expense
Cost report for a given cost centre for several months	Months	Types of expense
Contract costs report for a given cost centre	Individual contracts	Types of expense

This is a natural way to provide accounting information and the tables are immediately recognizable as conventional accounting reports. They are also clearly matrices. Since a relational events accounting system is not restricted to the conventional financial data, other less traditional tabular reports could be prepared by using the DBMS query and report generating facilities to access and combine tables from other subsystems with tables in the accounting database. The matrix framework provides windows each of which gives an ordered tabular view of a portion of the disaggregated data in the database. This can be contrasted with the traditional accounting model which analyzes and summarizes a restricted subset of the data linear fashion to produce the balance sheet and profit and loss account as end products. A relational events accounting system will also provide the conventional financial reports when such a view is requested, but the underlying data remains unaffected and it can subsequently be accessed (with other relevant data) for other purposes and processed in other ways.

THE CANONICAL ACCOUNTING MODEL

The enthusiastic assimilation of spreadsheet packages into the accountant's tool kit has encouraged the erroneous assumption that financial modelling's role is primarily in the realm of planning and 'what if' budgeting. There has been little recognition of the fact that models are fundamental to accounting.

The position is better appreciated by information specialists. A database information system is a physical model intended to represent reality, but database theory emphasizes the importance of a parallel conceptual model. McCarthy writes: 'A data model is intended to be a description of the logical structure of the object system as seen by the community of database users. It is a scheme that represents, with data, the organization of the conceptual world of interest' (1979, p. 668). In the past, accountants have not separated the conceptual accounting data model from the techniques and tools that they use (the physical model) but now a wish to emphasize this distinction is commonly expressed. Accountants, and accounting academics, frequently claim that the conversion from manual to computerized information systems is merely a change of the recording medium and method of processing which requires no change to their underlying conceptual data model.

A data model is not an optional extra in accounting. The distinguishing feature of accounting is its data model and there is a need for agreement on a *canonical* (i.e. a standard) version of it. As noted above, Mattessich considered the 'matrix formulation' in this way in 1957. The development of relational database systems since then has made the matrix framework even more suitable. Although a conceptual canonical accounting data model should be independent of the hardware on which physical systems are maintained, developments in technology create new opportunities for extending the facilities offered by information systems and it is important that this should be recognized and facilitated by the model. It is possible to continue with the traditional accounting model derived from handwritten books, but this is potentially damaging as it ties the conceptual model to a form of record keeping which is rapidly becoming obsolete and unduly restrictive when its capabilities are compared with those obtainable from more advanced database technology (Harper, 1985a, b and c; List,

1986). Technology should facilitate the development of accounting theory and practice but adherence to an outdated paradigm inhibits this.

The usefulness of the matrix framework has already been proved for financial planning. It is possible that the adoption of matrix notation for a new canonical accounting model will facilitate the integration of financial and managerial accounting (Forrester, 1984), the development of multi-dimensional accounting (Ijiri and Kelly, 1980), the move to an events accounting system (Sorter, 1969) and the wider use of appropriate mathematical techniques (Mattessich, 1964a; Mepham, 1980).

CONCLUSION

The major problems with attempting to apply conceptual matrix forms to recording and reporting accounting information can be overcome if the matrix is used to store aggregated data or (in the relational database version) to view aggregated data. This chapter has identified the main difficulties of developing matrix methods for accounting systems.

A computer-based accounting system has been designed which incorporates matrices to store the effects of transactions on account balances. By recording the effects of each transaction in one transaction matrix, the matrix becomes the summarized history of all the transactions that affect an accounting entity for a specified period of time. Transaction files are used to store the detailed records. It is then possible to obtain the details of each transaction for such reports as the journals and ledger, while the financial reports can be produced from the transaction matrix. A second (database) approach has also been outlined in which matrices can be materialized as summarized views of the disaggregated data in an events accounting system.

The reasons for incorporating matrices into computer-based systems and for using a matrix framework in accounting are many and varied. First, a matrix in which the balances of accounts are stored can give a total picture of the state of a firm at any time, provided of course that the matrix has been kept up-to-date. In an on-line system which uses the matrix to store account balances, financial statments and key financial ratios can be produced quickly and efficiently whenever they are requested. There is no need for lengthy processing or file searching – the amounts are stored in a convenient table form. Secondly, periodic financial reporting can be undertaken using the matrices – reference to transaction files is not necessary unless some specific account details are required. Thirdly, the detailed transaction records are stored once only, in the appropriate transaction files. All journals and specialized reports can be prepared from these detailed files on request. Fourthly, the account balances are stored in a form compatible with financial modelling languages and spreadsheet packages for budgeting and financial planning. The need to undertake detailed searching of computer files for *ex post* accounting data to enter into the matrix of a financial model is reduced or eliminated. Fifthly, the use of matrices is compatible with, and should further enhance the use of, relational database management systems in accounting. A matrix framework can provide a user with a convenient method of viewing an appropriate portion of a large, integrated database. Finally, it is argued that a matrix framework is suitable as the basis for developing a new canonical model in accounting. These benefits justify a strong consideration of the matrix form for incorporation into the design of computer-based accounting systems.

NOTES

1. Based on Goldberg and Leech (1984).
2. The question of how a computer stores the matrix *physically* is not considered in this chapter. The expression 'storing data in a matrix' refers to the conceptual or virtual storage.
3. This general mode is used consistently throughout this chapter. The description is then equally applicable to instructions in general purpose languages (such as BASIC, FORTRAN, COBOL) or commands in spreadsheet software (such as LOTUS 1-2-3, MULTIPLAN, EXCEL).
4. Based on the system designed in Goldberg and Leech (1984) and Leech, Colvin and Goldberg (1985).
5. Throughout this chapter the terms 'application program' and 'program' are used in a general sense. They refer to any computer-based software that may be coded or instructed to achieve the desired result.
6. In a commercial accounting system the processing of wages and salaries, for example is usually treated as a separate subsystem.

FURTHER READING

Goldberg, L. and Leech, S. A. (1984). *An Introduction to Accounting Method*. Longman Cheshire, Melbourne.
Mattessich, R. (1964). *Accounting and Analytical Methods*. Irwin, Homewood, Illinois.
Mepham, M. J. (1980). *Accounting Models*. Pitman, London.
Merrett, T. H. (1984). *Relational Information Systems*. Reston, Virginia.
Shank, J. K. (1972). *Matrix Methods in Accounting*. Addison-Wesley, Reading, Massachusetts.

DISCUSSION QUESTIONS

1. Discuss the major problems associated with the various approaches to matrix-based accounting systems in the period 1957–1980.
2. In this chapter, the design for an accounting system which incorporates a matrix approach into accounting sub-systems and which follows established accounting procedures was proposed. Critically evaluate the proposed design, including a discussion of the advantages and disadvantages.
3. In what ways would the use of a relational database management system support the argument for a matrix framework in accounting systems?
4. Is the recognition of a 'conceptual model' as distinct from a 'physical model' important in the design of accounting systems? Why? What difference, if any, would such a distinction make to the design of accounting systems?
5. Do you agree that there is need for a canonical model in accounting? Discuss the advantages and disadvantages of using matrices as the basis for a canonical model.

REFERENCES

Amernic, J. (1979). 'A matrix approach to asset and liability valuation', *Cost and Management*, March – April, pp. 25–31.
Barkman, A. I. (1977). 'Estimation on accounting and auditing using Markov chains', *Journal of Accountancy*, December, pp. 75–79.
Barton, A. (1975). *The Anatomy of Accounting*. University of Queensland Press, St Lucia, Queensland.
Boy, A. D. (1976). 'An input-output planning model that takes into account price-level changes', *Journal of Business Finance and Accounting*, Vol. 3, No. 1, Spring, pp. 15–31.
Buckley, J. W. and Lightner, K. M. (1973). *Accounting: An Information Systems Approach*. Dickenson, Encino, California.
Butterworth, J. E. (1972). 'The accounting system as an information function', *Journal of Accounting Research*, Vol. 10, no. 1, Spring, pp. 1–27.
Butterworth, J. E. and Sigloch, B. A. (1971). 'A generalized multi-stage input-output model and some derived equivalent systems', *Accounting Review*, Vol. 46, No. 4, October, pp. 700–16.
Charnes, A., Cooper, W. W. and Ijiri, Y. (1963). 'Breakeven budgeting and programming to goals', *Journal of Accounting Research*, Vol. 1, No. 1, Spring, pp. 16–43.
Churchill, N. (1964). 'Linear algebra and cost allocations: some examples', *Accounting Review*, Vol. 39, No. 4, October, pp. 894–904.
Codd, E. F. (1970). 'A relational model of data for large shared data banks', *Communications of ACM*, Vol. 13, No. 6, June, pp. 377–87.

Codd, E. F. (1972a). 'Further normalization of the data base relational model', *Courant Computer Science Symposia 6*, 'Data Base Systems,' New York University, Prentice-Hall, Englewood Cliffs, New Jersey, pp. 33–64.

Codd, E. F. (1972b). 'Relational completeness of data base sublanguages', *Courant Computer Science Symposia 6*, 'Data Base Systems', New York University, Prentice-Hall, Englewood Cliffs, New Jersey, pp. 65–98.

Colantoni, C. S., Manes, R. P. and Whinston, A. (1971). 'A unified approach to the theory of accounting and information systems', *Accounting Review*, Vol. 46, No. 1, January, pp. 90–102.

Corcoran, A. W. (1964). 'Matrix bookkeeping', *Journal of Accountancy*, March, pp. 60–66.

Corcoran, A. W. (1968). *Mathematical Applications in Accounting*. Harcourt Brace and World, New York.

Corcoran, A. W. and Leininger, W. E. (1975). 'Isolating accounting variances via partitioned matrices', *Accounting Review*, Vol. 50, No. 1, January, pp. 184–8.

De Morgan, A. (1869). *Elements of Arithmetic*, 5th ed, Appendix VII 'On the Main Principle of Book-keeping'. Taylor and Walton, London, pp 180–9.

Dennis, K. C. (1979). 'Hospitals must allocate bad debts properly', *Management Accounting*, July, pp. 11–14.

Doney, L. D. (1969). 'Integrating accounting and computerized data processing', *Accounting Review*, Vol. 44, No. 2, April, pp. 400–409.

Everest, G. C. and Weber, R. (1977). 'A relational approach to accounting models', *Accounting Review*, Vol. 52, No. 2, April, pp. 340–59.

Farag, S. M. (1967). *Input-Output Analysis: Applications to Business Accounting*. Centre for International Education and Research in Accounting, University of Illinois, Urbana, Illinois.

Farag, S. M. (1968). 'A planning model for the divisionalized enterprise', *Accounting Review*, Vol. 43, No. 2, April, pp 312–20.

Faux, M. C. (1966). 'A new approach to account training', *Accounting Review*, Vol. 41, No. 1, April, pp 129–32.

Forrester, D. A. R. (ed.) (1984). *Financial and Cost Accounting, Are they Compatible?* Strathclyde Convergencies, Glasgow.

Fuerst, E. (1955). 'The matrix as a tool in macro-accounting', *Review of Economics and Statistics*, Vol. 37, No. 1, February, pp. 35–47.

Gambling, T. E. (1968). 'A technological model for use in input-output analysis and cost accounting', *Management Accounting*, December, pp. 33–38.

Gambling, T. E. and Nour, A. (1970). 'A note on input-output analysis: its uses in macro-economics and micro-economics', *Accounting Review*, Vol. 45, No. 1, January, pp. 98–102.

Ghosh, B. C. (1978). 'Using matrix algebra for cost allocation and variance analysis', *Management Accounting*, June, pp. 248–9.

Goldberg, L. and Leech, S. A. (1984). *An Introduction to Accounting Method*, Longman Cheshire, Melbourne.

Harper, W. (1980). 'Matrix algebra as the accountant's tool in variance analysis – Part 1/Part 2', *Accountancy*, October, pp. 120–1, November, pp. 93–6.

Harper, W. (1985a). 'Using databases for accounting creatively', *Accountancy*, May pp. 104–6.

Harper, W. (1985b). 'Old accounting theory slows database advance', *Accountancy*, March, pp. 152–3.

Harper, W. (1985c). 'Set theory, ten green bottles and the accountant', *Accountancy*, July, pp. 111–2.

Haseman, W. D. and Whinston, A. B. (1976). 'Design of a multidimensional accounting system', *Accounting Review*, Vol. 51, No. 1, January, pp. 65–79.

Holmes, B. J. (1978). 'Input-output accounting', *The Accountant*, 1 June, pp. 753–4.

Ijiri, Y. (1965). *Management Goals and Accounting for Control*. North-Holland, Amsterdam.

Ijiri, Y. (1968). 'An application of input-output analysis to some problems in cost accounting', *Management Accounting*, April, pp. 49–61.

Ijiri, Y. and Kelly, E. C. (1980). 'Multidimensional accounting and distributed databases: their implications for organizations and society', *Accounting Organizations and Society*, Vol. 5, No. 1, pp. 115–23.

Jackson, J. (1956) 'The history of methods of exposition of double-entry book-keeping in England'. In Littleton, A. C. and B. S. Yamey, *Studies in the History of Accounting*. Sweet and Maxwell, London, pp. 288–312.

Johnson, G. L. and Gentry, J. A. (1970). *Finney and Miller's Principles of Accounting*, Prentice Hall, Englewood Cliffs, New Jersey.

Johnson, O. (1970) 'Towards an "events" theory of accounting', *Accounting Review*, Vol. 45, No. 4, October, pp. 641–53.

Kapoor, S. S. (1974) 'Matrix accounting model', *International Accountant*, June, pp. 45–52.

Kemeny, J. G., Schleifer, A., Snell, J. L. and Thompson, G. L. (1962). *Finite Mathematics with Business Applications*. Prentice Hall, Englewood Cliffs, New Jersey.

Kohler, E. L. (1952a). 'Accounting concepts and national income', *Accounting Review*, Vol. 27, No. 1, January, pp. 50–6.

Kohler, E. E. L. (1952). *A Dictionary for Accountants*. Prentice Hall, New York.

Konsynski, B. R. and Nawojski, C. A. (1978). 'A model of account transactions', *Proceedings 11th Hawaii International Conference on Systems Sciences*, Honolulu, pp. 47–9.

Kucic, A. R. and Battaglia, S. T. (1981). 'Matrix accounting for the statment of changes in financial position', *Management Accounting*, April, pp. 27–32.

Leech, S. A., Colvin, P. J. and Goldberg, L. (1985). *The TAC System*, Longman Cheshire, Melbourne.

Leech, S. A. (1986). 'The theory and development of a matrix-based accounting system', *Accounting and Business Research*, No. 64, Autumn, pp. 327–41.

Leontief, W. W. (1951). *The Structure of the American Economy, 1919–1939*, 2nd edn. Oxford University Press, New York.

Liao, M. (1976). 'A matrix approach to the depreciation lapse schedule preparation', *Accounting Review*, Vol. 51, No. 2, April, pp. 364–9.

Lieberman, A. Z. and Whinston, A. B. (1975). 'A structuring of an events-accounting information system', *Accounting Review*, Vol. 50, No. 2, April, pp. 246–58.

List, W. (1986). 'Exit double entry?' *Accountant's Magazine*, September, pp. 44–5.

Livingstone, J. L. (1968). 'Matrix algebra and cost allocation', *Accounting Review*, Vol. 43, No. 3, July, pp. 503–8.

Livingstone, J. L. (1969). 'Input-output analysis for cost accounting, planning and control', *Accounting Review*, Vol. 44, No. 1, January, pp. 48–64.

Lucas, H. (1969). 'Practical matrix accounting by computer', *The Accountant*, 26 July, pp. 112–4 and 2 August, pp. 140–2.

McCarthy, W. E. (1979). 'An equity-relationship view of accounting models', *Accounting Review*, Vol. 54, No. 4, October, pp. 667–86.

McCarthy, W. E. (1982). 'The REA accounting model: a generalized framework for accounting systems in a shared data environment', *Accounting Review*, Vol. 57, No. 3, July, pp. 554–78.

Manes, R. P. (1965). 'Comment on matrix theory and cost allocation', *Accounting Review*, Vol. 40, No. 3, July, pp. 640–3.

Mathews, R. L. (1967). 'A computer programming approach to the design of accounting systems', *Abacus*, Vol. 3, No. 2, December, pp. 133–52.

Mathews, R. L. (1971). *The Accounting Framework*. Cheshire, Melbourne.

Mattessich, R. (1957). 'Towards a general and axiomatic foundation of accountancy', *Accounting Research*, Vol. 8, No. 4, October, pp. 328–55.

Mattessich, R. (1958). 'Mathematical models in business accounting', *Accounting Review*, Vol. 33, No. 3, July, pp. 472–81.

Mattessich, R. (1964a). *Accounting and Analytical Methods*. Irwin, Homewood, Illinois.

Mattessich, R. (1964b). *Simulation of the Firm through a Budget Computer Program*. Irwin, Homewood, Illinois.

Mepham, M. J. (1966). 'Matrix algebra and accounting', *The Accountant*, 26 November, pp. 687–93 and 3 December, pp. 721–3.

Mepham, M. J. (1980). *Accounting Models*. Pitman, London.

Merrett, T. H. (1984). *Relational Information Systems*. Reston, Virginia.

Quesnay, F. (1760). 'Analyze du tableau economique'. In Oncken, A. (ed.) (1888). *Oeuvres Economiques et Philosophiques de F. Quesnay*. Baer, Frankfurt.

Richards, A. B. (1960). 'Input-output accounting for business', *Accounting Review*, Vol. 35, No. 3, July, pp. 429–36.

Shank, J. (1971). 'Income determination under uncertainty: an application of Markov chains', *Accounting Review*, Vol. 46, No. 1, January, pp. 57–74.

Shank, J. K. (1972). *Matrix Methods In Accounting*. Addison-Wesley, Reading, Massachusetts.

Sherwood, D. (1982). 'Modelling with matrices – the costing problem', *Accountancy*, June, pp. 60–4.

Sigloch, B. (1971). 'Input-output analysis and the cost model: a comment', *Accounting Review*, Vol. 46, No. 2, April, pp. 374–5.

Sorter, G. (1969). 'An "events" approach to basic accounting theory', *Accounting Review*, Vol. 44, No. 1, January, pp. 12–9.

Stone, R. (1952) 'Simple transaction models, information and computing', *Review of Economic Studies, 1951–52*, Vol. 19, pp. 67–84.

Williams, T. H. and Griffin, C. H. (1964). 'Matrix theory and cost allocation', *Accounting Review*, Vol. 39, No. 3, July, pp. 671–8.

Yamey, B. S. (1956), 'Introduction'. In Littleton, A. C. and Yamey, B. S. (eds) (1956). *Studies in the History of Accounting*. Irwin, Homewood, Illinois.

9 An 'events' approach to basic accounting theory

George H. Sorter

In 1966, after two years work, a committee of the American Accounting Association issued *A Statement of Basic Accounting Theory*.[1] Undoubtedly, the most startling recommendations were the sanctioning of current costs and the advocacy of two column (historical and current) reports. To this member of the committee, however, even more startling was that the near unanimous agreement on the recommendations was arrived at by following two very divergent paths originating from two very dissimilar basic concepts about accounting. This split is not confined to committee members but rather seems representative of a more widespread and pervasive difference in the world outside. The majority view of the committee and the predominant faction outside believes in what I here define as the 'value' approach to accounting. The minority view, of which I am sometimes the only member, I describe as the 'events' approach. This view, although implied by some in the past,[2] has never to my knowledge been explicitly stated but might have far-reaching implications. This chapter seeks to describe and contrast the two schools; present arguments for and illustrate the consequences of an 'events' approach to accounting theory; and examine the logic leading to the conclusions embodied in the *Statement of Basic Accounting Theory*. Hopefully, this will provide not only insights and help for the analysis and evaluation of the committee's monograph but perhaps also stimulate discussion and criticism of a new approach and suggest new avenues of research and experimentation to make accounting more responsive to present day conditions.

Source: *The Accounting Review* vol. 44, January 1969, pp. 12–19.
Published by the American Accounting Association.

TWO VIEWS – VALUE AND EVENTS

THE VALUE THEORY

The 'value' school within the committee, or as they would probably prefer to be termed the 'user need' school, assumed that users' needs are known and sufficiently well specified so that accounting theory can deductively arrive at and produce optimal input values for used and useful decision models. Most of the value theorists visualize accounting's purpose as producing optimum income and capital value or values.[3] This leads to the popular sport of proper matching of costs and revenue. The assumption is that 'proper matching' associates costs and revenue to produce the right income figure or figures – the figure or figures optimal for users' decision models.

Several criticisms may be levelled at this value approach.

1. There are many and varied uses of accounting data and it is therefore impossible to specify input values that are optimal for the wide range of possible uses.
2. For each specified use different users utilize a wide range of different decision models, that they have so far been unable to describe, define, or specify. Further, neither economists nor accountants have been able to advance the theoretically correct decision models.
3. The value theory is unnecessarily restrictive. Thus events such as leases or commitments have, until recently, tended to be excluded from the accounting universe, partially at least, because they did not affect income or net asset values.

    The orientation of accounting toward producing income and asset values which are nothing but simple attempts to adjust for the lag between cash outflows and cash inflows has impeded the development of more sophisticated lag models made possible by more sophisticated techniques.
4. The value theory is not useful in explaining many current developments in accounting. Income theory, for instance, does not provide a basis for the current sub-aggregates that are utilized in the income statement such as sales, cost of sales, etc. It has also not been helpful in explaining the advocacy of the fund statement or in helping the conglomerate and a host of other current problems.

THE EVENTS THEORY

Proponents of the 'events' theory suggest that the purpose of accounting is to provide information about relevant economic events that might be useful in a variety of possible decision models. They see the function of accounting at one level removed in the decision-making process. Instead of producing input values for unknown and perhaps unknowable decision models directly, accounting provides information about relevant economic events that allows individual users to generate their own input values for their own individual decision models. In other words, given the state of the arts, less rather than more aggregation is appropriate and the user, rather than the accountant, must aggregate, assign weights and values to the data consistent with his forecasts and utility functions. 'Events' proponents suggest that the loss of information generated by aggregation and valuation by the accountant is greater than the associated benefit. While they would agree that the accountants' suggested weights and values deserve to be communicated, they would insist that these weights be communicated in disaggregated form so that users always had the non-weighted raw data available as well.

This viewpoint seems particularly appropriate today when little is known about how accounting data is used but may even be preferred when more knowledge about decision models becomes available. It is possible to visualize reasonable decision models that are consistent with an 'events' approach rather than a 'value' approach. An investor, for instance, attempting to forecast the value of a firm at some future point may utilize two methods: (1) He may base his estimate of future values on the trend, size, and variability of current income or other aggregated values. (2) Alternatively, he may wish to use current accounting data to predict specific future events and then base his estimate of future values on these predicted events. In other words, he may wish to predict income or he may wish to predict sales, cost of sales, taxes, etc. The first model is more consistent with a value approach, the second with an events approach.

The criticism must be met that the 'events' approach relies just as heavily upon knowledge of users' models as does the 'value' approach. The argument goes as follows. Decisions as to what events are relevant (surely not all events can be recorded) must be made and can only be made with users' needs in mind. Thus, the users' needs must still be known. This is correct. But it seems clear that less need be known about decision models to decide whether or not an event might be relevant for a model than to have to decide how the data fits a specific decision model and what specific weights should be assigned.[4] In the lease example, under an 'events' approach, it is only necessary to decide that information about leases, commitments or orders are relevant to a host of decision models for such information to be included in accounting reports. It is unnecessary to justify how, if at all, this information should be weighted in an income valuation model.

TO AGGREGATE OR NOT TO AGGREGATE

As has been indicated, the real difference between the two schools lies in what level of aggregation and valuation is appropriate in accounting reports and who is to be the aggregator and evaluator. The question as to who is to aggregate or value is not unique to accounting. As Ijiri points out '... any aggregation generally involves loss of information in that the resulting total 'value' may be composed of many – possibly infinitely many – different *components*.'[5] It is interesting to note that in two widely different areas there have recently been thrusts toward presenting less aggregated data. In modern statistics it is no longer considered good form to merely report confidence intervals. Instead the plea is for full presentation of the underlying data or distributions.[6] Only the user can decide what is or is not significant, given his loss function. In weather forecasts, we are no longer told that it will or will not rain or snow. Instead we are given probability estimates and must ourselves decide whether or not to carry umbrellas or to send out work crews. We are given the underlying raw data and must assign values consistent with our individual utility functions.

Accounting income has variously been thought of as a measure of how much can be spent and still be as well off as before, as a measure of managerial efficiency or as a basis for forecasting future values. But each of these depends on individual expectations, individual preference functions and individual decision models not on some never clearly defined concept of 'proper matching of costs and revenues'. Unfortunately this attempt to match, the assigning of weights to generate values, the attempt to aggregate into an income figure, destroys potentially useful information about important underlying events and increases possible measurement errors and biases. Every item on an income statement is the result of at least two processes – the underlying event and the accountants' allocation of the event to a particular time period. This allocation has the purpose of matching in order to derive a 'true' income figure or figures. Lifo and Fifo for example are used in an attempt to produce better income figures. Both, however, destroy information about the consumption event. If either Lifo or Fifo is used consumption of two identical units bought at different prices will necessarily be described differently. A user interested in comparing consumption activity for two periods is unable to distinguish between variations caused by the measurement process, be it Lifo or Fifo, and real differences in the consumption levels.

Deferred tax attempts to secure proper matching of costs and revenues and thereby destroys information about current tax payments. Conventional absorption costing in an attempt to secure proper matching destroys information about production inputs and outputs since cost of goods sold and inventory become dependent on both the level of production and of sales.

The loss of information due to aggregation also holds for the balance sheet. Necessarily, every balance sheet account is an aggregation of two or more types of events (the events recorded on the debit and credit sides of the account). Very often the events so aggregated vary greatly in type, measureability and variability and therefore destroy much information about specific events. For instance, if current costs or values are used, acquisition and consumption activities as well as environmental changes are combined and the reconstructability of each specific event is impaired. Acquisitions and amortizations or acquisitions and dispositions are events differing widely in possible measurement error. By combining them in asset and liability accounts information about each is destroyed.

As already indicated, income and capital valuation are attempts to deal with lags between cash outflows and cash inflows. These appear to be unnecessarily crude and primitive given current advances in methodology and measurement technique. The presentation of less aggregated data suggested by the 'events' approach might stimulate investigation of more complicated but more useful lag and forecast models that could vary for different industries, firms, time periods, or indiviuals.

SOME CONSEQUENCES OF AN EVENTS APPROACH

This is not the proper medium in which to describe some possible long-range consequences of the 'events' approach. In a subsequent manuscript, I intend to speculate on the type of accounting reports appropriate to this approach. Even under the existing accounting framework there are several implications of 'events' theory which might help to explain this point of view.

THE BALANCE SHEET

It is currently the fashion to say that the balance sheet or position statement has lost most, if not all, of its significance. But not for event theorists. We view the balance sheet not as a value statement nor as a statement of financial position but rather as an indirect communication of all accounting events that have occurred since the inception of the accounting unit. This indirect communication is provided by summing the effect of all events on the names used in describing these events and then recording the subsequent balances. Inventory, thus, does not report either value or costs but rather describes the acquisition and consumption activities that have occurred. This view has several advantages. It does not purport to report something that is not achieved (i.e. value) and it does facilitate the understanding and analysis of what is described. If the inventory figure, for instance, is visualized as a representation of the inventory, under value theory the accountant must somehow rationalize the particular costs of value figure that he uses. If historical cost is used, the validity of a representation of inventory that ignores value inevitably crops up. If value is used the argument centres about the justification of this rather than some other value. It is certainly difficult to justify either historical costs or any one representation of value. This difficulty does not create so grave a problem for the 'event' theorist. Suppose original cost is used. Under an events notion this means simply that acquisition and consumption events, but not environmental changes, are recorded. Original costs need not be justified. One may certainly deplore the absence of information about environmental events (i.e. value changes) but one accepts information about the events that are described (i.e. acquisition and consumption) and uses them in whatever fashion is appropriate.

An 'events' approach to the balance sheet could lead to operational rules about balance sheet construction and presentation. The following represents a possible rule. *A balance sheet should be so constructed as to maximize the reconstructability of the events being aggregated.* Various users may thus generate information about particular events they are interested in. One purpose of the balance sheet is to facilitate the preparation of funds statements and like reports that provide information about important events.

THE INCOME STATEMENT

For value theorists the purpose of an income statement quite simply is to report income value or values. Under an 'events' approach the purpose of the income statement is to provide direct communication concerning the operating events or activities of the firm. Accounting utilizes two forms of communication: an indirect or effect communication of all events (the balance sheet) and direct, specific or event communication of certain critical events (income statement, cash statement, production statement, funds statement, etc). The concern of event theorists is not primarily with the final income figure but rather with describing critical operating activities of a firm. The preferred title would be 'statement of operating events'. Events theory can suggest an operational rule for income statements. For instance, *each event should be described in a manner facilitating the forecasting of that same event in a future time period given exogenous changes.* The deferred tax question would then be resolved by investigating which quantification more reliably forecasts future tax payments. Both Lifo and Fifo would be rejected because they impede the ability to forecast acquisitions and consumptions of inventory in the future.

The 'events' school can justify the present organization of the income statement which reports several sub-aggregates such as sales, cost of sales, etc., because these are considered critical operating events. Perhaps this is one instance when an events orientation has already affected the accounting structure.

THE FUNDS STATEMENT

Value theorists, rigidly faithful to their doctrine, have the most difficulty in justifying this statement. They state rather feebly that '... the basic purpose of the funds statement is to account for the change in working capital during the period covered by the statement.'[7] Such a concept certainly underrates the utility of this statement and leads to trivial discussions as to the proper definition of working capital. The 'events' school thinks of this statement as 'a statement of financial and investment events'. The working capital account merely represents a useful technique to organize the events and prepare the statement. The important consideration is whether a financing or investment event is relevant and should be reported, not whether working capital is affected by a given event. This again demonstrates the flexibility of an 'events' approach. Different financing or investment event may or may not be relevant for specific firms or at specific times. The content of the funds statement thus need not remain invariate for all times or for all firms.

A STATEMENT OF BASIC ACCOUNTING THEORY AND THE EVENTS THEORY

Most of the recommendations contained in *A Statement of Basic Accounting Theory* flow more logically from an 'events' rather than from a 'value' orientation. Why are standards or guidelines necessary at all if a 'value' approach is adopted? If users' needs are in fact well specified then accounting should provide the values that make the decision models operate optimally. The only relevant standard then would be the ability of the data to perform in the model. There would be no need for values to be verifiable or free from bias if they work well in a specified model. If, however, users' needs are not well specified suggesting an 'events' approach, then it is necessary to employ standards that limit the range and define the description of relevant events.

The need for two-column reporting under a 'value' approach is not clear. Presumably, the need arises because different columns are useful for different users; that is, historical cost data is useful for the stewardship function and current cost data for the investment function. This rather inadequate rationale has led to the assumption that the historical costs column was only advocated as a stop-gap measure until current value could sweep the day. This was not the intent of the committee.

Mult-column reporting seems eminently compatible with an 'events' view of accounting. The two column reports advocated by *ASOBAT* is a step in that direction. As the monograph states, 'the historical information reflects market transactions, the current cost information reflects market transactions plus 'unrealized' market influences, and the difference shows the effect of unrealized environmental influences.'[8] Since the historical cost column includes descriptions of events other than market transactions (i.e. depreciation, amortization, and other significant accruals) and because market transactions and environmental changes are not the only events that have relevance to the firm, the two columns advocated do not go far enough, but they represent a start.

Separate events should be reported in separate columns because (1) they vary in measurability, (2) they vary in controllability, and (3) they vary in importance from period to period. There is no question that market transactions and environmental changes, for instance, vary in measurability. Market transactions can be relatively satisfactorily described by single numbered quantifications (with relatively little measurement error). There is apt to be little variance around that single number. The same, however, cannot be said about environmental changes or forecasts where description by ranges or distributions could be more appropriate and where measurement errors could be material. As long as a single column is used there will be a tendency to continue to measure events by a single measurement process which is inappropriate for certain types of events and we shall continue to be faced with troubles in assessing measurement biases or errors.

These events also vary in controllability by the managers of a firm. Clearly, market transactions are more controllable than environmental changes but less controllable than conversions. If accounting reports are to be useful in evaluating management than a separation of events by controllability should help in fulfilling this objective.

Finally, the importance of the different classes of events may vary from period to period. An investor may predict a period of stability where certain environmental changes are expected to be minimal and in order to forecast adequately from accounting data he must then be able to separate the effect of environmental changes from market transactions. This he can do in multi-column reporting. As the importance of different types of events vary, users, according to their estimate of the future, can attach different weights to the different types of events.

At first blush multi-column reporting seems a drastic departure from current practices – but is it really? Presently we use multi-row reporting. We break down the income statement into many aggregates such as sales, cost of sales, S&A expenses, taxes, etc. We break down the balance sheet into many rows by classes of equities and assets. Very little research has been done as to what explains the current level of sub-aggregation and extreme proponents of the 'value' school would have a hard time rationalizing the present format of the income statement. Presently the income statement is organized around a functional event structure, and the balance sheet around a functional effect structure. Multi-column reporting would add a 'source of events' classification to both reports and instead of accounting reports consisting of a 7 by 1 matrix they would consist of a 7 by 5 matrix. This move from one matrix to another does not seem that revolutionary, and would be facilitated by an events approach.

CONCLUSION

Admittedly, the above represents only a rough and underdeveloped first approach toward a new orientation for accounting theory. Why, then, is it presented here and now? Only in the hope of encouraging the research activities suggested by this approach and also in the further hope that it might stimulate a re-examination of some essential if rarely expressed implicit tenets of present accounting thought. The areas of possible research opportunities indicated by an events approach are many. The following represent a few:

1. Test whether line by line prediction of events, i.e. the prediction of sales, cost of sales, etc., are more efficient in explaining the future value of a firm than the use of more aggregated figures such as income.
2. Investigate the present format of accounting reports to see how useful these formats could be, i.e. to what extent do the various subcategories of the income statement and balance sheet covary? To what extent do they provide additional information?
3. Attempt to develop more sophisticated models to explain the lag between cash outflows and cash inflows, i.e. utilizing fund statements, production statements, and others in an attempt to predict cash flows.
4. Investigate the information loss due to the aggregations presently used by accountants. How much information is lost by aggregating and

combining events to produce one income figure or to produce the different balance sheet amounts? A subsequent extension of this would be an investigation of the information loss due to expressing all economic activities in dollar terms.

5. Construct useful accounting reports based on an events approach.

Ultimately this paper will find its justification if what is presented here as the conclusion will serve as an introduction to the research activities and the re-examination advocated.

NOTES

1. American Accounting Association (1966). *A Statement of Basic Accounting Theory*. Report prepared by the Committee on Basic Accounting Theory, AAA.
2. This idea, like so many others, had its origins in the writings and thought of Professor William J. Vatter whom I hasten to absolve from any of its shortcomings.
3. Not all value theorists are income oriented. Chambers, for example, can be considered a 'value' but not an 'income' theorist.
4. '. . . a goal which by itself may not be so capable of definition as to determine a single perfect solution may nevertheless be clear enough and important enough to rule out some solutions . . .' From Guido Calabrese (1965) 'Fault, accidents, and the wonderful world of Blum and Calven', *Yale Law Journal*, December, p. 222.
5. Yuji Ijiri (1967). *The Foundations of Accounting Measurement*. Prentice Hall, p. 120.
6. See Howard Raiffa and Robert Schlaifer (1961). *Applied Statistical Decision Theory*. Harvard University, Division of Research, Graduate School of Business, p. 68.
7. Perry Mason (1961). '"Cash flow" analysis and the funds statement', *Accounting Research Study No. 2*. American Institute of Certified Public Accountants.
8. American Accounting Association, op. cit., p. 31.

10 Database accounting systems
Guido Geerts and William E. McCarthy

Almost fifteen years ago, McCrae (1976) spoke of the difference between systems and technology in making a case for the development of newer and more sophisticated accounting models:

> We must be careful to differentiate between accounting technology and accounting systems.
>
> The technology of accounting is concerned with the physical artifacts which are employed to process accounting data. These artifacts range all the way from quill pens to remote controlled computers. Accounting systems are concerned with the classifying and structuring of accounting data ... It is possible to change the accounting technology without changing the accounting system and vice versa. This is illustrated by the ... example set out later in this chapter. An unchanged system is processed on a changed technology.
>
> The clear distinction between system and technology is important since many accountants suffer from the delusion that because they have changed the accounting technology they must automatically have effected dramatic changes in the accounting system. This is not so. The new computer technology provides a dramatic improvement in the speed of data processing and automatic control but this potential cannot be realized without affecting major alterations in the accounting system. In other words the accountant must develop more sophisticated accounting models to benefit from computer technology (p. 39).

Specially commissioned for *IT and Accounting: The impact of information technology*.
Edited by Bernard C. Williams and Barry J. Spaul.
Published in 1991 by Chapman & Hall, London ISBN 0 412 39210 0.

The major alterations called for by McCrae have, by and large, not yet materialized in the modern EDP environment. Current systems (mainframe accounting software as well as PC accounting packages) consist simply of computerized versions of journalizing and posting routines which use double-entry principles to define procedures and the chart of accounts to classify meaning of economic events.

Most of the research aimed at better compatibility between accounting systems and information technology has concentrated on integrating 'events' accounting theories (Sorter, 1969) with *database* approaches to information management, approaches that assume that an enterprise chooses to manage its data as a centrally-controlled resource to be shared among a wide range of users with highly diverse needs. Accounting systems built with this type of orientation have included hierarchical models, network models and relational models (McCarthy, 1981).

A more generalized approach to the task of constructing events accounting systems in a database environment was proposed by McCarthy (1979) who built an accounting system using a conceptual schema – expressed in terms of Chen's (1976) entity relationship model – that could be mapped into any of the more specific approaches mentioned above. In 1982, McCarthy extended this approach by using data abstraction to develop a generalized semantic representation of accounting phenomena: the REA framework (McCarthy, 1982).

This chapter explains database accounting – as defined by McCarthy (1979, 1982) and later extended with implementation work (McCarthy, 1990) – and contrasts the use of such alternative accounting models with conventional book-keeping-oriented systems.

AN ALTERNATIVE VIEW OF ACCOUNTING REPRESENTATION

A chart of accounts and its accompanying double-entry procedures might be viewed simply as a scheme for organizing, classifying and aggregating financial data. Additionally, however, it represents the imposition upon an accountant of a particular mode of thinking about the economic affairs of an entity. For example, when queried about the 'things' that accounting deals with, accountants might list items such as 'prepaid revenues', 'retained earnings', or 'liabilties' because these, among others, constitute the elements in their predefined world of interest. Collectively, these account names and double-entry procedures represent a data model of an enterprise's economic aspects.

This predisposition toward certain types of 'book-keeping things' of interest will be discarded here. Instead this chapter will view an object financial system without 'traditional-accounting-coloured' glasses and use a *semantic model* for the creation of an accounting information system. Use of such a semantic framework assumes that an accounting system designer is trying to capture explicitly the object structure of the corporation being modelled. This object structure is normally reflected in a 'conceptual schema' of the targeted enterprise, and the purpose and architecture of these conceptual schemas is examined next.

CONCEPTUAL SCHEMAS OF BUSINESS ENTERPRISES

Conceptual schemas have claimed an increasingly important role in the development of information systems. But what are conceptual schemas and what is their function in the development of integrated databases for business enterprises? Consider first the classical ANSI/SPARC three-level architecture illustrated in Fig. 10.1 (Date, 1986, Chapter 2).

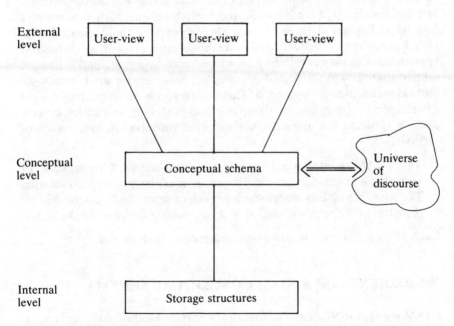

Fig. 10.1 ANSI/SPARC three-level architecture. (*Source*: Date, 1986, Chapter 2.)

While the external level presents the individual data views of various enterprise decision-makers, the conceptual level groups these views to a common enterprise-wide perspective called the conceptual schema. This global view has the explicit goal of modelling enterprise facts in a consistent and non-redundant fashion. The internal level corresponds with the more technical aspects of data storage such as the lengths of records and pointers. While the conceptual and external levels need to capture the problem-oriented aspects of the Universe of Discourse (UoD) – the part of reality being represented in the information system – the internal or physical level models the efficiency-oriented structures of computer storage (Falkenberg, 1981).

The conceptual schema is actually a model of the accounting UoD. Objects of interest – such as transactions, people, and financial resources which exist independently in the application world – should be represented directly in the schema. Identifying and structuring these representations correctly is the most important activity in the development of accounting information systems. Once the conceptual schema has been specified, designation of individual views for decision-makers and computer-oriented views for implementation can follow.

Different strategies exist for the specification of the conceptual schema. In the top-down approach, objects in the accounting world are identified first and modelled directly, while the bottom-up approach concentrates first on individual data needs and then integrates those views into a global perspective. Realistic design methodologies actually use these two approaches together (McCarthy, Rockwell and Armitage, 1989). For the sake of simplicity in the rest of this chapter, however, we will use only the more direct top-down approach. Our primary task in accounting system design then becomes one of identifying and modelling accounting objects directly. Toward this purpose, we will avail ourselves of two bodies of theory:

1. The NIAM model which provides a well-accepted framework of semantics and notational constructs for an accounting conceptual schema.
2. The REA accounting model which provides a semantically-oriented interpretation of the requisite objects in an accounting Universe of Discourse.

Each of these theories is addressed in a section that follows.

INGREDIENTS OF A NIAM CONCEPTUAL SCHEMA

NIAM stands for Nijssen's Information Analyses Methodology and can be considered as an integrated methodology for the development of an information system. A full treatment of NIAM is beyond the scope of this chapter, but interested readers may consult Verheijen and van Bekkum (1982), Wintraecken (1986) or Nijssen (1989). We will limit ourselves to an explication of NIAM's basic ideas. Before that explanation commences, however, we would like to stress some important overall characteristics of Nijssen's method:

1. NIAM provides a natural language interface for system analysis and design. Well-formed sentences are used during requirements analysis to aid communication between end-users and analysts. This interface is one of the keystones of the fact-based approach to system design (Kent, 1986; Leung and Nijssen, 1988).
2. A rich set of graphical constructs for schema specification is a key component of the methodology.
3. An algorithm is provided for the translation of a NIAM information structure diagram (ISD) to a fully normalized and optimal relational database specification. Fully normalized means that all relations are at least in 5th Normal Form (Date, 1986) while optimal means that the number of relations in the generated schema is minimal (Nijssen, 1989).

These characteristics provide most of the rationale for NIAM's widespread use in database design, especially in Europe and Australia.

BASIC CONCEPTS

The symbols in Fig. 10.2 cover the major aspects of a conceptual scheme in NIAM. A NOLOT expresses a set of non-printable objects with similar characteristics. Non-lexical objects refer to individual things in the UoD that are not utterable. A LOT by contrast contains a set of utterable objects. These can be used to describe and identify non-lexical objects. A binary fact is an association between two NOLOTs or between a LOT and a NOLOT. An association between two LOTS is never allowed.

The distinction between LOTS and NOLOTS leads to the two different kinds of binary association shown in Fig. 10.2(b): ideas and bridges. A bridge-type represents a set of similar binary associations between a NOLOT and a LOT. This association can be considered as a bridge between two different worlds. An idea-type connects two NOLOTS, and it is best considered as an abstract association.

Figure 10.2(c) illustrates two example associations. The first expresses the idea that warehouses are located in cities (or conversely that cities contain warehouses). The second association illustrates a bridge between the real world (where cities exist) and the representation world (where those cities are referred to by their names).

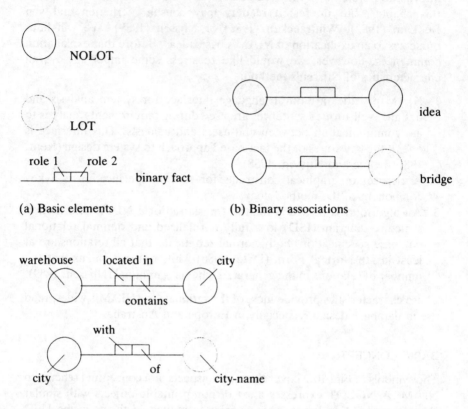

(a) Basic elements   (b) Binary associations

(c) Example

Fig. 10.2 NIAM constructs.

Consistent use of these concepts keeps clear the distinction between reality and a representation of reality. We consider this an important distinction that some data models fail to enforce.

CONSTRAINTS

Constraints specify the allowable ways in which data model constructs can be used to represent the real world. They are methods that enforce the semantic integrity of a conceptual schema. For our purposes in this chapter, consideration of a subset of available NIAM constraints suffices. We will treat successively cardinality and totality constraints.

Cardinality Constraints

A cardinality constraint expresses a restriction with respect to role populations. We limit ourselves first to the three examples presented in Fig. 10.3. Each example is followed by an equivalent set representation.

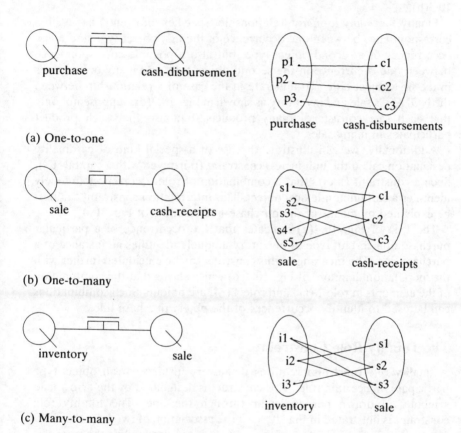

(a) One-to-one

(b) One-to-many

(c) Many-to-many

Fig. 10.3 Cardinality constraints.

Fig. 10.3(a) illustrates a *one-to-one* correspondence between two NOLOTs. Suppose for example a business enterprise has an operational rule that all purchases are to be paid for, in full, exactly five days after a receipt. Further, a payment corresponds with exactly one purchase. Each purchase event would correspond then to only one cash disbursement event and vice versa.

A *one-to-many* relationship specifies a correspondence between just a single occurrence in one role population and many occurrences in another role population. Suppose a situation where an enterprise bills its customers once a month for all sales during the preceding month and where customers must pay in full shortly thereafter. In this case, each cash receipt event would correspond to multiple sale events as illustrated in Fig. 10.3(b).

Finally, a *many-to-many* relationship specifies not only a possible correspondence between one occurrence of the first object-type and many occurrences of a second object-type, but also a possible correspondence between one occurrence in the second object-type and many occurrences in the first object-type. To illustrate in the case of a relationship between the NOLOT's sale and inventory as shown in Fig. 10.3(c), suppose not only that each sale consists of many products, but also that each product participates in many sales.

Additionally, we can illustrate the use of a special kind of cardinality designation called the **uniqueness constraint** (portrayed with a capital 'U'). Such a constraint asserts that a combination of role occurrences uniquely identifies a certain non-lexical object. This interrelation constraint can best be explained by means of the purchase-line example of Fig. 10.4.

The ISD of Fig. 10.4(a) indicates that the occurrence of a particular purchase of a certain type of inventory uniquely identifies an instance of a purchase line. The meaning of this construct can be elucidated further with the 'population diagram' of Fig. 10.4(b) which shows that the combination of the elements in role 1 (r1) and role 4 (r4) are unique. Such combinations can be used to identify occurrences of the object purchase line.

The Totality Role Constraint

A **totality role constraint** requires that every instance of an object-type participate in a certain role. This construct is designated by the arrowhead symbol ($>$) drawn perpendicular through the line. The totality role constraint is illustrated in Fig. 10.5 for the association of two lexical object-types with vendors. The first of these LOTs is required, while the second is not. From a practical viewpoint, these diagrams express the following integrity maintenance rule:

> If information concerning new vendors is added to the database, their names 'must' be added while their phone-numbers 'may' be omitted.

NIAM includes other types of integrity constraints dealing with semantic concerns of equality subsetting and exclusion (Nijssen, 1989). However, for our purposes here, the simple set we have explained thus far will suffice.

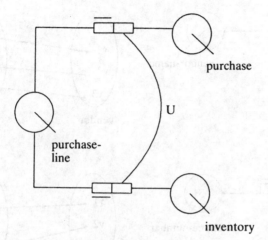

(a) Information structure diagram

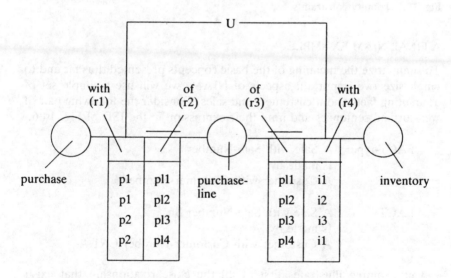

(b) Population diagram

Fig. 10.4 Uniqueness constraint.

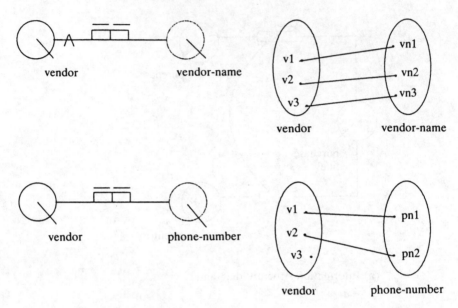

Fig. 10.5 Totality constraints.

A FINAL NIAM EXAMPLE

To summarize the meaning of the basic concepts presented thus far and to emphasize two important aspects of NIAM, we will use a simple set of accounting facts about customers and sales. Consider the following pair of well-formed sentences and note their expression in the ISD of Fig. 10.6.

FACT-type: A Sale with Sale-Number
             Is made by
             A Customer with Customer-Number.

FACT: A Sale with Sale-Number Sn1
             Is made by
             A Customer with Customer-Number CN1.

This example illustrates first of all the close relationship that exists between natural language expression and the ISD notation. This correspondence between these two representations makes natural language communication during systems analysis natural.

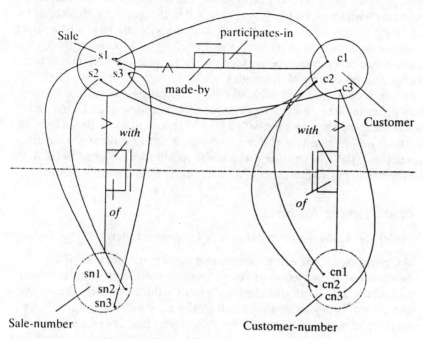

Fig. 10.6 Two world representation.

Secondly, the dotted line of the figure illustrates the distinction between the real world and the representation of the real world. This distinction in NIAM is sometimes obscured in database analysis and design. It is very important to proper design and use of accounting information systems, a fact noted well by Ijiri (1975) in his discussions of the differences between accounting principals and surrogates.

THE BOOK-KEEPING APPROACH TO ACCOUNTING vs AN REA SEMANTIC MODEL

Semantic models like NIAM are a recent addition to the science of representing real-world phenomena and making those representations available to decision-makers. What did people do before the advent of such models or even before the advent of computerized information systems?

In the case of accounting decision-makers, the answer to this question is obvious. Corporate book-keepers used charts-of-accounts and double-entry procedures to record phenomena such as sales with customers and purchases with vendors. However, as noted in the quote by McCrae at the beginning of this chapter, such book-keeping systems have not evolved along the path suggested by semantic modelling and database theory but have instead taken more the tack of simply running old systems on faster storage and processing technologies.

In this section, we will highlight the implications of such choices by showing a simple book-keeping example of an accounting UoD first and by then contrasting that example with a NIAM representation. In between the construction of these two systems, we will illustrate a theory of database accounting – the REA model – which was specifically designed to facilitate the construction of enterprise-wide accounting information systems.

A DEBIT–CREDIT EXAMPLE

Consider the following description of a fastener retailer:

> We purchased £200 worth of nuts and bolts from one vendor on
> Wednesday, then £300 worth of screws and nails from another vendor,
> and finally £25 worth of baling wire from a third supplier. We turned
> around on Thursday and sold half of the nuts and bolts plus all of the
> screws and nails to a customer for £500. Later that day, we sold the rest
> of the nuts and bolts to another customer for £150. On Friday, our first
> customer paid in full while the second one sent us £50, and on Saturday,
> we squared our accounts with the first two vendors.

Book-keeping analysis of the first Wednesday transaction would result in the following journal entry:

    Debit: Inventory   £200
           Credit: Accounts payable   £200

to record Wednesday's purchase of nuts and bolts

In Fig. 10.7, we illustrate how the rest of this retailer's weekly business would be transcribed with book-keeping terms. Readers should note that these T-accounts are a modelled representation of the enterprise's activities, albeit a very restricted one intended for a very limited audience of predefining accounting users. Most modern computerized general ledger systems retain this somewhat insular mindset. In McCrae's terms, they have switched technology but not system.

With a database approach, however, we would discard these debit–credit approaches and try to model the Universe of Discourse directly in terms of its facts and ideas. Nonetheless, even in the case where a natural

Inventory		Accounts Payable		Sales	
Wed. 200			Wed. 200		Thu. 500
Wed. 300			Wed. 300		Thu. 150
Wed. 25			Wed. 25		
	Thu. 400	Sat. 200			
	Thu. 100	Sat. 300			

Accounts receivable		Cost of goods sold		Cash	
Thu. 500		Thu. 400		Fri. 500	
Thu. 150		Thu. 100		Fri. 50	
	Fri. 500				Sat. 200
	Fri. 50				Sat. 300

Fig. 10.7 Book-keeping model.

language oriented approach such as NIAM is used, modelling a UoD with semantic constructs remains a difficult task. This is true for accounting information systems as well as for other systems. An important difference in the accounting sphere, however, is the availability of a semantically specified domain framework: the REA accounting model (McCarthy, 1982). This framework is discussed next.

DATABASE ACCOUNTING WITH THE REA MODEL

The REA accounting model is best considered as an 'occurrence template' for accounting transactions. It implies that accounting phenomena occur in well-defined constellations of associated objects which can be linked together and which can be used to produce traditional accounting numbers and reports. The obvious difference with conventional accounting systems is that the resulting accounting database is much more flexible and natural. The ISD in Fig. 10.8 reflects the REA framework in terms of binary semantic model. The term 'REA' is deduced from the three basic components of the framework: resources, events and agents. We will explain these terms briefly and then proceed to a discussion of this framework's use.

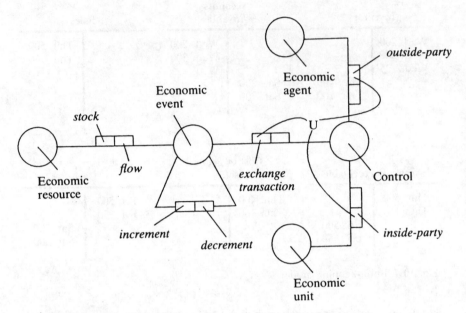

Fig. 10.8 The REA accounting model.

1. *Economic resources* are considered as objects that:
   (a) are scarce and have utility, and
   (b) are under the control of an enterprise
   (Ijiri, 1975, pp. 51–2).
2. *Economic events* are 'a class of phenomena which reflect changes in scarce means [economic resources] resulting from production, exchange, consumption and distribution' (Yu, 1976, p. 256).
3. *Economic agents* include persons and agencies who participate in the economic events of the enterprise or who are responsible for the participation of subordinates.
4. *Economic units* are a subset of agents – they are inside participants who work for or are part of the enterprise being accounted for.

   The control object expresses a three-way association among event, unit and agent. There is also a binary association between resources and events which reflects the stock-flow roles that these objects play in enterprise business. Finally, and perhaps hardest to understand in terms of its departure from book-keeping, there is a binary association required of every accounting event with another event: its dual transaction. Accounting theory (Ijiri, 1975; Mattessich, 1964) requires that transactions associated with resource outflows from a company (decrements) be paired with resource inflows (increments) and vice versa. This is the duality principle of accounting.

The REA framework is intended to be used for operational object analysis of an enterprise's information needs during the specification phase of system design. For example, if something is identified as an economic resource, it can be expected that two event sets, one an inflow and the other an outflow, also will be specified. Furthermore, each of these two event sets would require inside and outside participants, and additional events that would be linked via duality relationships, and so on.

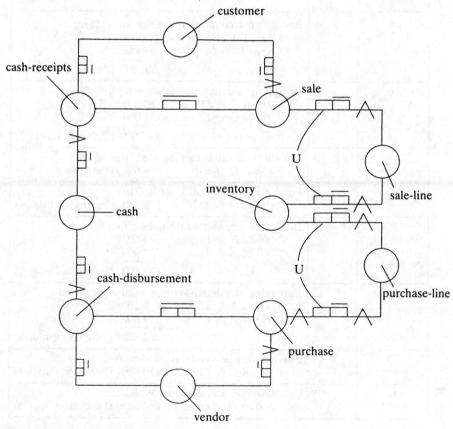

Fig. 10.9 REA instantiation.

In Fig. 10.9, the four transaction types of our fastener company – the Wednesday purchases, the Thursday sales, the Friday cash-receipts, and the Saturday cash-disbursements – are represented in such an integrated manner, beginning with the southeast part of the illustration and proceeding around counter-clockwise. For reasons of simplicity, inside participants (such as buyers, salespeople and cashiers) are neglected in this diagram. However, readers should be able to understand how each REA transaction template can be first instantiated and then linked to the other object constellations using the control, duality or stock-flow associations as the amalgamation points.

Transaction number	Date	Economic event
5	June 1	Bought on account merchandise from Oliver: 6 000 of A @ £2 £12 000 2 000 of B @ £4 8 000 £20 000 (Purchase Order 1)
6	2	Bought on account merchandise from Williams: 20 000 of E @ £1 £20 000 3 000 of C @ £9 27 000 £47 000 (Purchase Order 2)
7	3	Bought on account merchandise from Smith: 600 of D @ £10 £ 6 600 (Purchase Order 3)
19	9	Purchased on account from Smith: 600 of D @ £11 £ 6 000 (Purchase Order 4)
21	10	Bought on account merchandise from Oliver: 2 000 of B @ £4.30 £ 8 600 2 000 of A @ £2 4 000 £12 600 (Purchase Order 5)
30	17	Purchased merchandise on account from Oliver: 4 000 of A @ £2.30 £ 9 200 2 000 of B @ £4.30 8 600 £17 800 (Purchase Order 6)
33	18	Purchased from Williams on account: 1 000 of C @ £10 £10 000 (Purchase Order 7)
48	28	Purchased on account from Williams: 500 of C @ £9.25 £ 4 625 (Purchase Order 8)

Fig. 10.10 Purchase transactions.

AN EXTENDED REA EXAMPLE

Figures 10.7 and 10.9 contrast the structures of double-entry book-keeping and REA modelling, but a full appreciation of database accounting requires an extended example in which the reader may see final implementation ideas in very specific format. In this section we intend to provide such specifics with the NIAM modelling of purchasing transactions and the subsequent conversion of an ISD to a relational database. Our examples here will not be as broad as the fastener enterprise case, but the narrowing of scope will provide room for more details.

THE WILSON COMPANY – PURCHASE TRANSACTIONS

Figure 10.10 portrays a set of eight purchase transactions for a hypothetical enterprise called the Wilson Company. This example firm has been used previously by Gal and McCarthy (1983, 1986) in actual database accounting implementations. It includes a set of 55 transactions which occur during the first month (June) of a retail company's existence. Full Wilson details are given in McCarthy (1980) and are available upon request.

If we consider the set of purchase transactions as accounting phenomena to be modelled and if we use the REA framework of Fig. 10.8 as an occurrence template (again forsaking inside agents), the NIAM information structure diagram of Fig. 10.11 results (readers should note the central resource–event–agent constellation). With the exception of more detail, this is essentially the same modelling process we went through with the fastener company in Fig. 10.9.

ISD TO RELATIONAL DATABASE

As mentioned previously, a transformation algorithm exists that converts a conceptual NIAM schema into a fully normalized and optimal relational schema (Nijssen, 1989). Full explanation of this algorithm goes beyond the scope of this chapter, so we will limit ourselves to giving a cursory description of how the purchase REA-template in Fig. 10.11 can be translated to the relational model in Fig. 10.12.

1. Every NOLOT is represented as a relation, and a key must be selected to represent the non-lexical objects. That key must have the following characteristics:
   (a) the role at the side of the NOLOT must be mandatory, and
   (b) both roles of the binary association must have cardinality one.
   Keys are shown in Fig. 10.12 as double-headed arrows.

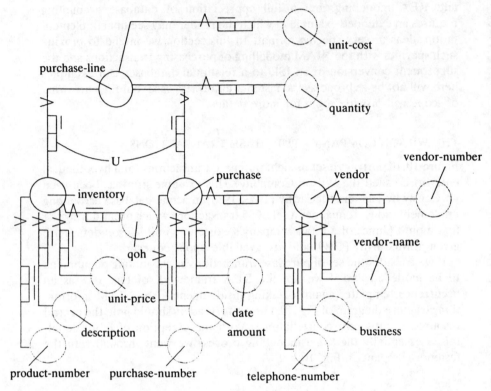

Fig. 10.11 NIAM model for purchase transactions.

2. Only LOTs with a uniqueness constraint on the role at the side of the NOLOT may be incorporated in the relation. Other cases are neglected in the example.
3. Non-mandatory roles are indicated by the symbol 'O' in the relational data model. Telephone_number in the relation customer is an example.
4. Finally, the associations between NOLOTS must be translated. Two kinds of interrelation connections are expressed in Fig. 10.12: equality (with an 'E') and subset (with an arrowhead). In our case these connections are implied by the mandatory constraints of Fig. 10.11. In simpler terms, the equality and subset symbols in the Wilson example equate to the following:

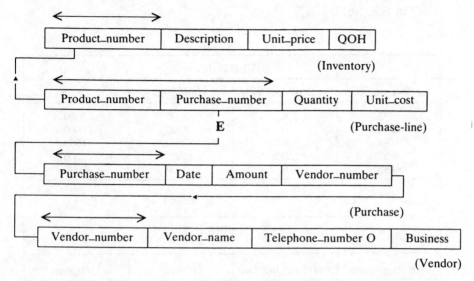

Fig. 10.12 Relational model for the purchase transaction.

(a) when a purchase occurs; it has to have designations of products, quantities and unit costs; and

(b) products and vendors exist independent of purchases, but when a purchase does occur, its vendor and products must already be known to the database.

Constraints like these enforce what database theorists call 'referential integrity'.

Fig. 10.13 shows the full Wilson extension for the database of Fig. 10.12. In examining the individual rows or tuples of these four tables, readers should remember again the purpose of conceptual schemas and databases – to represent to potential users the facts of a certain Universe of Discourse. By following around the individual values in these tuples, one can recreate part of the Wilson story for the month of June. Database users can do the same which was, of course, our primary goal in designing this type of accounting system.

PROCEDURAL SPECIFICATION FOR WILSON

In an operational enterprise, the structural components of a relational database are augmented by procedures that maintain data and aggregate it for eventual decision use. Two such procedures are shown in SQL (Date, 1986) in Fig. 10.14.

INVENTORY			
Product_number	Description	Unit_price	QOH
7432	A	3.00	2000
8519	B	5.00	1000
6784	C	12.00	1500
5862	D	15.00	200
4888	E	1.50	7000

PURCHASE-LINE			
Product_number	Purchase_number	Quantity	Unit_cost
7432	1	6 000	2.00
8519	1	2 000	4.00
4888	2	20 000	1.00
6784	2	3 000	9.00
5862	3	600	10.00
5862	4	600	11.00
8519	5	2 000	4.30
7432	5	2 000	2.00
7432	6	4 000	2.30
8519	6	2 000	4.30
6784	7	1 000	10.00
6784	8	500	9.25

PURCHASE			
Purchase_number	Date	Amount	Vendor_number
1	June 1	20 000	200
2	June 2	47 000	201
3	June 3	6 000	202
4	June 9	6 600	202
5	June 10	12 600	200
6	June 17	17 800	200
7	June 18	10 000	201
8	June 28	4 625	201

VENDOR			
Vendor_number	Vendor_name	Telephone_number	Business
200	Oliver	3244	wholesaler
201	Williams	1204	wholesaler
202	Smith	4502	wholesaler
203	Hodge	9861	trucker
204	Simmons	1243	cleaner
205	Green	7743	realtor
206	McKenzie	1288	pub-rel
207	Horvath	1324	off-equip
208	Shore	1917	car-dealer

Fig. 10.13 Relational database.

For data entry of the first purchase transaction of 1 June the SQL statements in Fig. 10.14(a) can be used. In real applications, such line-by-line coding would not be used with large amounts of new data. Instead, customized forms (in SQL-forms) would be provided. Notice that the application must compel the defined semantics. For example, no product_number can be inserted in the purchase-line relation if this number is not an occurrence of the inventory relation.

Once transactions are registered, information must be derived from stored data. In the case of the traditional book-keeping model, this occurs by aggregation after posting. This procedure is well-known and can be found in classical accounting textbooks.

The same information can easily be obtained in accounting databases by using conclusion-materialization hierarchies (McCarthy, 1984). Gal and McCarthy (1986) demonstrate these with a QBE implementation for the general ledger while Geerts (1990) illustrates an SQL implementation for a traditional report in current accounting environments: age-listings. A much simpler example of information retrieval with SQL is illustrated in Fig. 10.14(b): list the name(s) of the vendors who are wholesalers.

CONCLUSIONS AND DISCUSSION

In this chapter an alternative accounting model – called database accounting – was discussed and compared with the existing double-entry approach. We demonstrated first the importance of conceptual schemas in information systems design and use, and we proceeded to introduce a widely accepted methodology for schema specification: the NIAM model. We proceeded

Insert into PURCHASE values ('1', 'June 1', 20 000, '200');
Insert into PURCHASE-LINE values ('7432' '1', 6000, 2.00)
Insert into PURCHASE-LINE values ('8519', '1', 2000, 4.00)
Update INVENTORY set QOH = QOH + 6000 where product_number = 'A';
Update INVENTORY set QOH = QOH + 2000 where product_number = 'B';

(a) Date entry operations

QUERY
Select Vendor_name From VENDOR Where Business = 'wholesaler'

OUTPUT
Oliver Williams Smith

(b) Retrieval operations

Fig. 10.14 Database operations.

next to document how a semantically oriented domain theory – the REA accounting model – could be used to facilitate the development of accounting databases. These databases were then compared with more traditional methods in the context of two transaction sets, the first very simple and the second loaded with more detailed facts.

Out of this comparison of two approaches to accounting follows the conclusion that the database approach leads to a more natural representation of the Accounting Universe of Discourse. This is true for a variety of reasons documented by McCarthy (1990), the most prominent of which is that semantically developed accounting systems aspire to assist a much wider group of decision-makers than do debit–credit frameworks. They therefore cannot become encumbered with book-keeping artifacts which make little sense to non-accountants. While representation of disaggregate data and richer semantics requires more complex integrity-maintenance procedures, very diversified sets of information patterns can be followed, and the extra cost seems well worth it.

DISCUSSION QUESTIONS AND EXERCISES

1. Prepare the four-day financial statements for the fastener company. Make any assumptions about incomplete transactions that make sense.
2. Fill in the other three types of transactions for Wilson using your imagination for the facts. If you assume no other expenses and cash payments, you might have close to a whole system, and you should be able to prepare income and balance sheet estimates. Alternatively, you could look at a fully specified data model for Wilson (McCarthy, 1979, p. 675) in entity–relationship form and try to translate it to NIAM.
3. What kind of operations would be needed to produce financial statements from a full set of relations. If you have access to a relational DBMS on a micro or mainframe computer, you might try a partial implementation of these ideas. If your DBMS is strictly relational, however, you might have problems with LIFO or FIFO inventory costing as did Gal and McCarthy (1986). Why?
4. Why are debits and credits not needed in the REA model? Do you think accounting systems like this would ever win enthusiastic approval among accountants enamoured with more traditional methods?
5. Why would an REA system work better than book-keeping for a marketing or transportation decision-maker who was interested in data about inventory sales and shipments? Would this generalize to other non-accountants?
6. If you have had any exposure to expert systems or AI programming, try to discuss how semantic systems might interface with such tools.

ACKNOWLEDGEMENT

A significant portion of this chapter has been written directly from prior work of the authors (McCarthy, 1979, 1980, 1982). For readability purposes, quotations from those sources are not identified explicitly. Support for this work was provided by IBM-Belgium and Arthur Andersen & Co.

REFERENCES

Akoka, J. and Augustin, G. (1983). 'Le modèle comptable multidimensionnel l'approche entité-relation', *Revue Française de Gestion,* Juin–Juillet–Août, pp. 73–88.

Chen, P. P. (1976). 'The entity-relationship model – toward a unified view of data', *ACM Transactions on Database Systems,* 1 March, pp. 9–36.

Date, C. J. (1986). *An Introduction to Database Systems Volume I.* Addison Wesley, Reading, Mass.

Falkenberg, E. (1981). 'Some aspects of conceptual data modelling'. In Holsapple, C. W. and Whinston, A. B. (eds), *Data Base Management: Theory and Applications.* pp. 19–35.

Gal, G. and McCarthy, W. E. (1983). 'Declarative and procedural features of a CODASYL accounting system'. In Chen, P. (ed.), *Entity–Relationship Approach to Information Modeling and Analysis.* North–Holland, Amsterdam.

Gal, G. and McCarthy, W. E. (1986). 'Operation of a relational accounting system'. In Schwarz, B. N. (ed.), *Advances in Accounting.* JAI Press, Greenwich, Conn, pp. 83–112.

Geerts, G. (1990). *Het Gebruik van Tweede Generatie Gegevensmodellen bij het Ontwerp vaneen Events Accounting Information System.* Working Paper BEIF/ 23, Free University Brussels.

Ijiri, Y. (1975). *Theory of Accounting Measurement.* American Accounting Association, Sarasota, Florida.

Leung, C. M. R. and Nijssen, G. M. (1988). 'Relational database design using the NIAM conceptual schema', *Information Systems,* Vol. 13, No. 2, pp. 219–27.

Kent, W. (1986). 'The realities of data: basic properties of data reconsidered'. In Steel, J. R. and Meersman, R. (eds), *Database Semantics (DS–1).* North–Holland IFIP, Amsterdam, pp. 175–88.

Mark, L. (1983). 'What is the binary relationship approach?' In Davis, C. G., Jajodia, S., Ng, P. A. and Yeh, R. T. (eds), *Entity Relationship Approach to Software Engineering.* ER Institute, pp. 205–20.

Mark, L. (1987). 'E–R modeling versus binary modeling. A message from the church of binary methodists'. In *Proceedings of the Sixth International Conference on Entity–Relationship Approach,* New York, pp. 67–8.

Mattessich, R. (1964). *Accounting and Analytical Methods.* Richard D. Irwin, Homewood, Illinois.

McCarthy, W. E. (1979). 'An entity–relationship view of accounting models', *The Accounting Review,* Vol. 54, October, pp. 667–86.

McCarthy, W. E. (1980). *A Case Study Demonstrating the Applicability of Data Modeling to Accounting Object Systems.* Presentation for the Southeast Regional Meeting of the American Accounting Association, South Carolina. (Working Paper available.)

McCarthy, W. E. (1981). 'Multidimensional and disaggregate accounting systems', *MAS Communication,* July, pp. 7–13.

McCarthy, W. E. (1982). 'The REA accounting model: a generalized framework for accounting systems in a shared data environment', *The Accounting Review*, Vol. 57, July, pp. 554–78.

McCarthy, W. E. (1984). *Materialization of Account Balances in the REA Accounting Model*. Presentation to the British Accounting Association, University of East Anglia. (Working Paper available.)

McCarthy, W. E. (1990). *Once Upon a Time, at the Agleclap Store. . . .* Presentation to the 1990 AAA Senior Faculty Consortium, Phoenix, AZ. (Working Paper available.)

McCarthy, W. E., Rockwell, S. R. and Armitage, H. (1989). 'A structured methodology for the design of accounting transaction systems in a shared data environment', In *Proceedings STA 5*, Chicago, pp. 194–207. (Working Paper available.)

McCrae, T. W. (1976). *Computers and Accounting*. John Wiley and Sons.

Nijssen, G. M. (1989). *Conceptual Schema and Relational Database Design: A Fact Oriented Approach*. Prentice Hall.

Sorter, G. H. (1969). 'An events approach to basic accounting theory', *The Accounting Review*, Vol. 44, January, pp. 12–19.

Verheijen, G. M. A. and van Bekkum, J. (1982). 'NIAM: an information analysis method'. In Olle, T. W. and Sol, A. A. (eds), *Information Systems Design Methodologies: A Comparative Review*. North–Holland, Amsterdam, pp. 537–89.

Wintraecken, J. J. (1986). *Informatieanalyse volgens NIAM in Theorie en Praktijk*. Academic Service.

Yu, S. C. (1976). *The Structure of Accounting Theory*. University Press of Florida, Grainesville, Florida.

PART

4 Management Accounting

Recently several significant factors have combined to change the nature of management accounting. They include increased economic competition, not only from traditional Western economies but also from the emerging economies of the Pacific Ring. Japanese management practices in particular have had a dramatic effect on production methods. The recent increase in the practice of using payment by results for top management has also led to many changes in management practice. The development of new production technology has also led to huge changes in such areas as the allocation of fixed and variable costs, and on long- and short-run product viability.

This Part is concerned with the fact that a firm's cost accounting and management control systems should be designed and operated to provide information useful for planning and control decisions by management in the circumstances outlined above. These changes in the accountant's environment are likely to give rise to new information requirements. The management accountant is therefore faced with the task of developing new systems which design and maintain control systems to promote the planning and implementation of an organization's strategies and motivate managers to achieve their organizational targets.

The first chapter in this Part by Alan Gregory gives the reader an overview of the current management accounting environment. In outlining a model of a truly integrated control system which links the existing 'islands of automation' that may be common in the near future, he suggests that this may have important implications for management accounting. One consequence that might arise is the elimination of standard costing due to the non-occurrence of variances through the symbiotic operation of suppliers and purchasers linked with EDI.

Joan Ballantine's chapter on the use of spreadsheets by accountants gives one example of how far accountants have progressed with computerization in the last few years. The use of this type of software alone has, according to many experts, given rise to the large–scale adoption of personal computers in the financial sector. The paper examines the development of the use of spreadsheets and their progenitors, the paper worksheet.

In the third chapter of this Part Paul Collier presents a taxonomy of computing tools used by management. One of the real problems for students of management information systems is the multiplicity of definitions and organizational frameworks that different authors use. In his paper Collier attempts to give the reader an idea of where various concepts and groupings overlap and thus allow the reader to gain some understanding of how each type of system aids the manager in the decision-making process.

Chapter

11 Management accounting and information technology
Alan Gregory

INTRODUCTION

A satisfactory definition of management accounting is an elusive concept, but without being too contentious, we can probably safely assume that, *inter alia*, management accounting is concerned with the provision and analysis of information to assist the decision-making, problem-solving, planning, control and performance evaluation processes. Although this information will consist in the main of financial data, it is not exclusively so. (Some writers have argued that traditional management accounting places too much emphasis on financial information and not enough on non-financial indicators, e.g. Parker (1979).) Bromwich (1988) highlights the fact that information provision includes collecting data on the business, its competitors, evaluation of products from both the customers' and firm's perspectives, cost structure relative to competitors and product and resource life cycle costing. (Such data provision and analysis is often referred to as 'strategic management accounting'.)

It must also be recognized that management accounting does not stand apart from other aspects of organizational functioning, in that interaction occurs. Management accounting both influences and is influenced by such factors as organizational design, management information system choice, culture and management style. Furthermore, management accounting systems can have behavioural impacts which can be intended and un-intended (e.g. 'gaming' and other attempts to beat the system).[1] Whilst these issues are important, our focus here will be on what might be termed

Specially commissioned for *IT and Accounting: The impact of information technology*.
Edited by Bernard C. Williams and Barry J. Spaul.
Published in 1991 by Chapman & Hall, London ISBN 0 412 39210 0.

the 'neo-classical' decision-orientated framework of management accounting and the way in which information technology changes can be expected to impact upon each stage of the management accounting process.

The chapter now proceeds along the following lines. First, a brief review of information technology changes is given, and the possible expected impact of these changes on management accounting is then discussed. Finally, the results of recent research in this area are summarized and compared. The focus will be primarily upon manufacturing industry for two reasons, the first being that the majority of existing research is in this area, and the second that most general management accounting texts are mainly concerned with a manufacturing setting.

INFORMATION TECHNOLOGY CHANGES

Over the past ten years, advances in computer technology and software have created the potential for major changes in many industries. Although in particular increased automation in manufacturing has been facilitated, perhaps the key point is that greater integration of industrial and commercial processes has become possible. For some time, many firms have used computers for various aspects of their control and planning activities, for example performing engineering calculations required for product design, control of stock levels and production scheduling. Gradually, these systems have become more complex and comprehensive with perhaps the ultimate, but so far unachieved, objective of computer-integrated manufacturing (CIM). However, considerable progress has been made in establishing the complete computerization of some aspects of the design, manufacturing and product/service supply processes. Typically, many firms now operate computer-aided design (CAD), computer-aided engineering (CAE), and computer-aided manufacturing (CAM) systems. For example, Coulthurst (1989a) describes the successful development and use of CAD systems in Austin-Rover, Jaguar and Ford. CAE systems can be used to assess alternative production technologies and feed off the CAD system; thus the Ford system has computer links with component suppliers, so that they can use Ford specifications to design and test the feasibility of their own component products. In principle, the CAE system could transmit information direct to the CAM system which could directly control electronic workstations, facilitating a completely automated process of manufacturing with no human intervention. In practice, this has yet to be achieved and instead we have what Lee (1987) describes as 'islands of automation'.

However, extant technology has progressed as far as the flexible manufacturing system (FMS) which is a computer-controlled production line linking computer-controlled machines in such a way that product specifications can be quickly and efficiently altered. Japanese companies appear to have made extensive use of this type of technology, which is also being adopted by US and European firms; Lee offers the example of a General Electric plant in the US which is 'capable of producing diesel engines of substantially different sizes on the same automated production line, without substantial retooling and setups'. The benefits of all this can be dramatic; Coulthurst quotes the case of the Yamazaki Machinery Co. (Japan) which reduced the number of machines from 68 to 18, employees from 215 to 12, floor space to around 30% of former requirements and cut the average processing time from 35 to 1.5 days. However, he also warns that the expected benefits are not always realized, as in the case of General Motors which invested $60bn in advanced manufacturing technology (AMT).

Perhaps examples such as the latter help to draw attention to the fact that simply buying the latest 'high-tech' equipment and bolting it to the factory floor is not sufficient. The process of change has to be managed, the optimal investment decisions need to be made and the planning and control systems have to be set up in a manner compatible with the production technology employed.[2] In particular, each organizational function must have access to an integrated database which allows the control of the production schedules, stock levels, distribution and financing. One approach to this area is that of manufacturing resource planning (MRP II, so called to distinguish it from a partial stage of the process, material requirements planning (MRP)). Starting from a product demand forecast, MRP II uses computer-based models to generate a manufacturing plan and production schedule, which 'spins off' stock level requirements, material purchase requirements (allowing the automatic generation of orders) and capacity requirements. Advanced versions are also capable of generating accounting information; in essence, MRP II represents the automated version of the classic textbook 'master budget'. In addition, some MRP II systems allow actual results to be monitored against the original plan; appropriate amendments can then be made.

A logical outcome to this type of process is the just-in-time (JIT) system, a step made possible by the production scheduling possibilities offered by MRP II and the integration of databases allowed by advances in computing technology. The idea behind JIT is that stock levels can be eliminated by producing parts and sub-assemblies only when they are actually required for production. If the manufacturer's computer is linked to the supplier's (an example of electronic data interchange (EDI), then component deliveries can take place exactly when required on a flow basis rather than a stock delivery one. Perhaps the most frequently quoted example is that of Toyota (see Lee (1987), pp 19–22). Note that whilst AMT is not necessary for the successful operation of MRP II, which can be applied to any manufacturing technology, it is a requirement for JIT which requires an FMS in order to eliminate or drastically reduce set-up times; in the absence of this, optimal batch quantities will exist, necessitating the maintenance of stocks.

Kaplan and Atkinson (1989) point out that the use of JIT substantially to reduce stock levels saves factory space previously required for inter-process buffer stocks (WIP), and allows workstations to be moved closer together thus reducing conveyance time and distance. A related technique, OPT (developed by Goldratt), seeks to optimize factory throughput by eliminating bottlenecks rather than stock levels.[3]

A final point is that the use of JIT and OPT is not confined to manufacturing industry; for example, the use of electronic point-of-sale (EPOS) technology allows improvements in delivery scheduling and stock-holding in the retail industry.

THE LIKELY IMPACT OF INFORMATION TECHNOLOGY CHANGES ON MANAGEMENT ACCOUNTING

Clearly, the above changes should have a normative impact upon management accounting; the actual changes observed to date will be discussed later. Before embarking upon a detailed analysis of the impact of these changes, a few general observations are in order. First, AMT and other information technologies require large initial investments, which generally tend to produce benefits which are of a long-term nature (typically spanning over several product lifecycles) and include substantial real but intangible benefits (e.g. increased flexibility, greater product quality). Secondly, such investment needs to be appraised not against the status quo, but against the position which will result if the investment is not made. Thirdly, investment of this nature tends to change the cost structure of the firm; many costs become sunk once the investment is made, and in general 'fixed' costs tend to be substituted for 'variable' costs (whether these traditional definitions are of value is discussed below). Fourthly, many traditional management accounting practices are likely to become more questionable (e.g. overhead recovery on a labour hours basis), and finally, the traditional performance indicators found in management accounting texts may need to be either replaced completely, or supplemented by additional indicators. We shall now look at some of the key roles of management accounting, and the implications that information technology advances have for the type of management accounting devices that may be used in fulfilling those roles.

DECISION-MAKING

The type of decisions that face a manufacturing firm can be broadly categorized as investment decisions (including plant investment, divestment and shutdown decisions), product line decisions (including product introduction/discontinuation, special order or changed specification products, and component make-or-buy decisions), and product pricing and marketing type decisions.

The key features of investment decisions are the pattern and timescale of the benefits, and the sheer scale of the necessary investment. In theory, there is no problem here that cannot be addressed by the use of the usual net present value model; benefits can be stated in cash terms, and compared with the alternative cash flows of not making any investment (bearing in mind that domestic and foreign competitors may well do so).

However, as Seed (1988) points out:

The basic capital investment analysis model is sound but often misapplied. Firms commonly:

1. Attempt to justify projects rather than strategies
2. Fail to quantify the impact of not making investments
3. Prepare unrealistic forecasts to support investment justifications
4. Use incorrect discount . . . rates that provide a bias against longer term investments
5. Overlook various indirect and intangible benefits
6. Ignore terminal values
7. Inadequately monitor actual costs and benefits after expenditures are completed.

Many of these concerns appear to be shared by other authors, noting that the problems are compounded by practitioners' use of payback. For example, Kaplan and Atkinson (1989, p. 475) note that payback periods in the US are often as short as two to three years, whilst commenting on the UK experience[4] Primrose (1988) notes that the use of payback 'increases the difficulty of justifying AMT and will almost certainly result in wrong investment decisions being made'. He goes on to note that many AMT projects take several years to become fully operational, that plant installations may last for several product lifecycles and simultaneously produce several products and that 'the nature of the intangible benefits is such that they will invariably appear in a different department from that where the investment is made.' Note that none of these factors represent a negation of textbook NPV techniques; on the contrary, they emphasize the importance of a sound understanding of the key principles, in particular the consideration of all cash flow differences on a company-wide basis over the whole life of the project. Perhaps the most difficult practical aspect is the quantification of some of the 'intangible' benefits of the investment. These will include increased quality, greater flexibility and reduction of raw material and WIP stocks through the use of JIT techniques. Attempts to quantify these factors might include, *inter alia,* increased sales, lower material and labour costs, and smoother production flows; increased sales through customer satisfaction, reduced set-up times and greater productivity; less expenditure on warehousing and storage space, and saving on working capital respectively. Primrose notes that techniques like sensitivity analysis may be useful in the analysis of such problems.

Several authors (e.g. Kaplan and Atkinson (1989), Lee (1987), Seed (1988), Primrose (1988) and Coulthurst (1989b)) comment on the fact that many companies appear to use excessively high discount rates in the appraisal of AMT investment, which results in a negative bias against such projects because of their relatively long time horizons. Typical errors include the incorrect treatment of inflation – for example the application of market-derived (and hence money or nominal) discount rates to cash flows stated in real terms – and the inclusion of a non-systematic risk factor in the project discount rate. There is also some dispute about the true scale of the risk premium appropriate to UK investment, with estimates ranging from 9% (London Business School Risk Measurement Service) to 4.5% (ALCAR Consulting Group). If the latter figure is a more reasonable guide to the current risk premium, it may suggest that risk adjusted real discount rates are much higher than can be justified with reference to market expectations.[5]

With regard to product line decisions, many of the traditional 'marginalist' arguments still apply. However, as Kaplan and Atkinson note, many of these models are derived in somewhat simplistic settings which typically assume that material, labour and some overhead costs are 'variable', and further that these costs vary only with physical output; anything else is regarded as a 'fixed' cost. In order to facilitate product line decisions, a much more rigorous analysis of cost behaviour needs to be made. Johnson and Kaplan (1987) note that we need to become aware of how costs 'currently considered to be fixed or sunk' actually vary with decisions made about product output, mix and diversity.

It has become almost a fashion in the academic and practical literature to talk about 'cost drivers'. Cost drivers are those things that cause costs to vary. Whilst volume is one of these factors, others may include the number of specification changes, the relative size of production run, the number of customers, the standardization of components across products and so on. Whilst there is little dispute concerning the concept that costs can be driven by different factors, there is far from universal agreement on how this concept should be integrated into the management accounting process.[6] However, for our purposes, the following issues are of importance. First, direct labour costs are a declining percentage of total costs (the CAM-i survey of UK companies in advanced manufacturing environments find that the average has declined to 12%), whereas materials are a more significant percentage (CAM-i suggest a figure of just over 50%). It may well be the case that materials are now the only significant volume driven cost for many companies, with direct labour being virtually a fixed cost in the shorter term. Set-up costs may also have been reduced by investment in FMS, whilst design costs may also be cut through the use of CAD and CAE. Product specification changes and product design changes may thus be more frequent and feasible than was previously the case; the product costing implications are that some of the traditional opportunity cost prescriptions may actually be of more relevance, and because of the existence of computerized databases containing information on cost structure, may be more easily applied.[7] This could fulfil a very useful function in the managerial process, since the changing competitive environment may well require a series of short-run tactical decisions to be made on such product changes. The firm wedded to traditional absorption costing practices may well find itself at an informational disadvantage in this type of situation. Note also the increasingly important role here of strategic management accounting – it is no longer sufficient (if it ever has been) to be aware of one's own company's cost structure; there must also be an awareness of the competitive market-place, including the cost structure of rival firms (see Bromwich and Bhimani (1989, pp. 95–6)).

Much the same information set will be of necessity in product pricing and marketing decisions. It seems increasingly unlikely that firms will be able to employ successfully a naive cost-plus pricing policy. It is notable that many Japanese companies view the whole product production and pricing decision from the starting point of attempting to establish what the market price of a product under development is likely to be, and then working down to specifying a target cost necessary in order to make production of the product worthwhile. Part of the design and production process is then the search for necessary productivity and technology changes.

We might therefore conclude that developments in IT have re-emphasized the relevance of many of those approaches to decision-making which stem from the economics literature, but this needs important qualification. First, the strategic context must be more actively considered. Secondly, a more detailed analysis of cost behaviour is necessary; the old 'variable' and 'fixed' definitions are increasingly inadequate.

COST CONTROL

This is an area where much current management accounting practice, and not a little textbook theory, are beginning to look more impoverished and increasingly redundant. If we take the 'neo-classical' approach, we shall probably employ budgets which tend to follow financial accounting conventions, and control actual expenditure through a standard costing system. Despite various theoretical arguments which might be advanced, this approach is doubtless one that has flourished in practice and proved adequate in stable environments, typified by a slow rate of innovation and long product lives. Labour costs were probably a reasonably high percentage of total costs, and a good deal of the direct labour would have been regarded as a variable expense. Although many accounting texts may have opposed the practice, most firms would have also used direct labour hours to recover manufacturing overhead (although recovery on a machine hours basis was not uncommon). The logic of all this was reinforced by financial accounting requirements, in particular by SSAP 9 which specified that for stock valuation purposes, 'cost' included production overhead.

If we consider the changes which are likely as a result of advances in IT, it becomes apparent that one consequence is that WIP stock levels are likely to decline as a result of faster throughput and the adoption of JIT approaches. The logic of expending considerable time and effort on process costing systems (mainly designed to measure stock values anyway) looks increasingly shaky. Furthermore, as overheads increase and labour hours decrease the practice of loading on overhead recovery rates which 'may be three or four thousand per cent on direct labour or machine hours' (Bromwich (1988)) looks increasingly indefensible. Indeed, if the objectives of management accounting include the control of costs and the provision of information for decision-making purposes, we can argue that such allocation practices are likely to be counter-productive. Attention will tend to be focused upon the (probably wrong) objective of further labour reduction, instead of the investigation of why the overhead itself is increasing.[8] The problem here is that the overhead itself may well be capable of direct reduction (for example, by subcontracting out services currently provided internally).

A further issue is whether standard costing is actually a redundant control technique. When we consider that material is likely to be the only major variable cost, that JIT approaches will tend to mean long-term supply contracts being negotiated (so who needs a material price variance?), that AMT processes usually have built-in quality checks at each stage of the process and the widespread adoption of the 'zero-defects' approach to quality control in such environments (so what is the role of usage, mix and yield variances?), coupled with the fact that production runs are likely to become increasingly short, thereby limiting our experience on which to base 'standards' (although it must be admitted that the use of CAD/CAE overcomes this problem to a large extent), we may well reach the conclusion that standard costing is not going to achieve a great deal. We may do better to substitute other largely non-financial indicators of performance and efficiency. For example, Bromwich and Bhimani note that management accountants can 'no longer ignore information that is not expressible in financial terms. Data on product quality, customer satisfaction, delivery efficiency, vendor reliability, machine integrity and the contribution of workers to the enterprise all become crucial factors'; they go on to note that where internal accounting does not recognize such factors 'factory managers are beginning to ignore the accounting numbers entirely'.

As regards budgetary control, the principle that decisions give rise to budgets which reflect the costs and benefits which are estimated at the time the decision is made remains a sound one. Nonetheless, it is necessary that the budgeting system reflects the complexity of the internal manufacturing environment and the external market environment. Particular problems which IT changes pose for budgeting are the increased pace of change in product lifecycles (for example, greater product varieties, more frequent updating of product specifications, and generally shorter product lifecycles) coupled with the longer planning horizons which the scale of investment in AMT make necessary. Furthermore, there is the problem of how to deal with the intangible benefits which we noted in our discussion of decision-making, especially given that they may appear in a department other than that which incurs the investment and running costs. Finally, there is the difficulty posed by the changing cost structure associated with the adoption of AMT. Fixed overhead has always been a problematic cost for accounting control systems; the fact that this is increasing as a percentage of total cost suggests that a radical rethinking of the approach to this area may be due.

One possibility is to use databases to organize the budgeting activity on a matrix basis, with costs being measured across three dimensions, as shown in Fig. 11.1; obviously, not all the cost cells would be relevant for all situations. As an example, allocated costs would only be of relevance for stock valuation purposes. This type of flexible approach to budgeting would assist rather than constrain the decision-making and cost control processes. It would also be of use in post-audit of FMS investment and product investment where the traditional monthly/annual reporting cycles can be less than helpful. Bromwich (1988) has also suggested that those fixed overheads which are decision driven (and therefore effectively largely sunk costs when the decision has been made) could be treated in a similar way to that used for capital budgeting purposes. It is also essential that non-financial 'budgets' or targets are set for areas like customer satisfaction and quality.

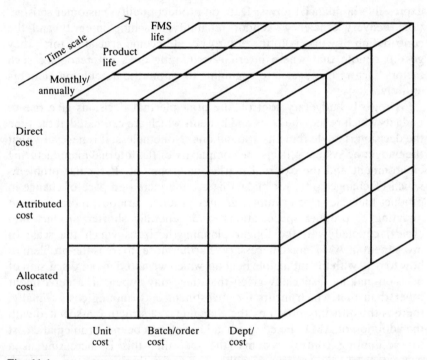

Fig. 11.1

PERFORMANCE EVALUATION

A positive move away from the current short-term emphasis is needed. Typically, many firms appear to rely upon measures like performance against budget and return on investment. Although the former can be defended, for example on the grounds of risk sharing (Demski and Feltham (1978)), the latter can lead to a distortion of investment decisions (for an explanation see Gregory (1988)). Performance evaluation is an area where the arrival of AMT adds urgency to the implementation of some existing prescriptions to reduce non-optimal short-term behaviour by managerial agents. This is particularly important where we are concerned with investment centre managers, where those managers have some influence or autonomy in the investment decision.

As we have concluded above, a long-term time horizon is essential when one is appraising AMT projects; however, adopting a benign approach to the investment analysis process will be futile if the performance evaluation system is malignant. A reliance upon ROI encourages managers with shorter time horizons to reject positive NPV projects because, even with constant cash flows, accounting returns increase through time due to the impact of straight-line depreciation. (The numerator, accounting profit, remains constant, but the denominator, accounting book value, decreases each year. Accounting return is thus initially below the IRR, increasing above the IRR as the asset life is used up.) This problem tends to be greater with many AMT investments because of the timing of cash flows (benefits may be slow to come through) and the scale of investment, which results in large depreciation charges and considerable increases in asset bases. Possible solutions to this problem include a comparison of actual and planned cash flows (Tomkins (1973)) or treating investment centres as lessees of centrally owned assets (Gregory (1987)).

When budgets are used as the basis of performance measurement, the suggestions made in the section on cost control should be borne in mind; again, it is important to relate performance to the timescale of the decision horizon, and not to some arbitrary one imposed by external reporting requirements. Finally, the need for a broader view of 'good performance' is necessary;[9] the use of non-financial budgets or targets would be a step in the right direction.

A BRIEF REVIEW OF THE EMPIRICAL EVIDENCE TO DATE

The rate of change in the technological environment has meant that there is a comparatively small amount of evidence available on which to base any conclusions. Bromwich and Bhimani (1989) summarize Chartered Institute of Management Accountants (CIMA) case studies on IT adoption as suggesting that 'the focus and breadth of management accounting ... is changing ... traditional boundaries based around scorekeeping activities are being enlarged to include many more factors and processes'. However, management accountants are still seen as being 'watchdogs' by many managers, rather than providers of information to support decision-making. Nonetheless, the use of IT appears to have assisted the problem-solving process.

Several UK studies on 'high-tech' firms suggest that some changes are taking place in the practice of management accounting, although these are not necessarily the ones we might expect to observe. Coates and Longden (1989), in a study of 20 UK and 5 US companies, found that there was 'considerable evidence that new and high technology growth companies do demand adaptation of traditional practices', principally concerned with improved information quality, which requires the use of up-to-date IT systems. Yet absorption costing remains a widely used device, with attempts being made to make it more 'accurate', although there seemed to be widespread recognition of the problems of arbitrariness. Some attempt was clearly being made to identify cost drivers, but the use of contribution margin after deducting attributable costs was also noted. Although all of the companies but one used DCF techniques, almost as many used payback; both approaches seemed to play a supportive role rather than a determining one when it came to strategic decisions, although DCF seemed to play a more prominent role in tactical decision-making.

The adaptation of JIT and MRP was noted to increase informational needs in respect of vendor reliability and quality, but in general no new techniques were noted, although adaptations of existing practice were.

In a study of ten electronics firms, Innes and Mitchell (1989) found that firms were moving from standard to actual costing systems, mainly for the reasons suggested under the section on cost control above. They also note that 'All the firms used at least some non-financial performance indicators', which included indicators of quality, delivery, throughput time of machines and launch time for new products. As regards investment appraisal, the findings were broadly similar to those of Coates and Longden. Innes and Mitchell discuss the use of strategic management accounting in some detail, finding the use of competitive analysis, 'design for cost' (in a way broadly similar to that used by Japanese firms) and the adoption of a more outward looking perspective. They also note that the role of the management accountant within the firms had changed, with closer contact and communication with non-accountants being noted.

Littler and Sweeting (1989) studied 25 new technology-based businesses in the UK and US, noting the importance of qualitative data and informal systems in the functioning of these firms. Accounting data appears to play a supporting role, and forms the basis for discussion. Further, they note that formal textbook techniques are often not used, and flexibility in management and budgeting seem to be of key importance.

It is difficult to reach many general conclusions from the empirical evidence to date. One encouraging sign is that some studies suggest that the management accounting is playing more of a team role, and interacting more with other managers, although this may be a misleading impression since it is possible that this is a function of firm size (Littler and Sweeting studied mainly smaller firms) rather than a real change in role. Conclusions reached on the use or otherwise of various techniques may also suffer from this flaw. One point that does emerge from the studies is that rapid change and increasing uncertainty about the nature of this change may make the use of any formal management accounting systems more difficult. This may well suggest the greater use of 'soft' or 'fuzzy' data to supplement the 'hard' or numeric data. This does not mean that companies should ignore the latter; some attempts clearly have to be made to assess long-run cash flows. If City financial analysts can and do perform such tasks, it should be possible for managers within the firm also to produce such numbers. How else will embittered company chairmen be able to complain convincingly that the City has undervalued their company?

CONCLUSIONS

The speed of technological change shows no sign of decreasing, and it seems likely that more firms will become affected by such change. From both theoretical and empirical perspectives, this change appears to have some impact on management accounting. Advances in information technology offer increased flexibility in the manufacturing and accounting spheres. However, this also means increasing complexity and greater uncertainty. In order to plan and control in this type of environment, we need to examine critically our available set of management accounting tools, discarding some that may have served us in the past, and adding new ones. These additions seem likely to include the substantial use of non-financial data. More complex and uncertain competitive environments might also suggest the greater use of existing techniques such as scenario modelling, simulation and sensitivity analysis, together with the need for more emphasis on the strategic aspects of management accounting. Some of those changes which we have posited from a normative perspective seem to be happening in practice, whilst others do not. This may, in part, reflect the over-emphasis of the formal content of management accounting systems (see Scapens (1988)); it may also reflect a reluctance to change on the part of management accountants. If there is a consensus view on this area, it is probably that this is a time of challenge and opportunity for management accounting; whether these challenges are successfully met and the opportunities taken advantage of remains to be seen.

NOTES

1. An exploration of this area is beyond the scope of this chapter. An excellent introduction can be found in Ezzamel and Hart (1987).
2. This should not be taken as implying that the effect on people of such changes is of only secondary importance. It is worth noting Coulthurst (1989a) who observes: 'Management style and labour relations appear to be at least as important in raising efficiency as is technology.'
3. Kaplan and Atkinson quote Goldratt as observing that 'cost accounting is the number one enemy of productivity', because managers are not penalized for stock build up in most accounting performance measures; furthermore, traditional standard absorption costing actively encourages this by generating positive overhead volume variances when production is greater than budget, no matter what the final product demand looks like.
4. A survey prepared for CAM-i (1988) noted that 65% of the companies questioned required AMT investment projects to pay back their costs within three years.
5. The term 'risk premium' here refers to the difference between the return on the all-share index (R_m) and the return on treasury bills (R_f), which may be used (given certain assumptions – see, for example, Brealey and Myers (1988)) in the capital asset pricing model to derive project discount rates.
6. As examples of alternative views on this issue, see Johnson and Kaplan (1987) and Bromwich and Bhimani (1989).
7. This is open to dispute. For example, Lee (1987) states that in this new environment 'absorption costing ... becomes the only meaningful costing method'. In contrast, Bromwich (1988) believes that for decision-making 'incremental costs and revenues need to be calculated in a way free of overhead allocation'; he also notes that allocation cannot be defended for what he terms 'decision-driven' fixed costs. (Decision-driven costs include capacity and infrastructure costs, which become sunk immediately the investment decision is made.)
8. Morgan and Weerakoon (1989) (amongst others) note that many Japanese companies allocate overhead on a labour hours basis *deliberately* to force departmental managers to substitute machinery for labour; they describe how Japanese managers are more concerned with using the management accounting system to affect the cost reduction priorities of middle and line managers, than with the accurate measurement of product cost.
9. For a discussion of this point see Parker (1979).

REFERENCES

Brealey, R. A. and Myers, S. C. (1988). *Principles of Corporate Finance,* 3rd edn. McGraw-Hill, Singapore.

Bromwich, M. (1988). 'Managerial accounting definition and scope – from a managerial view', *Management Accounting,* September, pp. 26–7.

Bromwich, M. and Bhimani, A. (1989). *Management Accounting: Evolution not Revolution.* Chartered Institute of Management Accountants, London.

CAM-i (1988). *Management Accounting in Advanced Manufacturing Environments: A Survey.* CAM-i, January.

Coates, J. B. and Longden, S. G. (1989). *Management Accounting: The Challenge of Technological Innovation 1.* Chartered Institute of Management Accountants, London.

Coulthurst, N. (1989a). 'The new factory', *Management Accounting,* March, pp. 30–4.

Coulthurst, N. (1989b). Justifying the new factory, *Management Accounting,* April, pp. 26–8.

Coulthurst, N. (1989c). 'Organising and accounting for the new factory', *Management Accounting,* May, pp. 38–41.

Demski, J. and Feltham, G. (1978). 'Economic incentives in budgetary control systems', *The Accounting Review,* April, pp. 336–59.

Ezzamel, M. and Hart, H. (1987). *Advanced Management Accounting – An Organisational Emphasis.* Cassell, London.

Foster, G. and Gupta, M. (1990) 'Manufacturing overhead cost driver analysis', *Journal of Accounting and Economics,* Vol. 12, pp. 309–37.

Gregory, A. (1987). 'Divisional performance measurement with divisions as lessees of head office assets', *Accounting and Business Research,* Summer, pp. 241–6.

Gregory, A. (1988). 'A review of divisional manager performance evaluation', *Management Accounting,* January, pp. 38–43.

Innes, J. and Mitchell, F. (1989). *Management Accounting: The Challenge of Technological Innovation 2.* Chartered Institute of Management Accountants, London.

Johnson, H. T. and Kaplan, R. S. (1987). *Relevance Lost: The Rise and Fall of Management Accounting.* Harvard Business School Press.

Kaplan, R. S. and Atkinson, A. A. (1989). *Advanced Management Accounting,* 2nd edn. Prentice Hall, Englewood Cliffs, New Jersey.

Lee, J. Y. (1987). *Managerial Accounting Changes for the 1990s.* Addison-Wesley, New York.

Littler, D. A. and Sweeting, R. C. (1989). *Management Accounting: The Challenge of Technological Innovation 3.* Chartered Institute of Management Accountants, London.

Morgan, M. J. and Weerakoon, S. H. (1989). 'Japanese management accounting: its contribution to the Japanese economic miracle', *Management Accounting,* June, pp. 40–3.

Parker, L. D. (1979). 'Divisional performance measurement: beyond an exclusive profit test', *Accounting and Business Research,* Autumn, pp. 309–19.

Primrose, P. L. (1988). 'AMT investment and costing systems', *Management Accounting,* October, pp. 26–7.

Scapens, R. (1988). 'Research into management accounting practice', *Management Accounting,* December, pp. 26–8.

Seed, A. H. (1988). *Adapting Management Accounting Practice to an Advanced Manufacturing Environment.* National Association of Accountants. 1988.

Tomkins, C. R. (1973). 'Financial planning in divisionalised companies', *Accountancy Age*, London.

12 The spreadsheet revolution and its impact on the budgeting process
Joan Ballantine

INTRODUCTION

Electronic spreadsheets have been around since the late 1970s and have proliferated in much of the business and financial community with applications in many areas such as accounting, finance, marketing, taxation and so on. Spreadsheet applications are, however, not solely confined to these areas, but are also used for example in engineering, educational, scientific and medical fields.

For many years accountants have been familiar with pencil and paper based spreadsheets or manual worksheets consisting of tables of information, it being the custom before the advent of electronic spreadsheets for professionals to work laboriously with these tools. Examples of applications which were suited to the use of manual worksheets included incomplete records accounting, costing, extended trial balances and budgetary projections. Today these same tasks are still carried out using the basic concept of the manual worksheet, but with the added dimension of computer power in the form of spreadsheets.

Despite the transition from manual to computer-based worksheets the principles of worksheet design and usage have changed little over the past fifty years. The typical manual worksheet provides the user with a matrix of columns and rows into which the data can be placed, and worked upon. Electronic worksheets, or spreadsheets as they are more commonly

Specially commissioned for *IT and Accounting: The Impact of information technology*.
Edited by Bernard C. Williams and Barry J. Spaul.
Published in 1991 by Chapman & Hall, London ISBN 0 412 39210 0.

referred to, display the same image as their manual counterpart – they are divided into a number of columns and rows, each of which contain data.

Both manual worksheets and electronic spreadsheets are used to model or represent particular dimensions of an organization or business – these dimensions might, for example, relate to the financial position, the expectations of the company for the future or the budgetary control aspects of the organization. The modelling process is particularly useful in that it gives the modeller the opportunity to view the organization as a manageable system and determine the relationships of subsystems to each other. The change from manual worksheets to electronic spreadsheets has, therefore, resulted in greater benefits but it has also had several drawbacks. These will be discussed later.

The first electronic spreadsheet program, Visicalc, was developed in 1978 by Dan Bricklin who was an MBA student at Harvard Business School. The concept of the spreadsheet was conceived whilst Bricklin and his fellow colleagues were given an assignment to complete. The nature of the assignment was to project the financial consequences of one company's acquisition of another. Clearly there would be many calculations involved and a great deal of 'what-if' scenarios had to be modelled to get a complete image of the entire situation. To project the data relevant to the exercise, Bricklin and his colleagues had to use a number of manual worksheets. These were laboriously filled in until the company and its acquisition were fully modelled.

From this experience Bricklin realized that much valuable time had been spent on repetitive calculations when changes to the input values of the model were made. If one or more input values were altered – for example, expenses for a given category or projected sales – the entire worksheet had to be recalculated manually: quite a task. It was this experience that gave Bricklin the idea of designing a computer program which would mimic the manual worksheet he had so painstakingly worked on.

Bricklin began work on the development of the first electronic worksheet with a friend called Bob Frankston in mid-1978. By the end of 1979 they had released Visicalc, the world's first electronic worksheet, available for use on microcomputers.

Originally written for the Apple II microcomputer, Visicalc quickly became a best-seller amongst microcomputer programs. The spreadsheet was based on large ruled sheets of paper which were organized into rows and columns. By organizing the spreadsheet in such a way, the authors provided a means by which information could be presented in a similar fashion to the paper version, yet allowing sensitivity analysis or 'what-if' analysis to be performed. The latter was accomplished by the dynamic interrelationship of the 'cells' and the reduction in computational time required to recalculate the spreadsheet when values within the model were altered in any way. The great success of Visicalc was due to both the price, which was kept to a minimum, and the great flexibility the package offered.

POPULARISATION OF THE CONCEPT

The rapid success of Visicalc led to the development of many other spreadsheet programs of a similar nature. In 1981, the first version of Supercalc was released by the Sorcim Corporation for CP/M computers. Shortly afterwards Multiplan appeared on the market. Both of these products tried to compete with Visicalc by offering additional features that it did not have. In 1982 the Lotus Corporation introduced a second generation product, Lotus 1–2–3, designed to run on the IBM PC. The product has since become the industry standard in spreadsheet software. The success of the original Lotus 1–2–3 was a combination of a number of features which were unique to Lotus at that time. It had an ability to communicate with other software, limited database facilities and the user could create graphs based on data held within the spreadsheet.

Later, other developments emerged in 1984 with the introduction of integrated software, examples being Framework by Ashton-Tate and Lotus Symphony by the Lotus Development Corporation. Essentially, integrated software means programs or packages of programs that perform a variety of different processing operations, using data which is compatible with whatever operation is being carried out. Integrated packages normally include spreadsheet, database, graphics and word processing facilities as a minimum, and may include other features such as communications. The success of integrated software has not been particularly spectacular.

BUDGETARY APPLICATIONS OF SPREADSHEETS

Spreadsheets have been applied successfully in many different fields to help solve a wide range of problems. Indeed any problem that involves repetitive and sometimes iterative calculations is a good candidate for a spreadsheet solution. The use of electronic spreadsheets has been particularly dominant in the financial sector, for example in the key areas of financial accounting, budgetary control, management accounting and financial management. Examples of applications which have utilized the power of the electronic spreadsheet include profit and loss accounts and balance sheet preparation, partnership accounts, incomplete records, cash flow forecasts, stock control, costing estimates, investment appraisal techniques, deferred tax computations, payroll calculations and so on.

Over the past fifteen years the financial sector has witnessed the emergence of the electronic spreadsheet as one of the key tools which has been utilized by a great number of managers and accountants. Indeed, without the spreadsheet facility many individuals in the business sector would find their work extremely difficult. One area in particular which has been greatly affected by the spreadsheet revolution is the area of budgeting, which has proved an ideal application for the spreadsheet modeller.

Before the introduction of the electronic spreadsheet manual worksheets were the main tool for those involved in budget development. Budgetary control systems were planned, analysed and summarized using several sheets of columnar paper, a pencil, rubber and calculator. The major problem users encountered with manual worksheets was the enormous task of recalculation when basic assumptions to the budget were made, or when input values were altered. Changes of this nature involved a complete manual recalculation of the entire worksheet, which ultimately proved to be not only very time-consuming but tedious and hence error-prone. There was also the problem of performing sensitivity or 'what-if' analysis. Sensitivity analysis involves altering key input values by specified amounts, often in a progressive fashion, to ascertain the effect on the criteria by which a particular project or probem is measured. For example, one method of applying sensitivity analysis to a budget is to recalculate the effect on profit it for example:

1. sales volumes are to increase/decrease by 10%;
2. running costs are expected to be 5% higher than originally estimated;
3. the cost of raw materials is to increase progressively by 1% each month over a twelve month period.

To carry out adequate sensitivity analysis it is necessary to alter key variables in the manual worksheet. This then leads to the problem already highlighted above, that of recalculating the worksheet manually.

The overall utility of the manual worksheet for budget construction was further reduced by other inherent limitations. Rarely did the user have sufficient time to test other valid assumptions, add further data to the problem, try other approaches or present information in an alternative manner.

The decreasing cost and increasing power of the desk-top microcomputer, coupled with the ready availability of spreadsheet software, has had the effect of further reducing the dependence on manual worksheets for budgets. Sophisticated spreadsheet packages which offer the user a vast array of features give rise to higher productivity and better utilization of time.

The spreadsheet modelling approach to the budgeting process can be considered in several stages. The first involves the definition of the objectives and scope of the budget model. In the case of a company-wide budgetary control system the objectives of such a model will be numerous, but at a minimum might include the following:

1. ensuring that a mechanism for comparison of actual figures is set up;
2. reporting to management the results of variances between actual and budgeted figures;
3. ensuring that a satisfactory system of feedback is enabled through the modelling process.

The second stage of the modelling process entails the identification of budget parameters and a definition of the relationships of variables to each other within the model. For example, in the budgetary control system described above parameters within the sales budget would probably include sales volumes, sales price and expected patterns of demand.

Having identified the parameters to the model the next stage is to determine and quantify the relationships of the model. These may be defined in terms of either a linear (or straight line effect, e.g. fixed costs) stepped (increasing, e.g. variable costs) or curved (e.g. the relationship between price and quantity demanded) relationship. The next stage is the task of assembling or constructing the budget model. This process involves assimilating all of the information gathered to date, i.e. the objectives and scope of the model, the parameters and relationships of the model, and relating these to the spreadsheet in a logical fashion. Testing of the model should be carried out after construction to ensure that incorrect relationships have not been defined and there are no inaccurate assumptions relating to the problem incorporation within the model.

At this stage the bulk of the work of model development has been carried out. The spreadsheet is now ready to use. The modeller will enter the input parameters relevant to the model and recalculate. At a glance the modeller can see the final outcome of the scenario he or she has just created. Different scenarios can be set up using the same model by simply changing the input parameter to the model. For example, the modeller can change the input parameters within the payroll budget by altering the hourly and daily rates of pay and the number of staff employed. Immediately the effect of such changes can be calculated and highlighted. Assumptions within a spreadsheet model can also be changed to create an alternative approach to the problem. For example, the assumptions relating to credit collection periods can be experimented with to see which combination of periods achieves the optimum solution in terms of cash flow.

ORGANIZATIONAL AND BEHAVIOURAL IMPACTS

The spreadsheet revolution has had a number of effects on organizations. Electronic spreadsheets have to a certain extent changed the way business and financial managers approach their work, by enabling them to be more creative and imaginative. Creativity is possible because of the nature of electronic spreadsheets, as they enable the user to perform detailed 'what-if' analysis with relative ease and without the constraint of performing manual calculations as with manual worksheets. The electronic spreadsheet presents minimal limitations on the user's imagination to model situations which can range from anything as complex as an organization diversifying into a new market to simple models which calculate depreciation. Key elements of the organization can be modelled, for example sales and production. Environmental factors can also be modelled to assess their impact on the organization – for example the rate of inflation or the prime borrowing rate can be built into the modelling process. Within limits, at the press of a button, managers can see the effect of a change in any of the key elements of the model, for example increases or decreases in the borrowing rate.

Limitations which the user may encounter when using spreadsheet software often relate to the facilities which particular packages offer in terms of functions available, such as graphical and database facilities and others. Many of the facilities available within spreadsheet software can serve to further enhance the users's creativity. For example, users have ability to produce graphical representations and desk-top publishing quality reports.

The way in which spreadsheet users think has also changed in some ways. Users today think in terms of rows and columns and the electronic spreadsheet, as opposed to the manual worksheet. Faced with a problem, a manager or accountant will ascertain whether the problem can first be solved using the electronic spreadsheet. Thinking is no longer constrained to the boundaries of a manual worksheet. Rather, the individual may now think in terms of modelling a problem using the spreadsheet as a tool.

Other changes in business and business structures have arisen out of the spreadsheet revolution. The use of electronic spreadsheets has had an impact on the process of decentralization of organizations and has contributed to the concept of end-user computing. Individuals are much less dependent on data processing departments to run financial or other models using large mainframe computers. Individuals now have the facility to create their own spreadsheet models using desk-top microcomputers. Decision-making has therefore become more decentralized with many individuals taking advantage of spreadsheet modelling for a variety of different applications.

The spreadsheet revolution has had an impact on both education and the professional accountancy practices. Increasingly we see more universities and colleges incorporating spreadsheet modelling within their business, finance and accounting programmes at both undergraduate and post-graduate levels. The accounting professions have also had to adapt and change their focus of attention. Many practices now use spreadsheets for incomplete records purposes, budget preparation, time allocation and charge out. As employers, accountancy practices have found the need to provide instruction for their accountancy trainees. Indeed some of the professional accountancy bodies require the accountancy student to undertake professional training in the use of electronic spreadsheets as part of their overall programme. The electronic spreadsheet is no longer regarded as a formidable object which can only be used by those who are computer literate. The user-friendly interface of the electronic spreadsheet gives the user a degree of mastery over the computer which undoubtedly has a positive effect.

SOME ADVANTAGES IN USING SPREADSHEETS

In addition to changing the way individuals approach their work the move from manual worksheets to electronic spreadsheets has resulted in numerous benefits. One of the greatest benefits of using the electronic spreadsheet as an alternative to the manual worksheet is the savings which can be made in terms of both time and cost. The initial set-up of time of a spreadsheet will vary depending on the complexity of the problem. In the case of a simple cash flow projection the set-up time may be as little as one or two hours, assuming the individual setting up the spreadsheet is clearly aware of the input values to the model and the relationships of variables within the model. Time savings which arise through using spreadsheets are more evident after the initial spreadsheet has been developed. After the initial development the user can experiment with different scenarios performing what-if analysis. Alterations to the spreadsheet model logic are only required where original assumptions to the model change.

In terms of cost savings electronic spreadsheets offer very sophisticated tools for a relatively low cost. The price of electronic spreadsheets vary from approximately 10% to 50% of the hardware costs of a personal computer system. This is relatively inexpensive in relation to the number of man hours saved by their usage. In addition reports can now be produced quarterly, monthly, weekly or even daily. Before the development of electronic spreadsheets, the production of daily reports on a daily basis for budgetary control purposes would not have been viable. The usage of manual worksheets required that the worksheet was typed manually and perhaps retyped if mistakes were discovered. Using the electronic spreadsheet for printing greatly reduces the time required to obtain printed output. The user simply specifies the area of the worksheet to be printed, sets the required print options through the spreadsheet – for example, headings within reports, footnotes, special print styles, etc. If changes to the spreadsheet are necessary the worksheet area to be reprinted is corrected, highlighted and reprinted quickly and efficiently.

Another major benefit of the electronic spreadsheet is that it has tended to encourage businesses to consider factors which were previously not considered in the budgeting process when using manual worksheets. The spreadsheet modelling approach tends to force the user to consider both internal and external environmental influences on the organization and model these. The process of sensitivity analysis is encouraged and this provides the modeller with a deeper appreciation of the nature of the business and the factors, both internal and external to the organization, which impinge upon it. Building spreadsheet models helps the modeller understand the real nature of the problem under review by identifying the causes, and the alternatives to and consequences of the solution.

Another advantage of the electronic spreadsheet is that it requires no general purpose language programming experience to use it. It follows that the individual, whether an accountant, engineer, doctor or academic, can use the electronic spreadsheet without a great deal of specialist training. Training takes little time and is cost-effective in comparison to the benefits to be reaped from the use of the spreadsheet.

Other benefits which arise from spreadsheet modelling include the ability for the modeller to see the overall effect of changes to the model immediately they are altered. The electronic spreadsheet is a flexible tool which does not force the user to set up models in a specific way.

SOME PITFALLS OR DANGERS OF SPREADSHEETS

Despite the great benefits which the electronic spreadsheet offers to a variety of professional and non-professionals alike, there are a few pitfalls or dangers which should be borne in mind when using the spreadsheet. One of the facts so often overlooked by the spreadsheet modeller is that many factors which affect an organization are qualitative as opposed to quantitative. Invariably these factors are hard to quantify and include within a spreadsheet model. For example, it is difficult to measure in monetary terms the quality of staff morale, the losses that could occur because of poor management practices and lack of motivation. The dangers of spreadsheet modelling are that decisions may be made purely on the basis of the information modelled in the spreadsheet, ignoring other important qualitative factors which may ultimately affect the organization. It is important to realize that these other qualitative factors should be taken into consideration in the decision-making process.

Another pitfall that electronic spreadsheet users should avoid is the trap of thinking that the spreadsheet can allow the user to make economic decisions based solely on the information that it provides. What the electronic spreadsheet can do is provide the user with useful information which is to be used in planning, decision-making and control situations. The spreadsheet should be viewed as a tool, or as a means to an end, and not as an end in itself. Ultimately it is the individual who is modelling the information who must make the final decision. There is also the danger that users of electronic spreadsheets may make incorrect decisions based on information arrived at using the spreadsheet. Incorrect or inaccurate data may be a result of a number of factors. First the spreadsheet developed may contain fundamental errors which have gone undetected. For example, a value may have been inserted where calculation should have been carried out. Secondly, the assumptions which are built into the spreadsheet model may have been stated incorrectly, an example being that relating to debtors collection periods. Finally the definition of the relationship of variables to each other may also be inaccurate. For example, the relationship between sales and purchase of raw materials in a production plant may be incorrect. Errors in spreadsheet construction generally arise where the individual setting up the spreadsheet has not defined the nature and scope of the problem in sufficient depth or has failed to identify all of the input parameters and the relationships of the model. If errors remain undetected management may find that they have made decisions which will work to the detriment of the organization.

Apart from not taking account of intangible or qualitative factors, electronic spreadsheets have no way of dealing with feelings that the user may have about a particular project. Whilst the position may look good from the spreadsheet point of view the individual reviewing the information may have mixed feelings or a hunch that something which is outside the parameters of the model may affect the output of the project. It is this aspect of human thought which the electronic spreadsheet cannot account for.

It is important to realize that there are several weaknesses which exhibit themselves when electronic spreadsheets are used for models which are large and complex. Large spreadsheets can become difficult to manipulate and may even become slow to operate when the hardware capability does not match the processing requirements. Large models can also be difficult to construct and the user can indeed get easily 'lost' in the logic of the entire model. Documentation of models is another point of concern for the user. Electronic spreadsheets provide no method of allowing the user to document the logic of the model or the relationships involved. If the user wants to document the spreadsheet model he or she must enter the documentation into a portion of the spreadsheet or use a word processing package.

RECENT ENHANCEMENTS

In their original form, electronic spreadsheets were designed and used for entering and manipulating data. Developments since the late 1970s have not changed the basic concept, but have resulted in many new features being incorporated which serve to enhance their usability. Particularly, in the last five years, there have been many additions to the spreadsheet 'family'. New packages have come onto the market and old ones have been upgraded. Among the many sophisticated features now available within electronic spreadsheets are those such as linked spreadsheets, three dimensional graphics, presentation quality printing and plotting capabilities, automation with sophisticated macro languages, spreadsheet debugging and auditing tools, and interfacing with other packages. In addition spreadsheet security has been increased, particularly on networked versions, and spreadsheet packages now offer more support for engineering and scientific applications by providing a larger set of commands and functions.

Most of the popular packages on the software market also include an extensive range of statistical, logical, calender, arithmetic, financial, trigonometric, index and string and special purpose functions. Many also have limited database management facilities which allow the user to create a database of information, perform database searches and data management statistical analysis and produce database reports. All of these enhancements have provided the spreadsheet user with a very powerful form of software at a very reasonable cost.

Other developments within the spreadsheet market in the 1980s have been the production of a wide range of application templates and add-ins which enable the spreadsheet user to perform many advanced functions. Application templates are commercially available as off-the-shelf models based on a particular spreadsheet package. They range from totally menu-driven systems through to systems that can be modified by the user. Examples include Ivy-Calc (a template which performs financial analysis and discounted cash flows, project appraisal and investment analysis).

Add-ins are programs that have been specifically designed to enable the developer to extend the spreadsheet's features and capabilities within a particular package. Examples of add-ins include Silverade and Oracle, relational database management programs, designed to be used with Supercalc. For Lotus 1–2–3, further examples are Macro Library Manager, which provides the facility for storing macros and formulas, and Allways, which enables the creation of presentation quality reports. The ability to incorporate graphical representations and text on the same page of output is a fairly new facility available within spreadsheet packages.

Because spreadsheets models are often large and complex this invariably increases the risk of errors and the likelihood that relationships within the model have not been defined correctly. To counteract this problem, spreadsheet auditing techniques and debugging functions have been developed. This has been one of the most significant developments to the area of spreadsheet modelling which will undoubtedly result in further enhancing the utility of spreadsheets. Auditing techniques are facilities which are available within electronic spreadsheets which enable users to check the logic of their models, audit relationships between variables, highlight errors, locate information, identify formulas that reference text or blank cells, locate problems and confusing patterns arising from spreadsheet design or layout, trace circular relationships and much more. All of these techniques are used at the testing phase of model developments. Previously spreadsheet models have been tested by double-checking the arithmetic, and by checking that the model reacts in a sensible or predictable fashion to changes in both input parameters and logic assumptions. The auditing features can now be used in conjunction with these tests to discover errors which have remained undetected.

Despite the sophistication and seemingly complex enhancements which have taken place in the spreadsheet world, as mentioned earlier, the underlying concept of the spreadsheet has remained intact. It is this basic simplicity of concept which has aided the rapid acceptance and use of the tool by many users. The sheer simplicity of spreadsheets have also allowed many non-computer literate professionals to learn how to use the tool quickly without the requirement to have an in-depth knowledge of computers or their workings.

CONCLUDING REMARKS

In conclusion the spreadsheet revolution has had quite a dramatic effect on the nature of the work of many individuals. The financial sector has been particularly influenced by the development of the electronic spreadsheet.

Those who have been exposed to the spreadsheet concept have adjusted to the idea in a fairly easy manner since they were already familiar with the concept via the manual worksheet. The electronic spreadsheet should, however, only be viewed as a useful tool which has applications for many different purposes. It should be seen as a means to an end and not as an end in itself. Users should be aware of the potential limitations of the tool and these should be borne in mind when modelling real-life situations.

FURTHER READING

Blewett, F. and Jarvis, R. (1989). *Microcomputers in Accounting.* Van Nostrand Reinhold (International)/The Institute of Chartered Accountants in England & Wales.

Bromwich, M. and Hopwood, A. (1986). *Research and Current Issues in Management Accounting.* Pitman.

Bryant, J. W. (1982). *Financial Modelling on Corporate Management.* John Wiley.

Kyd, C. W. (1986). *Financial Modelling Using Lotus 1–2–3.* Osborne McGraw-Hill.

Lehman, M. W., Lehman, C. M. and Daniel, T. E. (1987). *Using the Microcomputer in Managerial Accounting*, Lotus 1–2–3 edition. West Publishing Company.

Levy, S. (1989). 'A spreadsheet way of knowledge'. In Forester, T. (ed.), *Computers in the Human Context.* Basil Blackwell, Oxford.

Sherwood, D. (1984). *Financial Modelling.* Gee & Co.

Tjerkstra, R. J. (1987). *Electronic Spreadsheet Modelling for Business and Education. An Accounting Case Study.* Thomas Business Papers No. 6.

DISCUSSION QUESTIONS

1. Discuss the limitations of using electronic spreadsheets for budgetary control purposes.
2. Define the term 'modelling' as applied in the context of electronic spreadsheets. Briefly explain the process of developing a computer model using a spreadsheet.
3. What do you understand by the following terms in relation to spreadsheet modelling:
   (a) Model logic
   (b) Relationships
   (c) Parameters?

Give a practical example of each of the above to illustrate your explanation.
4. What do you understand by the term 'sensitivity analysis'? Illustrate by way of example how you would perform sensitivity analysis using a spreadsheet.
5. What benefits arise when using an electronic spreadsheet as opposed to a manual worksheet for budgeting purposes?
6. Describe the main areas of the financial sector where electronic spreadsheets are utilized. Give examples of applications in each of the areas outlined.

13 Using computers as management tools
Paul Collier

INTRODUCTION

The availability to management of computer-based workstations and support from information centres has lead to what Ahituv and Neumann (1990) characterize as the 'Age of the End User'. Throughout the 1980s managers as end-users took over greater responsibility for developing computer applications and planning information systems developments. Managers use computers as end-users in thrce main ways according to Rockhart and Flannery (1983):

1. non-programming end-users – who only access data through existing software;
2. command level users – who can manipulate data using command driven software tools like fourth generation languages, spreadsheets and graphics facilities; and
3. end-user programmers – who develop application programs of some sophistication.

Thus managers in the 1990s are using computers as tools, which assist their activities by providing information, support decisions, improve productivity and give access to expertise. These developments have given rise to a multiplicity of ill-defined terms. This chapter, after a brief historical overview of the development of computers as management tools and an analysis of management activities, outlines the major characteristics of the following terms: Electronic Data Processing (EDP); Management

Specially commissioned for *IT and Accounting: The Impact of information technology.*
Edited by Bernard C. Williams and Barry J. Spaul.
Published in 1991 by Chapman & Hall, London ISBN 0 412 39210 0.

Information System (MIS); Decision Support Systems (DSS); Executive Information Systems (EIS); Office Information Systems (OIS); and Expert Systems (ES), before developing a taxonomy, which defines the boundaries between them.

HISTORICAL PERSPECTIVE

The use of computers for commercial purposes begins in 1954 with the UNIVAC-1 and IBM 650. The usefulness of these computers as management tools was limited, due to the restrictions imposed by the valve technology and a reliance upon instruction code or assembly languages, to basic EDP applications which speeded up repetitive tasks like invoicing or payroll. In the late 1950s and early 1960s a new generation of computers based on transistors and high level languages like COBOL provided the scope for more sophisticated EDP applications. However, computers were still remote and concentrated in specialist centres. The third generation of computers arrived in 1964 with the IBM 360 series, which used miniaturized transistors on an integrated circuit board. These machines, and mini-computers which arrived in the early 1970s, coupled with database software, enhanced operating systems and more high level languages, enabled computers to provide management with an integrated MIS tailored to specific needs. Minicomputers meant that computers moved out of controlled environments and into the workplace, and the idea of linking computers through communications networks also came about. The increased computing power was also harnessed by management scientists to provide DSS, which enabled managers to explore the consequences of their actions and external events on corporate models. However, from the viewpoint of computers as management tools the most dramatic developments were stimulated by the arrival of the microchip in the late 1970s and the growth in microcomputer usage. These advances, linked with the development of advanced communication systems, microcomputer software and especially spreadsheets and fourth generation languages, led to a shift in computing away from specialists towards users as reflected in OIS and EIS.

Another result of these computing enhancements has been the development of artificial intelligence as reflected in this application of ES as an aid to management in specific domains of expertise.

MANAGEMENT ACTIVITIES

The major management activities in which computers can make a contribution are planning and control (although researchers like Mintzberg (1975) have indicated that these are not the sole activities).

Anthony (1965) defined the following categories of management planning and control:

1. strategic planning;
2. management control and planning; and
3. operational planning and control.

The operational level is concerned with activities with short time horizons relating to the present and past in a stable environment. Information is gathered from internal sources. The tactical level covers activities with a longer time scale, predominantly in the present and with a less certain environment than the operational level. The strategic level is concerned with longer-run relationships between the organization and its environment. Strategic information concerns the future, relates to an unstable environment and uses a variety of internal and external sources of information.

Inextricably linked with planning and control is decision-making. Computers provide information to aid decision-making by managers. As Simon (1960) stated this involves the interaction of intelligence, analysis and design, and selection and choice. Further, Simon classified decisions on a continuum ranging from structured, where the situation is well understood and there is a standard procedure, to unstructured, where cause and effect relationships are poorly understood. Figure 13.1 illustrates a framework with examples of typical decisions, which links decision-making and planning and control activities.

Computers and information systems as management aids must serve managers in carrying out these planning, control and decision-making activities. The characteristics of major management tools will now be discussed.

ELECTRONIC DATA PROCESSING (EDP)

EDP systems process data (the raw material for information) through a computer in order to produce information (data which is meaningful and useful to its recipient). The term in the widest context is generally used to describe the functions carried out by a computer department. However, a narrower view limits EDP to the automation of fundamental, routine

	Operational	Tactical	Strategic
Structured	Inventory re-ordering	Production scheduling	Financial planning
Less structured	Pricing	Budgeting	New product line
Unstructured	Customer complaints	Personnel management	Restructuring the company

Fig. 13.1 Decision-making linked to management activity.

processing to support operations, as for example updating account balances, calculating pay and maintaining inventory balances.

MANAGEMENT INFORMATION SYSTEMS (MIS)

Davis and Olson (1985), although accepting that there is no general consensus on a definition, define a management information system as 'an integrated, user–machine system for providing information to support operations, management, and decision-making functions in an organization. The system utilizes computer hardware and software; manual procedures; models for analysis, planning, control and decision-making; and a database.' The components of an MIS can be viewed from two perspectives: the functional subsystems, which link to form an MIS, and the management activities. The principal functional subsystems obviously vary depending on the type of business, but in a typical manufacturing organization the following might be expected: production, engineering, marketing, personnel, accounting, and treasury. In turn these consist of further integrated modules, for example accounting includes sales,

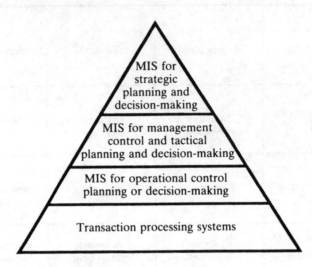

Fig. 13.2 Levels in the MIS.

purchases, inventory, fixed assets and payroll subsystems. An analysis by management activities, which distinguishes the EDP activity of transaction processing from the MIS, is illustrated in Fig. 13.2.

An MIS may be created in an organization once it is realised that information is a critical resource which must be properly managed through an integration of functional subsystems around one or a number of databases. Curtis (1989) linked MIS with the grid in Fig. 13.1. The MIS has a role in supporting managers in decision-making in all areas of the grid except for highly structured operational decisions, which could be automated, and items of an unstructured strategic nature, which are heavily reliant on subjective external information.

DECISION SUPPORT SYSTEMS

DSS derive from the interaction of three separate disciplines:

1. management science – provides problem-solving methodologies, especially through algebraic models;
2. computer science – permits the computerization of the models and the ability to explore numerous outcomes available through altering model variables and assumptions; and
3. ergonomics – assists the design of suitable man–machine interfaces.

Although the term DSS was first coined by Keen (see Freyenfeld (1984), no single definition exists. A simple definition of a DSS would be any computerized system which aids decision-making in organizations. However, more restrictive definitions have been proposed. Sprague and Watson (1986) summarized definitions of DSS as 'interactive computer-based systems, which help decision makers utilise data and models to solve unstructured problems'. The following four main characteristics of DSS are identified:

1. aimed at less structured problems as shown in the top portion of Fig. 13.2;
2. combine models and analytical techniques with traditional data access and retrieval;
3. interactive, user-friendly and targeted at non-computer people; and
4. flexible and adaptable to any approach a decision-taker may wish to adopt.

Several classifications of DSS have been made. Alter (1977) put forward a classification that was based on the split between computer science and management science. The categorization distinguished between data-oriented and model-oriented DSS. The data-oriented systems were sub-divided into data retrieval systems and data analysis systems. These involved accessing and analysing historic and current data held on files and small databases. Model-oriented systems distinguished between simulation models that permit the consequences of a range of actions to be explored, and suggestion models that offer the user a solution to a specific problem. In the analysis, simulation models were further classified into accounting models and representational models differentiated by whether or not the simulation model included elements beyond accounting definitions. Suggestion models were subdivided into optimization models that generated an optimum solution for achieving a set goal given certain constraints, and suggestion models that compute a specific suggested decision in structured repetitive situations, like a decis on to grant credit. Freyenfield (1984) approached the classification by linking what was currently available with the level in the hierarchy where it will be used and the decision-making method. Six types of DSS were identified:

1. Chief executive information systems (corresponding to EIS);
2. Commercial operational analysis and planning systems;
3. Industrial operational analysis and planning systems;
4. Preference determination systems;
5. Cognitive mapping systems; and
6. Expert advisory systems (ES).

A classification structure suggested by Finlay (1989) distinguishes between DSS on the basis of whether the system is dealing with information or intelligence. DSS are described under the headings of MIS or Management Intelligence Systems (MINTS). MIS provide information that the manager can interpret, while MINTS assist the manager with the interpretation of the information. The main elements of MIS and MINTS are as follows:

MIS

1. Data retrieval systems – comprise file-draw systems that provide rapid access to data, data analysis systems that give analysis of simple situations, and EIS (see below).
2. Extrapolatory systems – cover systems used to predict the future in a formalized manner. They are subdivided into definitional systems that use variables with predefined relationships, causal systems that use variables linked by cause and effect, and probabilistic systems where variables can have a range of values defined by a statistical distribution.

MINTS

1. Preference determination systems – deal with problems suited to decision tree or decision matrix approaches. To operate these techniques there must be clearly identifiable options with associated possible outcomes dependent on various criteria. The methodology structures the problem, identifies options and evaluates uncertainties.
2. Scenario development systems – the two main examples are cognitive mapping systems and ideas generation systems. In the former, linked concepts that have been extracted from the group with the problem by a facilitator are put into a cognitive map that highlights the disagreements and assists their resolution. In the latter, the computer supports brainstorming approaches to problems.

A by-product of DSS is enhanced interaction amongst managers, especially in examining the meaning of DSS output (see the study by Sanders *et al.* (1984) for example). However, this interaction usually takes place outside the DSS. Huber (1984) pointed out that improved communications technology enables the group processes in management decision-making to be directly supported from inside the system. Huber used the term Group DSS and defined it as 'a set of software, hardware and language components and procedures that support a group of people engaged in a decision related meeting'. Amongst the characteristics which differentiate a Group DSS from a DSS are:

1. communications linking of participants;
2. modelling systems that permit interactive ranking and voting;
3. models which are readily comprehensible to participants with different backgrounds and skills; and
4. decision aids that are flexible and offer the minimum constraints to problem specification and solution.

Although at present such systems are rare there are obvious applications, especially in strategic decision-making.

EXECUTIVE INFORMATION SYSTEMS (EIS)

EIS are user-friendly computerized systems designed specifically to provide top-level management with selected and summarized information from diverse sources. It permits the information to be accessed, analysed and presented in a way that assists top executives in managing and directing their organizations. This definition raises a number of areas that require expansion:

1. *User friendly*. EIS should be capable of being used interactively by executives dealing with business problems. This requires well-designed menus, and the use of devices like mice, icons, touch screens and number keypads.
2. *Top level management*. The system is aimed at senior executives directly responsible for strategy, control and decision-making in the organization.
3. *Diverse sources*. Information for an EIS will come from internal and external sources. In particular, an EIS will provide a direct link into external databases, of which there were over 4000 in the UK in 1989, to give the executive information on relevant factors like financial data on individual companies, exchange rates, stock market prices, key economic variables and regulatory constraints.
4. *Accessed*. An EIS must provide an executive with quick and easy access to information. This requires the structuring of an EIS database that is efficiently linked to existing systems and contains information in the form in which an executive thinks about the business. A classic feature of an EIS is the ability to 'drill down', a term referring to expanding areas identified for detailed examination. Thus an executive may identify from a summary screen of divsional performance a division that is underperforming. The EIS must permit the executive to explore this problem by accessing screens supporting the summarized data. Achieving this requircs skillful structuring of the EIS database.
5. *Analysed*. The information acquired by the executive must be capable

of analysis. The executive should be able to use models interactively to calculate ratios, growth rates, trends, forecasts, perform sensitivity analysis and explore 'what-if' scenarios.
6. *Presented*. The EIS should allow the executive to present the information extracted and the results of analyses in properly designed formats that make full use of colour graphics capabilities.

Studies (for example, Matthews (1988)) suggest that EIS are becoming more widely used in the UK and that many major multinational companies employ such systems.

OFFICE INFORMATION SYSTEMS (OIS)

OIS are synonymous with office automation (OA). OA is a general term used to refer to the application of information technology to office work. Alternative terms for OA include 'the electronic office', 'the paperless office' and 'the office of the future'. The purpose of office automation is to assist office workers to carry out their tasks more efficiently and effectively. Technological support for office workers is not new (for example telephones, photocopiers and typewriters offer this) but the 1980s saw the impact of the converging of microelectronics, communications and office equipment advances to provide integrated office systems which have provided new tools to managers. Unlike previous management tools, which have focused on operations and transactions directly connected with the production of goods and services, OIS are concerned with the administrative processes of the company. The full capabilities of OIS systems provided by this convergence of technologies are realized in an environment where workstations and other business equipment are linked via a communications network into the organization's internal and external computing services. Under these circumstances, Wetherbe *et al.* (1981) suggest that the OIS systems offer managers the following facilities:

1. document processing;
2. electronic mail systems;
3. executive support systems;
4. EIS and DSS facilities (as discussed previously).

More recently Peltu (1988) has emphasized the communications features of new office technologies like advanced telephony and video conferencing. Document processing is the most universal office function covered by OIS. It enables documents like letters, memoranda and reports to be prepared, amended and stored in the computer memory without necessarily being printed. The ability to amend text through the text editing facilities extends beyond mere addition and deletion of letters, words, sentences and paragraphs to encompass format changes to spacing, margins and other layout features by single commands. Facilities also exist to allow standard paragraphs to be called and reference to be made to computer lists like addresses to facilitate document preparation. As an extension of this, word processing systems have the ability to store and call standard formats, which could either be standard letters, for example debt reminders, orders or appointments, or standard forms such as timesheets, holiday requests and expense claims. In many systems dictionary facilities enable spelling to be checked and the storage of documents includes automatic disposal after a preset interval. Text processing also enables documents to be transferred, filed and retrieved electronically thus reducing the paper circulating in an office. Another key function is electronic mail, which allows text to be transmitted around an OIS network in a manner similar to a postal service with electronic addresses. Text, usually messages or memoranda, may be sent to individual addresses or broadcast to selected groups or all addresses on the network. Mail management software handles the creation, storage and deletion of messages and replies.

Executive support systems offer a range of aids aimed at assisting managers in improving their effectiveness. Typically the software available covers:

1. Diary – a daily diary for planning activities. As well as personal appointments, crucial dates of events for the organization would be held. Since the diary is in electronic form it is possible to allow other users to consult the diary and book appointments.
2. Directories – an internal telephone directory plus selected commonly used external numbers are available from the workstation.
3. Tickler files – software notepads with reminders. Information held might include projects and their deadlines, tasks delegated to staff and deadlines, outstanding action list and time records.
4. Calculator – a function enabling simple arithmetical and statistical routines to be performed at the workstation.
5. Spreadsheet – a simple software modelling device for situations involving few variables and simple relationships, which can be expressed in terms of rows and columns. Typically these are used to produce reports and explore scenarios ('what-if' analyses) and may form a component in EIS.

Telecommunications through advanced telephony and other systems offer possibilities for text, voice and image communication systems. For example, new telephone systems have automatic call rerouting, auto-redialling of engaged numbers, simplified dialling for commonly used numbers and teleconferencing facilities where several phone users can interact. Text transfer is also possible on a national and international basis over telecommunications networks through teletex, provided compatible terminals are installed. Similarly, facsimile (FAX) can transmit text and images, again assuming that special devices exist at each end. Finally video technologies offer the opportunity to project images for video conferencing, where remote participants can be seen, multimedia presentations of information linking computer and video output, and telewriting which allows text information to be communicated onto display screens. Thus OIS have provided management with integrated office systems which feature document generation and handling facilities, personal productivity tools, improved information sources and advanced communications.

EXPERT SYSTEMS (ES)

An ES is a computer system which has the knowledge-based component of an expert skill held in a form that enables the computer to offer intelligent advice or take an intelligent decision. The system should also be capable of justifying on demand its line of reasoning in a manner comprehensible to the enquirer. ES are best suited to structured problem areas which require for solution the use of a body of knowledge to which 'fuzzy logic' and heuristic rules (rules of thumb) can be applied. Typical application areas include diagnostics, advice, prediction and training. The importance of ES as management tools is emphasized by the findings of Feigenbaum and McCorduck (1984) who observed that 'most business management is done by symbolic inference, not calculation. In short, almost all the thinking is done by reasoning, and not calculating'.

There are three basic components in an expert system:

1. A knowledge base – a database holding the facts, heuristics and rules appertaining to a specific domain.
2. An inference engine – a program which solves problems by scheduling and controlling the selection process of applying rules that pertain to the solution of a problem.
3. A user interface – a system which provides an interface with the user and enables questions to be asked, knowledge and rules to be added to the ES and explains advice given.

The 1990 Department of Trade and Industry report *Expert Systems in Britain* categorized management applications of IT into those that save resources and those that multiply expertise. At present, the most widely applied have been the former (examples quoted include Blue Circle which has an ES for the process control of cement kilns that offers a 50p per tonne saving, and Glaxo's use of ES in pharmaceutical research) but in the future 'expertise-multiplying types of ES will eventually have a much wider impact on organisational performance'. Current applications of this type, including taxation and audit planning systems, are quoted by Connell (1987).

A TAXONOMY OF COMPUTERS AS MANAGEMENT TOOLS

The boundaries between the terms under which the use of computers as management tools has been discussed have not been clearly defined. This reflects the fact that EDP, MIS, DSS, EIS, OIS and ES are converging systems and technologies that are integrated into the firm's overall information systems strategy. Figure 13.3 puts forward the areas covered and interrelationships between the concepts. As with any taxonomy, the classifications are not prescriptive but merely serve to highlight the different uses of computers as management tools.

EDP DISTINGUISHED FROM MIS

EDP involves the production of operational information from a transaction processing system. Operational information is in standard formats, is routinely produced, derives from internal data and is targeted at operational control. Management information in contrast is aimed at assisting in the decision-making process which is inherent in all levels of management activity. Such information must be in a format suitable for the purpose of the user, is produced as needed, and is obtained from internal and external data sources. Nevertheless, the exact division between EDP and MIS is, as Davis and Olsen (1985) argue, conceptual – 'MIS is a concept and an orientation toward which an information system design moves rather than an absolute state.' Therefore the extent to which management information is produced is also a factor.

DSS DISTINGUISHED FROM MIS

There are numerous opinions on a division between these classes of management tools. For example, Naylor (1982) argues that DSS offer nothing which is not already inherent in management science and MIS and therefore the term is redundant. Others, like Keen and Scott-Morton (1978), focus on the nature of the decision, limiting DSS to unstructured

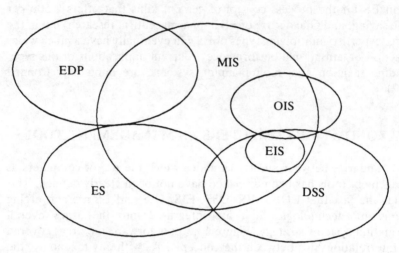

Fig. 13.3 The boundaries between terminology associated with computers as management tools.

and semistructured decisions as shown in the top half of Fig. 13.2 and leaving the rest as the concern of the MIS. Neumann and Hadass (1980) on the other hand support this approach by arguing that the organizational information system comprises the administrative data processing system and DSS. The former can be subdivided into the transaction processing system which supports operational activities, and the structured decision system (SDS) which deals with structured decisions. The DSS and SDS comprise the MIS with DSS limited to unstructured and semistructured decisions. However, Moore and Chang (1983) disagreed with these approaches and argued that MIS are institutionalized, whilst DSS deal with non-recurrent problems. The approach by Finlay (1989) was to divide MSS into MIS and MINTS components, the former providing information for managers and the latter helping the analysis and interpretation process. Thus DSS can be considered as partly within the MIS (see Fig 13.3) and partly as a MINTS.

DSS DISTINGUISHED FROM EIS

EIS are a subset of the MIS part of DSS. The objective of EIS is to provide executives with a system which can provide relevant information at several system levels and permit analysis and modelling of this data. EIS combine data retrieval and extrapolatory systems under Findlay's classification.

MIS DISTINGUISHED FROM OIS

OIS have features which are fundamentally different from MIS. For example, document processing and electronic mail involve a different unit of information to EDP and MIS approaches. The latter centre upon the processing of prespecified records, which although variable in content are consistent in structure. In contrast, the document processing and electronic mail parts of OIS process documents, messages and disparate pieces of information, which are consistent in neither structure nor form. OIS are reliant upon MIS and DSS for some of the management support features, which are traditionally linked with OIS. Therefore, Fig. 13.3 shows part of OIS outside and part linked with DSS, MIS and EIS.

THE PLACE FOR ES

Waterman (1985) identified four principal differences between ES and conventional EDP:

1. EDP involves the representation and use of data, while ES are concerned with the representation and use of knowledge;
2. EDP relies on algorithmic and algebraic relationships, whereas ES uses heuristics and fuzzy logic;
3. EDP is a repetitive process, while ES relies on an inferential process; and
4. EDP manipulates databases and ES manipulates knowledge bases.

However, according to Phelps (1986), ES have strong similarities with DSS even if the terminology is different. For example, the concept of relationships in the logic of a DSS is similar to the concept of a knowledge base of an ES. Applications of ES to management problems have largely been in more structured decision-making domains (for examples see Myers (1988) for an application to provide consultancy advice in making corporate capital investment decisions, or Sirinivasan and Kim (1988) where the ES made a credit granting decision). Under the DSS classifications, the former application would be a data retrieval system routed in the MIS part of DSS and the latter could not be DSS, as a decision is made not supported, but is obviously part of the MIS of the organization. ES as management tools also give advice on technical matters (for example, tax and the Data Protection Act (1984)) and can be used in training. Therefore ES are shown in Fig. 13.3 as part of MIS, part of the MIS section of DSS and part outside the other terms.

CONCLUSION

This review of the use of computers as management tools suggests that further developments aimed at integrating the various tools is necessary in order that organizations can have the comprehensive management support systems which are crucial in an era when information is a vital resource and its management can bring competitive advantages.

If end-user computing by management is to flourish it is important that information centres are developed so as to overcome the criticisms of excessive bureaucracy and an inability to distinguish worthwhile from trivial applications. To some extent this will come about as managers become better trained but greater impetus from senior management is needed. Otherwise, major developments of computers as management tools will probably result from improved man–machine interfaces, with extensions of voice input, touch screens and improvements in the user-friendliness of software, and new developments in the application of artificial intelligence (AI) to management tools. For example, AI could assist senior management using EIS by prompting the scrutiny of information and ensuring that analysis techniques were effectively used. Finally, the future will see the enhanced presentation of the results of the use of management tools by multimedia approaches, which combine text, graphics, video and other mediums.

FURTHER READING

Finlay, P. N. (1989). *Introducing Decision Support Systems*. NCC Blackwell, Oxford.

Peltu, M. (1988). *Successful Management of Office Automation*. NCC Publications, Manchester.

Waterman, D. A. (1986). *A Guide to Expert Systems*. Addison-Wesley, Reading, Massachusetts.

DISCUSSION QUESTIONS

1. Discuss the factors that distinguish MIS from EDP.
2. What are the major activities of managers and how are these enhanced by the use of computer tools?
3. Discuss the following statement: 'There is nothing new in DSS – all its attributes are to be found in management science and MIS.'

4. What is meant by the term 'end-user computing' and what factors have contributed to its growth in the 1980s?
5. Discuss whether OIS are management tools or merely secretarial and clerical support devices.
6. What are the main features of EIS? Outline the information which might be expected from an EIS for a UK supermarket chain.

REFERENCES

Ahituv, N. and Neumann, S. (1990). *Principles of Information Systems Management.* Wm. C. Brown, Dubuque, Indiana.

Alter, S. (1977). 'A taxonomy of decision support systems', *Sloan Management Review*, No. 1, Fall, pp. 39–56.

Anthony, R. N. (1965). *Planning and Control Systems: A Framework for Analysis.* Harvard University Press, Cambridge.

Connell, N. A. D. (1987). 'Expert systems in accountancy: a review of recent applications', *Accounting and Business Research*, Vol. 17, No. 67, pp.221–33.

Curtis, G. A. (1989). *Business Information Systems.* Addison-Wesley, Wokingham.

Davis, G. B. and Olson, M. H. (1985). *Management Information Systems: Conceptual Foundations, Structure and Development.* McGraw-Hill, New York.

Feigenbaum, E. A. and McCorduck, P. (1984). *The Fifth Generation*, Pan Books.

Finlay, P. N. (1989). *Introducing Decision Support Systems.* NCC Blackwell, Oxford.

Freyenfield, W. A. (1984). *Decision Support Systems.* NCC Publications, Manchester.

Huber, G. P. (1984). 'Issues in the design of group decision support systems', MIS Quarterly, Vol. 5, No. 1, pp. 195–204.

Keen, P. G. W. and Scott-Morton, M. S. (1978). *Decision Support Systems: An Organisational Perspective.* Addison-Wesley, Reading, Massachussets.

Matthews, R. (1988). *The board-room revolution: a market research report on director's information systems.* Metapraxis Ltd of Kingston, Kingston, England.

Mintzberg, H. (1975). 'The manager's job: folklore and fact', *Harvard Business Review*, Vol. 53, No. 4, pp. 49–61.

Moore, J. H. and Chang, M. G. (1983). 'Meta-design considerations in building DSS'. In Bennett, J. L. (ed.), *Building Decision Support Systems.* Addison-Wesley, Reading, Massachussets, pp. 173–204.

Myers, S. C. (1988). 'Notes on an expert system for capital budgeting', *Financial Management,* Vol. 17, No. 3, pp. 23–31.

Naylor, T. H. (1982). 'Decision support systems, or whatever happened to MIS?', *Interfaces*, Vol. 12, No. 4, pp. 92–4.

Neumann, S. and Hadass, M. (1980). 'DSS and strategic decisions', *California Management Review*, Vol. 22, No. 2, pp. 77–84.

Peltu, M. (1988) *Successful Management of Office Automation.* NCC Publications, Manchester.

Phelps, R. I. (1986). 'Artificial Intelligence – an overview of similarities with OR', *Journal of the Operational Research Society,* Vol. 37, pp. 13–20.

Rockhart, J. F. and Flannery, L. S. (1983). 'The management of end user computing', *Communications of the ACM,* Vol. 26, No. 10, pp. 776–84.

Sanders, G. L., Courtney, J. F., and Loy, S. L. (1984). 'The impact of decision support systems on organizational communications', *Information and Management,* Vol. 7, pp. 141–8.

Simon, H. A. (1960). *The New Science of Management Decisions.* Harper & Row, New York.

Sirinivasan, V. and Kim, Y. H. (1988). 'Designing expert financial systems: a case study of corporate credit management', *Financial Management,* Vol. 17, No. 3, pp. 32–50.

Sprague, R. H. Jr and Watson, H. J. (1986). *Decision Support Systems: Putting Theory into Practice.* Prentice Hall, New Jersey.

Waterman, D. A. (1985). 'How do ES differ from conventional programs?', *Expert systems,* Vol. 3, No. 1, pp. 12–21.

Wetherbe, J. C., Davis, C. K. and Dykman, C. A. (1981). 'Implementing automated office systems', *Journal of Systems Management,* Vol. 32, No. 8, pp. 6–13.

5 Tax and Law

This Part explores topics in the area of law and (the related area of) taxation and the involvement of computers in their business and accounting dimensions. In most aspects of business and accounting, computers have developed an essential and integrated role. Both the impact and the speed of these changes pose a real challenge for legislators and legal draughtsmen as they inevitably find themselves confronted with new and unforeseen problems in the midst of their attempts to revise the legal framework.

Law, like IT, permeates and influences almost all aspects of business and accounting, the two most important fields probably being contract and company law. Naturally these cover a very wide area from which two relevant aspects for accountancy have been selected. These give an indication of the impact of two information technologies, EDI (electronic data interchange) systems and expert systems on two areas of law, evidence and liability. Accordingly, the first chapter by Robert Bradgate looks at some of the legal issues surrounding the use of EDI. EDI is the direct electronic transmission of standard business documents in electronic form between two or more organizations. In a business environment this means the need for hard copy is eleminated entirely. By utilizing EDI, purchasers and sellers are operating in a near 'real-time' environment. This lack of paper documentation raises all sorts of problems for lawyers and auditors alike and it is some of these problems that Bradgate examines in detail.

In the second chapter Vijay Mital and Les Johnson examine the legal implications of professionals relying on expert systems. They consider in detail the mechanisms by which a court may examine errors of reasoning in expert systems used to help accounting and other professionals working in the 'financial–legal domain'. They convincingly argue that reliance on expert systems given current best practice in software engineering might not be regarded as 'reasonable' behaviour by the courts.

The final chapter in this Part by Dyerson and Roper looks at taxation and IT. More specifically it examines 'The computerization of PAYE'. It describes the two decades of work that has been put into the computerization of the 'pay as you earn' system in the UK. This chapter gives a real insight into the problems of developing and implementing a huge project of this nature, as well as allowing the reader to view the changes possible when taxation systems are automated to this extent.

Chapter

14 The evidential status of computer output and communications

Robert Bradgate

INTRODUCTION

As the business community makes ever greater use of computers, the courts are going to find increasingly that the disputes before them turn on evidence which has at some stage passed through or been processed by a computer. Unless the courts are able to take full account of such evidence, the law will fall out of step with business practice, and may become a brake on commercial progress. This was recognized by the Criminal Law Revision Committee: 'The increasing use of computers by the Post Office, local authorities, banks and business firms to store certain kinds of information will make it more difficult to prove certain matters such as cheque card frauds, unless it is possible for this to be done from computers'. (Criminal Law Revision Committee, 1972)

The problem of the admissibility of evidence from automatic systems first came to be considered twenty-one years ago (*The Statue of Liberty*, 1968); in the same year specific provision for computer evidence was made in Section 5 of the *Civil Evidence Act 1968* ('CEA'), and similar provision was made for criminal proceedings in Section 69 of the *Police and Criminal Evidence Act 1984* ('PACEA'). The purpose of those statutory provisions is to ensure that computer output is admissible in evidence and the British Government has expressed the view that there 'are no rules relevant to commercial activity in general which would prohibit a commercial firm from keeping all its records in computer readable form (UNCITRAL, 1985).

Source: an updated version of the article which appeared in *Computer Law and Practice*, **6**, pp. 142–8.
Published by Frank Cass & Co. Ltd.
© 1990 Robert Bradgate

However, the relative novelty of computers and electronic systems, and the unfamiliarity of the legal profession and judiciary with them, means that despite the existence of a detailed statutory code designed to ensure the admissibility of computer output, the detailed application of the rules has not yet been ascertained. Moreover, there is a widespread distrust of computers, shared by the general public, and reinforced by the publicity given to viruses, hackers and computer malfunctions. Paper, on which forgeries and alterations can be readily identified, seems reassuringly familiar and reliable. The purpose of this piece is to consider the evidential status of computer output, and, in particular, of EDI messages, in English law.

As noted above, computer output is admissible in evidence, but only where special conditions are satisfied. If those conditions are not satisfied, the computer evidence in question is wholly inadmissible, as underlined by the decision of the Court of Appeal in *R*. v *Harper and R*. v *Minors* (1989). Are special rules for computer evidence necessary and, if so, are the conditions established by the Section 5 CEA and Section 69 PACEA, and the rules made thereunder, appropriate? It will be suggested that the rules of evidence, whilst not prohibiting such computer storage, or the use of EDI, create unnecessary difficulties and thus pose an obstacle to the use of computers in business.

THE LEGAL STATUS OF COMPUTER EVIDENCE

Many commentators (Amory and Poullet, 1987; Kaiser, 1986) have assumed that, in the absence of special legislative provision, computer output would be inadmissible in English law due to the hearsay rule. This view is reinforced by the proximity of the 'computer evidence' provisions in both the CEA and PACEA to those regulating the use of certain classes of hearsay. However, it is suggested that computer output is not necessarily hearsay (Bradgate, 1989). Its status will depend, in each case, on the content of the computer record, the reason for using it in evidence and the way in which it was compiled.

The confusion between hearsay and computer evidence is unfortunate. It seems to have contributed to the decision in *R*. v *Pettigrew* (1980). It may also explain why it was felt necessary to create a special regime for computer evidence. There is ample support for the view that computer output is not *per se* hearsay (*R*. v *Wood,* 1982; *Castle* v *Cross,* 1984; *R*. v *Pettigrew,* 1980; Cross, 1985, p. 43–4) but the point can be confirmed by retreating to first principles. Evidence is hearsay where a statement in court repeats a statement made out of court in order to prove the truth of the content of the out-of-court statement. Thus if a witness repeats in evidence what he heard another person say in order to prove that what that person said was true, (e.g. A says 'I heard B say that C took the money' in order to prove that C did take the money) the evidence is hearsay. Similarly evidence contained in a document is hearsay if the document is produced to prove that statements made in the document are true. The evidence is excluded because the crucial aspect of the evidence – the truth of the out-of-court statement – cannot be tested by cross examination. In the example above, A can be challenged on the accuracy of his recollection, but not on the truth of B's statement. But if the evidence is given in court to prove that the out-of-court statement was made, it is not hearsay: the crucial aspect of A's evidence is now the fact that he heard B's accusation, and he can be cross-examined on that. Similarly, a document produced in court to prove that the document was written is not hearsay.

Applying these principles to computers, computer output is only hearsay where it repeats a statement made out of court by some person, such as the computer operator, in order to prove that the contents of that statement are true. It is not hearsay (a) if no person made the statement contained in the record or (*R* v *Wood,* 1982; *Castle* v *Cross,* 1984; Cross, 1985) (b) where the record is produced simply to prove that the statement was made.

Now consider the application of the hearsay rule to business communications and related disputes. A typical (simple) business transaction will generate several different categories of document. There will be the 'transaction documents' themselves – purchase order and acknowledgement which together form the basis of the agreement and record its essential terms. There will be other documents such as the delivery note and invoice, whose primary function is the transmission of information, but which may also have legal significance. Other documents may be required for administrative purposes: for instance to satisfy the requirements of Customs. Finally the businesses involved in the transaction may keep secondary records, based on the primary transaction documents, such as statements of account, stock records and so on. As a general rule, the transaction documents themselves will not be hearsay if they are adduced to prove the fact of the transaction or its terms. On the other hand, secondary records will be hearsay since, if produced to prove the existence of the transaction they 'testify' to the statement made out of court by the compiler of the record.

If a computer is used simply as an electronic filing cabinet to record details of transactions effected by other means – face to face, by telephone, fax or otherwise – the computer record is a secondary record and thus is hearsay. However, if the transaction is effected by computer–to–computer communication (EDI) then, when submitted, the record of the EDI messages can be treated as the equivalent of the transaction documents.

The position is not entirely free from doubt: it could be argued that if A sends a message to B by EDI the printout from B's machine is a hearsay repetition of the statement made by A's machine, but such an approach seems wholly artificial. Since the bulk of EDI messages are likely to be 'transaction messages', it is submitted that they evade the hearsay rule. Of course, if the EDI system is used to send a message such as 'our customer X says the goods you delivered are defective' that message is hearsay; but it is hearsay because it purports to prove the truth of what X said, not because it was generated by the computer.

Even where computer output is regarded as hearsay, it will generally be admissible in evidence, for the hearsay rule is now subject to a number of exceptions, and, in particular, most business records are admissible (see Section 4, *Civil Evidence Act 1968*; Section 24, *Criminal Justice Act 1988*) provided certain prescribed conditions are satisfied and proper procedures are followed. However, if the above analysis is correct, it follows that computer output is not necessarily hearsay, and that the records of many EDI messages will not be hearsay. It also follows that the question of the admissibility of computer output is separate from the question of the admissibility of hearsay. This has practical as well as theoretical significance. In both civil and criminal proceedings there are statutory provisions dealing specifically with the admissibility of computer output, and separate from the provisions allowing hearsay to be admitted.

In *R.* v *Harper and R.* v Minors (1989) the Court of Appeal held that in criminal cases hearsay computer output must satisfy the requirements of both Section 69 PACEA, concerned with computer output, and the separate provisions (now contained in Section 23–4 Criminal Justice Act 1988 (CJA) replacing Section 68 of PACEA) governing the admissibility of hearsay. The position in civil proceedings is less clear because the relevant provisions – Section 5 CEA, governing computer output, and Sections 2 and 4 governing hearsay – are worded differently, and different views have been expressed as to their interrelationship. The problem arises because Section 5 is worded positively:

> in any civil proceedings a statement contained in a document produced by a computer shall be admissible as evidence of any fact stated therein of which direct oral evidence would be admissible . . .

provided certain conditions are fulfilled (Kelmman and Sizer, 1982; Bradgate, 1988)

In addition, Section 4, dealing with the admissibility of 'second hand' hearsay, is expressed to be 'without prejudice' to the provisions of Section 5. It has therefore been suggested that any computer output which satisfies the requirements of Section 5 is admissible without satisfying the requirements of Section 2 or Section 4, even if it contains hearsay; and that computer output may be admitted under Section 2 or Section 4 even though it fails to meet the requirements of Section 5 (Duggan, 1986; Amory and Poullet, 1987). In contrast Tapper (Cross, 1985, p. 499) argues that the two sets of provisions are separate: computer output must always satisfy Section 5. This view is in line with the apparent policy of the legislation and has the merit of bringing the position in civil cases into line with that in criminal proceedings. It is submitted that it is the better view: as pointed out above, computer output is not necessarily hearsay and its admissibility should, logically, be and considered separately from the hearsay rules. Moreover, the clear statement that Section 4 is 'without prejudice to' the admissibility under Section 5 seems to indicate that evidence which does not satisfy the requirements of Section 4 can nevertheless be admitted under Section 5 provided it is contained in a document produced by computer. This is most unfortunate since the conditions in Section 4 are designed to ensure, so far as possible, accuracy of recording. Section 5 contains no equivalent safeguard (Cross, 1985).

What of non-hearsay? Logic might suggest that all computer output must satisfy the specialist computer provisions (in Section 5 CEA and Section 69 PACEA). However, in *R.* v *Spiby* (1990) the Court of Appeal reached a different conclusion. The facts of *Spiby* were relatively simple. *Spiby* was convicted of being involved in the import of cannabis resin. The evidence against him included a computer printout containing details of telephone calls made from the hotel room of one of the other conspirators in Cherbourg. The computer monitored calls, including the number dialled, in order to calculate the charge for the call. The hotel manager gave evidence that, although he was not a computer engineer, he understood how the machine functioned, that there had been no complaints from other guests about the charges made for telephone calls and that the machine had been functioning satisfactorily during the period in question. On the basis of that evidence, the computer printout was admitted and the defendant was convicted. He appealed on the grounds that the manager's evidence did not satisfy Section 69 PACEA and that the printout should therefore have been excluded.

The crucial factor here was that the computer system was fully automatic: there was no human intervention in the monitoring and recording of numbers dialled. There was therefore no question of the evidence being hearsay. It was real evidence. In two cases decided prior to 1984 (*R* v *Wood,* 1982; *Castle* v *Cross,* 1984; cf *R.* v *Pettigrew,* 1980) it had been held that documents produced by such automated systems could be admitted as real evidence, provided that the machine producing the evidence could be shown to be reliable.

The Court of Appeal held that the distinction between real and hearsay evidence survived the 1984 Act (which it obviously did), and that Section 69 only applied to hearsay evidence. The computer printout in question in this case was therefore admissible as real evidence without complying with the requirements of Section 69. If correct, the decision has the merit of narrowing the ambit of Section 69 and allowing non-hearsay computer output to be used in evidence without complying with its provisions. First, any record made by automatic recording or monitoring systems will be admissible as real evidence without the need to satisfy the requirements of Section 69 PACEA. This would apply, for instance, to the record in a bank's computer of a customer's transaction using an ATM and the customer's PIN. Second, and more signifiantly, the decision may facilitate the use in evidence of EDI messages, and, therefore, the adoption of EDI. Many EDI messages will be transaction messages – purchase orders, acknowledgements and so on. They are likely to be produced in evidence in the context of disputes about the existence of contracts, or the terms of those contracts. In such cases, the EDI message would not be hearsay. According to *Spiby* such messages would therefore be admissible in criminal cases without the need to comply with Section 69. Of course, most disputes arising out of the commercial use of EDI will be civil disputes where the governing statutory provision will be Section 5 CEA. As already noted, Section 5 is worded differently from Section 69 PACEA and so *Spiby* is not a binding precedent. However, the distinction between real evidence and hearsay would appear to be as applicable to civil proceedings as to criminal, suggesting that non-hearsay computer output could be admitted in civil cases without complying with Section 5 CEA. Moreover, insofar as Section 5 is worded differently from Section 69, the different wording appears to favour the admissibility of non-hearsay computer evidence in civil cases. As already noted, Section 69 is exclusionary in effect: evidence which does not satisfy the section is excluded. In contrast, Section 5 is permissive: the section does not appear to exclude evidence which does not satisfy its requirements.

However, the decision is difficult to reconcile with the wording of the 1984 Act. Section 69 makes no mention of hearsay evidence and seems to indicate that all such statements of fact, whether hearsay or not, must satisfy its requirements (Bradgate, 1991). It is even more difficult to reconcile the case with the policy of the 1984 Act for, if *Spiby* is correct, hearsay computer output must satisfy the requirements of both the section governing the use of computer output and the section governing the use of hearsay, whereas other computer output need satisfy neither requirement. The requirements imposed by Section 5 CEA and Section 69 PACEA are concerned with such matters as the operation of the computer, which seems to be equally applicable to hearsay and non-hearsay output, but according to *Spiby*, in the case of non-hearsay computer output it is not even necessary to show the court that the computer was at all times operating properly. If that position is correct, the imposition of an additional restriction on computerized hearsay (i.e. the need to show that the computer was operating properly) is almost impossible to justify or understand.

A second caveat must be that the law of evidence, and hearsay in particular, is notoriously difficult. In many cases it may be difficult to categorize a particular statement as hearsay or otherwise: often the categorization will depend on the purpose for which the evidence is adduced. The *Spiby* decision may therefore be difficult to apply in practice.

The status of non-hearsay computer output therefore cannot be taken as settled by *Spiby*. In any case, it is clear that hearsay output is admissible only if it satisfies the statutory requirements established under Section 5 CEA, in civil proceedings, or Section 69 of PACEA 1984, in criminal proceedings. The use of computer evidence is thus subject to extra conditions, not applied to other kinds of evidence. Why should this be so? The use of computers for the storage of information is probably close to being the norm; their use for the transmission of a business communications is becoming increasingly common. If a litigant seeks to produce a letter in evidence he can do so freely, unless he seeks to prove the truth of a factual statement contained in it (in which case it is hearsay). The letter can be used to prove that it was sent, that the sender and recipient were as identified in the letter, the date of the communication and the terms of any transaction effected by it. If his opponent seeks to challenge the accuracy of the letter as a record, he must adduce evidence in his turn to contradict it, and the question becomes one for the court to assess the weight of the two sides' evidence. But if that letter is transmited by EDI, the litigant seeking to rely on it can only adduce it if he first shows that the statutory conditions for admissibility are satisfied.

A secondary record, as defined above, compiled and stored on paper, is hearsay but is admissible if certain statutory conditions are fulfilled. Broadly these are designed to ensure the accuracy of the transmission of the information on which the record is based and the accuracy of the recording of that information by the compiler of the record. Generally, if the record was compiled in the ordinary course of a business, it will be admissible. The opposing litigant may challenge the accuracy of the record or allege that it has been altered, but he must at least adduce evidence to put the accuracy of the record in question. If he does so, again the court will balance the conflicting evidence. But if the record is kept instead on computer, the litigant seeking to adduce it must fulfill a second set of conditions. Regardless of any challenge, he must satisfy the court that the computer was at all times working satisfactorily. His opponent need adduce no evidence: he can sit back and, if the conditions are not satisfied, ask the court to exclude the record as inadmissible. It matters not that the hearsay conditions are satisfied and that the information recorded on the computer accurately records the transaction in question.

THE CONDITIONS FOR ADMISSIBILITY

The conditions applying in civil and criminal proceedings (Section 5 CEA and Section 69 PACEA respectively) are broadly similar. They are intended to establish a foundation upon which to admit the computer evidence by satisfying the court that the evidence is authentic and sufficiently reliable to be admitted. They deserve examination. Section 5 provided that 'in any civil proceedings a statement contained in a document produced by a computer shall be admissible as evidence of any fact stated therein of which direct oral evidence would be admissible . . .' provided:

1. the document was prepared during a period over which the computer was regularly used to process information for the purpose of any activities regularly carried on over that period;
2. information of the kind contained in the document, or from which it is derived, was over that period regularly supplied to the computer in the ordinary course of those activities;
3. throughout the period the computer was operating properly, or, if not, the reason for any malfunction or closedown was not such as to affect the accuracy of the document;
4. the information contained in the document reproduces or is derived from information supplied to the computer in the ordinary course of the activities for which it is used.

The litigant wishing to use computer output in evidence must satisfy the court that these conditions are fulfilled, either by oral evidence or by a certificate signed by a person occupying 'a responsible position in relation to the management of the activities for the purposes of which the computer was used' at the time the document was produced (not at the time the information was recorded), and must serve on all other parties to the litigation notice of his intention to adduce that evidence (see RSC 0 38 r22 and CCR 014 in Bradgate, 1988).

A number of criticisms can be levelled at the requirements of Section 5. The section is badly worded (Duggan has described it as 'cumbersome') and it contains a number of ambiguities. There is ample scope for a number of technical arguments over the meaning of its provisions, and it has been suggested that, although there is so far no reported case on the section, in a suitable case involving high stakes, some or all of those points could be taken and vital evidence stored in or produced by a computer might be excluded (VERDICT, 1987). It has also been suggested that where information is transmited from one computer to another Section 5 does not make output from the second computer admissible (UNICITRAL, 1985). The reason for this view is not clear, unless it is argued that the output of the second machine is a hearsay record of the message transmitted by the first, which cannot fulfill the conditions for admissibility of hearsay under Section 2 or Section 4 CEA. If correct, records of EDI messages would never be admissible. However, it seems to run counter to the wording of Section 5(3) which anticipates the storage or processing of information by a series of computers.

More fundamentally, it is suggested that the section addresses the wrong issues, with the result that it may exclude evidence which ought to be admitted, and admit that which should be excluded. The following points are worth noting.

1. 'Computer' is defined as 'any device for storing and processing information' (Section 5(6)). The implication of this, coupled with the wording of Section 5, seems to be that documents produced by a word processor are only admissible provided they satisfy the conditions laid down by Section 5. On the other hand it may be argued that the definition refers only to hardware and excludes software; or possibly that it includes the operating system but not applications software run on the system. If this is correct, defects in software do not affect the admissibility of computer output, even though it might be expected that software 'bugs' would be more likely than hardware failure to affect the accuracy of a document (*Eurodynamics Systems plc* v *General Automation Ltd,* 1988).
2. It may be that the section excludes evidence of matters known only to the computer, such as the system's real time clock record on a message.
   (a) The information in the computer document must reproduce or be derived from information 'supplied to' the computer, which would seem to exclude information recorded by automated systems.
   (b) The computer document is admissible as evidence of 'any fact stated therein of which direct oral evidence would be admissible'. It is not clear whether this means that there must be an identifiable person who could have given evidence of the matters recorded, or merely that the facts contained in the document are such that if there were a person with such knowledge he or she could give evidence (i.e. excluding opinion, evidence protected by privilege etc.).

3. 'Garbage in, garbage out', but although Section 5 lays down stringent conditions as to the operation of the 'computer' they fail to address important issues which might be expected to affect the reliability of computer records. The computer must have been 'regularly used' for activities 'regularly carried on'. 'Regularly' is not defined; there seems to be no good reason why output from a computer used for a 'one off' task should be excluded, provided the system can be shown to have been working accurately at the time in question. In contrast, both the means of supply of the information to the computer, and the accuracy of that initial input are ignored, although in deciding what weight to attach to the evidence, the court is directed to have regard to all the circumstances and, in particular, the contemporaneity of the recording of the data with the events described and the motive of any person to misrepresent the facts recorded: Section 6. Moreover, as noted above, the wording of the section seems to undermine the important safeguards contained in Section 4 and designed to promote accuracy in the initial compilation of the record. Similarly the requirements do not seem to address issues which might be considered to be of fundamental importance, such as the security of the system.

4. There seems to be some confusion in the legislation as to what exactly is the evidence in question: Section 5 refers to a document produced by a computer; it is not clear if this refers to the printout on which the evidence will normally be presented to the court, or to the record stored on disk or in the computer's memory.[1] The better view is that the relevant document is the computer readable original; the printout is a copy which is admissible to prove the contents of the original by virtue of Sections 6(1) and 10(2). This confusion may derive from the fact that the original proposal of the Criminal Law Reform Committee (Cmnd 2964) which preceded the passing of the CEA was that there was no need for special provision to be made for computer evidence; instead it should be treated as any other document. Thus the definition of 'document' was drafted sufficiently widely to include computer records in magnetic media.

The real problem is that the conditions in Section 5 which govern the admissibility of computer evidence are really concerned with the weight which ought to be attached to that evidence. It should be borne in mind that if one of the conditions is not fulfilled: for instance if there has been a malfunction so that the 'computer' was not operating 'properly' at all material times, then the evidence produced by the computer is not admissible: it is wholly excluded. Suppose that a litigant wishes to put in evidence a stock record. If that record is compiled manually, it will be admissible under Section 4 CEA, provided the compiler and the persons supplying the information on which it is based were acting under a duty. It makes no difference that the record is a 'one off', and the record is still admissible even if another party shows that it has been altered, or that unauthorized persons have had access to it. In contrast, if the same record is compiled by computer, it must be shown that the computer was 'regularly' used for that function: a 'one-off' record is inadmissible.

Despite these criticisms, Parliament followed the example of Section 5 and introduced a similar regime for computer evidence in criminal cases in Section 69 PACEA. It must be conceded that Section 69 is better drafted than Section 5. No attempt is made to define 'computer', tacit recognition no doubt of the fact that the pace of technological change would probably render any attempted definition obsolete before it could ever be tested in court. What is a 'computer' must therefore be left to the common sense of the judiciary, and as computers become more familiar this seems the wisest course, although no doubt wherever there is scope and an opportunity to exclude damning evidence, any number of technical and philosophical arguments as to the meaning of 'computer' will abound.

Another advantage of Section 69 is that it is couched in negative terms, making it instantly clear that evidence which does not satisfy its requirements is inadmissible and avoiding the difficulties posed by the CEA with regard to the relationship between the computer and hearsay provisions. However, Section 69 follows the lead of Section 5 in imposing conditions on the admissibility of computer evidence. It provides that 'In any proceedings, a statement in a document produced by a computer shall not be admissible as evidence of any fact stated therein unless it is shown

(a) that there are no reasonable grounds for believing that the statement is inaccurate because of improper use of the computer;
(b) that at all material times the computer was operating properly or, if not, that any respect in which it was not operating properly or was out of operation was not such as to affect the production of the document or the accuracy of its contents; and
(c) that any other conditions established by rules of court are satisfied.

Note that the person seeking to rely on the computer evidence (normally the prosecution) is faced with the burden of proving a negative: he must satisfy the court that there are no reasonable grounds for believing that the record is inaccurate due to improper operation. 'Improper operation' is not defined: presumably it would encompass hacking, but were that the only misuse covered by the words 'improper use' one would expect a phrase such as 'unauthorized use' to be used instead. Arguably, therefore, 'improper use' extends more widely to cover all forms of misuse. If this is correct, there appears to be considerable overlap between requirements (a) and (b) (it is interesting that there is no equivalent of requirement (a) in Section 5 and its related rules). There is no requirement that the other party adduce any evidence to challenge its accuracy. Quite how that negative could be proved is difficult to say: presumably a litigant would have to come to court armed with a complete description of the computer security system and a detailed log of its operations.

Thankfully the position has been somewhat ameliorated by a four-line comment by the Divisional Court of the Queens Bench Division in a 24-page judgement in *R.* v *Governor of Pentonville Prison ex p. Osman* (1989). The applicant, seeking habeas corpus to challenge his detention under the *Fugitive Offenders Act 1967,* challenged the evidence against him on a number of grounds. The evidence related to a complex series of frauds and part of it was contained in computer printouts of corporate and financial records. It was argued that the printouts were inadmissible because the Prosecution had failed to prove the proper operation of the computers, as required by Section 69. Lloyd, LJ dealt with the point briefly: 'Where a lengthy computer printout contains no internal evidence of malfunction and is retained, for example, by a bank or a stockbroker as part of its records it may be legitimate to infer that the computer which made the record was functioning correctly (see p. 727). Such a robust, and eminently sensible, approach provides some comfort. The reference to banks and stockbrokers should perhaps be read in the light of the facts of *Osman* where the records in question had been produced by such bodies. There seems no reason why the same principle should not apply to other records kept by a business in the ordinary course of its business. Note however that Lloyd LJ directed his comments to requirement (b); it is to be hoped that in future cases the courts can be persuaded to adopt a similar approach to the 'no improper use' requirement.

WHAT IS SPECIAL ABOUT COMPUTER EVIDENCE?

Can the imposition of special conditions on the admissibility of computer output be justified? What is it that is special about computer-generated documents that distinguishes them from their paper equivalents? It is submitted that the principle difference is in the ability to authenticate the document and assert its accuracy, and this problem can be seen to have three facets.

First, data stored in computer may be altered: by deliberate or negligent human action, whether by an authorized or unauthorized operator, or accidentally due to system failure or environmental factors relating to poor storage of magnetic media. Of course, paper-based records are also susceptible to alteration or deterioration. Where it is alleged that such alteration has taken place, the paper document remains admissible and the challenge goes to the question of its weight as evidence, to be decided on the basis of the evidence called to prove falsification or authenticity. In contrast, unless it can be shown that there is no chance of unauthorized use of a computer system, or of system failure, the same document stored on computer is inadmissible. It might be argued that such alteration is easier to detect in the case of paper than in the case of information stored on magnetic media, but whilst such an argument might be seen to justify the imposition of conditions relating to the security of computer systems and the storage of magnetic media, those issues are not directly addressed by Section 5 CEA or Section 69 PACEA. Even if system security is encompassed by 'improper use' in Section 69, there is no equivalent provision in Section 5; and if it is argued that the reference to 'proper operation' in Section 5 covers unauthorized access, the presence of a similar 'proper operation' requirement in Section 69 would seem to render the 'improper use' requirement otiose.

Second, in some situations there may be doubts about the accuracy of the original recording of information by the computer. Insofar as such doubts reflect concern for the accuracy of human recollection and the transmission of information, they apply equally to paper-based systems, and are addressed by the hearsay rules in Section 4 CEA and Section 24 CJA. One of the oddities of Section 5 CEA, as noted above, is that on one interpretation it allows the safeguards of Section 4 to be bypassed where a computer is used to compile and store a record. Where a computer is used, there may be a second cause for concern in that computer malfunction or operator error may cause the information to be recorded inaccurately. The proper operation requirements can be seen as addressing this problem.

Third, electronic data storage and interchange systems differ from their paper equivalents significantly with respect to the authentication of the record. A paper document can be authenticated by its author appending a signature. A number of ways have been suggested for authenticating EDI messages by electronic means (Heinriksen, 1983; Reed, 1990), and it is submitted that there is no good reason why such electronic signatures should not be equated to manual signatures for the purposes of legal rules attaching special significance to signed documents (Bradgate, 1989, p. 30; Millard, 1989). However, it must be conceded that electronic signatures based on smart cards, PINs or passwords, as opposed to biometric systems such as finger and palm printing and retinal scanning, are less secure than manual signatures simply because a PIN etc. can be passed on by one person to another.

However, authentication is, or should be, an entirely different question from admissibility and the fact that foolproof authentication of a computer record is rarely possible is no reason for imposing conditions on the admissibility of computer evidence. To put it rather crudely, a litigant faced with a printout of an EDI message is perfectly entitled to say 'That is not what I sent' or 'That didn't come from me' and challenge his opponent to prove its authenticity, but if authenticity can be proved the record should be admissible.

THE APPROACH IN OTHER JURISDICTIONS

In any case, the requirements established by Section 5 CEA and Section 69 PACEA do not purport to address the issue of authentication. That leaves only authenticity and, as noted above, there appears to be no good reason for treating computer records differently from paper documents. The treatment of computer evidence in other jurisdictions is instructive. In many civil law jurisdictions, all evidence is admissible unless specifically excluded (UNCITRAL, 1985; Amory and Poullet, 1987). A computer record may not always be acceptable as proof of the creation of an obligation, but that is a separate matter. In the United States there is no single rule but the general trend is to treat computer records as any other business record. Rules 803–4 of the *Uniform Rules of Evidence* allow the use in evidence of records provided (1) they were compiled in the ordinary course of business and reasonably contemporaneously with the events described and (2) no other evidence suggests that the evidence is un-reliable.[2] Other factors, such as the delay between recording and printout, and proper operation of the system, go to weight. In Australia, whilst some states (e.g. New South Wales) have applied specific rules to computer records, others have adopted a broader approach and allow computer records to be admitted in evidence in the same way as any other record produced in the course of a business. Amongst those states which have adopted specific legislation, some have simply adopted Section 5 CEA as a model,[3] whilst others have drafted their own provisions. Thus S. Australia's *Evidence Act* of 1979, whilst making special provision for computer output, at least improves considerably on the English legislation, in ways which suggest that the draftsmen had at least some awareness of the problems likely to affect computer operation. For instance, the conditions for admissibility take account of the manner of preparation of data for the computer (which must be 'systematic'); 'alterations to the mechanism or processes' of the computer which might be expected to affect the accuracy of the output; records of any alteration to the system must be kept; this would seem to take account of possible problems caused by software upgrades and patches; and the security of the system against unauthorized use.

CONCLUSION

Is a special regime for computer evidence justified? Computers are just one means of storing and transmitting information. They differ from traditional methods, based on paper, in that the means of both transmission and storage, using electromagnetic impulses, are intangible and even ephemeral. It has been shown that computer 'documents' are not necessarily hearsay, but the approach of English law has been to treat them as if they were, by excluding their evidence unless specified conditions are fulfilled. The reason for adopting this approach in the case of hearsay is the inherent unreliability of the evidence where the original maker of the reported statement cannot be cross-examined on it in court. Of course, nor can the computer be cross-examined, but to anthropomorphize the computer in this way borders on the superstitious. Provided it is used correctly there is no reason why documents produced by computer should be any less reliable than any others. Where the accuracy of the record is challenged, the human operator can be cross-examined; in the absence of such challenge, why should the evidence not be freely admissible?

The adoption of a special regime for 'computer evidence' necessitates the drawing of some fine distinctions. Why should a message sent by EDI be regarded as inherently less reliable than one sent by fax or telex? The only difference is in the storage media. To make and keep hard (paper) copies of EDI messages is to lose one of the main benefits of EDI, but if a contemporaneous print-out of the EDI message is made, there is no difference between the media, save possibly that the EDI message may have been generated automatically by the sender's computer. Equally, are the computer evidence rules to be applied to documents produced by word-processor? If so, how is the law to treat an electronic typewriter with limited memory? Or a till receipt produced by an electronic cash register?

Insofar as a special regime for computer evidence is justified, it is submitted that questions of accuracy of reproduction should be regarded as going to the weight of the evidence, not its admissibility. The distinction between admissibility and weight is an important one. Admissibility is a matter of law and is therefore a matter for the judge in a jury trial. Weight, on the other hand, is an issue for the jury in a criminal trial (Cross, 1985; p. 59) (subject to direction by the judge) and a decision on weight will be difficult to challenge on appeal. By making the admissibility of computer output subject to conditions which are really concerned with the weight of the evidence, the UK legislation places a double hurdle in the path of the litigant: even if the evidence satisfies the conditions and is admissible, the arbiter of fact may choose to disbelieve it in the face of contrary evidence. Even if a special regime is conceded, the existing UK legislation is open to criticism not only on the grounds of technicalities of drafting, but on the grounds that it asks the wrong questions.

Left to themselves the judiciary might have accommodated computer output within the existing rules of evidence without too much difficulty. Instead a special statutory regime was created. *Osman* suggests that the judiciary might be able to rescue litigants from some of the problems created by that regime. However, *Pettigrew* offers a caution against relying on the inherent flexibility of the common law. Last year saw the 21st anniversary of the law's first attempts to deal with computer evidence. Computers are grown up. Now that their use is so widespread there is a strong case for abandoning the special regime in favour of the approach originally advocated by the Law Reform Committee; but if we must have a special regime for computers, at least let it be one which asks the right questions.

NOTES

1. The definition of 'document' in Section 10 is capable of encompassing both.
2. The rules seem to be based on the decision in *King v Murdock Acceptance Corp.* 222 So.2d 393 (1969). The Rules have been adopted for use in the federal courts and in a majority of state courts.
3. Victoria, *Evidence Act 1958*, Section 55B; Queensland, *Evidence Act 1977*, Section 95.

REFERENCES

Amory and Poullet (1987) *Computers in the Law of Evidence – A Comparative Approach in Civil and Common Law Systems*, CLP 114 (*Note*: they do not appear to distinguish between hearsay and non-hearsay computer output).

Bradgate, R. (1988) 'Evidential problems of new technology in civil litigation', *Law Society Gazette*, **85** (6), p. 12.

Bradgate, R. (1989) Evidential Issues of EDI, in *EDI and the Law* (ed. Walden I.) Blenheim – Online Publications, pp. 9–14.

Bradgate, R. (1991) *Computer Law and Practice* (not yet published)

Castle v Cross (1984) Crim. L. R. 682.

Criminal Law Revision Committee (1972), *11th Report of the Criminal Law Revision Committee,* Cmnd 4991, para 259.

Cross, Sir R. (1985) *Cross on Evidence* (6th edn edited by Tapper C.), Butterworths.

Duggan, M. (1986) 'Computer Evidence', *Litigation,* **5,** 293.

Eurodynamics Systems plc v *General Automation Ltd.* (1988) (unreported), a decision of Steyn, J. in the High Court.

Heinriksen (1983) 'Signature and Evidence' (U.N. ECE doc TRADE WP.4/R98) in *Legal Acceptance of International Trade Data Transmitted by Electronic Means,* Special Paper No. 3 NORDIPRO, Universitets forlaget, pp. 40–101.

Kaiser (1986) *Evidential repercussions of Automated teller Machines,* CLP November/December, pp. 57–8.

Kelmman and Sizer (1982) *The Computer in Court,* Gower.

Millard (1989) *Contractual Issues of EDI.* In *EDI and the Law* (ed. Walden), Blenheim – Online Publications, p. 47.

Reed, C. (1990) *Authenticating Electronic Mail Messages: Some Evidential Problems,* 52 MLR 694.

R. v *Governor of Pentonville Prison ex p. Osman* (1989) 3 All E.R. 701.

R. v *Harper and R.* v *Minors* (1989) 2 All E.R. 208.

R. v *Pettigrew* (1980) 71 Cr. App R. 39.

R. v *Wood* (1982) 76 Cr APp rep 23.

The Statue of Liberty (recording made by automatic radar tracking system) (1968) 1 WLR 739.

UNCITRAL (1985) Response to UNCITRAL questionnaire on the legal value of computer records, *Report A/CN.9/265,* presented to the 18th session of UNCITRAL in Vienna.

VERDICT (1987) *VERDICT Report.*

Chapter

15 Professional negligence and the reasonableness defence in financial-legal expert systems: a developers' perspective
Vijay Mital and Les Johnson

Legal implications of professionals relying on expert systems have been extensively studied by analysts who have considered the 'macro' issues such as whether product liability can be invited for loss resulting from errors in expert systems, and apportionment of liability. These macro analyses do not distinguish programming errors from what we call 'errors of reasoning'. The latter errors may be considered to be advertent on the part of developers and/or user-professionals; may potentially be directly compared with the reasoning ascribable to a reasonably competent professional; and cannot be removed merely by better quality assurance in the sense prevalent in software engineering.

In this chapter we consider the mechanisms by which a court may examine errors of reasoning in expert systems used to assist professionals working in certain areas of financial services ('the financial-legal domain'). Our analysis of the 'micro' issues of liability shows that the advertent nature of errors of reasoning makes it difficult to argue that using the best possible quality assurance methods during development is sufficient to make the reliance on an expert system reasonable. However, certain valuable defences that are available to professionals acting unaided can be made out even when expert systems are employed as part of the reasoning process, though these defences will be disabled if certain conceptual

Source: *Proceedings of the Second National Conference on Law, Computers and Artificial Intelligence, 15–16 November 1990*, University of Exeter.
© 1990 Vijay Mital and Les Johnson

structures of the knowledge of professionals are not distinctively maintained in the knowledge-base. As such, opacity of a knowledge-base assists, rather than hinders, a plaintiff in establishing professional negligence. These considerations inevitably steer developers towards particular modelling paradigams.

INTRODUCTION

Financial services organizations are beginning to use expert systems ('ES') to assist professionals giving advice to or carrying out discretionary tasks for clients (Anon., 1988; Breeze, 1990). The *raison d'être* of these systems, which are becoming increasingly capable and sophisticated (Akelsen *et al.*, 1989; Clarke, 1989), is either substantially to supplement the skills of user professionals with knowledge obtained from others, or to take over a significant part of the reasoning task of the users. The verification process cannot be expected to remove all errors from a complex knowledge-base. It is predictable that some purported solutions which are wrong, but not obviously wrong, will be relied upon by users and their clients will suffer loss as a consequence.

Legal implications of errors in ES have been studied by a number of analysts (Reed, 1987; Frank, 1988; Turley, 1988; Cannataci, 1989; Cook and Whittaker, 1989; Tapper, 1989; Mykytyn *et al.*, 1990). They have looked at the 'macro' issues of liability, such as:

1. The branches of law under which an action may be founded.
2. Whether ES may be classified as 'goods' or 'products' on the one hand, or 'services' on the other, the former case potentially inviting strict liability. (This issue has caused the most controversy because an ES may, alone or with the intervention of a human, provide what would be called a service if a human provided it unaided; yet such a system may be mass-marketed in a manner similar to tangible products.)
3. The apportionment of liability between the various parties involved in the development, marketing and use of ES.

The macro analyses do not address certain issues of liability that are peculiar to those ES that attempt to emulate the reasoning process of professionals (or otherwise replicate its results) in domains where *empirically testing the result of a decision-making process is not the sole manner of legally judging the standard of the expertise used to arrive at that result*. It will be shown that such an ES is likely to be judged against the standard of the reasonably competent professional. However, the existence of a certain kind of error – 'errors of reasoning' – will make it difficult to argue that employing the best possible quality assurance methods during development is sufficient to make reliance on the ES reasonable.

Our analysis of the 'micro' issues of liability will involve studying the mechanisms by which a court may examine errors of reasoning and compare them with the supposed reasoning of what are regarded as reasonably competent professionals. It will be shown that certain valuable defences available to professionals acting unaided are still available where an ES is relied upon and there is an error of reasoning. However, these defences may be disabled if certain conceptual structures of the knowledge of professionals are not distinctively maintained in the knowledge-base by the use of second generation architectures.

LIABILITY FOR ERRORS OF REASONING IN FINANCIAL-LEGAL ES

Professionals in the domain of concern typically carry out tasks such as the following:

1. Making recommendations to a client aimed at achieving his financial goals, keeping his tax situation in mind.
2. Discretionary portfolio management, keeping track of changes in client's circumstances.
3. Monitoring of transactions for compliance with an organization's adopted interpretation of regulations governing its conduct with customers.

The expertise in these tasks is partly constituted by a knowledge of human affairs, partly by a knowledge of the financial environment and available financial services ('products'), and partly by a knowledge of the governing laws. The domain experts are professionals and have an expertise distinct from that of accountants and solicitors, though there is some overlap of function.[1] Hence we term the domain 'the financial-legal domain'.[2]

To see whether courts will impose strict or fault-based liability, it is sufficient to consider the cases most likely to occur in practice:

1. The case of a client seeking to recover from a financial services organization ('the FSO'), a professional employed by him/her which used the system.
2. The case where the system is developed outside the FSO and a client of the FSO seeks to make the developer organization ('the DO') liable; the contributors of knowledge are part of the DO.

The situation of the FSO and DO *inter se* is not considered because it is likely to be well regulated by means of contractual limitations of liability which may be effective given the relative positions of the parties.

RECOVERING FROM THE FSO

It would be unusual for a contract to make the FSO liable irrespective of fault. Nor will such a term be implied because a professional warrants no more than that he will use reasonable care and skill (*Greaves & Co.* v. *Baynham, Meikle & Partners*; *La Rossa* v. *Scientific Design Co.*). In most common law jurisdictions, the implied duty is virtually identical to the reasonableness demanded in the tort of negligent performance of service (Feldthusen, 1984). As such, ignoring the difficulties in invoking tortious liability when a contract exists, it makes little difference whether the action is framed in tort or contract. If liability is sought to be founded in the breach of a statutory duty, it is unlikely that the reasonableness test will be excluded. For instance, the various rules and regulations published by regulatory bodies pursuant to the Financial Services Act 1986 import the common law concept of reasonableness by the use of words such as 'reasonable grounds for believing that the transaction is suitable' and 'using reasonable care' (Lownicka and Powell, 1987).

Considerations of product liability are not relevant as between the client and the FSO. In an analogous situation it was said that the 'essence of the relationship between a hospital and its patients does not relate essentially to any product or piece of equipment it uses but to the professional services it provides' (*Silverhart* v. *Mount Zion Hospitals*, cited in Godes (1987).

RECOVERING FROM THE SYSTEM DEVELOPER

If the ES is mass-marketed, then there is a distinct possibility that the law relating to defects in products will apply (Frank, 1988; Cannataci, 1989; Cook and Whittaker, 1989). Equally so if the ES is said to be a custom-development but is essentially an altered version of a mass-marketed system (Birnbaum, 1988).

Assuming that a financial-legal ES is regarded as a 'product', fault is still the basis of liability under English common law, though the standard may be higher than in the case of provision of services. The Consumer Protection Act 1987, Part I of which is meant to implement the EC Directive of 25 July 1985, does not apply in cases where there is no risk of physical damage or injury. In the USA strict liability is rarely applied in cases of purely economic loss (Tapper, 1989, p. 256). Also, as will be shown later, the most powerful policy argument against a negligence standard, namely that the complexity of ES makes it difficult for an ordinary plaintiff to prove negligence (Godes, 1987; Birnbaum, 1988), does not generally apply in the case of financial-legal ES.

In any case, if it ever does become clear that treatment as a 'product' will import strict liability, developers will surely restrict themselves to one-off custom-developments: 'The easy answers are the extremes: ... a custom made expert system developed specifically for one user would most likely be subject to a negligence standard' (Turley, 1988).

ADVERTENT NATURE OF ERRORS OF REASONING

Financial-legal ES attempt to emulate (or otherwise replicate the results of) the supposed reasoning process of professionals. Some of the errors in such ES may have their origin in the system architecture, which may not fit the conceptual structures of the professionals' knowledge; some others may originate from the developers' or contributing experts' lack of appreciation of the richness of the expertise. We call these kinds of errors 'errors of reasoning' because:

1. They may be *advertent* in the sense that the developers and contributing experts may be aware of the kind of knowledge that the knowledge-base embodies, but may have taken a conscious decision that the embodied knowledge is adequate for operational purposes.
2. They can rarely be removed simply by a better quality control process in the sense prevalent in software engineering.

The court may hold in the case of errors of reasoning that the taking of the best available quality assurance measures during system development is not sufficient to make reliance on such systems reasonable. However, it is still possible to avail of certain valuable defences that are normally available to human professionals under the reasonableness test.

THE REASONABLENESS TEST

Reasonableness is a complex concept, varying substantially in scope and standard according to the legal and factual context in which fault-based liability is sought to be established. Still, we need to characterize certain notions and draw out some general principles, albeit at the expense of rigour.

Financial-legal decision-making aims at achieving a qualitative goal such as providing for inheritance tax liability or altering a portfolio to take maximum advantage of rising interest rates. If the decision-making does not adequately achieve the qualitative goal the path taken to make the decision has to be investigated to see if the skills employed corresponded to the requisite standard. As no direct test of skills is normally available, a *notional* peer review is applied to see whether the standards employed in similar situations by reasonably competent professionals of equal standing have been met. The distinction between what professionals actually do in practice and what the court thinks they ought to do is frequently blurred because it is the court that decides who is reasonably competent and that decision may well not select practitioners of average competence.

The test is relatively stringent as to the skills employed in appraising real-world facts. Widespread disagreement is not countenanced and the decision needs to conform to that which would be taken by a *majority* of professionals (*Chapman* v. *Walton*). However, skills in applying financial and legal knowledge to world facts are treated differently. Financial services organizations have different market positions and perspectives, and their interest in the outcome of problem-solving in identical factual situations can vary fundamentally. The law recognizes commercial realities to an extent, and it is normally sufficient that a *respectable minority* would do as the professional in question did. This is particularly true in cases of forecasts as to the movements of a volatile market (*Stafford* v. *Conti Commodity Services Ltd*).

MISSING NARROWLY IS EXCUSED, AIMING TO MISS IS NOT

Around the recommendations that are considered to be acceptably achieving some qualitative goal there lies a 'defendable penumbra' of recommendations that are justifiable in the sense that it is difficult to conclude that they are actually unreasonable. However, the presence of the defendable penumbra should not be thought of as a licence to err. It is essential that a professional is not biased and considers all the relevant facts of the situation before him.

It will be obvious that an allegation of aiming to miss is far easier to establish in the case of an ES, where it is predictable that a particular result will be repeated if the relevant facts recur, than in the case of a human whose pattern of behaviour needs to be studied over several transactions in order to arrive at the same conclusion. It is possible to lose the protection of the defendable penumbra if the embodied heuristics are such that a particular subset of relevant facts is sufficient to trigger a solution within the defendable penumbra, thereby excluding from consideration some of the relevant facts.

DELEGATION OF DUTY AND REASONABLENESS

The financial-legal profession is not *individually* regulated in the UK (unlike medicine and accountancy), and it is generally possible to delegate a part of the task to another employee of the organization to which the professional belongs.[3] However, the fact of delegation to a human agent does not diminish the standard of service reasonably expected by the client (Dugdale and Stanton, 1989, p. 262). An ES cannot stand in a better position than a human agent, and the client is reasonably entitled to expect the same minimum standard of skills. Conversely, unless a representation to that effect has been made, it is unreasonable for a client to expect a higher standard from a system assisting a professional than expected of a professional acting unaided (Willick, 1985).

TESTING A FINANCIAL-LEGAL KNOWLEDGE BASE FOR REASONABLENESS

For purposes of illustrating the relevant principles, it is sufficient to consider the following case:

The advice to a client originates wholly from an ES, the user-professional conveying it unamended. It is *admitted* that the advice was not capable of achieving the requisite qualitative goals and that the client suffered a loss as a result. The defence contends that the skills employed corresponded to the standard of a reasonably competent professional and that the error of reasoning made by the ES was such as would be excused if made by a human professional.

From the point of view of establishing reasonableness, this is probably the worst-case scenario because the professional wholly relies on the ES. Besides, it is simple to study because the *actual* chain of reasoning can be fully reconstructed by examining the knowledge-base alone (assuming that the relevant version of the system is still available, or that a proof-trace of the relevant recommendation session was preserved).

The court needs to take evidence as to the reasoning process employed by the ES. By analogy with the practice in computer copyright cases, a court may receive all such evidence as may reveal the structure of the system as well as its behaviour under particular stimuli, for the matter is directly at issue.

For the purpose of comparing with the workings of the ES the court needs to know the reasoning process of a reasonably competent professional. But does the court refer to the reasoning that is internal to the professional and which may, as some believe, be accessed by scientific psychology? Or is the court interested only in a rational reconstruction of reasoning through a process of argumentation in which the primary premises are (1) the steps that the witnesses who are regarded as reasonably competent say they would take; and (2) the justifications or rationalizations given by the witnesses for taking those steps? The answers to these questions are crucial because a knowledge engineer needs to know the nature of the paradigmatic reasoning against which an ES developed by him will be judged.

NOT INTERNAL MENTAL STATES

It must be made clear that in our chosen scenario the relevant reasoning employed in providing the questioned service can be wholly reconstructed by examining the knowledge-base alone. As such we are not concerned with the debate between the state of mind theory of negligence, which would make the state of mind of indifference and anxious care relevant, and the conduct theory, which considers these states of mind to be inconsequential.[4] There is no equivalent of the state of mind theory of negligence in the case of the reasonably competent professional who is a creature of the law. It is highly unlikely that evidence of scientific-psychologists and others who claim to be able to discover the internal workings or cognitive structures of the human mind can be admitted to elucidate the reasoning process of the reasonably competent professional, particularly in a domain where motor skills are not an essential part of the means of performing professional tasks. The court is interested in the exercise of professional skills by this mythical being only in so far as it is manifested in his conduct. It is the deviation from this gold standard of conduct that forms an element of negligent performance of service. Of course, the court may still use language that may be taken by a lay man to mean that internal states of the mind were being referred to. For instance, having assessed the evidence of witnesses who are regarded as reasonably competent, the court might conclude that:

1. 'In recommending a low-risk low-growth investment a reasonably competent professional is *guided* by the fact that the client is near retirement age.'
2. 'The reasonably competent professional does not *consider* the fact that some products do not result in his obtaining a commission.'

In the absence of evidence of scientific experts regarding the supposed internal workings of the human mind, the court is doing no more than ascribing a paradigmatic reasoning by assessing the rationalizations or justifications given by witnesses for the steps that they (or other competent professionals) would take in a particular situation. These rationalizations would consist of a description of the facts taken into consideration and one or more of the following:

1. The dedutive rules applied.
2. The defeasible principles applied.
3. The examples which were followed by direct application, or from which an analogy was made using certain relevant criteria.[5]

If advantage is to be taken of the defences available to human professionals acting unaided, it will be necessary for the defence to point out the particular error in the reasoning of the ES which is claimed to be excusable and relate it to some aspect of the ascribed reasoning process of the reasonably competent professional. However, this may be very difficult if the knowledge-base simply contains the heuristic knowledge acquired by the use of methodologies commonly employed in domains in which there is no legal reasoning element.

ADJUSTING KNOWLEDGE ACQUISITION METHODOLOGIES

Most knowledge acquisition methodologies are aimed at eliciting the so-called 'authentic' reasoning (Johnson, 1983). This involves a protocol analysis in which 'subjects are studied while they are in the process of solving problems . . . [t]hey are asked to report their problem-solving goals and the data they are considering at each point in time, but *are asked not to rationalise or to justify their actions*' (Musen, 1989, our emphasis). The ES community well recognizes that the acquisition methodologies generally dismiss the kind of explanation of his reasoning that a professional produces in his testimony when negligent performance of service is at issue (Gruber, 1989, p. 215).

The standard knowledge acquisition methodologies are not capable of being used in an unamended form in domains in which there is a pervasive normative element, i.e. where much significance is paid to what ought to be done and to the rationalizations or justifications given by professionals. In adversarial or contentious legal reasoning the normative element is paramount; however, the problem of knowledge acquisition is not encountered by developers of legal ES because they seek primarily to represent the formally recorded legal knowledge with a minimal heuristic element (Susskind, 1987). The financial-legal domain is a hybrid domain because justifiability of a solution is not everything and there is a significant body of heuristic knowledge. Knowledge acquisition methodologies have perforce to be used. However, the substantive and strategic heuristics must be supplemented and reconciled with the normative reasoning which is revealed by a process of rational reconstruction.

EXPLICITNESS WITHIN THE LIMITS OF CURRENT TECHNOLOGY

It is not being claimed here that each of the ascribable reasoning steps of a professional can be precisely mirrored in the knowledge-base, rendering trivial the task of examining whether the error of reasoning falls in the excusable category. This is not possible due to limitations inherent in the present state of ES technology. For instance, it is difficult to model defeasible principles because the techniques of non-monotonic reasoning are not yet sufficiently advanced. Reasoning by analogy in ES is also at the investigative stage. As for integration, 'researchers have only recently begun to write about the integration of [case-based reasoning] with other reasoning paradigms' (Rissland and Skalak, 1989).

We need to claim no more than that in the present state of technology, using what are called 'second-generation architectures' (Keravnou and Washbrook, 1989; Johnson and Mital, 1990), it is feasible identifiably to maintain references in the knowledge-base to *those conceptual structures that are significant to the finding of reasonableness*. Before going on to some of these conceptual structures, it is necessary to make a point that we think is obvious by now.

OPACITY ASSISTS, NOT HINDERS, PROVING NEGLIGENCE

When the whole or part of the task of providing a professional service is delegated, 'the duty is not one "to take reasonable care", but rather "to ensure that reasonable care has been taken". This duty is not satisfied simply by taking reasonable care when selecting the person to whom the work is delegated' (Dugdale and Stanton, 1989, p. 262). If a financial-legal ES is opaque, in the sense that its reasoning cannot readily be compared with the reasoning ascribable to a human, then, *unlike in the case of systems that control or interface with machines or do tasks beyond human capability*, the plaintiff may argue that the defendant could not have known whether reasonable care was taken in a particular instance.[6]

Opacity may be present for one of many reasons. Supposed 'rules' may be inducted or synthesized by some algorithmic process, or the knowledge may be 'compiled' into a relatively indiscriminate representational formalism like production-rules. It could also be present if a more sophisticated formalism like frames is used but knowledge is not organized at a conceptual level (Johnson, 1985; Johnson and Keravnou, 1988; Bylander and Chandrasekaran, 1987).

CONCEPTUAL STRUCTURES SIGNIFICANT TO REASONABLENESS

ARTICULATED REASONS MAY NOT BE THE OPERATIVE REASONS

The organizational motivations of a financial-legal professional may lead him to veer towards a particular solution for reasons which may not be articulated; instead, purported reasons, which the professional feels are more acceptable to an objective listener, may be expressed. For example, a professional may get a large commission for recommending an investment in unit trusts but little if he suggests the purchase of the equity of an investment trust. Though there is little historical data to bear this out, it is sometimes said that the ability of investment trusts to lever their investments in a particular market sector makes them slightly susceptible to localized downturns in the market. The expert may give this as a reason for ruling out investment trusts, even in a situation where the client is willing to take risks. A knowledge engineer, unless he is unusually knowledgeable about the domain, may not be able to spot the spurious nature of the articulated reason and may abstract heuristic knowledge from it. However, the notional peer review employed by a court will reject reasoning which is spurious by reference to the domain norms.

This decoupling of operative reasons from articulated reasons is present at both the conceptual and the epistemological levels in domains which attach significance to what *ought* to be done:

> ... 'a has a good cause of action versus b' may be said to justify awarding judgment for a versus b. Now the proposition 'Any bridge built according to specification R is stable' may equally be said to justify an engineer's action in building such a bridge. However the justification here is based on a prediction about what will happen rather than on an evaluation of what ought to be done. ... this difference arises from subject-matter, not logic ... (Cohen, 1970).

DEFENSIBILITY IS NOT A PRIMARY SELECTIONAL CRITERION

Financial-legal professionals often give stereotypical justifications that do not significantly narrow the solution space in the sense that a justification may apply to a large variety of purported solutions and continue to apply despite substantial changes in situational facts. The reason that professionals pay inordinate attention to such justifications is that, normally, they are sufficient to defend a challenged solution.

For instance, a justification in the following form may be given:

The client is a non-resident; off-shore funds are not subject to UK tax; in the recent past the returns from certain currency funds have been 'good'; continued 'healthy' growth is forecast; switching costs are low; the client is investing for medium-term growth. Therefore, a particular mix of off-shore currency funds is recommended.

Faced with such a justification, a court would ordinarily find it difficult to hold that the recommendation was unreasonable even if, say, equity-based funds were *admittedly* expected to grow at twice the rate expected for the recommended currency funds. The recommendation does not adequately achieve the qualitative goals of the client, but it can be said to be in the defendable penumbra. However, if the justification was used as a *selectional* criterion, the protection of the defendable penumbra might be lost. The cluster of concepts said to constitute a justification is coarse as it excludes the effect on the solution of many relevant factors, including the presence of higher yielding off-shore funds.

Defensively orientated knowledge must be separated from that which may validly be used in problem-solving. Mital and Johnson (1990a) present a methodology for differentiation and acquisition of defensive knowledge so that it may selectively be used to provide assurance to a user-organization that a purported solution is potentially defendable.

'UNSTRUCTURED DECISION-MAKING' AND JUDGEMENTAL REASONING

If a client is known to be impatient the professional may be loath to confuse him by exploring a multiplicity of alternative avenues of achieving his qualitative goals. For a more demanding client the professional may demonstrate that he has made an exhaustive search. If an ES is designed to be used at or near the point of service, it may be necessary to model such stylistic aspects – included within the 'unstructured decision-making aspects' – of the professional's expertise. However, mixing the un-structured decision-making with judgemental reasoning may be seen as unreasonable, for the former is unlikely to be a part of the reasoning ascribed by the court to a reasonably competent professional.

It may be noted that so-called intuitive reasoning or hunches, which are an integral part of most human expertise, are not generally sought to be modelled in ES which are meant at best to model the considered or deliberate judgemental reasoning of experts.[7] If we really could capture the intuitive aspects of human expertise we would have gone some way towards truly intelligent machines. But that day is not near.

ANALYTICAL PROBABILITY AND CONTINGENT REASONING

Like experts in many other domains, financial-legal professionals have to reason with incomplete facts. However, it does not appear possible to ascribe to professionals any form of analytical probabilistic reasoning because professionals *articulate* deterministic reasoning, albeit contingent on assumptions which are carefully carried forward.[8] For instance, a professional may say: 'There are indications that the client may be a non-resident, but I cannot be certain because all the relevant information is not presently available. I will therefore explore investment in off-shore funds. However, in case the client has spent more than 180 days in this country since last April, he should disregard the following portions of my advice . . .'

However, recommendations or actions can be contingent only on a certain class of assumptions regarding unknowns. Some unknowns may be so crucial to the reasoning that a declaration that advice has been given subject to assumptions regarding these unknowns may be construed by a court as not being part of the advice but as an unreasonable or unfair limitation of liability.

IMPLICATIONS OF NOT MODELLING SIGNIFICANT CONCEPTUAL STRUCTURES

The structure of the knowledge of financial-legal professionals is quite distinct from the structure that is expected by knowledge-engineers using representational paradigms developed for the traditional ES domains like science and medicine (Johnson and Mital, 1990). The omission of direct reference to conceptual structures leads to difficulties during knowledge acquisition and subsequent stages of development (Keravnou and Johnson, 1986; Gruber and Cohen, 1987). However, our concern here is not with the difficulties experienced in knowledge-engineering, which can frequently be surmounted by extra effort. The point which we wish to make is that, in onerous applications, there clearly exist imperative legal reasons for using second-generation paradigms that recognize and maintain significant conceptual structures.

The authors have presented the above analysis from the developers' perspective. It is important to mention the context in which the analysis has been carried out. The authors are building upon their experience of designing and developing ES in the financial-legal domain, including those which are in commercial use (Anon., 1988). Their current work forms part of the wider research and development effort being carried out by the Knowledge Based Systems Group at Brunel University. This includes developing second-generation architectures for financial-legal ES (Johnson and Mital, 1990) and building knowledge insertion tools to automate a part of the task of building large financial ES (Mital and Johnson, 1990b; Mital and Stylianou, 1990; Mital, 1990).

CONCLUSIONS

We have shown that while it is essential to be aware of the issues of liability in general (i.e. the macro issues of liability), it is also necessary to go beneath the surface of the technology when considering a particular ES development or use. The nature of the application and the knowledge employed to perform the tasks have to be analysed in detail. Only then can users and developers know what liability they face and how it may be limited.

NOTES

1. Where function overlaps financial-legal professionals use mainly off-the-shelf or standard financial and legal devices to provide the service. Accountants and solicitors may instead employ tailored devices.
2. The legal reasoning in the financial-legal domain is aimed at determining commercial conduct and differs significantly from the legal reasoning in adversarial, or notionally adversarial situations, that has been more widely researched in the context of ES (Gardner, 1987). In the latter there is minimal heuristic content (Susskind, 1987) with most developers acting as their own domain experts. See Waterman *et al.* (1986) for the difference in the fundamental models of the two types of legal reasoning, and Johnson and Mital (1990) for the nature of conduct-orientated heuristics.
3. In the USA the SEC has refused to give a declaration that an expert system designed to make specific recommendations would not have to register as a financial adviser (Warner, 1988).
4. In American jurisdictions, where the distinction between these two views is the starkest because juries have to be instructed as to the elements of negligence, the conduct theory clearly prevails (Harper and James, 1956, pp. 896–9; Prosser, 1971, p. 153). There are some English judgements seemingly accepting the state of mind theory. For instance, it has been said that negligence is an 'attitude of mental indifference to obvious risks' (*Hudston* v. *Viney*). But no English court seems to have taken the state of mind theory to the logical conclusion of admitting expert evidence, e.g. evidence of psychologists, to establish indifference or anxious care (cf. Harper and James, 1956, p. 898).

5. Financial-legal professionals expound some of their knowledge in the form of illustrations and examples which may be based on previously encountered situations or may be hypothetical. If the particularized knowledge does not precisely cover the situation at issue, then it may be necessary to reason by analogy. Of course, in the case of frequently applied examples, it may be possible to abstract widely applicable principles (Ehrenzweig, 1971).

6. As reasonableness is a community standard, it is relevant to note that those practically involved with ES have recognized that it is unreasonable to rely on a system that cannot 'justify its conclusions' (Schwartz *et al.*, 1987) or which 'claims to provide answers by methods which are not clear to any competent professional' (Stamper, 1988).

7. Researchers into associated memory technology and certain kinds of neural networks believe that eventually the intuitive aspects of human reasoning may be captured. However, even if that elusive goal is achieved, it may not be entirely fruitful. While intuition can play an important role in decision-making, humans also make mistakes based on intuition (Turban, 1988). In normative domains it is dangerous to mimic the supposed workings of the brain at a level which does not allow professionals to see whether valid reasoning has been carried out.

8. Cohen (1977) discusses the kind of probabilistic reasoning that may be countenanced by a court in an adversarial situation; however, this discussion does not extend to conduct-orientated situations.

DISCUSSION QUESTIONS

1. Introducing a computer in a workplace may change the mode of working. Many authors believe that asking a computer to do everything that it can be programmed to do can make the overall work mode unsatisfactory and non-optimal. Identify the functions in a busy tax accountancy practice which may possibly be delegated to a computer. Which of these functions would you hesitate to entrust to a computer?

2. Assume that you have identified the commercial need for the development of an expert system for tax planning/advice. Discuss the factors that would cause you to nominate particular persons as the contributors of knowledge to the system. What difficulties would there by in the way of these persons describing their expertise in detail to those not initiated in the art? What do you think it is, precisely, that experts know that trainee accountants do not?

3. Human experts are not infallible. When can giving wrong advice be legally excused? What kinds of mistakes are inexcusable on the part of

one who holds himself out to be a competent tax accountant? Draw analogies in your discussion with the facts of some recent cases on liability for negligent statements made by professionals.

4. Assuming that no higher standard of performance is expected when an expert system is used as part of a decision-making process, when can there be legal liability due to an error originating from an expert system even though a human acting alone would be excused for the same wrong advice?

5. First-generation expert systems expressed expertise in the form of rules. Representing knowledge as rules does allow certain tasks to be performed, but does not actually model the way that human experts perform sophisticated tasks. Discuss why more closely modelling expertise makes a complex expert system (a) more acceptable to a user, (b) more readily defendable in a court of law, and (c) easier to develop.

REFERENCES

Akelsen, S., Hartvigsen, G. and Richardsen, P. W. (1989). 'Knowledge-based systems for commercial line insurance', *Artificial Intelligence Communications*, Vol. 2, No. 2, pp. 98–109.

Anon, (1988). 'News', *Expert Systems*, Vol. 5, No. 1, pp. 58–9.

Birnbaum, L. N. (1988). 'Strict products liability and computer software', *Computer/Law Journal*, Vol. 8, pp. 135–56.

Breeze, P. (1990). 'Be your own expert', *Money Management*, January, pp. 47–9.

Bylander, T. and Chandrasekaran, B. (1987). 'Generic tasks for knowledge based reasoning: the "right" level of abstraction for knowledge acquisition', *International Journal of Man-Machine Studies*, Vol. 26, pp. 231–44.

Cannataci, J. A. (1989). 'Law liability and expert systems', *Artificial Intelligence & Society*, Vol. 3, pp. 169–83.

Chapman v. *Walton* (1833). 10 Bingham 57.

Clarke, G. (1989). *Expert Systems in the City*. IBC Financial Books, London.

Cohen, L. J. (1970). *The Implications of Induction*. Methuen, London.

Cohen, L. J. (1977). *The Probable and the Provable*. Clarendon Press, Oxford.

Cook, D. F. and Whittaker, A. D. (1989). 'Legal issues of expert system use', *Applied Artificial Intelligence*, Vol. 3, No. 1, pp. 69–81.

Dugdale, A. M. and Stanton, K. M. (1989). *Professional Negligence*. Butterworths, London.

Ehrenzweig, A. A. (1971). *Psychoanalytic Jurisprudence*. A. W. Sijthoff-Leiden, Amsterdam.

Feldthusen, B. (1984). *Economic Negligence*, Carswell Legal Publications, Agincourt, Ontario.

Frank, S. J. (1988). 'What AI practitioners should know about the law', *Artificial Intelligence Magazine*, Summer, pp. 109–13.

Gardner, A. von der Leith, (1987). *An Artificial Intelligence Approach to Legal Reasoning*, MIT Press, Cambridge, MA.

Godes, J. N. (1987). 'Developing a new set of liability rules for a new generation of technology: assessing liability for computer-related injuries in the health care field', *Computer/Law Journal*, pp. 517–34.

Greaves & Co. (Contractors) Ltd v. *Baynham, Meikle & Partners* [1975] 3 All ER 99.

Gruber, T. R. (1989). *The Acquisition of Strategic Knowledge*. Academic Press, London.

Gruber, T. R. and Cohen, P. R. (1987). 'Design for acquisition: principles of knowledge-system design to facilitate knowledge acquisition', *International Journal of Man-Machine Studies*, Vol. 26, pp. 143–59.

Harper, F. V. and James, F. (1956). *The Law of Torts*, Little Brown and Company, Boston.

Hudston v. *Viney* [1921] 1 Ch. 98.

Johnson, P. E. (1983). 'What kind of expert should a system be?', *Journal of Medicine and Philosophy*, Vol. 8, pp. 77–97.

Johnson, L. (1985). 'The need for competence models in the design of expert consultant systems', *International Journal of Systems Research and Information Science*, Vol. 1, No. 1, pp. 23–36.

Johnson, L. and Keravnou, E. T. (1988). *Expert Systems Architectures*, Kogan Page, London.

Johnson, L. and Mital, V. (1990). 'Developing second-generation architectures for financial-legal KBS: a modelling approach', *Brunel University Technical Report*, No. CSTR-90-3 (available from authors) to be published in *International Journal of Systems Research and Information Science*.

Keravnou, E. T. and Washbrook, J. (1989). 'An analysis of the architectural requirements of second-generation expert systems', *The Knowledge Engineering Review*, Vol. 3, No. 4, pp. 205–33.

La Rossa v. *Scientific Design Co.* 402 F.2d 484 (3rd Cir., 1968).

Lownicka, E. Z. and Powell, J. L. (1987). *Encyclopaedia of Financial Services Law*, Sweet & Maxwell, London (see latest updates).

Mital, V. and Johnson, L. (1990a). 'Structuring financial expert systems to defend against negligence'. In Addis, T. R. and Muir, R. M. (eds.), *Research and Development in Expert Systems VII (Proceedings of Expert Systems 90)*. Cambridge University Press, Cambridge.

Mital, V. and Johnson, L. (1990b). 'Automating the acquisition of financial-legal knowledge: combining heuristics with normative rationalisations', *Brunel University Technical Report*, CSTR-90-8 (available from authors).

Mital, V. (1990). 'Case-based design and conceptual information retrieval in domains with weak theory: financial-legal and litigation support applications', *Brunel University Technical Report*, CSTR-90-7 (available from author).

Musen, M. A. (1989). *Automated Generation of Model-Based Knowledge-Acquisition Tools*. Morgan Kaufman, San Mateo, CA.

Mykytyn, K., Mykytyn, P. P. Jr and Slinkman, C. W. (1990). 'Expert systems: a question of liability?', *Management Information Systems Quarterly*, March, pp. 27–42.

Prosser, W. L. (1971). *Handbook of The Law of Torts*. West Publishing Company, St. Paul, MN.

Reed, C. (1987). 'The liability of expert system producers', *Computer Law & Practice*, Vol. 4, pp. 12–14.

Rissland, E. L. and Skalak, D. B. (1989). 'Combining case-based and rule-based reasoning: a heuristic approach'. In *Proceedings of The Eleventh Joint Conference on Artificial Intelligence*, IJCAI, Detroit, pp. 524–30.

Schwartz, W. B., Patil, R. S. and Szolovits, P. (1987). 'Artificial intelligence in medicine: where do we stand?' *Jurimetrics*, Vol. 27, No. 4, pp. 362–9.

Silverhart v. *Mount Zion Hospitals* (1971). 20 Cal. App. 3d 1022.

Stafford v. *Conti Commodity Services Ltd* [1981] 1 All ER 691.

Stamper, R. (1988). 'Pathology of AI: responsible use of artificial intelligence in professional work', *Artificial Intelligence & Society*, Vol. 2, pp. 3–16.

Susskind, R. E. (1987). *Expert Systems in Law*. Clarendon Press.

Tapper, C. (1989). *Computer Law*. Longman.

Turban, E. (1988). *Decision Support and Expert Systems*. Macmillan.

Turley, T. M. (1988). 'Expert software systems: the legal implications', *Computer/Law Journal*, Vol. 8, pp. 455–77.

Warner, E. (1988) 'Expert systems and the law', *High Technology Business*, October, pp. 32–5.

Waterman, D. A., Paul J. and Peterson, M. (1986). 'Expert systems for legal decision making', *Expert Systems*, Vol. 3, No. 4, pp. 212–26.

Willick, M. S. (1985). 'Professional malpractice and the unauthorised practice of profession: some legal and ethical aspects of the use of computers as decision-aids'. In Walter, C. (ed.), *Computing Power and Legal Reasoning*. West Publishing Company, pp. 817–63.

Chapter

16 Building competencies: the computerization of PAYE

Romano Dyerson and Michael Roper

PREFACE

This paper focuses on the computerization of PAYE by the Inland Revenue, and is partly based on interviews conducted at the Department during the first half of 1990. Information has been gathered from various levels in the Inland Revenue, including senior management at Whitehall, the Development Centre at Telford, and District Office staff. To preserve confidentiality individuals have not been identified by name.

The paper could not have been written without the generosity of Inland Revenue staff in agreeing to meet with us. We would like to thank staff for their co-operation during interviews, and willingness to relay comments on our work.

INTRODUCTION

Inland Revenue's computerization of PAYE (COP) is the 'quiet man' of government IT projects undertaken over the last two decades. Six hundred district offices have been connected to a nationwide computer network serving 30m PAYE records, almost on budget and within the time allotted.

This chapter was prepared as a paper within the Technology and Firm Organization research programme at London Business School. This is a multi-disciplinary programme of the Centre for Business Strategy and the Institute for Organization Research. It is part of the ESRC/DTI initiative on Technology and the Firm, and their financial support is gratefully acknowledged. We would like to thank Matthew Bishop, Paul Geroski, and particularly Peter Grindley and Jonathan Hopper for their comments and assistance.

Success on this scale contrasts with the difficulties encountered by other departments such as the DVLC or DSS, yet the Inland Revenue's achievements have largely escaped public attention.

While the technology used on COP was not particularly path-breaking, the manner of its implementation represented a marked departure from civil service modes of planning and execution. Inland Revenue used technology incrementally, computerizing the manual system rather than seeking radical organizational change. Clear and focused aims enabled the Department to merge quite disparate forms of knowledge: formal programming and systems expertise, with day-to-day user experience.

Several features of project management contributed to this integration. Consultants were full members of the project team, facilitating the transfer of skills. High turnover of development staff – the traditional bugbear of government IT projects – was avoided by fostering a sense of 'esprit de corps' and extensive on-the-job promotion. Further features of good practice included the early securing of users' co-operation, and the effective control of suppliers. Management issues such as these are important in all technology projects, whether 'leading edge' or adoptive, public or private sector.

COP's most enduring legacy has been a capability to exploit further opportunities for cost reduction and service improvements. For example computerization was extended to Schedule D in 1984, and the Department has recently begun to consider radical initiatives such as the development of a common interface of PAYE and other taxes at district level. Changes like these are possible because the Department possesses a development team in which business needs are meshed with technical skills.

This paper begins with a brief history of PAYE and previous computerization attempts, and then discusses the scope and objectives of COP. Sections 4 and 5 explore the main features and strategic implications of project organization. The Sections which follow are: Background to COP, COP and Objectives, Project Management, Strategy Issues, Conclusion.

BACKGROUND

PAYE AND THE PRESSURE FOR CHANGE

Pay As You Earn (PAYE) tax was first introduced in 1944, and while the following thirty years saw substantial changes in the scope and rates of the tax, its administrative infrastructure remained little changed. It was a decentralized system, which by the 1980s relied on a network of some 500 District Offices. Liability was worked out manually, with data being written on index or 'Concards' and filed at District Office level. Computerization was not intended to change the nature of this system, but to increase efficiency, promote flexibility and thereby raise responsiveness. Technology would, for example, enable the Inland Revenue to reduce from months to days, the time required for tax rate changes.

Agreement for the computerization of PAYE was secured as long ago as 1962. A rising working population, expanding the general tax base, had begun to place increasing strain on the manual procedures of assessment and collection.[1] As the workforce shifted towards salaried employment the burdens on the PAYE system increased dramatically: by 1980 PAYE accounted for 85% of the total revenue raised from income tax, compared to just 25% in 1953.[2] The 1960s impetus for computerization also sprang from the growth of the welfare state and interest in using the taxation system for social ends. This increased the administrative load and exacerbated problems of recruiting and retaining skilled staff.[3]

However, from the later 1970s, worries about mounting administrative costs and error rates came to dominate concern over staff shortages. Overall administration costs compared unfavourably with many other countries, partly because of the extra labour involved in a system based on calculating liability throughout the year ('cumulative assessment'). Costs were almost twice as high as in the US, which relied on year end self-assessment and more extensive use of computers. Collection costs were also rising during the later 1970s when the Department began considering again the automation of PAYE: during 1978–9 alone they rose by 13%.[4] The search for efficiencies began with staff numbers, which were growing by almost 10% per annum during the mid 1970s.[5] By 1978 the Permanent Secretary of Inland Revenue, Sir William Pile, felt that the manual system was close to breakdown. He envisaged that the degree of error would increase and service would decline with the sheer 'weight that is being put on it'.

PRE-COP HISTORY

Table 16.1 provides a brief chronology of PAYE computerization. From the chronology one can see that the Department has spent the best part of thirty years at first establishing, and then extending its skills in computerization. Between 1962 and 1969 skills were originally developed in drawing up and implementing plans for a series of single site regional centres, geared around mainframe computers. The first centre of this kind, 'Centre 1', opened in 1968 at East Kilbride. At this site, collection and

Table 16.1 Inland Revenue chronology

1944	PAYE introduced
1962	Plan for nine batch processing centres
1968	Centre 1 established at East Kilbride, Scotland
1970	PAYE computerization suspended for review of tax credit system
1974	Tax credit scheme abandoned
1977	Small trial for on-line work
1978	Cumbernauld centre established
1978/79	Detailed feasibility study
1979	Shipley centre established
1980	Government reviews PAYE automation proposals
1982	Telford established as main development centre
1983	West Midlands pilot involving 14 local offices commences
1984	National implementation of COP approved/CODA and NTS added
1988	COP successfully implemented nationally through 11 regional centres
1989	CODA/NTS implementation completed

Adapted in part from Matheson, in Pitt & Smith, 1984.

processing procedures were batch automated for 2m Scottish PAYE taxpayers.

In 1970 the incoming conservative government brought with it proposals to rationalize the *ad hoc* tax and benefit structure into a unified system under a tax credit scheme. Implementation of the regional centres was suspended in 1970 – before the second of the nine centres could be constructed – and officially cancelled in 1971. However, the Government's loss of a general election in early 1974 meant that the credit scheme proposals were never acted upon. This left PAYE computerization in limbo.[6] Computer technology had moved forward from the Department's early area of expertise to on-line, distributed systems. Revising or simply reviving the Department's earlier skills, however, fell foul of public expenditure constraints. This effectively curtailed the large scale computerization of PAYE records until the end of the decade.

On a more modest scale, the Department expanded their existing skills in two directions: the automation of general accounting procedures and a small trial of on-line technology. Accounting operations for all routine work on PAYE, Schedule D and Corporation Tax were shifted away from local tax offices to three central sites, over a two year (1978-1980) period. Following a year of development, attempts to computerize the assessment of Schedule D were abandoned in 1978. Consequently, only two computer centres were established at Cumbernauld and Shipley in 1978 and 1979 respectively.[7]

In 1977 funding was secured to undertake a small pilot project to investigate the potential of on-line technology on a limited range of daily

PAYE processing tasks. This involved connecting six local tax offices, via VDUs, to a central computer at Liverpool. The success of this pilot gave rise to a full feasibility study over 1978–1979, leading to the Computerization of PAYE project (COP).

COP AND ITS OBJECTIVES

AIMS

> Every bit of your income and allowances, each one of you, will be on somebody's Concards, kept in a little drawer in a desk and filled-in in ink by the clerical officer or the executive officer who is looking after it. What we want is a button to press so that it is registered on the file instantaneously by pressing another button. (Sir William Pile, Inland Revenue Permanent Secretary, 1980.[8])

Inland Revenue completed its feasibility study into PAYE computerization in late 1979. Four basic objectives were identified: efficiency, flexibility, staff satisfaction and service. Equal weight was not attached to each aim simultaneously, indeed a factor contributing to COP's success is that the Department sought staff reductions through process innovation before considering service improvements and further efficiencies. We sketch the operational objectives and relationship between them in more detail below.

Efficiency

Initially, the primary aim of COP was to reduce administrative costs. The feasibility study estimated that COP could enable PAYE staff reductions of 20%, and the project was given the go-ahead on this basis.[9] By this stage however, the momentum for reductions did not derive from the problem of rising staff numbers. In fact by 1982, a combination of policy changes (for example the abolition of reduced rate band) and government cut-backs meant that staff numbers had returned to the levels of the mid 1970s. Thus while spiralling staff numbers during the late 1970s provided the initial motivation for computerization, by the time of COP's inception in 1980, the aim was to yield economies irrespective of whether numbers were increasing in real terms. In all public sector computerization projects during the 1980s, the present Director General (and ex-COP/CODA Project Manager) Steve Matheson has remarked, 'the driving force . . . has been the efficiency aspect rather than anything else, and bluntly, reduction in headcount'. Computerization is process oriented and must pay for itself in staff losses.

PAYE was an obvious candidate for computerization, since it was already rule-based and so could be codified relatively easily. However as Table 16.2 indicates, in fact PAYE was a much less staff intensive tax than Schedule D. The scope for reductions under Schedule D was much greater, and provided a strong motivation for further computerization once the Department had established a platform of IT skills on the basic PAYE functions.

Table 16.2 PAYE/Schedule D staff costs

%	PAYE	Schedule D
Taxes collected	62	21
Inspector force	67	46
Collector force	46	30

Source: PAC, 1978

While efficiency objectives centred on staff reduction, COP was also expected to increase accuracy. Error rates had risen to 'disturbingly high' levels in the later 1970s and early 1980s and Inland Revenue was under considerable public pressure to improve the situation.[10] COP provided a partial solution, addressing the 10% of arithmetic and transcription errors.[11] On-line links between the regional mainframes were favoured because they would remove the scope for error as records were translated from written form to computer code.[12]

Flexibility

Two types of flexibility were sought through COP: policy flexibility to enable major overhauls of the taxation system, and short-term operational flexibility. Major reforms were constantly under discussion during the 1970s.[13] In 1977 the Department established a committee in parallel to the feasibility study, to consider which options should be built into the proposed system. These included local income tax instead of rates, the combining of tax and social security benefits, an overhaul of taxation relating to savings and investments, and self-assessment.

COP also set out to enhance operational flexibility. Minor, year in year out changes would be implemented more swiftly and simply. As the *Financial Times* explained in 1980, 'what the Inland Revenue wants to see is a situation whereby the Chancellor can announce structural changes in tax during a Budget speech and the individual adjustments of rates stemming from that speech can be made within a few hours.'[14]

Staff Satisfaction

In common with other public sector computerization projects, (for example at the DSS) Inland Revenue stressed the importance of enhancing staff satisfaction through computerization. Experience with the West Midlands on-line pilots had convinced them that staff enjoyed using the systems. It was believed that computers would make work 'easier and pleasanter' for District Office staff in two ways.[15] First, computers would alleviate the routine work and second, the provision of 'up to date' equipment would in itself enhance job satisfaction. Though there was much public discussion about the need to increase staff satisfaction, it was taken for granted that computerization would achieve this.[16]

Service

Service improvements were also viewed initially as a follow-on from operational efficiencies. Handwritten forms would become unnecessary and the printing and layout of forms would improve. More important, incorrect assessments would be made less often and could be rectified more quickly when they did occur. When questioned about the effect of COP on service, Inland Revenue managers tended to return to the issue of administration costs. As Sir Lawrence Airey explained, the main benefit to the taxpayer would be 'a handsome yield in terms of reduced costs of operation.'[17]

Accordingly, little change was envisaged in the procedures or rules governing PAYE. The objective was simple: to substitute automated for manual methods, leaving a slimmed down but basically unchanged organizational structure. As the Permanent Secretary remarked above, Concards would be replaced by electronic data storage, pen-pushing by button-pressing. The primary motive and justification for COP was cost reduction, which would be achieved through process innovation. As we shall see below however, the case of COP illustrates a reverse product cycle, where the successful attainment of cost efficiencies paves the way for service oriented benefits.[18]

THE COP PROJECT

COP's basic function is to automate the assessment of PAYE tax and enable the easy storage, retrieval and transfer of PAYE records. Simple objectives help explain why the project was implemented successfully. Inland Revenue managers called for a freeze on policy changes during implementation in the 1980 feasibility study, on the grounds that computerization should precede changes to the assessment system.[19] The Project Manager Steve Matheson was adamant that COP should mirror the manual procedures because this would make it easier to specify user requirements, and reduce the impact of changes on staff.[20] So while the Department's aims were ambitious in terms of the scale and timing of the roll-out, it did not seek immediate changes in the way the business itself was conducted.

In terms of functionality and policy change then, COP steered a cautious path. The implementation strategy was also incremental. Development would take place stage by stage. Testing and on-line operation were clearly separated on the grounds that development would inevitably be 'messy', and that any disruption to users would undermine their acceptance of the systems. Adherence to schedules was also emphasized. As the project manager Steve Matheson explained in 1981, 'the main risk is delay, and delay involves costs . . . Delay in getting the thing completed . . . would be delay in achieving the full staff savings.'[21]

While COP's planners stressed organizational continuity through clear goals and incremental means, in one respect the 1980 feasibility study was comparatively radical. It specified that on-line links between mainframes should be incorporated from the very start, even though this increased the technical complexity and the consequent risk of failure. Favouring ICL but lacking confidence in their ability to provide on-line links, the Government called for the deferral of on-line links in their feasibility study review. In late 1980 an amended strategy was agreed.[22] Phase One would involve the installation of mainframes at regional centres, linked to terminals in District Offices. Construction of the regional centres would be staggered, enabling early problems to be sorted out and subsequent hardware developments to be incorporated.[23]

Phase Two would entail the installation of on-line links between the mainframes.[24] The revised timetable stipulated that Phase One should be complete by 1987 and the final completion date was pushed back to 1990. Under pressure from the CCTA and Treasury, Inland Revenue made Phase Two conditional on the successful completion of Phase One. The Department would only be permitted to proceed with networking, Steve Matheson explained, once the ICL equipment proved 'that it was safe and we might achieve the higher savings.'[25] Doubt about ICL's ability and experience in networking thus resulted in a stage by stage introduction of the technology.

Following the success of the pilot during Phase One of COP, in April

1984 ministers approved three extensions to the programme. First, assessment of Schedule D (CODA) was added.[26] As with COP, CODA would be implemented incrementally, pilot schemes in two regions during 1987 preceding nationwide implementation the following year. Second, a National Tracing System was added. This is a register of national insurance number and personal details which acts as a central referencing system for other applications. Third, ministers sanctioned the on-line links which the Department had called for in its 1980 strategy.

Inland Revenue worked back from the organization in preparing its computerization plans, aiming to minimize the disruption to end-users while delivering the necessary staff reductions. Clear objectives and adherence to schedules would ensure that savings were not jeopardized, while the decision to automate the existing system and avoid on-line development helped secure user acceptance. The one area where COP's project managers were technologically ambitious was in favouring immediate on-line links. Forced into a more incremental strategy than they had themselves originally proposed, however, project managers were able to build on the implementation expertise gained during COP.

SYSTEM CONFIGURATION

The feasibility study initially proposed a regionally distributed processing system. Twelve (later eleven) regional centres were to be set up, each housing an ICL mainframe, and connected via VDUs to a network of local tax offices. District processing tasks such as recoding and data storage would be taken over by the regional centres. Local offices would retain an input function, together with enquiry and supervisory roles through direct on-line links to their regional centre. Not all processing tasks would take place on an on-line basis. Batch processing would be used for functions outside the scope of the day to day work of local offices; including the issuing of returns and recording exercises in anticipation of future changes.

The 1980 review modified the original system configuration in two ways. Firstly, rather than a single district office network per regional mainframe, each region would operate four or five networks. This simplified the overall complexity of the system: each network would be responsible for 400–500 terminals, rather than 2000. Secondly, linkages between regional centres through a nationwide data transfer network were postponed. Instead, data transfer between regions would take place via tape delivery. Though by 1984 on-line linkages were reinstated. Figure 16.1 illustrates the final configuration settled on.

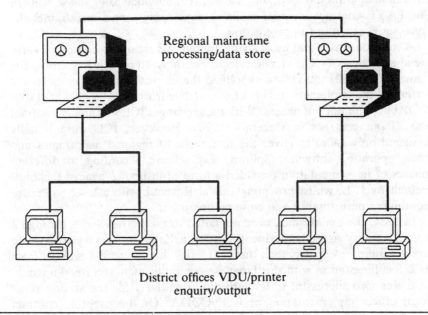

District offices VDU/printer
enquiry/output

Key: ———————— On-line direct links

Fig. 16.1 1980 system configuration.

EQUIPMENT

At the time of the COP tender, ICL was the sole supplier of computers for public sector contracts. As the one remaining British manufacturer of mainframe computers the company had benefited from preferential treatment by government keen to ensure its survival. But in 1980 ICL was under significant pressure. It faced two problems: the presence of potential rivals lobbying for open procurement and new EEC legislation at the start of 1981 that would ban the Government from protectionist action. This left Inland Revenue in an unusually strong position to secure favourable contract terms for COP.

The Government's decision was complicated by doubts over ICL's technical ability for the project. Officials at the Inland Revenue had previously circulated tender specifications to a number of computer manufacturers. The Press had picked up on this and argued that IBM was better placed to fulfil the contract terms, since it had had previous experience in the related area of banking and insurance. Furthermore, the company had proposed installing hardware and software that had been proven in operational use.[27] In contrast, ICL intended using the security of the PAYE contract in order to finish developing a new mainframe, the 2966 series, than not in production.[28]

A solution was found by delaying announcement of the contract award, pending review of COP's technical specifications. Reporting in October the same year (1980) the review simplified the original system specifications, extended the implementation completion date from 1987 to 1990, and split COP into a number of phases. With these changes ICL was finally awarded the £150m contract in December 1980. However, ICL were initially assigned only £40m to cover the first cache of regional mainframes and their operating software. Splitting expenditure according to different phases of implementation provided a form of insurance against technical default by ICL, whilst providing Inland Revenue with a lever to ensure continuing performance and close co-operation.

In 1984, the mainframes were upgraded to the Estriel Series through a supplementary agreement. Incorporating a faster processing ability and greater memory capacity than the 2900 series, it was the first product from ICL'S collaboration with the Japanese computer manufacturer Fujitsu.[29] ICL was also successful in tendering competitively for the second stage local office implementation of COP/CODA. Of the eventual contract breakdown ICL supplied twelve mainframes and its consortium partners, Logica and Newbury supplied software for the network and VDUs respectively. In a separate tender, Plessey developed and installed a data communications management system at East Kilbride as part of the upgrade to on-line information transfer.

Table 16.3 Implementation Timetable

Task	Date
Procurement and initial design	Nov 1980–Nov 1981
Detailed design and development	Dec 1981–Dec 1983
Implementation in initial districts and performance review	Jan–Dec 1984
Delivery and acceptance of balance of first region's equipment	Jan–Mar 1985
Implementation in remaining regions	Apr 1985–end 1987/ early 1988

Source: Matheson, in Pitt and Smith, 1984, p. 95

PROGRESS

COP met all its implementation milestones, as Table 16.3 indicates. Support contracts were signed with two external software firms at the beginning of 1981: PACTEL, which provided assistance on project control systems and support, and Computer Sciences Corporation (CSC), which provided technical expertise. 1981 was spent preparing a detailed user specification in conjunction with the consultants and the London operating division responsible for PAYE, and contracting the mainframes and terminals. In June 1982 Inland Revenue opened its National Development Centre at Telford, which acted as a test bed for the PAYE scheme and doubles up as the West Midlands processing centre. 1982–3 was spent on detailed design and development at Telford.

By mid 1983 the Department had completed design, programming and testing of the initial computer system, and in October a pilot scheme involving 14 District offices opened in the West Midlands. Designed to test user acceptance, the pilot was to operate up to 1985. By December 1983 – ahead of schedule – VDUs had been installed, staff had been trained, and taxpayer records had been created in preparation for live operation during 1984. Table 16.4 provides details on the full implementation of COP/CODA, completed in 1989. Based on the original 1980 timetable, COP has been installed a year earlier than intended, together with the successful addition of CODA within the schedule. At the same time, an additional 10 000 VDUs (38 000 in total) have been installed in local tax offices, connected to 50 mainframe computers.[30] Between 1988 and 1989 the original mainframe site, Centre One at East Kilbride, has been up-rated and converted to on-line operation. The COP/CODA system has been reported as operating with 99% reliability.[31]

Table 16.4 COP/CODA Implementation

Project	No. of Offices	Implementation period
COP	477	1983–1988
CODA	606*	1984–1989

Source: NAO, 1987
*includes 427 PAYE offices, 129 sch. D

PROJECT COSTS

Viewed in strictly financial terms, there has been some slippage from the original investment proposals. However estimated benefits have remained on target. Net savings of 6800 staff have been achieved as a result of computerization, against a background of general administrative rationalization during the implementation period. Care has to be taken with these figures. The desired headcount was only achieved because of the incorporation of CODA into the programme, which allowed additional labour shedding. Table 16.5 provides a breakdown of the changing investment estimates over the implementation period

It should be noted that Table 16.5 is based on 1987 estimates of final expenditure. Detailed final expenditure figures for 1989 are not available, but are estimated to have risen to £340m at 1987 prices.[32] Based on 1987 figures, the programme has incurred a 9% increase in real terms. Of course, this has to be measured against the technological improvements discussed above.

From Table 16.5 we can see that technology costs have declined in real terms from the original estimate. This reflects general cost falls in the computer industry over the implementation period. Over the three years reported in Table 16.5 staff costs have increased as a proportion of the total cost estimates. In real terms, over the period measured, staff costs have risen by 27%. Table 16.6 indicates that rising staff costs reflect the increasing use of consultants during implementation.

Table 16.5 COP/CODA Cost Estimates

Category	1980[1] £m	%[2]	1984 £m	%	1986 £m	%
equipment[3]	158	54	122	43	154	48
staff, consultants	75	26	91	32	95	30
accommodation	53	18	63	22	62	19
other	7	2	8	3	8	3
	293	100	284	100	319	100

[1] 1986 prices, up to 1987 end
[2] Rounded
[3] Hardware and operational software.
Source: adapted from NAO, 1987

From Table 16.6 it is apparent that there has been a fivefold increase in the number of consultants. Over the same period internal staff numbers have approximately doubled.[33] Accordingly, consultants have been employed at a faster rate during implementation than internal staff. In cost terms, consultants as a proportion of total staff costs, have increased from less than a fifth to about a third. Based on the original proposals, staffing requirements for COP/CODA would appear to have been underestimated.

Table 16.6 Average Number of
Consultants

Year	Consultants		% Total staff	
	No	£m*	%No	%£m
1982–83	30	2.0	3.1	18.0
1983–84	30	2.1	2.9	16.9
1984–85	50	3.4	4.3	22.2
1985–86	115	8.2	7.7	34.2
1986–87	159	11.5	7.7	34.3

* Includes special projects as well as
consultants on secondment
Source: Inland Revenue, NAO, 1987

One difficulty during implementation has been the shortage of specialists within the computer industry in general, and the civil service particularly. This has made it difficult for COP/CODA to attract sufficiently qualified staff to the project. Rather than accept the resulting slippage amongst target implementation dates due to the incorporation of CODA and the NTS, there has been an increase in the numbers of consultants employed. Though consultants are on average four times more expensive than equivalent internal staff, it is argued that their employment has had a positive effect on implementation. In the short term the extra costs involved in employing consultants are outweighed by the benefits to the project as a whole from remaining on schedule. On a general level, the increased costs arose from the unexpected expansion of the project in 1984, which made the original staffing estimates over-optimistic.

PROJECT MANAGEMENT

Project management on COP/CODA was characterized by both the devolution and centralization of power. On the one hand, the Project Manager Steve Matheson played the role of 'champion', particularly where issues of finance or relations with suppliers and other government departments was concerned. At the same time, autonomy was given to development staff and users were encouraged to participate in the project. This devolution of power was reflected in the character of technical support, recruitment of development staff, and labour strategy. Below we explore this balance between autonomy and control, and how it was achieved during implementation.

PROJECT CONTROL

In contrast to other government IT initiatives which have suffered from high turnover of senior staff, Steve Matheson remained with the programme from the beginning of the feasibility study in 1978 to the addition of CODA in 1984.[34] During this time he sought direct control over staffing on the grounds that this would help achieve the necessary integration between in-house and external expertise. Liaison with ministers, trade unions, suppliers and all the Telford development teams took place through Matheson. He also controlled the budget, which enhanced flexibility by enabling resource priorities to be changed relatively easily during development. For example when ICL was developing the Estriel series, Matheson reallocated resources to test the new generation of mainframes. Similarly, key decisions about the building of the National Tracing System could be made without having to wait for committee approval.

A further element in COP's success was the direct involvement of all senior personnel – consultants and civil servants – in project control. At the inception of the program a COP Steering Group (COPSG) was established, and met quarterly throughout with the brief to evaluate progress and give direction.[35] Though Matheson himself was not a member, he was always present at COPSG meetings, and set the agenda. COPSG was to provide early warning of hitches in implementation and facilitate speedy action by directly involving the decision makers. COPSG's most significant function however was to tie the external contractors in to the project by making them accountable at a senior level.[36] Matheson used it as 'a big stick' to exert pressure on contractors, who did not want their performance questioned publicly at senior levels. In the event this stick was never wielded, and although there were occasions where Project staff threatened to air grievances at the Steering Group, contractors usually acceded to demands before this point. At a lower level a Coordinating Committee – chaired by Matheson – met monthly to monitor progress. Practical aspects of implementation were dealt with by a project executive, which met weekly.[37]

Basic project control methods were flexible, allowing COP/CODA managers to organize their schedules within the overall timetable. Project control was finalized in early 1981 after a Feasibility Study Review involving PACTEL. On their suggestion the standard government methodology (PROMPT) was rejected in favour of a newly emerging and unproven automated system – since adopted by other government departments – called Artemis. Artemis reports summarizing the activities and deadlines of each line manager were sent on a weekly basis. At first staff viewed this as an imposition, but Matheson observes that attitudes changed once they realised 'it was *they* that were pushing in the dates and the targets and it was *they* who had to commit to them'. Automated schedules facilitated the devolution of responsibility for adhering to timetables, helping to avoid the over-runs common in other government IT projects.[38]

DEVELOPMENT METHODS

Systems development support was mainly provided by the Computer Science Corporation (CSC), which used Digital Systems Development Methodology (DSDM). This development guide had two main advantages. First, it facilitated the accurate gauging of user needs. Operating through data flow diagrams, DSDM enabled systems requirements to be specified in a form which could be easily understood both by technicians and users. Second, DSDM helped to promote an incremental development process. It established a modular and clear systems architecture, controlled changes to the systems base, and validated the systems overall, enshrining the principle of 'build a little, test a little'. The end result was a systems development environment which, while slow in getting off the ground, avoided the costly and disruptive task of re-specifying user requirements later in the development process.[39]

Standardization of development functions was a further area where Inland Revenue made substantial progress. This was necessary in the project's early stages because of the acute shortage of skilled IT staff. Users were drawn from District offices around the country and trained as on-line programmers at Telford. Their inexperience meant that development tasks had to be broken down into small units, called 'functional decomposition'. Although this was an extremely resource-consuming policy, it brought a number of benefits. Functional decomposition provided a platform for internal skills build-up, ensured that errors could be more easily traced, and prevented contract programmers from writing idiosyncratic code (and therefore from making themselves indispensable).[40]

Finally, the efforts of in-house staff were concentrated on developing 'middleware', which is the interface between the mainframe operating systems and the applications software. Developing the operating shell themselves assisted the Department to tailor the systems to its needs, and generated the expertise needed to build in subsequent applications. It meant that internal staff rather than consultants held the key to the systems.

SKILLS TRANSFER

Integration of user experience with technical skill was a key factor in ensuring successful development work on COP/CODA. User requirements were accurately gauged and users were encouraged to 'go native' by developing a degree of technical competence. Integration was fostered through the way consultants were managed, and through recruitment and training strategies. These are examined in turn below.

Inland Revenue concentrated its resources on establishing programming and middle level IT skills, but left problems of systems design and other formal expertise to consultants. At the beginning of the project Matheson all but exhausted the contingency budget hiring database specialists, communications specialists, continual flow modellers and senior designers. There was never any attempt to acquire this kind of expertise internally. Consultants were not employed 'stop gap' in times of crisis or shortage, but were full members of the development team from the very start.[41]

Integration and continuity of expertise was vital to the development process, and has played an important longer term role in aligning the formal expertise with business needs. Throughout the project Inland Revenue stayed with PACTEL and CSC. While their growing involvement was the major source of cost increases following the addition of CODA, the Department rightly judged that the benefits of skills build-up outweighed the marginal savings which might have been gained through open competition. Consultancy fees were re-negotiated on an annual basis, and were broadly in line with other government departments.[42] Inland Revenue seems then to have achieved a satisfactory compromise between cost and staff continuity.

By 1986 there were 751 in-house staff in post at Telford, together with 109 consultants. As the PAC noted, 'the consultants themselves will have no incentive to transfer skills which they are under contract to provide'.[43] Recognizing this early in the programme, the Department set out to tie the consultants in to the development teams. Time was specifically provided for 'tasking' so that internal staff might learn from the consultants on the job. More importantly, consultants were employed at 'line' level. They were answerable to Inland Revenue project managers, directed internal staff themselves, and were subject to the same assessment arrangements. As the Telford Development Centre's Controller explained,

> We have deliberately from the start set out to have mixed teams of consultants and in-house staff working together. We do not put the consultants all in one place and ask them to deliver a part of the project and put our own staff in another place and ask them to deliver another part of the project. We put the two together with firm deadlines,

integrated teams, and in that situation all our in-house staff will be learning from the special expertise of the consultants working with them.[44]

This emphasis on learning required careful management of both the consultants and staff, and gave rise to an informal rule that consultants must always be 'better than anybody we've got on-site in-house'. There were two reasons for this policy. First, skills transfer could only take place if there was effective leadership by the consultants. Second, the Department recognized that placing staff alongside consultants on a fraction of the salary would have a poor effect on morale if the consultants were not demonstrably superior in skill. This in turn necessitated careful recruitment and supervision of the consultants by Inland Revenue managers. Consultants were sacked if they lacked ability or could not fit in at Telford. Action had to be prompt 'in order to carry the staff with you', and ensure that they were working under consultants who they could learn from.

Behind the attention to morale and motivation lay a belief that the long term future of IT in the Department depended on the continuity of in-house staff. Turnover at Telford was low for a public sector IT project; a function partly of the development office's remote location.[45] In the early days it was easy to retain staff because as Matheson says, 'the only thing in Telford town centre ... was the shopping precinct'. However as the programme began to take shape, staff became 'hooked on the excitement of it all' (Steve Matheson). In contrast to the rest of the Civil Service, on the job promotion of internal staff was encouraged.[46] Consultants have also been promoted up through the organization. This has resulted in substantial one-off cost increases but has helped to bridge the gap between formal expertise and knowledge of the Department's business.[47]

While its overall record on consultancy is good, in common with other Civil Service IT projects, Inland Revenue has occasionally departed from its stated policy of only employing external labour to provide specialized skills. For example after CODA was added to the project in 1984, the Department found itself short of programmers and resorted to extensive contract programming. By February 1986 over half the 102 consultants employed at Telford were engaged on routine work.[48] This caused 'huge resentment' among internal staff, who were generally more proficient in Telford's procedures than the newcomers, but who earned substantially less. Employment of outsiders on routine tasks broke the motivational principle that external staff should always possess superior ability.

In overcoming the skills shortage, recruitment staff were helped by the relaxation of civil service rule binding them to central procurement. In early 1986 they embarked on a campaign of local Executive Officer (EO) recruitment, and by April 1986 EOs were being recruited at the rate of 100 per year, compared to only 29 supplied by the Civil Service Commission during 1985–6. By September 1986 Inland Revenue had significantly reduced the numbers of consultants.[49] Action on recruitment coincided with a review of IT training throughout the Department, and the development of a comprehensive training strategy for IT staff. Today the majority of programmers at Telford are trained internally.[50]

IMPLEMENTATION STRATEGY

Inland Revenue adopted a strategy of maximum consultation and information sharing with the civil service unions, from the very earliest days of the feasibility study when job losses were first discussed. Steve Matheson believes that although time consuming, it paid 'huge dividends' in terms of staff motivation and stability because there were 'no surprises' once the roll-out began. As with the DSS, there was initial strike action over the computerization proposals. In January 1984 Inland Revenue staff struck as on-line trials commenced in the West Midlands. While the action centred ostensibly on whether computerization of District Office tasks constituted a re-definition of the job for which clerks had originally contracted, the fundamental issue at stake was whether the Department would give a guarantee of no redundancies under a New Technology Agreement (NTA). A court decision on the matter found against the unions, but despite its undoubtedly strong hand after the court victory, Inland Revenue opted to sign a NTA shortly afterwards in which they gave their strongest endeavour not to make compulsory redundancies.[51]

Lasting up to 1988, the NTA covered all applications of new technology. It provided for staff reduction by natural wastage, an objective which the Department has honoured since then as well. Provisions were also made for health and safety, consultation mechanisms, and flexible working arrangements enabling a nine day fortnight.[52] Later in the implementation process, Inland Revenue allowed union representatives to choose the type of monitors which staff would use, commissioned work on possible VDU hazards, and provided new office furniture for all users. Damaging strikes during the roll-out period were avoided by dealing with uncertainty over staff reductions early in the project, and offering incentives to users as part of the implementation.

STRATEGY ISSUES

Delivered on time, almost within budget, and with considerably more functionality than originally planned, Inland Revenue's computerization programme is undoubtedly a success. Where the original 1981 specifications called for computerization of PAYE alone, for a marginal cost increase the Department has also computerized Schedule D, provided on-line links, and established the National Tracing System. The case illustrates how instances of short term, incremental process changes can be exploited in order to effect radical and long term changes in service.

COP/CODA was incremental both in its goals and implementation strategy. It mirrors the manual system in that the District Office structure has remained, PAYE and Schedule D continue to be functionally split, and assessments are worked out using the same rules. Instead of records being housed in filing cabinets however, they are on-line and assessment is calculated automatically. The method of assessment lent itself to computerization because it was already rule-based, unlike Supplementary Benefit at the DSS, which had to be codified before computerization could take place. In terms of the technology, COP/CODA would have been more radical had the Government not intervened in 1981 to defer on-line links. This externally imposed restraint was advantageous to Inland Revenue because it allowed them to gain experience developing software for the ICL mainframes, and incorporate new technology, before embarking on networks. The outcome of the Government review was thus a mainframe based system which bore some resemblance to the already existent East Kilbride processing centre. Gradually over the 1980s then, Inland Revenue extended the skills gained in running and maintaining one mainframe processing centre to a number of regional computing centres. It began with familiar technology and used it to increase operational efficiency without making radical changes to the organization.

So the programme's success is partly due to cautious implementation and limited objectives. However a number of more proactive features in project management were also significant. Skills build-up and integration of external with internal staff are the two most important of these, and have in turn contributed to the growth of technical capabilities.

LEARNING

Bridging the gap between user requirements and technical specialists is necessary for effective development, and depends on cross-flows of tacit and formal knowledge. Two major learning processes seem to have taken place over the programme. First, the transfer of formal development and implementation expertise to internal staff. Second, the extension of existing capabilities through such devices as retraining office staff as programmers and functional decomposition.

The formal knowledge required in working through the specifications of the computer system, its design and implementation, had to be brought in, but consultants were used proactively. They were involved in the programme even during the planning stage, but care was taken to avoid over reliance by emphasizing the transfer of their skills to internal staff. Missing however, was the informal knowledge necessary to tailor computerization plans with organizational needs. An appreciation of the type of work involved in assessing PAYE could not simply be brought in. To this end, the recruitment of programmers from district offices around the country at the beginning of the project, training them under supervision of the consultants, and promoting them on the job, helped ensure that at least some of the staff responsible for systems development had practical experience of business needs.

Building up internal capability over time is important for a number of reasons. External consultants can be four to five times more expensive than internal staff. Furthermore, without a core of internal skill, project progression can become dependent upon the actions and inclinations of external staff – particularly when acute skill shortages prevail in the labour market. Internal skill provides a platform from which future technological developments can be assessed in terms of the organization's needs.[53] A stronger base is established than could be achieved through reliance on outside experts, because internal capability assimilates a mixture of general and organization specific knowledge.

For example, experimentation and development has recently taken place on computerizing and linking the collection systems with the COP/CODA network under the initiative 'BROCS' (Business Review Of Collection Services). In general the technical focus is shifting towards powerful, distributed processors, relational databases and intelligent terminals, operating through an extensive national communication network. Ultimately these moves will lead to significant changes in service, such as common interfaces for corporation and PAYE tax.

INTEGRATION

Tight integration between programmers, consultants, Inland Revenue Project Managers, and the Steering Group was apparent throughout the programme. It was facilitated by highly visible senior managers who generated commitment to the project's success; the nature of feedback mechanisms between senior management and project managers; and a flattening of the hierarchy through the project management structure. The Department's approach to project management involved concentrating power at senior levels in some areas and encouraging autonomy in others. At Telford Matheson took particular interest in the areas where integration was likely to be most problematic: external recruitment and pro-motion, where the ability to 'fit in' had important consequences for internal staff morale, and establishing user requirements. In other areas however, project managers were able to exercise autonomy. Senior managers encouraged development staff to find solutions to their own problems, offering assistance with resources.[54] Project control mechanisms assisted this process of delegation by enabling project managers to adjust their schedules within the overall time frame. In contrast to the hierarchical model with its emphasis on downward information flows, senior levels played an active role in co-ordinating resources but technical responsibilities were maintained at project team level.

Integration between consultants and internal staff was handled particularly well during COP/CODA. Bearing in mind the example of the DVLC, which originally bought its technology off the shelf and was totally dependent on consultants for expertise, Inland Revenue involved con-sultants from the feasibility stage but made sure that they committed themselves to the Department's aims and timetable. Pressure was placed on consultants at senior levels through mechanisms like the Steering Group, while at Telford itself, the greenfield site and insistence on mixed development teams ensured that external staff did not maintain a monopoly on technical expertise.

COP/CODA's success has been accomplished through a management style which balanced the Department's existing skills with new abilities. Early experience of a single regional processing centre was utilized in the national plan for on-line operation. Internal personnel were supplemented by consultants and in this way, the Department built upon existing competencies. Matheson's undoubtedly energetic personality was a component in achieving the integration between end-users and technicians necessary for learning to take place. However his technique was only viable because the project involving a relatively small development team which could be hand picked. Growth in the IT division since then, from 300 in the mid 1980s to around 1 400 today, along with changes in senior personnel, have rendered this kind of personal control impossible. Recent modifications in the management structure have been designed to re-establish effective control by splitting the IT division into smaller projects.[55] Recognizing the importance of integrating user experience with specialist knowledge, the present Controller of Telford is attempting once again to flatten the hierarchy.

CONCLUSION

Inland Revenue has more than fulfilled its 1980 plan for computerization. The manual, card based system of tax administration has been replaced by a range of sophisticated computer functions. Over 500 District Offices and 11 Regional Centres have been linked into a national network encompassing both PAYE and Schedule D. Filing and referencing functions have been automated through the National Tracing System.

Throughout the project senior management emphasized learning and integration, aided the build up of longer term competencies. A focus on the organization's priorities rather than the technology *per se* led to clear objectives and realistic timetables. End-users were brought into the planning process early on, and given sufficient education to ensure that their needs could be communicated to technical specialists. Contractors and senior management were tied to the project through a quasi-public forum; internal specialists were treated sensitively by highly selective recruitment of outside expertise; and the cooperation of end-users was sought through union agreements.

Having successfully computerized PAYE, the Inland Revenue continues to build upon its competencies in a balanced manner. Project teams have been set up to computerize the collection services, whilst relational databases are being used to improved fraud control. Having extended computerization in these directions, the Inland Revenue is now able to consider changes to the organization itself. For example, integration of PAYE and Schedule D at the District Office level is under discussion. Though the Inland Revenue has taken an incremental approach to technology, the overall effect of increased flexibility in the working environment will be quite radical.

APPENDIX A GLOSSARY OF TERMS

BROCS   Business Review of Collection Services
CCTA   Central Computer and Telecommunication Agency
CODA   Computerization of Schedule D
COP   Computerization of PAYE
COPSG   Computerization of PAYE Steering Group
DSS   Department of Social Security
DVLC   Driver and Vehicle Licensing Centre
EO   Executive Officer
GDP   Gross Domestic Product
ICL   International Computers Limited

IR   Inland Revenue
IT   Information Technology
ITSG   Information Technology Steering Group
NTS   National Tracing System
NAO   National Audit Office
NTA   New Technology Agreement
PAC   Public Accounts Committee
PAYE   Pay As You Earn Tax
PSA   Property Services Agency
SCPS   Society of Civil and Public Servants
VDU   Visual Display Unit

APPENDIX B INLAND REVENUE COMPUTER INSTALLATIONS

Telford
    ICL environment
    COP/CODA & NTS
    Maintenance/enhancement
    Design, development, testing of assessment & collection projects
Worthing
    IBM environment
    Statistics of income and wealth
    Staff payroll
    Management, financial and accounting systems
Basingstoke
    Unix environment
    Small systems testing centre
Liverpool
    Tax deduction scheme for subcontractors in construction industry

APPENDIX C PAYE PROCESSING CENTRES

Region	Location	Go-live date
West Midlands	Telford	Oct. 1983
Eastern Counties	Peterborough	Aug. 1985
Wales	Llanishen	Oct. 1985
South East	West Byfleet	Dec. 1985
Scotland/N. Ireland	Livingston	Jun. 1986
Greater Manchester	Wythenshawe	Jun. 1986
South Yorkshire	Wentworth	Sep. 1986
South West	Exeter	Oct. 1986
North West	Netherton	Jan. 1987
North	Faverdale	Mar. 1987
London	Peterborough	Mar. 1987
Scotland	East Kilbride	Oct. 1988

NOTES

1. Inland Revenue's operational problems were particularly acute in 1968 when three PAYE recoding exercises had to be undertaken.
2. *Financial Times*, 9/8/80; PAC 1980; PAC 1978, para. 1282. In 1980 there were 26.5 million PAYE accounts, *Financial Times*, 9/8/80.
3. S. Matheson, 'Computerisation of the Pay As You Earn System', in Pitt and Smith (1984) *The Computer Revolution in Public Administration*, p. 93; *Times*, 20/3/68; 20/5/69.
4. *Financial Times*, 9/8/80. By 1980 collection costs overall were running at around 2% of net revenue collected. Cost/yield ratios should be treated with care. For example as the Chairman of IR Sir William Pile pointed out in regard to the 1977 figures, rising unemployment had lowered the yield while simultaneously absorbing staff resources. (PAC 1978, para. 1282).
5. PAC, 1976, para. 80.
6. Though on a smaller scale, work proceeded on a London Employers PAYE Collection system run on computers from Liverpool, originally set up in 1971 to service a deduction scheme for subcontractors in the construction industry.
7. This project was estimated to save 2 000 staff, or £9m at 1978 prices.
8. PAC, 1980, para. 2743.
9. In 1980 PAYE staff numbered 34 500, and COP was expected to achieve net savings of 6 800. NAO, 1989, sec. 2.11–12, p. 8.
10. A 1980 report found that there was a 27% error rate on assessments,

12% of codings were inaccurate, and 24% of examinations of returns contained errors. Errors were generally in favour of the taxpayer, representing a net loss to the Revenue of £7m per annum (PAC 1980, p. ix; *Financial Times*, 9/8/80; PAC 1982, para. 2208).

11. PAC, 1984, para. 3546.
12. This had apparently been one of the problems with the East Kilbride mainframe already operating. Inland Revenue 1980, 123rd Report, p. 22.
13. *Financial Times*, 9/8/80; PAC 1978, Qs 1278. Self-assessment was particularly attractive because it meant that the cost of assessment would be borne primarily by the individual rather than the state.
14. *Financial Times*, 9/8/80.
15. Sir Lawrence Airey, PAC 1984, para. 3580.
16. PAC, 1987, p.i; NAO 1987, p. 7. Evidence from the DSS indicates that computerization may often result in **reduced** job satisfaction, because of the time which staff spent inputting via keyboard.
17. PAC, 1984, para. 3596.
18. The most important of these is the integration of assessment functions (for example self-employed income and PAYE), and the merging of assessment and collection, so that taxpayers may deal with just one contact point instead of four or five.
19. Matheson (1984) p. 95. In the event this did not occur; among other things, child tax allowances were abolished half way through implementation.
20. *Financial Times*, 9/8/80.
21. PAC, 1981, para. 2891.
22. *Financial Times*, 9/8/80; *Times* and *Financial Times*, 30/10/80; PAC 1981, para. 2891.
23. *Financial Times*, 6/11/80.
24. The main disadvantage of the amended strategy was that staff savings had to be revised downward by 900, owing to the extra operating staff needed to input data manually at regional centres.
25. *Times*, 30/10/80, 31/12/80; *Financial Times*, 6/11/80; PAC 1981, PARA. 2888–2890.
26. This utilized the COP computers, with the information needed for collection being passed on to the Accounts Office computers at Cumbernauld.
27. In fact IBM at the time, lacked the necessary database handling capability. Other companies which had the potential ability, such as Tandem, were discouraged from serious lobbying because of the industrial support policy then in operation.
28. PAC, 1981, para. 2854.
29. The 2966 computer had a 1 Mips (Million instructions per second)

capacity, compared to the Estriel 3.5 Mips (Morris and Hough, 1987).
30. *Financial Times*, 20/7/89.
31. *Financial Times*, 20/7/89.
32. Norman Lamont, answer to House of Commons, 27 January 1989
33. From 925 in 1982 to 1890 (estimated) in 1987.
34. The DSS Operational Strategy has had three Directors in the decade since its inception.
35. Matheson (1984) p. 102. The ITSG included the Chairman of the Board, three deputy secretaries; the Deputy Chairman (Policy), Director General (Technical and Data Processing) and Director General (Management), two under secretaries; the Director of Data Processing and the Director of Operations, and the Director of the CCTA. Other members were the managing directors of PACTEL and CSC, an under secretary from the PSA, and representatives from ICL and British Telecom.
36. Matheson (1984) p. 101–2.
37. Matheson (1984) p. 101–2.
38. Morris and Hough (1987) p. 163, p. 173.
39. Morris and Hough (1987) p. 170–1.
40. Morris and Hough (1987) p. 164–5.
41. Morris and Hough (1987) p. 162; NAO 1987, para. 5.25.
42. A NAO report for 1986–7 showed that consultants were on average four times more expensive than equivalent internal staff. *NAO* 1987, 5.24–5.30.
43. PAC 1987, p. ix.
44. PAC 1987, para. 1783.
45. NAO 1987, para. 2.8, 5.9; PAC 1987, para. 1751.
46. Morris and Hough (1987) p. 164.
47. PAC 1987, para. 1751.
48. NAO 1987, para. 5.26.
49. Earlier recruitment initiatives included the establishment of a Youth Training Scheme at Telford, and the appointment of new graduates as trainee programmers, supplied via a consultant. However the latter initiative was ended following industrial action by the SCPS (NAO 1987, para. 5.26).
50. NAO 1987, para. 5.18–19.
51. *Financial Times*, 24/1/8; 2/2/84.
52. Willman (1986) p. 34–5; *Financial Times*, 14/6/85.
53. As Edith Penrose (1966) pointed out in a slightly different context, internal productive resources can generate a momentum of expanding capabilities within the organisation.
54. Matheson (1984) p. 18.
55. This has included the management of BROCS, criticized by the NAO in 1987 for its thin dispersal of IT specialists.

REFERENCES

Board of Inland Revenue (1980) *Report of the Commissioners of Her Majesty's Inland Revenue for the Year Ended 31st March 1980: One Hundred and Twenty-Third Report*, February, Cmnd 8160, House of Commons.

Board of Inland Revenue (1982) *Report of the Commissioners of Her Majesty's Inland Revenue for the Year Ended 31st December 1982: One Hundred and Twenty-Fifth Report*, December, Cmnd 8947, House of Commons.

Board of Inland Revenue (1983) *Report of the Commissioners of Her Majesty's Inland Revenue for the Year Ended 31st December 1983: One Hundred and Twenty-Sixth Report*, December, Cmnd 9305, House of Commons.

Dyerson, R. and Roper, M. (1989) 'Computerization at the DSS 1977–89: The operational strategy', *Technology Project Papers*, No. 4, London Business School.

Grindley, P. (1989) 'Technical change within the firm: A framework for research and management, *Technology Project Papers*, No. 1, London Business School.

Matheson, S. 'Computerization of the PAYE System'. In Pitt, D. C. and Smith, B. C. (1984) *The Computer Revolution in Public Administration*, Wheatsheaf.

National Audit Office (1987) *Inland Revenue: Control of Major Developments in Use of Information Technology*, January, HC 132, House of Commons.

Morris, P. W. G. and Hough, G. H. (1987) *The Anatomy of Major Projects: A Study of the Reality of Project Management*, Wiley Chichester, UK.

Penrose, E. (1966) *The Theory of the Growth of the Firm*, Basil Blackwell, Oxford, ch. 5.

Public Accounts Committee (1977) *Tenth Report From The Committee of Public Accounts*, July, HC 536, House of Commons.

Public Accounts Committee (1978) *Sixth Report From The Committee of Public Accounts: Board of Inland Revenue*, July, HC 574, House of Commons.

Public Accounts Committee (1981) *Twelfth Report From The Committee of Public Accounts: Board of Inland Revenue*, May, HC 318, House of Commons.

Public Accounts Committee (1981) *First Report From The Committee of Public Accounts: Government Financial Assistance for ICL*, November, House of Commons.

Public Accounts Committee (1982) *Twenty-second Report From The Committee of Public Accounts: Board of Inland Revenue*, July, HC 339, House of Commons.

Public Accounts Committee (1984) *Thirty-fifth Report From The Committee of Public Accounts: Quality Control Over District Office Procedures*, July, HC 594, House of Commons.

Public Accounts Committee (1987) *Fourteenth Report From The Committee of Public Accounts: Control of Major Developments in use of Information Technology*, April, HC 262, House of Commons.

Public Accounts Committee (1987) *Twelfth Report From The Committee of Public Accounts: Matters Relating to the Inland Revenue Department*, November, HC 157, House of Commons.

Public Accounts Committee (1988) *Forty-fifth Report From The Committee of Public Accounts: Inland Revenue Department*, October, HC 546, House of Commons.

Willman, P. (1985) *New Technology and Industrial Relations: A Review of the Literature*, London Business School.

6 Quantitative Methods

Any programme of study in a social science will, today, contain an element of quantitative methods. This normally includes inferential statistics as well as implementations of management science or operational research techniques. The orientation of the programme will dictate the contents of this component. In the case of sociology, it is likely to be mainly inferential statistics, while accounting and business courses are drawn more towards management science tools such as linear programming, critical path analysis and queuing theory in addition to various forms of financial modelling.

Operations research, the forerunner of operational research/management science (OR/MS), evolved during the inter-war years, primarily as a military discipline aimed at determining the results of military operations. It is worth noting that originally it did not have a purely quantitative orientation.

By the 1950s OR/MS, in its current form, was emerging as a business discipline concerned mainly with the implementation of mathematically based methods and procedures developed during the Second World War for the movement of men and materiel. The simultaneous development of IT greatly benefited OR/MS and many organizations were able to improve their manufacturing processes and develop better markets for their products.

OR/MS has, however, the character of Jekyll and Hyde. Whilst it aids and facilitates the process of enquiry about the world through structured methods and models, the lack of a critical perspective may eventually lead to a conceptualization of the world in a mathematical and mechanical metaphor. There are many that believe that this is appropriate for accountancy arguing that the rigorous processing of 'value-free' data allowed by quantitative methods guarantees a kind of truth. The major problem in accounting, as in other social sciences, remains one of data capture, in other words how to preserve the richness of data whilst maintaining an ability to process it.

This Part contains chapters which deal both with the quantitative/qualitative issue as well as the IT dimension. In some ways, it might be argued that the exploration of the IT dimension encourages enquiry into the quantitative/qualitative dichotomy. The first chapter by Valerie Belton acts as a general introduction and focuses on the effectively symbiotic development of IT and OR/MS. The widespread use of financial modelling facilitated by the development of end-user computing highlights a particular OR/MS problem that is addressed by Bob Berry and Alyson McLintock. They suggest that too little attention is given to the development of adequate model logic through insufficient validation and critical reflection. Finally, Bryan Pfaffenberger offers a critical reflection on quantitative methods and the social construction of technology to complete the four-way exploration.

17 Operational research and information technology – impacts and interactions
Valerie Belton

INTRODUCTION – THE CHANGING FACE OF OR

Operational research (OR), also known as management science (MS), is traditionally associated with the application of quantitative techniques to the analysis of managerial problems. It has its origins in the analysis of operations in the Second World War and was subsequently introduced first to industry and later to government and commerce with some considerable success. More recently a Community OR Unit has been established, an idea initiated by Rosenhead (1986) and established during his Presidency of the OR Society, with the support of the Society. The aim of this unit is to make OR available to non-profit-making bodies, such as tenants' organizations and community groups.

The definition of Operational Research which appeared in the *Journal of the Operational Research Society* of Great Britain up until April 1984 said:

> Operational Research is the application of the methods of science to complex problems arising in the direction and management of large systems of men, machines, materials and money in industry, business, government and defence. The distinctive approach is to develop a scientific model of the system, incorporating measurements of factors such as chance and risk, with which to predict and compare the

Specially commissioned for *IT and Acccounting: The impact of information technology.*
Edited by Bernard C. Williams and Barry J. Spaul.
Published in 1991 by Chapman & Hall, London ISBN 0 412 39210 0.

outcomes of alternative decisions, strategies or controls. The purpose is to help management determine its policy and actions scientifically.

Operational research has traditionally been associated with optimization and techniques such as linear and non-linear programming, critical path analysis, queuing theory, and so on. In much of continental Europe and the USA OR is regarded as a branch of mathematics.

However, this is a very restricted view of operational research as practised in Britain today. The early 1980s saw much debate about the role of OR; a paper by Tobin *et al.* (1980) discusses the changing role of OR in British Airways. In 1983 the Operational Research Society established a Commission on the Future Practice of Operational Research, which had as part of its terms of reference an investigation of the changing state of OR in practice (see Mitchell *et al.* (1986). The Commission found that the aims of OR in practice were characterized by statements such as the following:

1. to help structure messy problems;
2. to research into the facts of an uncertain topic;
3. to help an understanding of a sphere of activity;
4. to design systems (usually of a non-routine nature);
5. to facilitate change;
6. to help introduce new technologies and ideas (particularly in the field of information technology);
7. to provide an independent view on a contentious issue;
8. to provide technical solutions to technical problems.

A shared view of OR in practice was as a means of enhancing the clients' understanding of their own problems.

Note that none of these aims make direct mention of optimization or the use of techniques which so commonly characterize other disciplines' views of OR.

OR AND COMPUTERS

The introduction of OR and computers to business began at about the same time, in the period following the Second World War. In the very early days OR did not use computers – the emphasis was on problem-solving. This often involved the construction of analogue models which simulated the way in which a physical process worked. These models were used to try out different ways of operating, providing the basis for reports from the OR group to management. They were often very large, sophisticated constructions; Jones *et al.* (1955) describe a model used to investigate the flow of materials in a steelworks. The model was a system of flexible pipes connecting bunkers which represented the various operations in the steelworks, for example the blast furnaces. Lead shot flowed through the model representing the materials, the rate of flow being controlled by various mechanisms. The model required a scaffolding 30 feet high to support it and used two tons of lead shot when operating. The user could investigate the way the system operated by controlling the rate of flow of lead shot which represented, for example, the rate at which iron ore was unloaded from the ships.

The rapid development of mainframe computing power in the 1950s and early 1960s enabled a parallel development in OR techniques. At this time OR was at the forefront of developments in technology, pioneering the introduction of computers in a number of organizations, in particular their use as tools to aid management decision-making. Two examples are the introduction of linear programming in the oil industry and simulation in the steel industry. Ranyard (1988) gives an excellent account of the history of OR and computing, which goes into more depth than is possible here. OR continued to take on a pioneering role as technological developments progressed. The OR group at British Airways led the introduction of interactive planning models in the early 1970s using a timesharing system based around a minicomputer, as described by Tobin (1975). The advent of the microcomputer in the early 1980s again saw OR at the leading edge in introducing systems into organizations. The micro was received enthusiastically by OR groups, giving them full control over their computing facilities at relatively low cost. The large number of meetings and publications (see the *Journal of the Operational Research Society*, April 1981 and April 1983) on microcomputer issues during the early 1980s reflects the extent of the enthusiasm and involvement. In recent years OR groups have taken a leading role in the introduction of expert systems as managerial tools; O'Keefe (1985) discusses mutual benefits of OR and expert systems and Zahedi (1987) forecasts the convergence of the two fields. Many applications have featured in the OR literature in the last five years; for example, Bowen and Payling (1987) describe an expert system for performance review of hospitals, Finlay and King (1989) a system for screening applications for an MBA programme.

THE IMPACT OF IT ON OR

The above brief account of the history of OR and computers paints a picture of OR in an active role in the introduction of new technology and systems. This is indeed the case. However, at the same time the technology itself has influenced the way in which OR is practised. The example of interactive planning models in British Airways was an early indication of the way in which OR was to develop, in large part facilitated by the developing technology. The role of the OR analyst has for the most part changed from that of an expert advisor to that of a facilitator. The expert advisor operated by taking away a manager's problem, perhaps building a model of it, solving it, and some time later returning to the manager with the 'best' solution. There are numerous accounts of why this is an inappropriate way of working – for example, see Tobin *et al.* (1980). The facilitator may operate in a number of ways and at all levels of the organization, but the important difference from the expert advisor is that the facilitator works *with* the client in developing a model or system, and possibly also in using it. The important impact of developing IT on OR is that is has constantly enhanced and extended the potential of the facilitating role. This may take many forms, all of which could be grouped under the heading of decision support. Although OR can by no means claim the entire field of decision support systems as its own, it has made a number of very significant contributions. The following section outlines briefly the concept of a decision support system and discusses the contributions of OR to these systems in some detail. The final section reviews how IT has been an enabling factor in these developments and comments on the impact they have had on the practice of OR.

OR CONTRIBUTIONS TO DECISION SUPPORT

The term decision support systems (DSS) was first used by Keen in the late 1970s. His book *Decision Support Systems* (1978) written with Scott-Morton has become a classic text on the subject. They describe a decision support system as:

> ... a coherent system of computer-based technology (hardware, software and supporting documentation) used by managers as an aid to decision making in semi-structured tasks.

A semi-structured task is one which requires some element of human judgement, one which cannot be wholly automated.

A DSS comprises three elements as illustrated in Fig. 17.1: a model, a database and a user interface. OR analysts have been developing such systems since the mid-1970s, the British Airways' planning system referred to above being one of the earliest examples. We will now look in more detail at some examples.

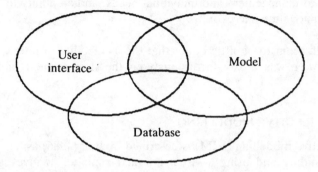

Fig. 17.1 The components of a decision support system.

INTERACTIVE SYSTEMS

A good example of the type of interactive system which was developed by OR analysts in the days before microcomputers is described by Williams (1979). This is a system which was developed for a Danish shipyard building supertankers. The company was one of Europe's most efficient yards, rapid construction time being the key element in its success. Sections of a ship were assembled in large welding halls, over a number of days, and on completion they were lifted over in complete sections, out of the hall and along to the dry dock where the ship itself was being assembled. Planning the construction of the mid-ship sections was relatively straightforward as they were relatively uniform in shape and did not differ from one ship to the next. The problem arose in planning the forepeak and stern sections which were very different in size and shape from one ship to the next. The question facing the planners was where in the hall each section should be placed for assembly. Once assembly had begun it was not possible to move a section until completed and a wrong decision, constraining the space available, could have a significant knock-on effect. The system which was developed acted as an aid to the planners: it allowed them to use their expertise in locating the shapes within the hall, whilst providing a record of their decisions, carrying out necessary computations of workload, and prompting action as necessary. The conclusion of the paper states:

> The value of this project . . . lay in the scope it afforded the company to build on its own considerable planning expertise . . . The role of OR was recognised as a key contributory factor to the success of this project, not

for the considerable element of technical underpinning contained in the final system, but rather for an analytical approach to problem diagnosis, a response to management and individual needs, and an ability to introduce innovation successfully.

There would seem to be little doubt that the availability of interactive computing power was a key factor enabling the development of this system.

VISUAL INTERACTIVE MODELLING

Visual interactive modelling (VIM) is described by Bell (1986) as '. . . the process of building and using a visual interactive model to investigate issues important to decision makers. The VI model has three essential components: a mathematical model; a visual display of the status of the model; interactions that permit the status of the model to be changed.' He goes on to say that VIM is '. . . most useful for semi-structured problems where the objective of the analyst is to incorporate the knowledge of the decision maker in the problem solving loop.' The above definition and claim clearly sets VIM within the bounds of decision support systems as defined by Keen and Scott-Morton. The unique feature is the emphasis on the nature of the user interface. The pioneering work in VIM was done by Hurrion (1978, 1980), now at the University of Warwick, and by the Operational Research Group in British Leyland (see Fiddy *et al.*, 1981) who developed the first commercial Visual Interactive Simulation package, known as See-Why. Bell has written a number of papers reviewing VIM (1986 and forthcoming) and its applications (1985).

I will illustrate the concept of VIM by a simple simulation model of a pub.[1] The actors in this model are the customers and the barstaff. The screen display seen in Fig. 17.2 shows the layout of the pub and the current positions of the actors. Customers may be drinking, seated at tables, at the bar being served, in a queue waiting to be served, or in the washroom. Bar staff are busy serving customers, or washing glasses, or they are idle. The number of clean glasses available and the number waiting to be washed is also shown. Information on the rate at which customers arrive at the pub, how long they stay, how many drinks they have, how long it takes to serve a customer, and so on, are available in the model. As the model is run (in fast-time), events are displayed on the screen, for example, as customers finish their drinks they may get up and leave the pub, or join the queue at the bar to buy another. The user can see if queues build up, and if resources are adequate. They can make changes to the model, for example, by adding another server, and immediately see the effect on the

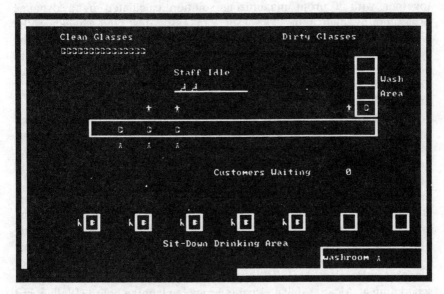

Fig. 17.2 Visual interactive simulation of a pub.

system. As a consequence of using such a model the user often comes to understand the system better and is able to make a more informed decision about how it should be operated.

The approach has been widely used in practice with considerable success (see Bell, 1985); unfortunately, there are few applications described in the literature. Lembersky and Chi (1984) describe an early application, called VISION, originally developed on a mainframe and later implemented on a mini then a micro. VISION is a system which is used in the timber processing industry to inform decisions about cutting tree stems (which can be up to 100 feet in length) into logs which are then allocated to processes resulting in different end-products (lumber, plywood, paper). A single stem can be cut and allocated in many different ways, each resulting in a different revenue. Factors to be taken into account are the geometric profile of the stem (length, diameter, curvature, taper) quality variations along the length, and the return to be had from allocating different quality and shape of logs to different end products. The system is used as a training tool and as a means of investigating alternative processing strategies. The user is shown a realistic representation of a stem on the screen, which can be inspected by rolling and rotating it, and he or she would then cut (by positioning a saw displayed on the screen) and allocate it. The economic consequences of the decision are calculated and reported to the user, together with a profit maximizing solution calculated by a dynamic programming algorithm. The user can easily test and challenge the algorithm's solutions using the visual display if they wish. The use of the system enabled management and operators in Weyerhauser Company to develop a new, more cost-effective strategy for cutting the West Coast Douglas fir, a very high value timber, resulting in a measured benefit of 7 million US dollars per annum.

A more recent application of visual interactive modelling developed by Lembersky (forthcoming) and colleagues is a form of customer support in the retail home improvement (DIY) business. Using three dimensional graphics the customer can build up a design for a shelving system, or an outdoor deck, with the assistance of a salesperson. The system automatically checks that the construction is sound and does not violate any legal restrictions. When the customer is satisfied with the appearance the system will determine the cost, materials required and optimal cutting pattern; if they are not happy with this then modifications can be made.

Other uses of VI models reported in the literature are manpower planning in Barclays Bank (Billington, 1987), and production planning and scheduling at Alcan, using a visual interactive planning board (Walker and Woolven, forthcoming).

The development of these models has clearly depended on the availability of interactive computing facilities with appropriate graphical displays. Some current systems, for example WITNESS (Clark, forthcoming), allow the analyst to construct the model and display interactively with the client. If this is not possible, then an approach of rapid prototyping may be used – the analyst and client discuss the requirements of a system, possibly including the drawing of mock screens on paper, the analyst then quickly (possibly in a few hours) develops a rough working system and tries this out with the client. A series of refinements and modifications, in close consultation with the client, takes place until a satisfactory system is arrived at. This rapid prototyping approach, earlier referred to as the evolutionary approach, is often referred to in the OR literature (Tobin *et al.*, 1980; Ranyard, 1988).

GROUP DECISION SUPPORT SYSTEMS

Group decision support system (GDSS) is a term which has emerged to describe the process of working interactively on a problem with a group of decision-makers with the support of a computer system. The period during which the group comes together is referred to as a workshop or decision conference. As with DSS, GDSS are by no means the sole premise of the OR world; however, OR analysts have made a significant contribution to the field. (Phillips (1990) and Ackermann (1990) give full accounts of the nature of the process of group decision support. In general the workshop will involve the building and use of a model, or the development and use of a previously constructed model. The group may be comprised of managers from the same company, at all levels of the organization, or it may be an inter-organizational group. The nature of models used is wide ranging, different consultants having their own distinctive toolbag and style. We will look briefly at two approaches used in this context, multiple criteria decision analysis (MCDA) and strategic options development and analysis (SODA). Ackermann and Belton (1990) give a fuller description of the two approaches.

An important aspect of the approaches is that they are being used in work with groups and that the technology is appropriate to support that work. Compared to some work with GDSS done in the USA, utilizing networks of computers in a boardroom configuration (see Phillips, 1990), the technology utilized is relatively modest – usually a single micro-computer with powerful display facilities (a large screen or colour projector) or a number of stand-alone machines with which small groups can work interactively.

Multiple Criteria Decision Analysis

By MCDA we mean any approach which seeks to take explicit account of multiple, conflicting criteria in supporting an investigation of a decision problem. There are many such approaches and it is not possible to describe them all here; Belton (1990), however, contains a tutorial account of those currently most widely used in practice. An application of MCDA to the Bank of England's decision to relocate one of its departments out of London is described by Butterworth (1989) and a decision about the allocation of the contract to develop an international cash management system is described by Belton (1985).

A workshop which involved the use of such an approach would typically involve the building of a model of the criteria which are relevant to the problem, identifying a number of alternatives which are to be considered, an evaluation of the performance of the alternatives against the criteria, an evaluation of priorities, a synthesis of all this information and a detailed investigation of the impact of changing judgements and priorities. The process involves much cycling through the above stages as new information comes to light, new insights arise, and discussion leads to redefinition of some concepts and the inclusion of new ones and so on. The computer plays a significant, but low-key role in enabling the rapid processing of new data and the provision of an effective interface for feedback to the decision-making group. The visual interactive approach, described above, has been incorporated into MCDA, with the same anticipated benefits (see Korhonen and Laasko, 1986; Belton and Vickers, 1989; Mareschal and Brans, forthcoming).

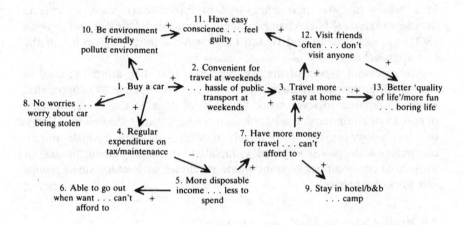

Fig. 17.3 Cognitive map.

Strategic Options Decision Analysis

SODA is an approach designed to help OR consultants work with messy problems, based on the modelling technique of cognitive mapping, using the COPE software (Eden, 1985). Cognitive mapping aims to portray beliefs, values, attitudes and the relationships between them in a way which facilitates investigation (see Eden *et al.*, 1983). A map is constructed by an analyst through discussion with a client – an illustrative map is shown in Fig. 17.3 which reflects someone's personal decision about whether or not to buy a car.

Each concept in the map is noted together with its psychological opposite (which may not match the logical opposite). The arrows represent the client's perceptions of causality, an arrow with a + by it implying that the first pole of the concept at the tail of the arrow leads to the first pole of the concept at the head of the arrow. For example, in Fig. 17.3, we see that the act of buying a car leads to the need to spend on regular maintenance and to the capability of travelling more conveniently at weekends. A negative arrow (with a minus sign by it) implies that the concept at the tail leads to the opposite pole of the concept at the head. Thus, buying a car leads to polluting the environment (the opposite pole of being environmentally friendly). Building the map is itself helpful in straightening out one's thinking; further analysis will help identify, for example, feedback loops and significant issues and beliefs, highlighting where these lead to contradictions or conflicts.

When working with a group of clients, individual maps may be built initially and then merged to form a group map which will be used in group workshops as a tool to facilitate the investigation of the issues which members of the group perceive to be of importance.

The ability to construct and make appropriate use of the model embodied in the cognitive map is combined with skills of managing the processes involved in getting a group to work together with the aim of achieving consensus and commitment to action. A detailed description of the approach is given by Eden (1989) and applications are described in Eden (1985) and Eden and Simpson (1989).

Once again the computer plays an important, but low-key, role in enabling the rapid handling and analysis of large amounts of qualitative data.

REFLECTIONS ON THE IMPACT OF IT ON OR – OUT OF THE BACKROOM?

An image of OR which is still prevalent is that of backroom workers. In the early days of OR this was largely enforced by the technology available. Mainframe computers and massive analogue models similar to the lead-shot model described earlier could not be brought to the manager's desk. The widespread availability of computing facilities, initiated by on-line computing and minicomputers, culminating in the era of the micro-computer, means that substantial computing power can be made available relatively easily wherever it is needed. Networks and constantly improving options for the display of output offer options for working easily with groups as well as individuals. As the examples given above suggest this technology has enabled OR to move out of the backroom into a range of environments, using a variety of approaches. The examples of planning in the Danish shipyard and tree cutting at Weyerhauser are systems which are in use at the forefront of operations, essentially on the shopfloor. The discussion of decision conferencing illustrates a move into management's own empire, interactively supporting decision-making, problem-solving or analysis of issues with a group, often of senior managers. The example of VIM to support DIY decisions (Lembersky, 1990) demonstrates a move into another new environment, that of the retail world and the consumer.

The main factors relating to IT which have enabled this move are, I believe, as follows:

1. The facility to work directly with the client which is brought about by ready access to systems which permit the interactive development of models, quickly.
2. Systems which allow for the rapid development of effective user interfaces, often incorporating visual interactive displays. The impact of an effective display is manyfold and deeply significant – a good display is a means of enhancing learning about a problem, leading to increased understanding of the system being modelled, including the user's values and priorities, and consequently to improved decision-making.

I do not believe that these factors are on their own responsible for this changing way of working. The development of the technology has, in a way which is inextricably linked, been accompanied by a development in the skills, experience and mode of working of management, leading to an increasing acceptance of and enthusiasm for IT. Nor do I believe that the changes are simply a consequence of the available technology, although undoubtedly they are greatly assisted by it – Walton's (1977) account of the potential of analogue LP (linear programming) solvers, and Bryant's (1988) description of Walton's work illustrate a very different approach to interactive modelling.

The consequence of the increased involvement of the client in the development of models and systems is a greater degree of ownership of the model, which in general leads to a greater commitment to action. The consequence of increased interaction with the model, often facilitated by effective displays, is a greater degree of learning and understanding, leading to more effective decision-making.

THE FUTURE

Where do we go from here? What of OR and developments in IT? It is well recognized, as reported by the Commission on the Future Practice of OR (Mitchell *et al.*, 1986) that the nature of OR in practice is ever-changing as a result of the dissemination of methods to other disciplines and the migration of subject areas as they become well established in their own right, or absorbed by other parts of the organization. This process is matched by a movement into new areas and consideration of new issues, much of which is likely to be associated with further developments in IT. The move to a more interactive process of developing models and decision support systems has been the main thesis of this chapter – as the technology develops further, in particular the available software, it is possible that clients will soon be in a position to develop their own systems without assistance, as speculated by Lockett (1984). Indeed, spreadsheets, expert systems shells, large-scale project management systems, user-friendly LP packages, and so on, have already made this possible to a large extent. This does not mean that OR analysts will become redundant, rather that their role will change. OR will continue to work at the leading edge of technology, innovating, tackling messy problems, breaking new ground, helping clients to understand their own problems better and to do their jobs better. Some work will draw on new technology, for example, designing more effective decision support systems; some will concern the implementation of the technology, for example Lockett (1989) proposes an exciting role for OR in generating new ideas in the field of information systems.

SUMMARY

This chapter presents a personal view of the development of OR and its interaction with the development of IT; it tries to avoid discussing the impact of IT on OR, or vice versa. The argument is essentially that whilst in the early days of OR and business computing, the association of OR with computing contributed to a large extent to the image of OR analysts as backroom workers, as the technology has become more widely available, more portable and more powerful, it has enabled OR to move out of the backroom to meet the action, whether it is on the shop floor, in the manager's office or the boardroom. Most of this activity can be encompassed under the umbrella of decision support systems, a field to which OR has brought a number of important contributions, in particular, visual interactive systems and systems for working interactively with groups. OR has been involved with the leading edge of IT since the introduction of computers to business, on the one hand utilizing IT to enhance its own role and on the other leading in the application of IT. There seems to be little doubt that in the future that role will continue.

NOTE

1. The model was created by K. Concannon using the GENETIK software.

DISCUSSION QUESTIONS

1. This chapter has discussed a changing role for the OR analyst – from 'expert' to 'facilitator' – in which the development of IT has been a significant enabling factor. What do you think are the skills necessary to be a successful OR analyst in the 1990s? Compare and contrast this with the position in the early days of OR. (Recommended reading: Tobin *et al.* (1980), Mitchell *et al.* (1986).)
2. Choose a specific application and describe the nature of a decision support system you might expect an OR analyst to develop today. How does this compare with one which might have been developed, say, 15–20 years ago?
   Suggested application areas:
   (a) managing a portfolio of financial investments.
   (b) a production planning system
   (c) a blending problem (e.g. animal feed)
   (d) a relocation decision (e.g. where to site the new head office)
   (e) a queuing system (e.g. passport control and personal security checking at an airport)
3. In what ways do you think OR has benefited by developments in IT? In what ways has it been disadvantaged?
4. Compare and contrast the impacts of IT on the OR profession and on the accounting profession.

REFERENCES

Ackerman, F. (1990). 'The role of computers in group decision support'. In Eden, C. and Radford, J. (eds), *Tackling Strategic Problems*. Sage, London, UK.

Ackerman, F. and Belton, V. (1990). *Managing corporate knowledge using SODA and VISA*. Working Paper, University of Strathclyde, Department of Management Science.

Bell, P. C. (1985). 'Visual interactive modelling in operational research: success and opportunities', *Journal of the Operational Research Society*, Vol. 36, No. 11, pp. 975–82.

Bell, P. C. (1986). 'Visual interactive modelling in 1986'. In Belton, V. and O'Keefe, R. M. (eds), *Recent Developments in Operational Research*. Pergamon Press, Oxford, UK.

Bell, P. C. (forthcoming). 'Visual interactive modelling: the past, the present and the prospects', *European Journal of Operational Research*.

Belton, V. (1985). 'The use of a simple multiple criteria model to assist in selection from a shortlist', *Journal of the Operational Research Society*, Vol. 36, No. 4, pp. 265–74.

Belton, V. (1990). 'MCDA – practically the only way to choose'. In Eglese, R. and Hendry, L. (eds), *Operational Research Tutorial Papers*. Operational Research Society, Birmingham, UK.

Belton, V. and Vickers, S. P. (1989). 'VISA – VIM for MCDA'. In Lockett, A. G. and Islei, (eds), *Improving Decision Making in Organizations*, Springer-Verlag, Berlin.

Billington, J. N. (1987). 'Visual interactive modelling and manpower planning', *European Journal of Operational Research* Vol. 30 (7), pp. 77–84.

Bowen, T. and Payling, L. (1987). 'Expert systems for performance review', *Journal of the Operational Research Society*, Vol. 38, No. 10, pp. 929–34.

Bryant, J. (1988). 'Frameworks of inquiry: OR practice across the hard-soft divide', *Journal of the Operational Research Society*, Vol. 39, No. 5, pp. 423–36.

Butterworth, N. J. (1989). 'Giving up "The Smoke"; a major institution investigates alternatives to being sited in the City', *Journal of the Operational Research Society*, Vol. 40, No. 8, pp. 711–18.

Clark, M. (forthcoming). 'WITNESS: unlocking the power of visual interactive simulation', *European Journal of Operational Research*.

Eden, C. (1985). 'Perish the thought!', *Journal of the Operational Research Society*, Vol. 36, No. 9, pp. 809–19.

Eden, C. (1989). 'Using cognitive mapping for strategic options development and analysis (SODA)'. In Rosenhead, J. R. (ed.), *Rational Analysis for a Problematic World*. Wiley, Chichester, UK.

Eden, C. and Simpson, P. (1989). 'SODA and cognitive mapping in practice'. In Rosenhead, J. R. (ed.), *Rational Analysis for a Problematic World*. Wiley, Chichester, UK.

Eden, C., Jones, S. and Sims, D. (1983). *Messing About In Problems*. Pergamon Press, Oxford, UK.

Fiddy, E., Bright, J. G. and Hurrion, R. D. (1981). 'See-Why: interactive simulation on the screen', Proceedings of the Institute of Mechanical Engineers, C293/81, pp. 867–72.

Finlay, P. N. and King, M. (1989). 'Experiences in developing an expert system for MBA admissions', *Journal of the Operational Research Society*, Vol. 40, No. 7, pp. 625–36.

Hurrion, R. D. (1978). 'An investigation of visual interactive simulation methods using the job-shop scheduling problem', *Journal of the Operational Research Society*, Vol. 29, No. 11, pp. 1085–93.

Hurrion, R. D. (1980). 'Visual interactive (computer) solutions for the travelling salesman problem', *Journal of the Operational Research Society*, Vol. 31, No. 6, pp. 537–9.

Jones, H. G., Davies, W. M. and Dickerson, P. D. (1955). 'The study of materials handling systems by a lead-shot analogue', *Journal of the Iron and Steel Institute*, Vol. 180 (July), pp. 255–62.

Keen, P. G. W. and Scott-Morton, M. S. (1978). *Decision Support Systems: An Organisational Perspective*. Addison-Wesley, Reading, Mass.

Korhonen, P. and Laasko, J. (1986). 'A visual interactive method for solving the multiple criteria problem', *European Journal of Operational Research*, Vol. 24 (2), pp. 277–87.

Lembersky, M. R. (forthcoming). 'Enhancing Point-of-Sale Productivity and Satisfaction in Retail Stores', *European Journal of Operation Research*.

Lembersky, M. R. and Chi, U. H. (1984). 'Decision simulators speed implementation and improve operations', *Interfaces*, Vol. 27, No. 4, pp. 1–15.

Lockett, A. G. (1984). 'Self starters in OR/MS – a growth area', *Interfaces*, Vol. 14 (May–June), pp. 59–61.

Lockett, A. G. (1989). 'Information systems and operational research'. In Jackson, M. C., Keys, P. and Cropper, S. A. (eds), *Operational Research and the Social Sciences*. Plenum Press, New York.

Mareschal, B. and Brans, J. P. (forthcoming). 'Bankadvisor – an industrial evaluation system', *European Journal of Operational Research*.

Mitchell, G. H. and members of the Commission on the Future Practice of OR (1986). 'Report of the Commission on the Future Practice of Operational Research', *Journal of the Operational Research Society*, Vol. 37, No. 9, pp. 827–86.

O'Keefe, R. M. (1985). 'Expert systems and operational research – mutual benefits', *Journal of the Operational Research Society*, Vol. 36, No. 2, pp. 125–30.

Phillips, L. D. (1990). 'Decision analysis for group decision support'. In Eden, C. and Radford, J. (eds), *Tackling Strategic Problems*. Sage, London, UK.

Ranyard, J. C. (1988). 'A history of OR and computing', *Journal of the Operational Research Society*, Vol. 39, No. 12, pp. 1073–86.

Rosenhead, J. R. (1986). 'Custom and practice', *Journal of the Operational Research Society*, Vol. 37, No. 4, pp. 335–44.

Tobin, N. R. (1975). 'Timesharing, interactive models and operational research', *Operational Research Quarterly*, Vol. 27, No. 3, pp. 531–46.

Tobin, N. R., Rapley, K. and Teather, W. (1980). 'The changing role of OR', *Journal of the Operational Research Society*, Vol. 31, No. 4, pp. 279–88.

Walker, L. J. and Woolven, J. D. (forthcoming). 'Using a visual interactive planning board', *European Journal of Operational Research*.

Walton, J. H. D. (1977). 'Interactive LP models in management – an analogue approach', *Omega*, Vol. 5, pp. 293–307.

Williams, A. J. (1979). 'A case study in OR/client involvement', *Journal of the Operational Research Society*, Vol. 30, No. 11, pp. 941–2.

Zahedi, F. (1987). 'Artificial intelligence and the management science practitioner: the economics of expert systems and the contributions of OR/MS', *Interfaces*, Vol. 17 (September/October), pp. 72–81.

Chapter

18 Financial modelling – use or abuse

Robert H. Berry and Alyson J. McLintock

INTRODUCTION

Financial modelling is a widely written about topic. For example, in just two professional journals, *Accountancy* and *Management Accounting* over 100 articles on this subject have appeared over the last eight years. Some of the literature highlights the range of model types in use and the financial problem areas analysed (Ashford, Berry and Dyson, 1988). Other writers comment on the rate of growth of use of financial models and on the technology involved (Grinyer, 1983). Still others discuss modelling techniques and methods of application (Naylor, 1979). This chapter emphasizes what the authors see as the neglected area of financial modelling – the model building process.

Financial modelling is carried out by individuals with varied back-grounds. Some describe themselves as operational researchers or econometricians, some as accountants. The operational research and econometrics literature contains rich discussions of the model building process. Eden and his colleagues provide an accessible example (Eden, Jones and Sims, 1983). Unfortunately these discussions have not been adequately reflected in the general accounting and finance literature. Of the 100 articles in the professional literature referred to above, most contained descriptions of computer hardware and software. None contained an adequate discussion of the methodology of model building.

It can of course be argued that if the practice of model building is being carried out with an appropriate methodology, then lack of discussion in the

Specially commissioned for *IT and Accounting: The impact of information technology*.
Edited by Bernard C. Williams and Barry J. Spaul.
Published in 1991 by Chapman & Hall, London ISBN 0 412 39210 0.

accounting literature is irrelevent. This ignores both the need to communicate to the next generation of practitioners, and the evidence emerging that all is not as it should be in the world of financial modelling (McLintock and Berry, 1990).

THE FINANCIAL MODELLING PROCESS

Financial modelling is an activity with a very long history. Since a model is nothing more than a representation of key features of reality, profit and loss accounts, balance sheets, breakeven charts, and many other routine accounting representations are financial models. The breakeven chart is an example of a model which is worth pursuing since it can be used to demonstrate all the key activities involved in the process of building a financial model.

The following is a simple example of a breakeven analysis. The aim is to show profit, revenue and cost for a range of activity levels. Table 18.1 shows the formulae used in the analysis. Fig. 18.1 shows the traditional model solution and display mechanism, the breakeven chart.

Table 18.1 Breakeven analysis

Output range:	q	$= 0 \ldots 110$	
Parameters:	P	$= 2.5$	Sale price
	VCPU	$= 1$	Variable cost per unit
Equations:	TR_q	$= P \times q$	Total revenue
	VC_q	$= VCPU \times q$	Variable cost
	FC	$= 50$	Fixed cost
	TC_q	$= FC + VC$	Total cost

The basic insight in breakeven analysis is that level of activity, in this case quantity of product produced, affects both costs and revenue. Developing this basic understanding constitutes the first and crucial part of the modelling exercise.

The next stage is to develop a model form, a set of equations which reflect the basic understanding already achieved. In this example there are four equations. There is an accounting identity: the fact that total cost is the sum of fixed and variable costs. There are also three behavioural equations, showing how total revenue and variable cost respond to changes in activity level, and how fixed cost remains constant. The variable cost and revenue equations exhibit strictly proportional behaviour. That is to say they can be represented on a graph as straight lines passing through the origin.

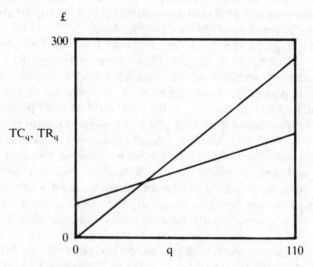

Fig. 18.1 Breakeven chart.

The choice of model form can reflect many considerations. There has to be a reflection of the way the real world behaves, but there is always a degree of simplification. Thus use of linear relationships can reflect a belief that the variables being considered are linked in a linear fashion in general, or that they are linked in this fashion over the activity range of interest. There might also be a desire to use linear equations because they are easier to solve.

The third stage of the modelling exercise involves putting parameter values into the equation forms. In this example a value of fixed cost must be specified, as must the slope coefficients in the total revenue and variable cost equations. Price per unit, variable cost per unit and fixed cost must be estimated. This phase of the modelling activity involves the modeller in confronting the problem of statistical estimation: how to use real-world data to find values of unknown coefficients.

The fourth stage of the modelling process is solving the model. In the breakeven example a graphical solution has been produced. More commonly a set of numerical values that satisfy the equations in the model are produced. The process of solving the model can sometimes cause problems. If the set of equations is recursive (solving the first generates the data necessary to solve the second and so on . . .) solution is simple. If the set of equations is simultaneous but linear then a matrix algebra approach should serve. If, however, the equation set is simultaneous and non-linear then an iterative procedure is often necessary. Then issues of convergence have to be taken into account. Potential solution difficulties, as hinted above, can be a major determinant of choice of model form.

The next stage of the modelling exercise is to validate the model. Validation involves two stages. First there must be a check on the computational accuracy of the process of model solution. Secondly, and more importantly, there must be a comparison of the outputs of the model with what happens in the real world. It must be emphasized here that the real world data with which the model's output is compared must not be the data used in deciding on equation forms or in estimating model parameters. If the same data set is used both to construct and test a model, then all that is tested is arithmetical accuracy. Data from a hold-out sample (data at hand when the model building process was being carried out, but not examined or used in any way) or additional newly collected data must be used for testing purposes.

There is a further aspect of the validation problem. So far phrases such as 'real-world data' have been used as if obtaining such data and comparing model outputs with it are unproblematic procedures. The problem is that model builders operate with perceptions of the world, their own and those of others. It is often the case that a model is built by analysts to be used by, or at least to serve the purposes of another group of individuals. Because of differences in background and training it is possible that analysts and users will see the world in different ways. For this reason validation is a much broader activity than described so far. Model form and model structure must be made obvious to users and not kept as a 'black box'. The user group must see that their interpretation of the world is consistent with what goes on in the model. Further the adequacy of the performance of the model must be judged by what the users consider important, rather than by some 'ballpark', average error criterion.

If the validation phase in the model building process is judged a failure, then the earlier parts of the modelling process must be reconsidered. If the validation phase is judged a success, then the model can be put to use. The typical use of a financial model is conditional forecasting, that is to say answering 'what would happen if' type questions. At some stage during the use of the model, it might be observed that the forecasting performance of the model is worsening. In this case it will again be necessary to reconsider the earlier stages of the model building process. Gradual or abrupt worsening in model performance can occur because the nature of the firm being modelled and its environment have changed or because perceptions of what is required have changed. Model building then is an iterative process, which may never terminate.

FINANCIAL MODELLING AND THE COMPUTER

Despite the fact that breakeven analysis is a financial modelling exercise in every important sense, it is not what many people think of as financial modelling. The model has typically been solved and the solution displayed using pen and paper, whereas most people think that financial modelling involves the use of the computer. Thus financial modelling is seen by many as starting with the large mainframe computer based corporate models of Sun Alliance and the like. These early models were gigantic endeavours, involving several man years of effort and much computer time. The financial element generally involved the production of pro forma financial statements for a firm. However, marketing and production modules were also typically present.

The models were often massive constructs, involving many equations and a very disaggregated view of the firm. Because of the opacity of mainframe operating systems and the programming languages in use, accountants and managers ceased to be key members of the modelling team and were replaced by computer literate model building specialists. This separation of model builder from senior management and potential users led to much modelling effort being misdirected. Models were built, only to fall quickly into disuse, either because during the process of construction user ownership of the problem had been lost, or because the process of use was too difficult, time-consuming or demeaning to the user to be supported.

These problems spawned several solution attempts. They largely took two forms. The first was a more careful analysis of the conditions likely to lead to a model building exercise being useful. This led to a recognition of the political and behavioural dimensions of the model building process. The second was an attempt to develop modelling languages, computer packages which had powerful analytical tools combined with a user-friendly method of use.

Good descriptions of these large models and of the details of these model building processes are rare in the literature. Often commercial confidentiality stood in the way. However, the growth of this type of modelling activity is well documented. Further, it was observed that over time as modelling tools developed and became easier to use, and as computers became more accessible – often due to the use of time-sharing bureaux – managers and accountants began gradually to recover

	A	B
1	Breakeven analysis	
2		
3	Price	2.5
4	VCPU	=B3*0.4
5	Fixed	=50
6		
7		
8	Quantity	Profit
9	10	=(B3*A9)−(B4*A9)−B5
10	=A9+10	=(B3*A10)−(B4*A10)−B5
11	=A10+10	=(B3*A11)−(B4*A11)−B5
12	=A11+10	=(B3*A12)−(B4*A12)−B5
13	=A12+10	=(B3*A13)−(B4*A13)−B5
14	=A13+10	=(B3*A14)−(B4*A14)−B5
15	=A14+10	=(B3*A15)−(B4*A15)−B5
16	=A15+10	=(B3*A16)−(B4*A16)−B5
17	=A16+10	=(B3*A17)−(B4*A17)−B5
18	=A17+10	=(B3*A18)−(B4*A18)−B5
19	=A18+10	=(B3*A19)−(B4*A19)−B5

Fig. 18.2 Spreadsheet formulae.

their role as key members of the model building team (Grinyer and Wooller, 1978).

MODELLING AND THE MICRO

The late 1970s saw a dramatic change in the financial modelling environment. This was the development of the microcomputer. Significant computer power at dramatically reduced cost became available. In business terms the Apple II machine with its 48K of memory, twin floppy drives running under DOS (Apple's disk operating system) and each capable of holding over 100K of data on small floppy disks, colour screen, and simple, built-in BASIC interpreter, was a revelation. Managers and accountants could have computer power on their desks. There was no longer any need to deal with computers at arm's length through the good offices of a large data processing department. The Apples were quickly joined by a host of other micro systems. Many used the CP/M operating system which quickly became an industry standard. As the computers arrived so did the software suppliers. Cut-down versions of main-frame packages began to appear. More importantly so did new products which related directly to the new microcomputer environment. One such was VISICALC on the Apple. VISICALC was the first (1978) commercially available spreadsheet package. It took the business world by storm and was quickly followed by similar packages for CP/M machines, such as SUPERCALC and CALCSTAR. Accountants in particular were delighted with this electronic representation of their traditional A3 sheet of analysis paper. Their budgets, cash flow projections, and other tools quickly migrated into the computer-based spreadsheet format.

The microcomputers of the early 1990s differ from these earlier machines in power rather than kind. A user of an IBM PC clone experiences a very similar situation to that facing Apple users of the late 1970s. The dramatic change was that from mainframe to micro use.

The simple breakeven analysis looked at earlier could easily be handled by these early spreadsheets. Indeed it featured as an example of what was possible in the documentation that accompanied the SUPERCALC pack-age. The breakeven model's representation in a spreadsheet format is shown in Fig. 18.2. Figure 18.3 shows the output. These correspond to Table 18.1 and Fig. 18.1 which showed the traditional form of model and output.

The usual reasons for preferring a computer solution of a model – speed and ability to handle more complex equation forms – hardly apply here. Carrying out a 'what if' analysis with the earlier diagrammatic representa-tion merely requires drawing a new straight line on a graph. With the spreadsheet, the contents of a cell must be altered and the return key pressed to generate automatic recalculation of all other cells. However, for the solution of larger models the combination of micro and spreadsheet clearly offers substantial potential advantages.

One potential disadvantage to the use of computers and spreadsheets can also be seen from this breakeven example. Neither spreadsheet display, output or equations conveys the form of the model being used as clearly as does the traditional, graphical presentation given earlier. When a breakeven graph is used, discussion moves quickly from the results to the

	A	B	
1	Breakeven analysis		
2			
3	Price	2.5	
4	VCPU	1	
5	Fixed	50	
6			
7			
8	Quantity	Profit	
9	10	−35	
10	20	−20	
11	30	−5	
12	40	10	
13	50	25	
14	60	40	
15	70	55	
16	80	70	
17	90	85	
18	100	100	
19	110	115	

Fig. 18.3 Spreadsheet solution.

assumptions built into the model, how competition might affect the revenue curve, how diseconomies might affect the cost curves. Presenting similar material in spreadsheet format does not generate the same critical and questioning attitude among non-model builders. The assumptions are not as transparent, and the fact that a computer has been used tends to give a false sense of security. This problem is gradually being overcome as spreadsheets normally have an integrated graphics facility. The presence of such a facility, however, does not necessarily mean that it is used!

The substantial manipulative power given to the potential modeller by the combined micro and spreadsheet was rapidly appreciated. In the magazine advertising of the early 1980s there was a mass of advertisements showing an executive sitting in front of a microcomputer using VISICALC or one of its many clones. The image was managerial, not analytic. The advertiser's target was the manager, financial or otherwise, rather than the technical expert. There is also harder evidence which supports the view that modelling was becoming micro based and once again the function of the accountant and manager. For example, Hobson (1983) and Lewis (1984) emphasized the growing importance of the microcomputer. Also Grinyer (1983) in his survey of financial modelling found that by 1982 accountants had become the dominant category of financial model builders. Grinyer's general conclusion was: '... one gets a consistent picture of accountants, planners, and other users developing their own models, changing the logic as required, and using them themselves, rather than relying on computer specialists.'

While the advertising image is now less common, and the various surveys which appear no longer highlight the role of the accountant and manager as modellers, these are the results of a general acceptance of the phenomenon, not of its decline. The accountant as model builder, with the micro as the standard piece of hardware, is now seen as the norm.

THE ACCOUNTANT AS MODEL BUILDER

The problem with the statement that the accountant is once again playing a significant model building role is that it says little about the nature of the model building activity being carried out by this new breed of computer-based modeller. The assumption is that the model building activity is of good quality, or if not, is at least a learning experience on the way to better things. Unfortunately there is little in the way of evidence around to indicate what is going on. These model builders, like their mainframe based predecessors, don't publish case studies.

Berry (1986) describes one model building exercise from the early 1980s. An accountant, acting as a financial consultant to an overseas company interested in establishing a manufacturing operation in the UK, had a problem. He had produced a set of monthly profit and loss and cash flow forecasts for the first two years of the proposed operation's life. These indicated the need for substantial loan finance. The process of producing these forecasts, which covered four sheets of partly typed, partly hand-written A3 analysis paper, had been laborious. The accountant wanted assistance in producing similar sets of output based on different sets of assumptions about the way the firm would develop. Given that potential lenders might want additional assumptions analysed, a method of generating output quickly was required. The accountant felt that a computer model would solve his problem.

The accountant was introduced to CALCSTAR running under CP/M on a Superbrain micro. He took to the system immediately. Lack of keyboard skills proved no problem. Within a matter of hours data and simple examples of formulae were being input and processed.

Problems, however, arose when the accountant had to enter details of the model which represented the processes expected to be at work during the first two years of the new firm's life. Such a model clearly existed, since the original analysis sheets contained output based on it. Unfortunately, it existed only in the mind of the accountant. Form and structure had apparently never been written down. Specifying and entering the accounting identities involved proved no problem, but the process generating the sales series, the links to costs, and the mechanisms generating many cash flow items, seemed difficult for the accountant to specify. The accountant seemed to find it difficult even to talk about linkages between variables in anything but the broadest terms.

To overcome the problem of specifying the model prior to entering it onto the spreadsheet, a statistical analysis of the output on the original analysis sheets was carried out for the accountant while he quizzed management in the parent company about the likely behaviour of sales. The outcome of this effort was a list of sales values, a series of fixed cost items, some strictly proportional behavioural relationships, and, for the cash flow series, very simple lags. During discussions it became clear that the assignment of cost items between fixed and variable categories was relatively arbitrary. Unsurprisingly early trials with the model showed that implicit purchasing and production behaviour was likely to be unrealistic.

Discussions about the model with the accountant proved difficult. Pressure from the accountant to work with the computer and generate more output rather than discuss the implications of existing output was the rule. It seemed that the accountant had no criteria for choosing between alternative model forms or model structures. Furthermore it seemed as if ease of model use only served to distract the accountant from the need to think more carefully about the model specification.

This example, together with a variety of anecdotal evidence prompted McLintock and Berry (1990) to carry out an examination of the model building activities of accountants in professional offices in East Anglia. The research involved a postal survey to indicate the extent of modelling activity and the range of areas of application, and a series of follow-up interviews to discuss the nature of the model building process being applied. Respondents worked in a range of size of offices, some of which were local firms, others were local offices of national partnerships.

The survey indicated that there were relatively few specialist computer personnel employed in the various offices but that a substantial computer-based, financial modelling activity was being carried out. The implication that financial modelling was an activity carried out by accountants rather than technical specialists was strongly reinforced by the interview evidence. Even in those firms with specialist computer staff, the accountants were heavily involved with the modelling process. The survey and interview evidence also indicates that the accountants had not received any formal training in model building, tending rather to rely for guidance on manuals provided with computer packages.

The research also indicates that the micro has virtually displaced the mainframe, whether wholly owned or time-shared as a financial modelling platform. The most common computer was the IBM PC or one of its clones. There was no relationship between size of office and type of hardware in use. By far the most commonly used piece of software was a spreadsheet. Supercalc and Lotus 1–2–3 were each used by about a third of users. There was very little use of BASIC and none of any other high level programming language, and there was no reported use of any specialist financial modelling language.

As far as area of application is concerned, the results indicate that financial modelling is mainly applied to short- and medium-term profit and cash flow forecasting. An interesting sidelight on pattern of use is that accountants make far greater use of financial modelling to satisfy client needs than to satisfy their own.

The follow-up interviews painted a clear picture of the rather limited nature of the modelling process being carried out. The basic understanding of the problem to be modelled tended to be an inherited set of accounting identities and a traditional set of links between variables. The use of ratio measures to estimate strictly proportional behavioural relationships was the beginning and end of the estimation phase. The only attempt to communicate model form and structure to users, prior to model solution, is typically a letter setting out assumptions which will be used in solving the model. This serves more as a contract to define the limit of the task the accountant is taking on. It indemnifies the accountant against claims by the client that more was expected. The only formal expression of model and structure is when equations are entered into the spreadsheet. As far as model validation goes, while there is testing of arithmetical accuracy of the spreadsheet solution, there is no evidence of any more serious attempt to compare model output to historical data on firm behaviour.

The overall picture is of an accountant computerizing conventional financial accounting identities, and using traditional fixed variable distinctions to provide a behavioural dimension. The lack of an attempt to see whether the resulting model in any way represents real-world behaviour clearly distinguishes this type of modelling exercise from that carried out by modelling specialists such as econometricians or operational researchers.

What the computer has added to the traditional non-computerized modelling activities of accountants is merely speed. This speed is utilized to produce multiple 'what if' scenarios. However, since the ability of the model to represent adequately the behaviour of the organization being modelled is never checked, the 'what if' answers are without value. It is one thing to build a model designed to represent the behaviour of a specific organization, test that the model does have this capability, and then use the model to ask 'what might happen if ...' questions. It is quite another to enter accounting identities and ratios on a spreadsheet, fail to check whether ratio relations do adequately capture the behaviour of a specific organization over time, and then use the model to make recommendations to users in the organization in question.

The research did not attempt to discover what value client organizations derive from these modelling exercises. There must, however, be some concern that the mere fact of computerization adds a gloss to an otherwise irrelevant exercise, and may mislead client and users.

AN APPROPRIATE MODELLING PROCESS

It seems clear that there is a financial modelling process in operation which has the capacity to mislead model users. This capacity is the more so since the use of a computer can seem to provide a guarantee of the quality of the modelling exercise to a naive model user. This situation can only be remedied if greater attention is paid by the model builder to all the stages of the model building process which have been outlined in this chapter.

The technical stages of the model building process can be represented as a series of concentric circles (Fig. 18.4). The closer the activity is to the centre the more serious are errors for the likely success of the modelling activity.

At the centre is the process of developing an understanding of the organization being modelled, its environment and the problem definitions owned by the various participants in the model building process. It is clearly possible that conflicting views may be present. The model builder can exercise choice, attempt to reconcile, or develop multiple models. Whichever course of action is chosen the model builder has become a player in the organizational game. It is at this stage of developing and communicating an understanding of the problem situation that the big

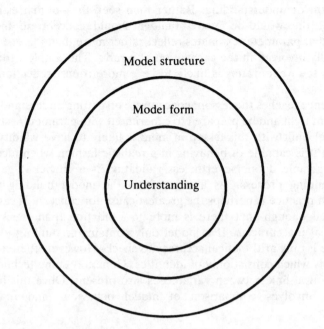

Fig. 18.4 Model construction schema.

mistakes in model building are made. Anything which displays the model builder's tentative understanding and makes it available for discussion by interested parties is of use here. Techniques such as cognitive mapping can help, but cannot overcome a lack of perceptiveness on the part of the model builder (Eden, Jones and Sims, 1983). The model building process apparently practised by accountants is seriously deficient at this stage. Professional accounting training, by providing ready-made solutions, almost appears to get in the way of developing new understanding.

One level out from the centre is the process of building the model form. It should be remembered that the world is not necessarily a linear system. Start-up situations, competitive behaviour, economies and diseconomies of scale and scope imply non-linearities. An incorrect choice of model form can cause the answers to 'what if' questions to be seriously in error. However, the error is likely to be of lesser magnitude than those caused by a lack of understanding.

At one level further removed from the centre is the process of estimating model structure. Here a mass of statistical techniques are available – and are probably best ignored. Parameter estimates are just that, estimates.

They are also liable to become out of date more rapidly than either model form or understanding. Rather than seek the optimal estimation technique, the would-be model builder should concentrate more on ensuring that parameter estimates reflect rather more than the one year of data usually involved in the calculation of a ratio. The simplest trend line through a few years ratios is likely to be a more robust reflection of the world.

Experience teaches the lesson: concentrate on getting understanding and model form right and be prepared to experiment with parameter estimates.

A model built with this lesson in mind is likely to have validity in the sense that it is capable of behaving in a realistic fashion when faced with hold out sample data. Nevertheless validation is a crucial stage of the model building process. Its absence from the model building process adopted in practice is perhaps the greatest cause for concern. It cannot be emphasized enough that there is more to validation than checking for arithmetical inaccuracies. If a model only contains accounting identities then there is only arithmetical accuracy to check. However, there are very few models which consist only of identities. Generally some technological or behavioural link between variables is also present. Once this happens validation involves comparison of model behaviour and real-world behaviour.

DISCUSSION QUESTIONS

1. Is there such a thing as an unconditional forecast?
2. What approaches are available to assist the model builder to communicate model form and structure to naive model users?
3. Under what circumstances might a ratio link between sales level and size of asset base fail to predict adequately asset growth?
4. Find out how the Gauss Seidel iterative solution process works and identify conditions which might generate non-convergence.

REFERENCES

Ashford, R. W., Berry, R. H. and Dyson, R. G. (1988). 'Operational research and financial management', *European Journal of Operational Research*, Vol. 36, pp. 143–52.

Berry, R. H. (1986). 'Raising finance for a small business: a spreadsheet case history'. Unpublished Working Paper, University of East Anglia.

Eden, C., Jones, S. and Sims, D. (1983) *Messing About In Problems*. Pergamon Press.

Grinyer, P. H. (1983). 'Financial modelling for planning in the UK', *Long Range Planning*, Vol. 16, pp. 58–72.

Grinyer, P. H. and Wooller, J. (1978). *Corporate Models Today*. Institute of Chartered Accountants of England and Wales.

Hobson, T. (1983). 'Financial modelling on microcomputers', *Journal of the Operational Research Society*, Vol. 34, pp. 289–97.

Lewis, C. D. (1984). *Managing With Micros*, 2nd edn, Blackwell.

McLintock, A. J. and Berry, R. H. (1990). 'The use of financial modelling in the accounting profession'. Unpublished Working Paper. University of East Anglia.

Naylor, T. H. (1979). *Corporate Planning Models*. Addison-Wesley.

Sherwood, D. (1983). *Financial Modelling*. Gee.

19 Technology in qualitative research: an overview
Bryan Pfaffenberger

INTRODUCTION

Despite a major shift toward quantitative analyses in the decades following the Second World War (Collins, 1975), no obituary has yet appeared for *qualitative research*, a research strategy that 'fundamentally depends on watching people in their own territory and interacting with them in their own language, on their own terms' (Kirk and Miller, 1986, p. 1). On the contrary, something of a renaissance is well under way in qualitative research. This renaissance stems, or so argues the anthropologist Cliffort Geertz, from scholars' interest in looking less for the 'sort of thing that connects planets and pendulums' and more 'for the sort that connects chrysanthemums and swords' (Winkler, 1985, p. 5). Qualitative studies, at their best, provide the inside view of social behaviour – the meaningful 'connecting links' (Smith and Manning, 1982, p. xviii) – that make the observable (and quantifiable) patterns of behaviour intelligible to the observer.

Social scientists who use qualitative strategies, however, face what Sproull and Sproull (1982, p. 283) accurately call a 'cruel trade-off' between the richness of qualitative data and the tedium involved in analysing it (e.g. Miles, 1979, pp. 593–5). Visual anthropology aside, nearly all qualitative techniques produce text, and in copious amounts. To 'capture' qualitative data is to write it down, to make it into field notes, life histories, interview transcriptions, case histories, protocol analyses and

Source: Pfaffenburger, Bryan (1988) *Microcomputer Applications in Qualitative Research*, Qualitative Research Methods Series, 14, pp. 11–24.
© 1988 Sage Publications, Inc.

rank listings. Acknowledging this point, Geertz (quoted in Lyman, 1984, p. 75) recently argued that the participant-observer is more accurately described as a participant-writer. Unfortunately, to analyse this textually captured data is to engage in a paper-pushing enterprise of monstrous proportions. If the job is to be done properly, the researcher is in for such tormenting jobs as manually searching thousands of pages of notes for an obscure passage, recoding all the field notes to suit a newly discovered framework of coding categories, and rewriting the notes to flesh out events from memory.

The inherent difficulty of qualitative data analysis keeps qualitative researchers at arm's length from their data and, arguably, it retards the growth of analytical sophistication. Not a few qualitative researchers have brought back reams of data from the field only to ignore the bulk of it. And despite Merton's (1968, p. 444) call for a new level of discussion and sophistication in qualitative research methods, by 1984 qualitative data analysis still involved little more than 'underlining, shuffling paper, re-reading, and cutting and pasting' (Conrad and Reinharz, 1984, p. 7). The very richness of qualitative research is, in short, its bane.

Quantitative researchers used to suffer in much the same way. Before computer statistical packages were devised in the early 1960s, quantitative studies in sociology were all but restricted to small data sets and simple analytical strategies. In 1946, for example, two-thirds of sociology journal articles that employed statistical methods used only totals, percentages and simple cross-tabulations. Although more sophisticated techniques such as multiple regression analysis were known, they could not be applied without 'mechanical calculators and small armies of graduate students to operate them' (Collins, 1982, p. 439). General-purpose statistical packages such as SPSS, however, put the use of sophisticated techniques (and large data sets) within the reach of any social scientist who had access to a mainframe computer. Overall, the result was an impressive expansion in the quality of survey analysis – even though, as Martin Levin (1986) notes, some researchers have come to rely more on the statistical packages's 'mindless' ability to cross-tabulate all variables than spend time developing a well-crafted, thoughtful analysis.

Now that high quality text-processing programmes are becoming available for qualitative data analysis, it seems likely that qualitative researchers will enjoy the same two benefits that quantitative researchers receive from the computer: the ability, first, to work quickly and conveniently with much larger units of data, and second, to apply more sophisticated analytical techniques. Yet the computer's potential in qualitative research is still just that, a potential. Although qualitative researchers are taking to microcomputers and word processing in huge numbers, the more sophisticated text-processing applications (such as the production of key-word-in-context concordances and word frequency analysis) are seldom used and, in the main, poorly understood. Furthermore, the methodological texts available on such applications (e.g. Hockey, 1980; Oakman, 1984; Feldman and Norman, 1987) concentrate on literary applications to the virtual exclusion of social science topics. A clear need exists for a brief survey of text-processing applications in a social science context.

THE NEED FOR A CRITICAL PERSPECTIVE

To realize the promise of text-processing applications for qualitative research fully, however, it is necessary to adopt a critical perspective on this new technology. At the minimum, qualitative researchers should take great care to grasp just what today's hardware and software can be expected to do – and what such tools *cannot* do. Consider, for example, the fact that computers represent and process text as if it were data in the most general sense – that is, an inherently *meaningless* collection of representations. The word 'cat', for instance, is represented, stored and processed as a sequence (a 'string' in computer parlance) of three binary numbers. What is not stored is all the information that allows us to make the connection between those three letters and such things as crunchies, Garfield, kitty litter, and a Broadway show. Efforts to represent such connections have made impressive strides in recent years, but the formidable complexity of human semantic systems ensures that a meaning-sensitive text-processing technology is still many years away – if, indeed, it is feasible at all. In practice, therefore, a qualitative researcher must understand that a computer-assisted search of a text for the word 'birth' will retrieve all passages in which the string 'birth' appears; however, it will not retrieve passages that mention 'parturition' but omit 'birth' – unless it is specifically instructed to do so. So long as limitations of this sort are clearly understood, search techniques and other applications can be used with some profit.

There is more to a critical perspective on technology, however, than a mere awareness of an application's limitations. Such an approach requires reflection about the computer's likely impact on qualitative research. After all, quantitative social scientists still wonder whether the computer, rather than people, has dictated the trajectory of sociological theory in recent decades (Levin, 1986). To approach this question, however, requires nothing less than a complete rethinking of the culturally provided views we tend to hold on the relationship between technology and social behaviour.

Studies of Western views of this relationship reveal two propositions that, on the surface, appear to be grossly contradictory. The first, which Winner (1986, pp. 5–6) calls *technological somnambulism*, holds that the human relationship to technology is simply 'too obvious to merit serious reflection'. It consists only of 'making', which is of interest only to engineers and technicians, and 'use', which amounts only to an 'occasional, innocuous, [and] nonstructuring occurrence'. Use is understood to be a straightforward matter: you pick up a tool, use it, and put it down. In this view, a given technology is by definition culturally, morally and politically neutral. It is, as Buchanan (1965, p. 163) puts it, 'essentially amoral, an instrument which can be used for good or ill', and so the impact of a technology depends on the ethical awareness of the people using it.

The second proposition, *technological determinism*, takes what appears to be precisely the opposite position, namely that technology is a powerful and autonomous agent that dictates in some detail the patterns of human social and cultural life (e.g. White, 1959) – and usually for the worse. Modern technology, moreover, is often assumed to be even more autonomous – indeed, out of control – since it unfolds along a pathway afforded by the 'grand avenue' of scientific advance (Ellul, 1962). Civilization, in this view, is yoked to a runaway beast that is stripping us of our humanity: the cold, detached values of scientific technology (efficiency and economy) have taken precedence over aesthetic values, respect for the environment, and concern for social justice. Folk versions of this view take the form of assertions such as 'the use of computers is depersonalizing and isolating.'

Underlying the apparent contradiction, however, is – surprisingly – a hidden unity: both views gravely understate or disguise the *social* dimension of technology (Pfaffenberger, forthcoming). Both see technology as an autonomous thing; it either has no relationship to society (technological somnambulism) or stands to society as does an independent variable to a dependent variable (technological determinism). This view represents a remarkable denial of the human dimension of technology; to put it in Marxist terms, technology is *fetishized*. What is in reality produced by relations among people appears before us in a fantastic form as relations among things (Godelier, 1972, p. xxv).

Yet this human dimension is becoming increasingly readable as scholars strip away the facade of ideology that disguises it. Increasingly, technology is defined, not as material culture (e.g. a thing), but as a socially and culturally constituted system of knowledge (Layton, 1974) and social relationships. And its 'impact on society' is coming to be studied, not on the basis of the simplistic assumptions of technological somnambulism or determinism, but by terms supplied by the sociology of scientific knowledge (Pinch and Bijker, 1984). The sociology of science demonstrates that scientific 'truth' is socially constructed by political processes of academic negotiation (Mulkay, 1979) and, what is more, by the surrounding culture's prominent role in providing metaphors and analogies for the expression or constitution of scientific 'facts' (e.g. Holton, 1973; Manning, 1979). Radical interpretations of this evidence go so far as to deny that science possesses a privileged epistemological status; it is simply one 'knowledge culture' among others (Collins and Pinch, 1979). Such perspectives amount to a refusal to accept science's myths about itself at face value (Goonatilake, 1984).

Technology is socially constructed in precisely the same way, and it therefore deserves the same kind of analysis. The myth that technology advances uncontrollably along a 'grand avenue' made possible by scientific advances has been shown to be misleading, if not false, in numerous studies. Noble (1986), for instance, has shown that, as new technologies are developed, engineers confront a variety of design options. Pressures external to the design process itself – economic considerations, management goals, and even culturally defined notions of how a technology should be used – impinge on the selection of one option over another. In his important book, Noble shows how American companies rejected a GE-developed machine tool automation system called record/playback in favour of a numerical control system. The record/playback system required the service of a highly skilled machinist, whose movements would be recorded and, later, played back automatically. Corporate management, however, was more interested in an approach to industrial automation that could eliminate skilled (and unionized) machinists altogether, replacing them by non-unionized, semiskilled 'button pushers'. Numerical control techniques did precisely that, and more: they took decision-making power away from workers and put it in the hands of central management. For engineers, too, such techniques had the additional appeal of 'technical sweetness', computerized numerical control techniques were clearly the way of the future, while record/playback was merely an attempt to capture the past. Industrial automation, in sum, could have preserved a role for well-paid, skilled machinists; that it did not do so testifies to the role of social choices in shaping the technology we end up getting.

Once created, however, the opportunity for social choice diminishes. An implemented technology carries with it a powerful vision of the society in which it is to be used, replete with an equally powerful endowment of symbolic meaning and, sometimes, an obligatory plan for the way people will have to arrange themselves to use it. A technology thus embodies what Noble (1986, p. xi) calls a 'frozen fragment of human and social endeavour', replete with a set of values, a vision of how the technology should be used, and often a plan for the social relationships required to weave the technology into human life. It presents us with what Winner (1986) calls a 'form of life', a set of social and symbolic circumstances in which people – to the extent that they adopt the technology – are more or less obliged to carry on their daily affairs.

To make this point, however, is not to assume – as would a technological determinist – that the impact of a given technology is certain or that it will everywhere be the same. Such an argument would be specious, for reasons that deserve clarification here. Technological determinism holds, in essence, that the independent variable, technology (i.e a thing, something extraneous to society), affects the dependent variable, society. Yet – textbook definitions of technology aside – the new studies in the history of technology have shown that technology is not a thing, an object external to social behaviour. On the contrary, technology *is* social behaviour. If technology is social behaviour, then in assessing its impact we are not talking about the impact of a 'thing' on 'society'. We are talking about the *relationship between one form of social behaviour and others* (MacKenzie and Wajcman, 1985, p. 3). This relationship is complex, shot through with meaning, indeterminate, and – one might add – a perfect subject in itself for interpretive, qualitative analysis.

These new findings in the history and sociology of technology are of more than passing relevance to the use of computer hardware and software in qualitative research. The hallmark of qualitative studies, after all, is their careful concern with epistemological issues; to do qualitative research well means becoming aware of what Bob Scholte calls 'pre-understanding', the tacit social assumptions, cultural biases, and outright prejudices that we carry to the field (Scholte, 1974, p. 441). What these new findings have made clear is that technology is loaded with pre-understandings – and what is more, they are all the more dangerous because they are denied, hidden and submerged from view in ordinary, day-to-day discourse. To use a microcomputer in qualitative research, then, is to use a form of social behaviour whose most remarkable characteristic is its built-in denial that it is a form of social behaviour, coupled with its simultaneous symbolic assertion that it is, instead, a disembodied thing. What we must consider, then, as Godelier (1972, p. xxv) puts it perfectly, is:

> the effect *in* and for consciousness of the disguising of social relations *in* and *behind* their appearances. Now these appearances are the *necessary* point of departure of the representations of their ... relations that individuals *spontaneously* form for themselves. Such images thus constitute the social reality within which these individuals live, and serve them as a means of *acting* within and upon this social reality.

In short, when we introduce a microcomputer into the heart of qualitative research, namely writing and rewriting, we are acting in a social and symbolic system that is founded on the denial of the technology's social and symbolic aspects. The responsible use of this technology requires, therefore, considerable efforts in the direction of what Scholte (1974) calls 'hermeneutical reflection and concern for epistemological error'. Such efforts are the hallmark of qualitative studies anyway, but there is ample reason – as the foregoing argument should make clear – to turn an especially wary eye on microcomputer hardware and software.

An example should help to demonstrate that the foregoing is more than academic hot air and that there really is a need for this critical approach to microcomputing. The *sine qua non* of scholarly involvement in computing is, of course, word processing. In the grip of somnambulism, writers typically regard word processing programs as straightforward and handy tools for the creation, revision and printing of text. Alternatively, they view the technology as a new, even revolutionary, device that will all but automatically raise their productivity or improve their writing (the determinist view). What they do *not* tend to perceive, however, is word processing's programs with characteristics that are empirically verifiable to be inimical to the writing process.

Word processing software was initially developed with the engineering ethos in mind – namely to rescue people from mindless drudgery, and so to benefit civilization. This laudable goal, one that engineers profess with evident conviction, takes on a more sinister implication in the hands of some managers, who sometimes see labour-saving or 'user-friendly' technologies as opportunities to 'deskill' workers. It takes a skilled typist to produe a handsomely formatted typescript with letter perfect formatting; the word processor, however, handles all the difficult formatting operations automatically and relieves the operator of the need for spelling skills. All that is required of the word processor operator is speed – and to make sure the speed is achieved consistently, office word processors are increasingly networked or monitored so that a supervisor can accurately determine a typist's performance. As one such supervisor commented proudly to Jane Barker and Hazel Downing (1985, p. 160), this technology and its supervisorial regime produces results so that 'a less experienced typist is able to produce the same quality of work as a really skilled girl (sic) and almost as quickly'.

Word processing was designed, in short, in collapse the time float between the *typing* of a manuscript and the production of a well-formatted, attractive-looking printout. This goal was accomplished, in part, by removing the human dimension of skill as an intervening variable between keyboarding and printing. And it does its job quite well. The more recent achievements in this area include 'what-you-see-is-what-you-get' word processing software and desk-top publishing software, which graphically (and accurately) represents the printed page on the screen. What is far from clear, however, is whether this technology – which was shaped by the social and economic environment in which it arose – is an effective tool for *writing*.

When word processing software became widely available for micro-computers, there was no end to the gushing enthusiasm with which people involved in writing – writers and writing teachers – received the technology. By making text revision vastly easier and facilitating the production of multiple drafts, word processing would encourage writers to produce higher quality work. Carefully controlled experiments on the use of word processing software in composition instruction have, however, produced disappointing results (e.g. Collier, 1983). One study even found that students do more revision when they use pencils and paper! The reasons for these results are just now becoming clear (Pfaffenberger, 1987a). Word processing software was designed for typists, not writers; a typist need see only the section of a page being typed, but a writer (as research on the composing process has revealed) needs to cycle back and forth between writing the text and reviewing the document's structure (Flower and Hayes, 1981). Archaic though they may be, pieces of paper are vastly superior to the limited view of a text that one gets on a 24-line computer display; it is far easier to see the overall structure of a piece when one can flip easily among loose pages. Of course, a writer using word processing software can easily print the document for review, but here another problem emerges: the automatic text formatting capabilities of the software produce what appears to be a beautifully printed, finished document, tacitly introducing the authority of the printed text into the writing process at a premature stage. Word processing, in sum, defeats the writing process by focusing the writer's attention on words and sentences and, when revision is contemplated, by presenting the writer with a typescript that powerfully symbolizes completed work.

The key point here is that once a writer becomes conscious of these built-in, socially shaped characteristics of word processing, it is quite easy to devise strategies to mitigate their ill consequences. Once you know, for instance, that word processing programs tend to concentrate revision efforts on the word and sentence levels to the detriment of overall structural coherence, it is obvious that you should pay more attention to the structure of large text domains when using a word processing pro-gram. The authoritative appearance of the well-formatted document can be similarly combated by such strategies as printing on yellow paper (suggesting that the text is a draft) or eschewing right margin justification and other symbols of finished work.

The cure for all such problems, in sum, is critical awareness – relentless critical awareness. A technology is like a colonial power – it tells you that it is working in your best interests and, all the while, it is functioning insidiously to dim your critical perception of the world around you. You will remain its victim so long as you fail to conceptualize adequately what it's up to.

It should be stressed that no attempt is made here to introduce the reader to microcomputers or academic word processing (see, instead, Pfaffenberger (1986) or, for a treatment designed for literary scholars, Feldman and Norman (1987); nor will 'how-to' instruction be found for specific software packages. Moreover, some familiarity with micro-computers and, at the minimum, word processing is assumed. Finally, it is not intended to discuss or evaluate specific microcomputers or micro-computer programs. Where specific programs such as ZyIndex, Notebook II, and WordCruncher are mentioned, the intention is merely to illustrate the properties (and pre-understandings) that are common to all or most programs of their type. Specific programs will, after all, come and go, but the generic categories into which such programs can be placed show a stability that counters the intuitive assumption of volatility and innovation in the microcomputer market-place. This pattern is now quite clear in the business market, where the features and performances of relational database managers, multifunction spreadsheet packages, and professional word processing programs have stabilized to a remarkable degree and can be discussed profitability in generic terms, even for training purposes (for an example of such an approach, see Pfaffenberger (1987b).

WHY MICROCOMPUTERS?

Although larger computers have been (and will continue to be) useful for qualitative research applications, microcomputers have three major advantages for qualitative research.

First, battery-powered (but still quite powerful) microcomputers can be taken directly to the field, where they can be used for the *direct entry* of field notes, interview transcriptions and the like. The significance of this point cannot be overstated. The major obstacle to computer-assisted applications in qualitative research prior to the microcomputer was the expense of transcribing huge quantities of handwritten or typed field notes to computer-readable form. To be sure, optical character reading (OCR) devices such as the Kurzweil 4000 can automatically create transcriptions from clear typescript, but the better OCR machines are expensive, the transcription process is slow and tedious, and even the best ones will make errors. It makes much more sense to write up the notes in computer-readable form in the first place.

Some fieldworkers will prefer not to bring portable computers into field research situations, fearing that the machine would intrude on the observation process (e.g. Lyman, 1984). Even so, there are still good grounds to recommend the use of portable computers and the direct entry of field notes, in so far as it is possible. The notes taken during field observation sessions are usually cryptic, so retyping them into the computer immediately afterwards will not add significantly to the paperwork dimension of fieldwork. The more copious field notes, such as after-the-fact reflections and field journals, are usually created after the field session is over for the day. These notes can be entered directly into the computer without qualms.

One other potential problem with computer-based research notes deserves mention here. To use a microcomputer to store field notes is to transform the experience of a social world into lexical form – or more specifically, into lexical forms that can be keyboarded (Altheide, 1985). As such, it biases a researcher's note-taking activities against some fruitful non-textual exercises, such as those described by an anthropologist: 'I'm always drawing diagrams, sketching things, describing the theatre of things ... If you are writing longhand, rich designs can flow directly from the material you are working with' (quoted in Lyman, 1984, p. 83). Typing one's notes into the computer, at least with most programs, strips away the graphics. The cure is to realize that there may still be a place for handwriting, doodling and graphically 'describing the theatre of things' even in a highly computerized research operation. There's no reason to restrict one's note-taking activities to the computer when drawing sketches on paper may still have a place in the research.

The second advantage of microcomputers for qualitative researchers is that a surprisingly wide variety of useful (and inexpensive) application packages are available in microcomputer formats. Software originally intended for business purposes, such as word processing and database management programs, are useful for qualitative computing (so long as their limitations are kept in mind). And software developed specifically for literary analysis and qualitative computing, such as key-word-in-context concordance programs, is now making its migration from mainframe to microcomputer formats. And all the while, microcomputers are becoming smaller, cheaper, more portable and more powerful.

The third advantage of microcomputers is that, owing to their low cost, social scientists can afford to own them outright. Collins (1982) under-scores the significance of this point in Marxist terms. To own a microcomputer is, for a computer-using social scientist, to own and control the scholarly means of production. The use of a mainframe, in contrast, means paying stiff time-sharing costs ('renting the means of production') that discourage exploratory data analysis. It may also mean accepting the software-purchasing decisions of an academic computing centre, which is all but certain to have priorities that differ from the researcher's. And as Peter Lyman (1984) found to his dismay, using a mainframe may even mean accepting the possibility that a technically adept intruder – that is, a 'hacker' – could gain access to one's field notes, thus violating their confidentiality. To own one's own microcomputer is, in a way that is far from trivial, to control one's own means of knowledge production.

Microcomputers, in sum, are ideally suited for qualitative research, but it bears mentioning that – like any research technology – it makes good sense to scrutinize the pre-understandings that they bring to the research process. And here we are much informed by the work of Sherry Turkle (1980, 1982). In interviewing dozens of personal computer users, Turkle encountered some men who seem to have become trapped by the machine. They saw in it a comforting but infantile world of retreat, in which it was possible to establish the total control, coupled with a sense of prowess and achievement, that could not be achieved in social life. Turkle notes that, although these men felt that becoming adept at the computer gave them an enhanced sense of self-esteem and competence, it was a Pyrrhic victory: the world they had conquered – a world of amateur programming and adventure games – bore little relation to the world of social relations and did nothing to improve their competence there.

Turkle's work clearly sounds a warning note: the microcomputer is known to have snared some men in something of a psychological trap. Yet there are grounds, I would argue, to sound a more general alarm. The men Turkle interviewed clearly saw the microcomputer as an instrument by which they could create their own rite of passage, moving themselves to a new status in which they saw themselves as more competent, more efficacious and more in control. In this context, one can only note Cynthia Cockburn's argument (1985) that for men in Western culture, this is precisely the role provided by all forms of highly sophisticated technical expertise. It is, she argues, a key element of men's 'formative processes' and becomes, once acquired, men's 'social property'. To use the micro-computer, then, is to use a symbol that tacitly communicates means of potency, male prowess, control, legitimacy, efficacy, expertise and achievement. As Michael Agar puts it (1983), to use the microcomputer is tantamount to speaking in what Bernstein (1981) would call an elaborated code, a code that is so closely associated with intelligence and competence that it impresses people, even if you use it to state the obvious.

It should now be clear why so much work involving the computer in social science amounts, as critics often say, to the study of trivial issues with highly sophisticated techniques. In the academic environment, where survival requires constructing an impression of competence, using the computer is as irresistible as using other socially meaningful symbols of scientific or scholarly competence, such as big words and the passive voice. Trouble starts, however, when the concern for elaborating the code overwhelms concern for the substance of what is being said.

There's no easy formula for knowing when you've lost the necessary perspective, although the expenditure of large amounts of unproductive time in front of a computer display screen is suggestive. The point of applying the computer to qualitative research, after all, is not to become involved in the microcomputer, but on the contrary to become involved in the research data. So long as the microcomputer furthers and deepens that involvement, it is playing a positive role. But when the microcomputer starts to loom larger in significance than the original goals of the research, when it demands less engagement in the research data and more engagement in the computer, the time has come to reflect on these goals and to re-establish contact with the values and commitments that initially motivated your engagement with the human social world.

REFERENCES

Agar, M. (1983). 'Microcomputers as field tools', *Computers in the Humanities*, Vol. 17, pp. 19–26.

Altheide, D. L. (1985). 'Keyboarding as a social form', *Computers and the Social Sciences*, Vol. 3.

Barker, J. and Downing, H. (1985). 'Word processing and the transformation of patriarchal relations of control in the office'. In MacKenzie, D. and Wajcman, J. (eds.), *The Social Shaping of Technology*. Open University Press, Philadelphia, pp. 147–69.

Bernstein, J. (1981). *The Analytical Engine*. William Morrow, New York.

Buchanan, R. A. (1965). *Technology and Social Progress*. Pergamon Press, Oxford.

Cockburn, C. (1985). 'The material of male power'. in MacKenzie, D. and Wajcman, J. (eds), *The Social Shaping of Technology*. Open University Press, Philadelphia, pp. 165–72.

Collier, R. M. (1983). 'The word processor and revision strategies', *College Composition and Communication*, Vol. 34, pp. 149–55.

Collins, H. (1986). 'Expert systems and the science of knowledge'. In Bijker, W. B., Hughes, T. P. and Pinch, T. J. (eds), *The Social Construction of Technological Systems: New Directions in the Sociology and History of Technology*. MIT Press, Cambridge, Mass.

Collins, H. and Pinch, T. J. (1979). 'The construction of the paranormal: nothing unscientific is happening'. In Wallis, R. (ed.), *On the Margins of Science: The Social Construction of Rejected Knowledge.* University of Keele, Keele, pp. 237–70.

Collins, T. W. (1982). 'Social science research and the microcomputer', *Sociological Methods and Research*, Vol. 9, pp. 438–60.

Conrad, P. and Reinharz, S. (1984). 'Computers and qualitative data', *Qualitative Sociology*, Vol. 7, pp. 3–15.

Ellul, J. (1962) 'The technological order', *Technology and Culture*, Vol. 3, pp. 394–421.

Feldman, P. R. and Norman, B. (1987). *The Wordworthy Computer: Classroom and Research Applications in Language and Literature.* Knopf, New York.

Flower, L. and Hayes, J. R. (1981). 'A cognitive process theory of writing', *College Composition and Communication*, Vol. 32, pp. 365–87.

Godelier, M. (1972). *Rationality and Irrationality in Economics.* Monthly Review Press, New York.

Goonatilake, S. (1984). *Aborted Discovery: Science and Creativity in the Third World.* Zed, London.

Hockey, S. (1980). *A Guide to Computer Applications in the Humanities.* Johns Hopkins University Press, Baltimore.

Holton, G. (1973). *Thematic Origins of Scientific Thought: Kepler to Einstein.* Harvard University Press, Cambridge, Mass.

Kirk, J. and Miller, M. (1986). *Reliability and Validity in Qualitative Research* (Sage University Paper, Qualitative Research Methods series, Vol. 1). Sage, Beverly Hills, Calif.

Layton, E. (1974). 'Technology as knowledge', *Technology and Culture*, Vol. 15, pp. 31–414.

Levin, M. L. (1986). 'Technological determinism in social data analysis', *Computers and the Social Sciences*, Vol. 2, pp. 201–7.

Lyman, P. (1984). 'Reading, writing, and word processing: toward a phenomenology of the computer age', *Qualitative Sociology*, Vol. 7, pp. 75–89.

Mackenzie, D. and Wajcman, J. (eds) (1985). 'Introduction'. In *The Social Shaping of Technology.* Open University Press, Philadelphia.

Manning, P. K. (1979). 'Metaphors of the field: varieties of organizational discourse', *Administrative Science Quarterly*, Vol. 24, pp. 660–71.

Merton, R. K. (1968). *Social Theory and Social Structure.* Free Press, New York.

Miles, M. (1979). 'Qualitative data as an attractive nuisance: the problem of analysis', *Administrative Science Quarterly*, Vol. 24, pp. 590–601.

Mulkay, M. (1979). *Science and the Sociology of Knowledge.* Allen and Unwin, London.

Noble, D. (1986). *Forces of Production: A Social History of Industrial Automation.* Oxford University Press, New York.

Oakman, R. (1984). *Computer Methods for Literary Research*, 2nd edn. University of Georgia Press, Athens.

Pfaffenberger, B. (1987a). 'Word processing and text revision: interpreting the empirical evidence', *Computers and Composition Journal*, Vol. 1, pp. 105–18.

Pfaffenberger, B. (1987b). *Personal Computer Applications: A Strategy for the Information Society*. Little-Brown, Boston.

Pfaffenberger, B. (forthcoming). 'Fetishized objects and humanized nature: toward an anthropology of technology'. *Man*.

Pinch, T. and Bijker, W. (1984). 'The social construction of facts and artifacts: or how the sociology of science and the sociology of technology might benefit each other', *Social Studies of Science*, Vol. 14, pp. 399–441.

Scholte, B. (1974). 'Toward a reflexive and critical anthropology'. In Hymes, D. (ed.), *Reinventing Anthropology*. Random House, New York, pp. 430–57.

Smith, R. B. and Manning, P. K. (1982). 'Preface'. In Smith, R. B. and Manning P. K. (eds), *Qualitative Methods*, (Vol. II of *Handbook of Social Science Methods*). Ballinger, Cambridge, Mass., pp. xvii–xx.

Sproull, L. S. and Sproull, R. F. (1982). 'Managing and analyzing behavioural records: explorations in nonnumeric data analysis', *Human Organization*, Vol. 41, pp. 283–90.

Turkle, S. (1984). *The Second Self: Computers and the Human Spirit*. Simon and Schuster, New York.

White, L. (1959). *The Evolution of Culture*. McGraw-Hill, New York.

Winkler, K. J. (1985). 'Questioning the science in social science, scholars signal a "turn to interpretation"', *Chronicle of Higher Education* (26 June 1985), p. 5.

Winner, L. (1986). *The Whale and the Reacter*. University of Chicago Press, Chicago.

7 Business Organization and Policy

Over the last forty years, IT has evolved through several stages or generations which may be defined in many different ways. From the organizational viewpoint, the significant stages are as follows:

1. 1950s 1960s: Off-line batch processing undertaken by specialists in a background EDP department. Data input and output undertaken in EDP department.
2. 1970s: On-line processing undertaken by a specialist EDP department in the background. Data input and output undertaken usually in user department.
3. 1980s: End-user computing. Some or all processing undertaken by user department. Data input and output undertaken in user department.

It is in fact the 1980s that are normally associated with the 'IT revolution', probably because it marks the time when computers reached the mass population. It was characterized by the arrival of very cheap computing resources in the form of microchips which were installed in a variety of machines for control or data processing purposes. The effect was equivalent to the invention of small reliable electric motors which allowed the abolition of belt-drive systems in factories. Suddenly, users could be freed from the central bureaucratic constraints of EDP departments and acquire a considerable amount of freedom. The relative cheapness of the technology further encouraged its acquisition for facilitative or supportive modes of operation rather than previous authoritarian modes where users effectively supported EDP departments.

A similar revolution looks set for the 1990s. Over the last few years, computer-based networks have been developing to the point where national computing infrastructures (analogous to transport networks) are almost in place. These vary in sophistication, with some of them quite primitive at present. Nonetheless the effects of being able to move information and data rapidly across national networks in electronic form is being felt, for example, in retail outlets where restocking, which is sensitive to subtle changes in customer taste, can be carried out quickly and accurately based on point-of-sale data.

The first chapter in this Part, by John Child, dates from the early 1980s and reflects the impact of the first IT revolution (the microchip). It remains interesting because it raises not only general issues concerned with principles of technical change but also it gives the reader of the 1990s an invaluable socio-technical hindsight of the 1980s.

In contrast, the second chapter by John Taylor and Howard Williams is forward looking. It addresses the forthcoming second IT revolution based on the establishment of a computer-based network infrastructure. Using case study material they illustrate how networks have and are likely to continue changing the perception, organization and interrelationship of firms.

The final chapter by Nigel Bryant and Rob Lambert gives a consultant's view on the possibilities for change in small businesses that can arise from the use of IT. It draws on the first IT (microchip) revolution and it charts the impact of small stand-alone computers (where previously only bureau services were available) on the activities of small organizations.

20 New technology and developments in management organization
John Child

INTRODUCTION

New technology, using miniaturized electronic circuitry to process information, is now being applied to a wide range of manufacturing and service operations. A number of investigations have already been carried out into the accompanying changes in employment, skill requirements and organization of work among non-managerial workers, particularly in manufacturing (e.g. Wilkinson, 1983). Less is known about the potential of new technology for changes in management organization, though some important indications are provided by case studies (e.g. Buchanan and Boddy, 1983) and experiments now under way in industry.

Problems of management organization have increased as companies have grown larger, diversified their activities, taken on new specialist skills and faced pressures to innovate in a more hostile competitive environment. Diversification and the employment of specialists have made it more difficult to ensure adequate communication and integration of effort. The continued growth of managerial, administrative and staff employment, even during a contraction in direct employment, has led to the elongation of management hierarchies. In these circumstances, larger companies had to give considerable attention during the 1960s and 1970s to ways of improving integration, coordination and control.

One philosophy favoured for a while was that management organization

Source: *OMEGA International Journal of Management Science*, **12**(3), pp. 211–23.

should itself encompass the several dimensions contained in this growing complexity. This gave rise to multi-dimensional management organization, of which the 'matrix' is the best-known form. Product, regional and functional lines of responsibility and authority were formally identified, and their incorporation into a formal structure was expected to assist co-ordination and control along each dimension. However, the result often turned out to be cumbersome, with a great deal of time being spent in meetings, paperworking proliferating, and initiative being constrained both by these time-consuming activities and by a lack of clarity as to where priorities lay (Knight, 1977). With the premium that is placed today upon developing new competitive opportunities and responding more flexibly to market demands, many companies are now having second thoughts about matrix organization structures (Hunsicker, 1982). Indeed, they have been roundly condemned by Peters and Watersman (1982) on the basis of their study of 'excellent' American companies. The view is emerging that other ways need to be found of coping with complexity in management.

In the early heady days of the 1950s, some believed that computers would provide a solution to the problem. Leavitt and Whisler (1958), looking forward to 'management in the 1980s', argued that the introduction of computers would permit a return to compact centralized decision-making because their rapid collation and transmission of information enabled decisions to be made centrally on a better informed basis. They also predicted a considerable saving in middle management staff, as decision-making powers were removed upwards and as computers took over the information processing roles of such staff. In the event, however, most computer applications were for a long time confined to routine accounting and administrative operations, and did not extend into the heart of management information processing. The introduction of computers did not lead to any consistent changes in managerial decision levels (Robey, 1977); their most evident impact on management organization came instead with the growth of central data processing and systems departments.

It has become appreciated that new technology does not of itself have independent effects on work and organization. The consequences it appears to have result from decisions to select equipment with certain processing capabilities, and from decisions as to how these capabilities are to be developed and used. Buchanan and Boddy (1983) argue from their case study evidence that there is real choice over how computers are applied to organizations. Robey (1977) in fact concluded from his review of research that the form taken by management structure could be explained in terms of the contingencies within which an organization's tasks are performed rather than by the presence or not of a computer. Factors of a cultural and political nature can also create open-endedness in the outcomes of investment in technology. For example, managers may be conservative in initiating changes in organization that could benefit from the technology (Bessant and Dickson, 1982).

Despite the lack of consistent changes in management organization arising from previous eras of computing, and despite the open-endedness in how technology is applied, there are novel features in the introduction of present new technology under contemporary conditions which provide some basis for suggesting that particular developments in management organization could ensue. First, the cheapness, reliability, speed of operation, accuracy, compactness and low energy consumption of new technology has greatly extended its range of applications, and encouraged a burgeoning of complementary software development. Technology is for the first time becoming available which not only offers possibilities of close operational control in a wide range of industries, but which also extends to the efficiency of management organization itself via developments such as organization-wide integrated databases, the efficient use of telecommunications, network architectures, personal computing, and end-user programing languages. Secondly, present-day competitive and cost pressures have increased the determination of many employers to overcome inertia and resistance to new patterns of work and organization for which the aid of new technology can be enlisted. It is particularly significant that new technology is today being introduced when the balance of industrial power has moved substantially in the employer's favour and when indeed even managerial redundancies have become commonplace.

RELEVANCE OF CHANGES AT THE OPERATIONAL LEVEL

Managers will normally have several goals in mind when introducing new technology into their companies' operations. The emphasis between these is likely to vary according to the priorities and purposes of their organization and the context in which it operates. However, case studies (e.g. Buchanan and Boddy, 1983) and surveys (e.g. Northcott *et al.*, 1982) suggest that the following are usually prominent: (a) reducing operating costs and improving efficiency; (b) increasing flexibility; (c) raising the quality and consistency of products; (d) improving control over operational processes. The achievement of each of these goals through new technology has relevance for management organization.

Improvements in *costs* and *efficiency* can be secured in several ways. New technology may permit reductions in manpower via a substitution for direct labour (Francis *et al.*, 1982); or via partial substitution for labour as in word processing (IDS, 1980) and in laboratory automation (Harvey and Child, 1983); or via the more economical allocation of manpower on the basis of superior workflow information such as that provided by electronic-point-of-sale (EPOS) systems in retailing (Cosyns *et al.*, 1983). New technologies can also reduce costs by permitting improved stock control, the reduction of waste due to operator error, and better plant utilization via computerized scheduling. Advanced manufacturing systems offer a combination of these advantages on the basis of integrating the different elements of design, production, handling, storage and stock control (Lamming and Bessant, 1983). They also offer greatly improved flexibility.

In an industry like engineering, many firms now have to compete on the basis of offering custom-built products produced in smaller batches and often involving complex machining. Achieving *flexibility* in production has therefore become an increasingly important goal. One of the most attractive features offered by new computer-controlled technology is the ability to run a range of production items through a single facility with the minimum of cost and delay when changing from one specification to another. A somewhat comparable advantage in flexibility is now being sought in banking with experiments in computerizing customer files and linking these to VDUs used by bank staff. By providing individualized customer profiles, this facility would enable staff to adjust rapidly to the financial circumstances and history of each customer, and on that basis to make decisions rapidly on whether to grant loans or to offer other services.

Improvements in *quality* can be gained from the introduction of highly accurate automated equipment conducting repeatable operations, or from the use of microelectronics for more precise process control. These are examples which tend to substitute for human intervention. However, quality can also be enhanced when electronic assessment complements human judgement. This can apply to some forms of testing in manufacturing and to service work where, for example, the electronic monitoring of patients can complement a physician's judgement.

The new technology is one of information processing which depends upon the quality of its data inputs. If accurate measurement can be obtained, the ability to communicate information swiftly across distances, and the capacity to apply computational or synthesizing routines when required, clearly enhance the potential for managerial *control*. An implication of this is that senior managers may now no longer have to rely upon operators and middle managers for control data or for their interpretation if this data can be captured directly at the point of operations. For example, EPOS systems in retailing can, via capturing data through the scanning of bar-coded or magnetically ticketed items, transmit control data on itemized sales, on throughput at each point of sale, and on stocks, directly to store managers and to central buying departments in a company's head office.

The use of new technology at the operational level in pursuit of the goals mentioned has implications for management organization, but these are importantly mediated by the form of work organization that is adopted. Work organization refers here particularly to the division of labour, the level of worker discretion and the form of supervision through which work is accomplished. The important point is that work organization will not be simply, or even primarily, a function of technology. It is likely to vary according to the nature of the task, but will also be influenced by management's views on the scope workers should have to use skills and control the parameters of ther work, and reformed by a continuing process of negotiation and informal adjustment in the workplace.

Studies which have been completed into computer numerical control (CNC) serve to illustrate the relevance of these factors. Different forms of work organization have been found in CNC applications. Sorge *et al.* (1983) conclude, with respect to the nature of the task, that situations where production is moving towards smaller batch sizes and more frequent batch changes require increased flexibility at the level of the machine and the operator: each CNC operator is liable to have to deal with a greater and more frequently changing range of jobs. This degree of requisite flexibility, they argue, cannot be handled so adequately by a specialist machine programming department operating remotely from within the management structure. Second, Wilkinson (1983) illustrates how managerial policies on the appropriate degree of shopfloor control and use of workers' skills can vary between different sites and how indeed the views of middle-level production management on these matters can diverge from those held by top management. Differences in management policy helped to account for the differences in work organization that Wilkinson observed. Third, both Wilkinson's case studies and those reported by Rose and Jones (1984) indicate how the organization of work actually adopted in conjunction with new technology emerged from local negotiations and accommodations. The outcome did not necessarily bear a close resemblance to management's original intentions.

The varied and partly open-ended relationship of new operations technologies to work organization qualifies their implications for management organization. For example, there is a choice as to how far workers are given the facility to override, edit and even develop computer programs applied to their work. These might be CNC programs, programmed instructions linked to banks' customer files, or other applications. The more that workers are given, or assume, this discretion, the less is the role of specialist programmers or planners in workplace operations. The role of the supervisor can develop in more than one direction when the computer programming of operations is installed.

Foremen may, for example, be downgraded to serve primarily as facilitators ensuring that jigs, tools and materials are available; or they may be upgraded to use terminals to compile programs and to initiate changes in these (Sorge *et al.*, 1983). Jones (1982) has in fact noted how the respective roles of workers, supervisors and programmers vary even between plants all undertaking small-batch engineering and using similar numerical control technology. In general, it appears that where frequent batch changes, a high incidence of new work and variability in materials or phsyical conditions create a requirement for flexibility at the point of production, the use of new technology is more likely to be left to the initiative of workers, assuming that they possess appropriate competences and are willing to acquire new skills. In situations where a high degree of autonomy is left to the worker or work group, it should be possible to reduce the number of supervisors considerably, especially if they are not required to enter progress data, if improved stocking and scheduling avoids the need to chase up shortages and if newer equipment (sometimes incorporating self-diagnostic routines) results in fewer crises due to breakdown.

Some new technology offers improvements in respect of all four managerial goals mentioned, and as a result has wide ramifications for management organization. Lamming and Bessant (1983), for example, discuss the management implications of advanced manufacturing technologies, such as flexible manufacturing systems, which bring together a number of automated and computerized applications. These include robotics and automated transfer; automated assembly, testing and warehousing; advanced monitoring and process control; computerized planning; and computer-aided design. These technologies offer potential cost savings through a displacement of labour, faster throughput and lower inventory, better consistency and quality due to the accuracy of automated equipment and improved flexibility combined with greater control over work in progress.

The adoption of advanced manufacturing technologies has been slow in Britain, but is expected nevertheless to spread. Three-quarters of factory managers polled by MORI in December 1982 said they were considering introducing flexible manufacturing systems (*Sunday Times*, 12 December 1982). While no doubt overstated, this is a clear expression of interest. Early experience noted by Lamming and Bessant (1983) suggest that with advanced manufacturing technology, customary management structures become largely redundant in the areas of supervision, control and monitoring. With a reduced need for high percentage inspection, the quality control function can be reduced and its associated systems simplified. The displacement of operators by automated machines only requiring a low level of manning reduces the need for traditional supervision and enables line management to concentrate more on manufacturing technique and technical performance. Where machines can be flexibly programmed and linked together, production scheduling is simplified and can deal in terms of immediate requirements rather than weeks ahead. If production control data can be secured directly from the plant, and if the reliability and consistency of equipment is greater, the time and staff taken up with chasing around to keep the work to schedule and spent in progress meetings should decline significantly. Point of manufacture data capture devices increase the accuracy and currency of information in a similar manner to EPOS terminals in retailing. The computerized processing of this information should enhance the cost accounting service to management while at the same time reducing the need for clerical accounting staff.

Some functions are likely to expand with these technological developments. One is in-company training to ensure that employees acquire the new skills which are required, and to assist staff generally to adjust to new systems and roles. Another is the area concerned with systems development and programming of computerized equipment. Maintenance of equipment and instrumentation may also expand or at least require the development of new competences. Buchanan and Boddy (1983) found that in such areas the computerization of operations gave rise to new specialist groups and hierarchies. This qualifies the general expectation (discussed later) that new technology should permit the contraction of management hierarchies and simplification of management structures.

Advanced manufacturing technology therefore offers the prospect of an overall simplification of management organization in production and production support functions, though an elaboration in certain other areas. Its logic also calls for increased integration between these functions, including design, purchasing and despatch. A comparable simplification in the organization and staffing of operating areas, combined with a strengthening of the system development activity, is now under way in certain services. These are services (a) where new technology can eliminate the need for paper-processing or its equivalent, and (b) where the public will accept automation as a substitute for personal service delivery. Examples of (a) are found in banking with the progressive automation of cheque clearing and counter transactions, and in retailing with the computerization of purchase order and stock systems. An example of (b) is automated telling in banking, leading to the possibility of completely unstaffed local 'lobby' bank outlets.

MANAGEMENT STRUCTURE

CENTRALIZATION VS DECENTRALIZATION

The long-standing debate over the merits of centralized vs delegated decision-making pointed to a tension between efficiency and flexibility. The case for centralization rested partly on its efficiency: centralized decision-making involves fewer people, less formalization and less investment in systems for maintaining control and integration. The case for delegation rested partly on its flexibility: when decisions are left to people who are closer to the action, they can respond to changing circumstances without the delay that ensues from having to make a case for action which is passed up the hierarchy for authorization. Moreover, behavioural scientists have pointed to the motivational benefits which delegated responsibility offers, while it is also consistent with the principle of enhancing the participation of people in decisions relevant to them and to which they can contribute with some knowledge and experience.

The use of new technology to improve information systems, such as those monitoring production processes, retail sales or distribution, offers an opportunity to resolve some of the tension between efficiency and flexibility in decision-making. The technology itself could be used to facilitate either a re-centralization of decision-making or its more effective delegation. Leavitt and Whisler (1958) at an early stage predicted re-centralization is assisted when comprehensive and current information can be passed directly to senior management, particularly if the problem of data overload and complexity is mitigated by the availability of computer programs to integrate data and draw key analyses from them. Centralization is also rendered more feasible to the extent that use of the new technologies can simplify management structures and so reduce senior managers' spans of control.

There is, however, no overwhelming technical reason why information technology cannot be used to facilitate more effective delegation. This can be done in two main respects. First, by linking each unit within an organization into a common network so allowing its members to be immediately aware of the situation of other units and elicit any comments swiftly. The precise recording of such communication which information technology offers can both protect the local unit from the charge of failing to consult or making its intentions clear, and provide confirmation of any intervention higher management wished to make. This reduction in ambiguity should encourage local initiative and discourage intervention from the centre. Second, the improved analytical facilities provided by information technology, such as programs for sensitivity analysis and financial modelling, when combined with improved data, could be used to enhance the capacity of local units to make 'sound' judgements in their decision-making. This capacity may previously have only been available to senior managers located in a corporate office and served by staff assistants.

In practice, the choice of whether to use new technology to assist centralization or decentralization is likely to be swayed by (a) the managerial ethos of the organization reflecting factors such as entrepreneurial and family control which, as in retailing, promotes centralization (Child *et al.*, 1984), and (b) task contingencies. In regard to the latter, Robey (1977) concluded that task contingencies, such as variability of production and the number of environments served, largely governed whether computerization was used to support centralization or decentralization. Computerization was associated with centralization when operations were standardized and the configuration of relevant environments simple. Some other studies also suggest that greater centralization tends to be found, other things being equal, when production throughputs are more standardized (e.g. Child, 1973, and Sorge *et al.*, 1983). Information technology is of less assistance to top-level decision-makers when novel and unpredictable conditions arise in the organization's operations. The programmed forms in which it presents information may prove inadequate to account for new circumstances, and even if they are, a personal on-the-spot assessment of new configurations is required for an informed decision to be made.

THE SIZE AND SHAPE OF MANAGEMENT STRUCTURE

Although the problem of controlling the growth of managerial overheads has been recognized for some time now (cf. Child, 1978), it has not yet been resolved. A survey by the Institute of Administrative Management found that among 180 UK companies, administrative and managerial costs had risen by 4% in real terms during the five years to 1981. This was a somewhat faster rate than in continental European and US companies (Kransdorff, 1983). Signs of disillusion with matrix management structures were noted earlier; these structures are an attempt to address the need for improved integration by duplicating managerial and coordinative positions which also adds to overheads.

The introduction of information technology is expected to assist in revising the growth of managerial and related overheads in three main respects. First, office automation can lead to economies in clerical and secretarial staff, including their supervisors. For example, the introduction of word processors has reduced the number of typing jobs (IDS, 1980, and Labour Research, 1983). A survey conducted for the Equal Opportunities Commission (Bird, 1980) examined the impact of new office technology on female employment and concluded that by 1990 some 17% of typing and secretarial jobs were likely to be lost.

Second, information technology should assist moves towards simpler and smaller management structures by virtue of the advantages for the processes of control and integration. In regard to control, these include a reduced need to rely on supervisors for monitoring and contingency handling and to employ middle managers for processing information. The introduction of superior communications technologies may permit a simplification of management structures by providing a requisite degree of integration and information sharing between functions without the need to rely on coordinating roles and hierarchies such as those embodied in the matrix form. Experiments which use microprocessors and communications technology to provide for a network of homeworkers are also directed towards overhead economies and the reduction of the full-time managerial structure down to a smaller, less complex core.

Third, the increasing use of personal microcomputers and terminals connected into networks raises doubts about the continuation of large central data processing departments. These departments developed because specialists were required to handle the unwieldy and inflexible computers of the 1960s. Initiative in the use of personal computers is, by constrast, lodged within management and main-line departments themselves. This implies a reduction in the size of central EDP departments and a change in their role towards providing a central servicing function dealing with technical problems and specialist assistance in developing new applications initiated by users (International Data Corporation, 1983).

Some British employers have expressed approval of the kind of management structures which new technology is expected to facilitate. For example, Sir Adrian Cadbury has argued in favour of a concentration of organization staffing on core activities (with other activities being bought in), as well as flexible working arrangements which include individualized contracts for a given amount of work or time given (Cadbury, 1983). He sees these developments as providing the basis for achieving greater participation and consensus within the smaller core organization that remains. Large scale is known to encourage bureaucratic complexity and rigidities, as well as poor industrial relations, and a reversal to smaller scale therefore holds out the prospect of more organic organizational relationships.

DISCUSSION

New technology has the potential to ease those problems of organization which have assumed greater proportions with the development of large complex companies and public institutions. It can considerably improve the transmission, storage and analysis of information and it offers the prospect of smaller organizations.

The scenario that has been outlined in this paper is an attractive one for senior management, for those key staff who will retain prospects of long-term employment and for those who willingly accept the risks of working independently on short-term contracts. It is not so attractive for others whose jobs will be displaced by new technology. However, it is unlikely that the changes projected will apply equally to all kinds of organizations. Their expected effects on industrial relations and management structure may not always be realized and their implementation may be particularly impeded by certain characteristics of the British situation. These qualifications may be illustrated in turn.

An important class of organizations offers personal services of a kind which have to be adapted to individual needs: for example, public sector organizations offering health, educational and social services, and commercial organizations such as travel agents and hotels. The ability of the service provider to respond creatively to the requirements of the client is an integral component of these services, the more so when they involve matters of major concern to individuals such as health. While new technology is already being used to effect economies in the administration and routine operations of such organizations, it is less likely to reduce staff in direct service provision. New technology is more likely to complement than to substitute for the work of such staff, and their present role is often underpinned both by public expectations and professional ideologies (Child *et al.*, 1984). Such organizations will be less affected by the developments outlined in this chapter.

Technical and professional staff who presently feel distracted from their work by the unwanted middle management duties of information provision, dealing with paperwork and attending meetings (Torrington and Weightman, 1982) may well welcome the assistance of information technology with relief. They are likely to preserve long-term employment as members of the more compact management structures which have been envisaged, occupying strategic positions such as senior engineer and senior systems analyst. It does not necessarily follow, however, that people in these roles, and other key occupational groups such as instrumentation maintenance staff, will refrain from using their strategic positions in the firm to bargain collectively in a robust manner for their own benefit. To this extent the new model of management organization may be considerably less 'organic' and consensual than has been envisaged.

There may also be limitations to the extent that the body of line middle managers can be cut and decision-making re-centralized within general management. When operational conditions continue to be marked by uncertainty and a high level of variability, reliance may still have to be placed on what Jones has called the 'tacit knowledge' of middle managers and supervisors (as well as workers) which is founded primarily on their practical experience (Jones, 1983). In these situations there will be limits to the assistance which programmed computer control can usefully provide. Decisions will be required of people on the spot. This of course also qualifies the assumption that decision-making can necessarily be re-centralized with the aid of new technology. The question has in any case to be asked to what extent senior managers should take on the burden of additional decisions rather than using any saving of time provided by information technology in order to devote the extra capacity to longer-term issues.

Progress towards the developments outlined in this chapter may be less straightforward than some descriptions of the 'microelectronics revolution' suggest, both because of unanticipated problems such as these, and also because of features peculiar to the British situation. The example of a confectionery company is instructive. This company has invested heavily in microelectronic process control, and is seeking to link operating information systems to managerial ones. It envisages a reduction in its production management heirarchy to only three main levels of control: operator, manager of each plant or line, and factory manager. This would eliminate one or two levels of control, reduce the numbers in production management and simplify the management structure. While some progress has been made towards this goal, with the numbers of operators and first-line supervisors greatly reduced, it has been delayed by technical and behavioural problems. For example, on the technical side, software development to enable consolidation of production data into a central computer has proved to be a slow process partly because of inadequate software in some bought-in production measuring equipment. On the behavioural side, operators in one of the most recently modernized plants were not using the production and plant data now provided for monitoring and control purposes. Instead they were still tending to devote too much of their time to more mundane activities and to direct visual surveillance of plant. Among the probable sources of this behaviour were: (a) insufficient training to acquire the new skills for analysing and using data; and (b) traditional narrowly defined boundaries of competence, which had never extended to the operation of a plant as a whole system.

Despite considerable governmental assistance, the rate of application of new technology in Britain has been slower than in some other countries (Bessant, 1982). Behavioural factors such as those just illustrated, which create a gap between the potential of new technology and its realization, are sustained by a number of institutional and cultural factors. The organization of work in Britain, in shopfloor, technical and managerial activities, is characterized by a high degree of specialization and a narrow bounding of occupations. Although this phenomenon has deep historical roots, it continues to be sustained today by the British system of education and vocational training (Child *et al.*, 1983). This constrains the extent to which the greater adaptability and the integration of information offered by new technology can be matched by a complementary broadening in the responsibilities of employees and departmental managers. Not only has British vocational training tended to create narrowly bounded competences, but the numbers being trained and the standards of training compare unfavourably with competitors such as West Germany (Prais and Wagner, 1983). Even the government's New Training Initiative is unlikely to overcome a shortage of skills required to make best use of new technology.

A less tangible, but none the less real, obstacle to applying information technology in British management lies in the individualism and tolerance for ambiguity which have been identified as among the salient cultural characteristics of British managers and employees (Hofstede, 1980). A penchant towards ambiguity and imprecision contrasts with the need of information technologies in their present stage of development to have precise inputs, and also with the way in which the improved processing of information itself removes some of the grounds for ambiguity. The control and integration potential of these technologies sits uneasily with individualism. On these grounds, a greater resistance to the introduction and adequate use of information technology is to be expected in British organizations.

In short, a new technology offers a technical potential for resolving significant problems in management organization. The sheer weight of economic pressures for increased efficiency will ensure that this potential is realized in those organizations which survive, though in Britain the process of adjustment may be more difficult than elsewhere.

DISCUSSION QUESTIONS

1. Discuss whether new technology can provide the means to institute considerable changes in management organization.
2. What are the main areas and applications of IT in organizations?
3. Describe possible effects on management structures arising from advantages offered by IT.
4. Comment on whether you think Britain is at any particular disadvantage,

compared with other countries, when it comes to achieving the full management potential of new technology.

REFERENCES

Bessant, J. (1982). *Microprocessors in Production Processes*. Policy Studies Institute, London.

Bessant, J. and Dickson, K. (1982). *Issues in the Adoption of Microelectronics*. Frances Pinter, London.

Bird, E. (1980). *The Impact of Telecommunications and Information Technology on Equal Opportunities*. Equal Opportunities Commission.

Buchanan, D. A. and Boddy, D. (1983). *Organisations in the Computer Age: Technological Imperatives and Strategic Choice*. Gower, Aldershot.

Cadbury, Sir A. (1983). 'Cadbury Schweppes: more than chocolate and tonic', *Harvard Business Review*, January–February, pp. 134–44.

Child, J. (1973). 'Predicting and understanding organization structure', *Administrative Science Quarterly*, Vol. 18, pp. 168–85.

Child, J. (1978). 'The non-productive component within the productive sector: A problem of management control'. In Fores, M. and Glover, D. (eds), *Manufacturing and Management*, HMSO, London, pp. 51–67.

Child, J., Fores, M., Glover, I. and Lawrence, P. (1983). 'A price to pay? Professionalism and work organization in Britain and West Germany', *Sociology*, Vol. 17, pp. 63–78.

Child, J. Loveridge, R., Harvey, J. and Spencer, A. (1984). 'Microelectronics and the quality of employment in services'. In Marstrand, P. (ed.), *New Technology and the Future of Work*. Published for the British Association by Frances Pinter, London.

Cosyns, J., Loveridge, R. and Child, J. (1983). *New Technology in Retail Distribution – The Implications at Enterprise Level*. Report to the EEC, University of Aston Management Centre.

Francis, A., Snell, M., Willman, P. and Winch, G. (1982). 'Management, industrial relations and new technology for the BL Metro'. Unpublished paper, Imperial College, Department of Social and Economic Studies, November.

Harvey, J. and Child, J. (1983). 'Green Hospital, Woodall, Biochemistry Laboratory: a case study'. Unpublished document, University of Aston Management Centre.

Hofstede, G. (1980). *Culture's Consequences: International Differences in Work-related Values*. Sage, Beverly Hills, Calif.

Hunsicker, J. Q. (1982). 'The matrix in retreat', *The Financial Times*, 25 October, p. 14.

IDS (1980). *Changing Technology*. Study No. 22. Incomes Data Services, London.

International Data Corporation (1983). 'The wired workplace'. Supplement to *Management Today*, December.

Jones, B. (1982). 'Destruction or redistribution of engineering skills? The case of numerical control'. In Wood, S. (ed.), *The Degradation of Work?* Hutchinson, London, pp. 179–200.

Jones, B. (1983). 'Skills, tacit knowledge and the automation of metalworking'. Production paper given to University of Aston Management Centre, November.

Knight, K. (ed.) (1977). *Matrix Management.* Gower, Farnborough.

Kransdorff, A. (1983). 'Now for the white-collar shake-out', *The Financial Times*, 18 April, p. 10.

Labour Research (1983). *New Technology Special*, 72, November.

Lamming, R. and Bessant, J. (1983). 'Some management implications of advanced manufacturing technology'. Unpublished paper, Department of Business Studies, Brighton Polytechnic.

Leavitt, H. J. and Whisler, T. L. (1958). 'Management in the 1980s', *Harvard Business Review*, Vol. 36, pp. 41–8.

Northcott, J., Rogers, P. with Zeilinger, A. (1982). *Micro-electronics in Industry: Survey Statistics.* Policy Studies Institute, London.

Peters, T. J. and Waterman, R. H. Jr (1982). *In Search of Excellence: Lessons from American's Best-Run Companies.* Harper and Row, New York.

Prais, S. J. and Wagner, K. (1983). 'Some practical aspects of human capital investment: training standards in five occupations in Britain and Germany. *National Institute Economic Review*, 105, August, pp. 46–65.

Robey, D. (1977). 'Computers and management structure: some empirical findings re-examined', *Human Relations*, Vol. 30, pp. 963–76.

Rose, M. and Jones, B. (1984). 'Managerial strategy and trade union response in plant-level reorganization of work.' In Knight, D., Collinson, D. and Willmott, H. (eds), *Job Redesign: The Organization and Control of Work.* Heinemann, London.

Sorge, A., Hartmann, G., Warner, M. and Nicholas, I. (1983). *Microelectronics and Manpower in Manufacturing.* Gower, Aldershot.

Torrington, D. and Weightman, J. (1982). 'Technical atrophy in middle management', *Journal of General Management*, Vol. 7, pp. 5–17.

Wilkinson, B. (1983). *The Shopfloor Politics of New Technology.* Heinemann, London.

21 The networked firm
John Taylor and Howard Williams

INTRODUCTION

The emergence of the networked firm is a relatively recent phenomenon. It is centred upon the widespread adoption of computer networking and its use in the design and implementation of business strategies. In the networked firm computer networks, and the new information flows they support, are a central feature of business activity. Computer networks not only mediate intra-organizational activity but also the transactions between customers and suppliers. In the context of an increasingly competitive and unstable operating environment computer networks allow the strategic realignment of the firm thus bringing about new patterns of economic activity and industrial organization.

The purpose of this chapter is twofold. First it is to set out a conceptual framework for understanding the adoption of computer networks and their importance as a source of innovations which give rise to the networked firm. Secondly, and by reference to primary survey material and case study evidence, to illustrate some of the forms of innovation that are occurring.[1]

Specially commissioned for *IT and Accounting: The impact of information technology*. Edited by Bernard C. Williams and Barry J. Spaul.
Published in 1991 by Chapman & Hall, London ISBN 0 412 39210 0.

BACKGROUND

The ever increasing power of information technology (IT) at ever decreasing prices is resulting in the widespread diffusion and adoption of the technology by firms. Increasingly the use of IT within firms is going beyond well-established functions such as accountancy and finance into other areas of activity, such as marketing, production and distribution. Moreover, advances in the technology are allowing new applications to be developed and implemented, again going beyond the traditional batch processing of transactions.

Importantly these advances in the technology and the applications supported have brought about not only a greater ability to process information but also facilitate a more rapid and effective communication of information. Therefore IT might better now be characterized as information and communication technologies (ICTs).

As a result of these broad technological advances, firms are being confronted with opportunities to reconfigure their existing activities around the adoption of ICTs. The argument here is that ICTs can be used to reshape existing activities and, in so doing, change the capabilities of the firm. For example, the introduction of computer-aided design and manufacturing technologies in the design and production process can radically alter the capabilities of the firm. Further, the wiespread diffusion of ICTs can allow firms to consider deeper changes such as in the nature of the organizational structure and its decision-making processes.

Importantly the availability of new and advanced ICTs is occurring at a time when individual firms are being confronted with new sets of uncertainties and thereby increased instability in their operating environment. For individual firms these new uncertainties have centred around a number of issues, including;

1. changing sources of value added
2. greater competitive pressures
3. the changing nature, including the stability, of consumer behaviour
4. a changing geographical distribution of markets
5. a changing technological basis of products and services
6. increased internationalization
7. changing regulatory environments.

As a result the traditional and well-rehearsed company strategies, designed to minimize uncertainty, are at best of only limited value in adapting to a rapidly changing environment. Such traditional strategies are predicated upon stable markets, stable regulatory frameworks and stable technologies.

Inevitably, therefore, these change processes necessitate the design and implementation of new management strategies aimed at recapturing greater degrees of certainty and maintaining the competitive position of the firm. The development of these strategies, however, is seemingly confounded by the very nature of the change process themselves. Firms are simultaneously required to be responsive and sensitive to an increasing number of highly differentiated competitive markets (geographically, culturally and temporally) whilst at the same time becoming more managerially integrated and cohesive as organizations. In essence firms are being pulled between the need to develop and support a wide product range tailored to individual customer requirements whilst at the same time maintaining relatively low costs derived from economies of scale in production (Prahalad and Doz, 1988). These developments in the private sector are also being mirrored by changes in public administration (see, for example, Taylor and Williams, 1989, 1990).

In devising new strategies what is increasingly evident is that the division of labour and functions within the firm, which hitherto have provided a coherent structure for their incremental development, are being radically challenged. Thus firms are seeking to define and implement new products, processes and patterns of behaviour. It is in this change process that the adoption of ICTs can be seen to be significant in allowing firms to find new forms of industrial organization, and of particular interest here is the emergence of the networked firm.

THE NETWORKED FIRM

The emergence of new uncertainties and instabilities has brought into sharp focus the internal rigidities of the firm. The need for the firm to be responsive and sensitive to the increasing vagaries of consumer behaviour, and the consequences of this for upstream (backward) linkages introduces a perspective of the firm as existing in a set of complex interdependent relationships. Both to understand the firm as ring-fenced, and to perceive the production process from raw material to finished good as a set of discrete activities, are increasingly mistaken. The boundaries that have hitherto traditionally delineated the functional structure of the firm, its management hierarchies, and the boundaries between firms are becoming increasingly blurred. Moreover, the actions of one firm can be seen to affect intimately those of others. As a result a new concept of the firm is sought which places emphasis upon systems and the interconnections which exist between firms, functions and customers (Rada, 1984). This new concept gives rise to the notion of the 'networked firm'. The concept of the networked firm emphasizes the nature of transactions within and between firms.

Analytically the transactions of a firm can be seen to embrace both the primary activities of the firm as well as the coordination and control of such activities (Williamson, 1975; Beniger 1986). Jonscher (1985) has observed that the ever increasing division of labour within the wider economy as well as in individual firms has brought about a more formal separation of 'co-ordination tasks' from 'production tasks'. For example, in an artisan production system different functional activities and decision-making processes involved in the design, manufacture and selling of products are not formally differentiated. In contrast advanced capitalist economies are, to a certain extent, characterized by the sophisticated division of activities and the existence of complex decision-making processes.

The transactions of a firm necessarily involve the exchange, and therefore flow, of information within and between functions as well as between firms and their suppliers and customers. The nature and shape of the transactional structure of the firm can be seen to have at least two important dimensions. First, the transactional costs incurred by the firm are a key determinant in whether the firm undertakes an activity itself or relies upon the market. By comparing the internal transaction costs with those of going through the market a firm can seek to minimize its transaction costs through the choice of activities conducted in-house and those contracted for through the market. Secondly the nature and pattern of those transactions within the firm give form to both the responsiveness of the firm to its customers and cohesion of the organization as a whole. Aoki (1986) has contrasted the transactional nature of US firms with those of Japanese firms in terms of the responsiveness of firms to changing market conditions.

The transactional structure and embedded information flows within and between firms provide a framework within which to analyse the adoption and use of information and communication technologies. Of particular significance here are computer networks, the synthesis of computing and telecommunication technologies, which by their very nature can be seen as transactional systems and therefore supporting the transactional structure of firms. Importantly such an understanding of computer networks goes beyond one which focuses upon the technology and sees the transactional nature of computer networking simply as 'bit-hauling'.

In essence the transactions and information flows supported by computer networks can be understood as flows of capital and labour. Given this perspective computer networks can be seen to have certain characteristics. In particular, computer networks sever the need to co-locate capital and labour, permit simultaneous access to capital resources, facilitate the instantaneous transfer of productivity gains from one location to another and allow for the codification and routinization of decision-making (Hepworth, 1986; Willinger and Zuscovitch, 1988). In consequence computer networks can be seen to be of considerable economic and managerial significance, a powerful source of innovations and competitive advantage.

The adoption of computer networking can be seen to provide the basis for a broad set of organizational innovations which manifest themselves in a variety of ways. Porter and Miller (1985) argue that IT can enhance the competitive position of a firm through its impact upon the value-added chain. In reviewing different activities within the value-added chain Porter and Miller (1985) identify specific IT applications which can bring about enhanced competitive positions. For example, they illustrate how the integration of IT, such as microprocessors, into a wide range of equipment allows for the remote analysis and diagnosis of performance. In this way field service activities can be enhanced and costs reduced.

In elaborating and extending the framework offered by Porter and Miller, Antonelli (1988) argues that within the firm the use of computer networking has become a major source of competitive advantage the net results of which far outweigh the additional costs of new investments in telecommunications and computer hardware and software. Specifically Antonelli cites the following advantages deriving from the application of computer networking (Antonelli, 1988, p. 20):

1. *Reductions in the amount of working capital* per unit of sale using telematics for logistic functions to reduce the level of stocks of finished products, intermediate and primary inputs and the order-invoice time lags.
2. *Better specialization of business units* in a few product lines more appropriate to the factor endowment of each unit.
3. *Purchasing economies of scale* as inputs are purchased centrally, at better prices and on better payment and delivery conditions.
4. *Integrated manufacturing and marketing* as excess capacity or production failures in one factory can be compensated by other markets or other factories.
5. *Financial economies of scale* generated by centralized financial management of highly diversified financial activities, with dramatic effects in terms of reduction of currency fluctuation risks, optimization of financial liquidity, optimization of the borrowing capacity of affiliates and head office, increase of contractual power in dealings with banks and the creation of an internal intra-corporate clearing house.
6. *Economies of scale* in data processing made possible by an integrated management of hardware and software capacities, skills and working time.

Whilst the work of Antonelli largely focuses upon new opportunities to realize economies of scale, the typology of innovations emanating from computer networking innovations offered by Gillespie and Williams (1988) focuses upon particular activities of the firm. They illustrate the manner in which computer networking can be seen as a source of innovations in the following areas: products, production processes, distribution, customer transactions and strategic management.

Further they argue that since technology is essentially configurational, yet interacting with the processes, structures and culture of the organization, its delivery of organizational benefits is neither guaranteed nor secured merely by the installation of a computer network. In consequence the range of innovation achieved is in no sense technologically determined but is shaped by managerial resources, organizational characteristics, technological parameters and broader regulatory settings.

In summary, computer networking can be seen as a powerful source of innovations permitting the organization to adjust to changed market conditions and new sources of uncertainty. However, the transition from one organizational format to another is not smooth nor automatic and necessarily involves the firm and those firms with which it has inter-dependencies to restructure the nature and scope of their activities.

THE ADOPTION OF COMPUTER NETWORKS

The networked firm, and the importance of computer networking in underpinning its emergence, raise questions about the nature of the adoption and diffusion of computer networks within and between organizations. This process of adoption and diffusion can be understood on two levels, the formal and strategic, and the detailed and technical.

At the formal and strategic level a number of different strategies exist for the adoption of computer networking. The initial strategic focus in the adoption of computer networking is upon internal applications. The transition to inter-organizational networking can be seen to be shaped both by the nature of the relationships between firms and by the broad regulatory structures defining the provision of telecommunications services. Morgan (1990) identifies three stages of network development:

1. *Internal networking* where the emphasis is upon using telecommunications to abbreviate the development cycle of new products or services and to make a more coherent entity by 'bonding' employees in different divisions. The need for concomitant organizational innovation is important in securing the advantages of intra-corporate networking.

2. *Upstream external networks* where the emphasis is upon forging stronger and longer-term procurement relations with suppliers, especially key suppliers. Electronic data interchange (EDI) is a major example here.
3. *Downstream external networking* where the emphasis is upon using telecommunications as an interface with the market, for example in the financial services sector.

Irwin and Merenda (1988), writing from a US perspective, sees the development trajectory of computer networking somewhat differently. His analysis again starts with the adoption of computer networking for internal purposes but the subsequent stage, according to Irwin, is the use of the network as an income generator in its own right. This second stage reflects differences in the regulatory structures surrounding the provision of telecommunication services in the US, for example the relative ease with which firms are able to resell surplus telecommunications capacity thereby generating additional revenues. The final stage of development suggested by Irwin is the reshaping of customer/supplier linkages. The computer network development trajectory of a number of major US corporations is given in Fig. 21.1.

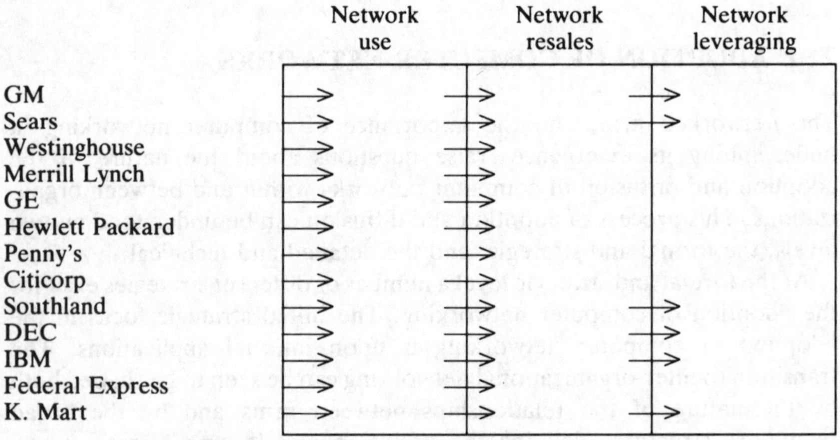

	Network use	Network resales	Network leveraging
GM	→	→	→
Sears	→	→	→
Westinghouse	→	→	
Merrill Lynch	→	→	
GE	→	→	
Hewlett Packard	→	→	
Penny's	→	→	
Citicorp	→	→	
Southland	→	→	→
DEC	→	→	→
IBM	→	→	→
Federal Express	→	→	
K. Mart	→	→	→

Fig. 21.1 Network evolution.

In developing and extending these formal and strategic explanations of the adoption of computer networking the authors have laid emphasis upon evolutionary patterns of adoption, where the initial phases of adoption define both the technological and informational parameters of future development. At the initial stage of adoption computer networks appear to be used in functionally specific ways, that is within, rather than as a challenge to the existing and specific activities of the firm. As a result adoption may occur in a fragmented way within the same organization. Furthermore, this fragmented adoption may result in a single organization supporting technically different systems. Therefore any strategic concern in this initial stage of adoption is concerned with particular functions and typically couched in terms of increased *efficiency*.

Subsequently, computer networks and the information flows they support come to form an integral part of procedures used to evaluate existing functional activities. Thus the focus of computer network use moves away from data specific activities within a function, towards departmental information systems and increased *effectiveness*. In this way the technology tends to become integrated into the generality of functional activities in the organization. Whilst the technology appears to remain located within particular functions, at this point, its deeper penetration into functional activities begins to raise more strategic questions about the process of information systems integration in the wider organizational context.

The final stage of this evolutionary model sees the broad integration of computer network resources, including the new information flows they support, throughout the organization. As a result the information flows conveyed by the technology become central to the reshaping of the organization, its relationships both internally and externally and its *competitive advantage*. Thus the focus here is on strategic and corporate information systems through which the organization can design, evaluate and implement change.

At a second and more detailed level the technical trajectory of computer networks provides important insights into their adoption. Given the close relationship between the technological nature of the computer network and its broader organizational significance the technical objectives of computer network development provide a proxy measure of other change processes. On the basis of primary research (a large-scale postal survey and detailed case studies) the authors have recently examined both the uptake of computer networks and their technical trajectory. At a first level these characteristics indicate the size and shape of information activities, and the nature of their integration into the organization. It is towards these concerns that the observations below are directed. However, these observations are drawn from a preliminary analysis of survey data and should be treated as such.

Of the survey respondents 40.5% had a computer network in 1989. Of these organizations 40% had installed their network after 1985, perhaps indicating the beginnings of a more rapid diffusion of the technology.

Also emerging from the survey is prima facie evidence that the number of users within the respondent organizations has grown over the period 1982 to 1989. This suggests a deeper penetration of the technology into the processes and activities of the firm, again reflecting an expanding range of information activities. For example, the number of organizations with fewer than ten computer network users has fallen from 70% to 24% between 1982 and 1989, whereas those with more than 50 users has risen from 11% to 40%.

The proportion of transactions which are on-line (i.e. real-time transactions) gives a proxy measure of the extent to which network applications are integrated into the day-to-day activities of the organization. In 1982 over 50% of respondents had some on-line capability compared to 92% in 1989. Whereas only 13% of respondents had all on-line transactions in 1982 this had grown to 28% by 1989. The growth in on-line transactions is more starkly illustrated by including all those respondents with 90% or more on-line transactions. Here the growth between 1982 and 1989 is from 14% to 40%.

In terms of computer hardware the growth in the number of mainframes and front-end processors indicates the increasing dependence of firms upon information and communications technology infrastructures. To strengthen this point evidence is emerging of the need to provide network management tools, to provide back-up, and the development of a capability to recover from technical disaster situations rapidly with the minimum loss of information resources. What is evident from the survey data is that a growing number of organizations have more than one mainframe and the number of front-end processors has also increased. In 1982 13% of respondents had more than one mainframe and only 22% had a front-end processor. By 1989 35% of organizations had two or more mainframes and 53% of respondents had front-end processors.

Within the context of the research, 'intelligent terminals' (e.g. personal computers attached to the network) were used to indicate the degree of computing sophistication amongst users within an organization. In 1982 only 20% of respondents had intelligent terminals yet the figure for 1989 is 88%.

The availability of services beyond data processing is limited. For example, in 1989 43% of respondents with a computer network do not support electronic mail, 50% do not support relational databases, and 25% do not support spreadsheets. So, whereas other data indicates an expanding and deepening of information activities within organizations, these data begin to suggest limits to the size and shape of these information activities.

In terms of the functional use of computer network applications the continuing dominance of finance and administrative functions is clearly demonstrated. For example, beyond data processing finance functions are the major users of spreadsheets (66%), word processing (45%), relational databases (30%), electronic mail (22%). The relatively circumscribed use of the network by other functions reinforces the notion that the diffusion of computer networks is at an early stage and that the realization of potential innovations remains largely anticipatory.

From a regional perspective, variation in the technical infrastructures of organizations is sharp, though less at the level of the general adoption of computer networks, and more in terms of the number of users and the proportion of transactions on-line. In 1982, whilst 18% of respondents in the City of London had 100 users or more, no respondents in north east England had computer networks with that number of users. By 1989 40% of respondents in the City of London had computer networks with over 100 users compared to just 15% in north east England. In north east England 16% of respondents in 1989 were on-line (i.e. 100% on-line transactions) compared with 41% in the City of London.

COMPUTER NETWORKS: CASE STUDY EXAMPLES

In the detailed study of computer networking in a number of case study organizations the authors have explored the innovation process around a number of themes, specifically the management of process, structure and territory. Importantly these case studies provide a focus upon the organization. The *management of process* is concerned with those routine activities that link the corporate hierarchy; the *management of structure* is directed towards the delineation of those roles and responsibilities which constitute the corporate hierarchy; the *management of territory* is concerned with the space-economy of the organization and the nature of the claims, by the organization, upon particular geographically defined markets.

THE MANAGEMENT OF PROCESS

A good example of the management of process is provided by the circulation control system for the delivery of library services from one of the case studies. Circulation control systems seek to integrate the details of stock-holding against issuing, receipts, reservations, overdues, borrowers overdue, catalogue searches, and the production of statistical information about, for example, the 'recovery rate' of overdue books and the 'success rate' for different kinds of reservation, not only for each library but for the service as a whole, or whatever combination of libraries is thought relevant. Traditionally these systems have been manually based, contained within each library, and committing labour resources essentially to back-office activities.

A networked solution to circulation control has allowed the library service to remain geographically dispersed yet to be integrated around an information axis. This development in the circulation control system is facilitating change in a number of ways. First, it is enabling local book stocks to be tailored to local customer requirements allowing spatial differentiation rather than duplication in the book stock. Considerable differences in customer preferences occur in different locations and information flows are permitting these to be both formally identified and subsequently better matched to local book stocks. As a result the number of duplicate books has been reduced and the savings made spent on extending the range of books available. Secondly, issue analysis permits product range experimentation through innovative book classification mixing and thereby increasing consumption. Importantly, here the effective product range is augmented and customer satisfaction enhanced without any increase in the overall capital stock of books being required. In effect the system is facilitating an intensification in the use of the book stock. Thirdly, the technology is also permitting more rapid and reliable book circulation from within existing stock. The implication here is that the number of duplicate copies of a book can be reduced. Thus finance is released to deepen rather than duplicate the overall stock. Fourthly, the total collection is made available via the computer network to all users regardless of the location. The stock has thus moved from one which is spatially differentiated to one which can be conceptualized as 'virtually' unified permitting access regardless of the physical locations of the books, and the user. Fifthly, the emerging 'new library service' is being further enhanced by the release of staff from the 'back-office' jobs to positions where broader advisory and information functions are central.

In short, the adoption of a networked solution to the delivery of library services can permit new spatial structures to evolve which are both increasingly sensitive to the differentiated needs of local communities yet do not deny users the advantages of a large integrated collection because of their location.

THE MANAGEMENT OF STRUCTURE

The changing responsibilities of a function are illustrated by the retail outlets of a case study firm. The original rationale for these retail outlets was to provide a contact point for customers to facilitate the payment of bills. Thus originally the technology was designed to capture and transmit minimal data, e.g. account number and the fact that the bill had been paid.

Any other contact between the customer and the organization had to be directed through one of four district offices by telephone. It was the district offices that had the functional responsibility to accept and authorize contract work, and thereby commit engineering resources.

The most recent phase in the evolution of the computer network has seen these outlets fully integrated into this network, thereby permitting access to a wide range of computer applications. Of particular importance is the engineering resource management system. Direct access to this facility means that these outlets are now able to manage a wide range of maintenance and repair activities through from the initial order to the committing of engineering resources. Thus these outlets have begun to adopt a far more important role in the delivery of services and the development of business.

As the functional responsibilities of these outlets have evolved so the nature of employment has changed with the emphasis moving away from back-office clerical staff to those able to handle a broad range of customer enquiries. In parallel, as the importance of these outlets as point of contact between the organization and its customers grows, so the role of the district office is being diminished. Locational decisions which saw the establishment of district offices in the outskirts of towns are now being challenged. The rising significance of the shops necessarily means that town centre (shopping centre) locations are of increasing importance.

In a further example the widespread diffusion of computer networks has brought about radical organizational change and the redefinition of functional responsibilities. Computer networking in this case has facilitated the development of two parallel structures, one concerned with the final consumers of product, and the other with its manufacture and delivery.

The first of these structures includes sales and marketing, product development, advertising, market research and brand management. This structure is designed to create and manage an information resource centred upon consumer behaviour in highly differentiated geographical markets and it accounts for between 20% and 40% of product costs. The information resources of this first parallel structure are central to the better specification of consumer requirements, the enhanced support of customers in terms of order handling, the definition of new product opportunities, the formal modelling of markets, the redefinition of sub-national markets, and the better definition of the retail environment, including product synergies and shelf displays. In effect this new structure seeks to provide information 'haloes' around the existing products of the firm, and a catalytic informational basis from which to define both new products and markets.

The second parallel structure is concerned with the procurement, manufacture and delivery of products. The scope of its activities account for about two-thirds of employment, and between 60% and 80% of total product costs. This parallel structure is designed to operate at the European level and realize economies of scale. Within this procurement–manufacturing–delivery organization there has been a process of functional integration so that the entire structure operates in a coherent and cost-effective manner in a cross national context. It is here that the computer network has been used centrally in the implementation of radical structural change in the organization.

THE MANAGEMENT OF TERRITORY

A good example of territorial management comes from a case study firm which established a particular geography to underpin its claim upon different markets. As the nature of these markets changed so the firm was reorganised geographically. The early development of the firm was consequent upon it being the least-cost producer in locally defined markets. As a result the expansion of the firm involved its spatial duplication in different geographically defined markets. Each 'branch' plant was relatively autonomous designing and manufacturing non-standard products tailored to local requirements. The use of the computer network at this stage of the firm's development was restricted to the finance function and applications were orientated towards cost control. The network sought to reinforce the strategic objective of being least-cost producer.

Over a period of three years, these locally defined markets collapsed and the firm was left with an organization suited to securing its growth in market conditions which no longer prevailed. In particular the orientation of the firm was towards markets in northern and western England and to manufacture on a ten week order-to-delivery cycle. The new market conditions manifested themselves in a shift in the market towards south eastern England and the manufacture of product on a three day order-to-delivery cycle.

The response of the firm to these structural changes in its market was interwoven with the development of its computer network. The firm had to bring about the spatial reorganization and integration of its production, as well as its sales and marketing, in order to achieve the requirements of a three day order-to-delivery cycle. This reorganization was centred upon a new spatial information strategy capable of assembling, analysing and integrating information externally and assimilating it with similar information of its own internal operations. The computer network underpinned the implementation of this new strategy.

At a detailed level the firm reorganized its manufacturing plants so that each had the prime responsibility for a particular product range. The firm was therefore able to achieve economies of scale in production. The branch plants despatched their output to warehouses which were responsible for deliveries to the market. The sales function was centralized and its geographical focus reoriented towards the market in south east England.

The interrelationship between these spatially fragmented functions of manufacturing, distribution and sales is managed through information flows over the computer network. New relationships have been established whereby the production activities of the company are determined by the actual number of daily sales. As a result daily fluctuations in production reflect changes in demand.

More recently the company sought to align its sales activities with several of the large merchant chains through the development of inter-corporate networking. In so doing the company has attempted to use its computer network to exert greater influence on the market and secure for itself the distribution of product into newly claimed territories.

The spatial restructuring of the company has occurred within the parameters set it by existing locations. Through the use of computer networked information flows the firm has managed to reassert its territorial claims in markets in south east England. Importantly this realignment of the firm's territorial claims has occurred without the need to locate investments in these new markets. In short, the development of computer networking has allowed spatial reorganization, ensured the integration of different functions, and permitted the assertion of new territorial claims.

CONCLUSIONS

The emergence and significance of the networked firm stem from a changing set of economic, organizational and functional relationships each of which is characterized by relatively higher degrees of uncertainty. The emergence of the networked firm provides a focus upon the nature of transactions within and between firms in these conditions of uncertainty and offers up a framework within which to understand the adoption and use of computer networking. As mentioned earlier, however, it is evident that whilst computer networking can be seen as a source of innovation, its configurational nature means that any benefits of computer networking are neither guaranteed nor secured merely by its technical adoption.

The use of computer networking, however, undoubtedly opens up opportunities for innovation which can have a profound impact upon the nature of the organization and its relationships with customers and suppliers. The results of empirical work discussed above suggest ways in which computer networking is being used to transform the nature of organizational activities. It is in these ways that computer networking is significant to the management agenda of the 1990s and beyond.

NOTE

1. The work reported here was funded by the Economic and Social Research Council under its Programme on Information and Communication Technologies. The authors wish to acknowledge the support of Professor John Goddard, Irene Hardill, Pooran Wynazyck of the Centre for Urgan and Regional Development Studies at the University of Newcastle upon Tyne, and Roberta Capello of the Boconni University in Milan, Italy.

FURTHER READING

Bakis, H. (1987). 'Telecommunications and the global firm. In Hamilton, F. I. (ed.), *Industrial Change in Advanced Economies*, Croom Helm, London.

Belussi, F. (1987). *Benetton: Information Technology in Production and Distribution, a Case Study of the Innovative Potential of Traditional Sectors*. SPRU Occasional Paper No. 25, University of Sussex.

Capello, R., Taylor, J. and Williams, H. (1990). 'Computer networks and competitive advantage in building societies', *International Journal of Information Management*, Vol. 10, pp. 54–66.

OECD/Berkeley Roundtable/CEC: DGXIII (1990). *Information Networks and Competitive Advantage*, Vols 1, 2 and 3. Available from either the European Commission or OECD.

Taylor, J. and Williams, H. (1990). 'Themes and issues in the information polity', *Journal of Information Technology*, September.

REFERENCES

Aoki, M. (1986). 'Horizontal vs. vertical information structures of the firm', *American Economic Review*, Vol. 76, No. 5, pp. 971–83.

Antonelli, C. (1988). *New Information Technology and Industrial Change: The Italian Case*. Kluwer Academic Press, Dordecht.

Beniger, J. R. (1986). *The Control Revolution: Technological and Economic Origins of the Information Society*. Harvard University Press.

Gillespie, A. E. and Williams, H. (1988). 'Telecommunications and the reconstruction of regional comparative advantage', *Environment and Planning A*, Vol. 20, pp. 1311–21.

Hepworth, M. E. (1986). 'The geography of technical change in the information economy', *Regional Studies*, Vol. 20, pp. 407–24.

Irwin, M. and Merenda, M. J. (1988). 'The corporate network: an emerging trend for the nineties', *Communications in the 1990s*, 10th International Conference, IDATE, Montpellier, France, November 1988.

Jonscher, C. (1985). 'Information resources and economic productivity', *Information Economics and Policy*, Vol. 1, pp. 13–35.

Morgan, K. (1990). 'Shaping the infrastructure, large firms, advanced networks and the dilemmas of freedom'. *The Future of the Network*, PICT Conference, Polytechnic of Central London (CICS), May 1990.

Porter, M. and Miller, V. (1985). 'How information gives you competitive advantage', *Harvard Business Review*, Vol. 85, No. 4, pp. 149–60.

Prahalad, C. and Doz, Y. (1988). *The Multinational Mission*. Macmillan.

Rada, J. (1984). 'Development, telecommunications and the emerging information economy', *Second World Conference on Transborder Data Flow Policies*, Rome, June 1984.

Taylor, J. and Williams, H. (1989). 'Telematics, organisation and the local government mission', *Local Government Studies*, May/June, pp. 75–93.

Taylor, J. and Williams, H. (1990). 'Themes and issues in the information policy', *Journal of Information Technology*, September.

Williamson, O. E. (1975). *Markets and Hierarchies: Analysis and Anti-Trust Implications*. Free Press, New York.

Willinger, M. and Zuscovitch, E. (1988). 'Towards the economics of information intensive production systems: the case of advanced materials'. In Dosi, G. *et al.* (eds), *Technical Change and Economic Theory*. Pinter, London, pp. 239–55.

22 The impact of information technology on small businesses and entrepreneurs

Nigel Bryant and Robert Lambert

The last twenty years have seen the introduction of technology become increasing important to the overall operation of small businesses. We will consider three areas in relation to information technology and small businesses which contribute toward a positive impact on the operation of a particular small business. These are the changing contribution of IT to small businesses, the systematic approach to identifying potential applications in a small business, and the successful incorporation of information technology into a small business's operations.

THE CHANGING CONTRIBUTION OF IT TO SMALL BUSINESSES

The performance of an organization and the ability of its managers to manage effectively is significantly affected by the quality of its computer systems. This is particularly true in today's world for several reasons. Businesses have become increasingly complex. They need to respond more quickly to environmental changes and they have significant staff restraints placed upon them. Businesses look toward technology to facilitate these changes. Recent developments in computer

Specially commissioned for *IT and Accounting: The impact of information technology*.
Edited by Bernard C. Williams and Barry J. Spaul.
Published in 1991 by Chapman & Hall, London ISBN 0 412 39210 0.

technology affect both the way an organization presents its products, for example bank service tills, and the way it organizes itself internally, for example the increasing use of personal computers and electronic communications.

These applications and the beneficial impact they have upon organizations are derived from three key characteristics of computer systems. They can perform repetitive logical tasks at high speed. They can store and allow fast access to large volumes of data in a compact form. They are increasingly taking advantage of electronic forms of communication.

The earliest business computers in the 1960s made use of this high speed processing to perform such tasks as payrolls and invoicing. Such tasks have little need for intelligence, merely an ability to carry out the same mathematical operations over and over again. In the case of payrolls the process is very straightforward: take gross pay, deduct tax allowance, calculate PAYE, deduct tax, add allowance, deduct any other amounts necessary to give net pay, print pay slip. This is easy enough for one employee. The early mainframes could repeat this process for ten thousand employees and so were very popular with large organizations such as local authorities, water boards, etc. Now, personal computers can handle the payroll of a company with 1 to 1 000 employees.

The computers of the 1960s were massive machines with limited processing capabilities, ideal for repetitive tasks as mentioned above. They could access thousands of employee records which were held on magnetic tape. Because the medium was tape, the processing had to be sequential. In other words the payroll system started at the beginning of the tape with Mr Aardvark, calculated all the salaries and wages and ended at the end of the tape with Miss or Mrs Zuckerman. The advent of disc storage meant that information anywhere on the disc could be retrieved very quickly, rather like choosing a track on a compact disk or LP. Thus later computers were used for storing and retrieving data such as customer records, product information, supplier's names and addresses, etc. Of course, the old payroll systems are still there producing the payslips.

A further development, after fast processing and massive memories, was the introduction of links between computers enabling direct communications between computers and their respective users. Thus, it was possible for a computer-user in Manchester to access information in London and, even, New York or Tokyo, and use the information to create a report which is then directed via cable and satellite to a computer in Melbourne.

Many of these systems were developed for and used in large organizations. However, more and more smaller businesses are adopting computer technology to improve the way they do business. This has been made economically possible by recent developments in computing which have resulted in a personal computer with some business applications costing around £1 000.

Small businesses now have the advantage when implementing IT. Unlike large organizations, small businesses can be flexible and responsive. A decision to spend money on a computer can be made locally without recourse to 'the technology committee'. If there is a perceived need to buy a computer, then finance can be allocated by reducing expenditure elsewhere. Again there is no need for long and tedious presentations to 'the technology committee'.

Personal computers can help small businesses become more efficient and effective. A particular characteristic of a small business is that the owner/ manager is the key decision-maker for the organization. A personal computer can provide easy access to the essential business information needed to develop and control the business. The owner/manager can respond more quickly to signals generated such as levels of debtors or falling sales without the problems of departmental boundaries often found in large organizations. A single personal computer can carry out the day-to-day chores of a small business such as generating invoices freeing the owner/manager's time. However, the latest generation of computers can undertake more sophisticated tasks such as financial planning and fore-casting as an aid to decision-making, thus helping the small businessman monitor and control the business more effectively.

To summarize, computer technology is becoming a more viable option for use within smaller businesses for three reasons: costs are falling; the range of applications is growing and these applications are becoming available to small businesses with limited budgets; it is small businesses particularly that can benefit because the decision to invest can be made quickly and easily.

TYPICAL APPLICATIONS IN A SMALL BUSINESS

The term software includes everything from a few lines of program, written in a language like BASIC, to an enormous program which will handle three-dimensional design of solid objects. We will concentrate on business software which lies somewhere between the two extremes. Business software can be considered under three headings: business applications (e.g. invoicing); general software (e.g. spreadsheets); industry-specific software (e.g. estate agent packages).

Whilst all businesses may appear outwardly different, they all have things in common. All businesses employ staff, take money in and pay money out. In addition, most companies will have stock of some sort. It might be a few sheets of stationery or a large quantity of raw materials, work in progress and finished goods. Nonetheless, there are common components of businesses such as payrolls, ledgers, accounts and stock control. These can be classified broadly as financial accounting systems, cash systems and inventory systems. Each of these areas has relevant software available.

Often people running small businesses find it difficult to maintain complete and accurate accounts, frequently suggesting that they are too busy or that accounting is tedious. One solution is for a small business to maintain its accounts on a personal computer. Many business advantages can be gained by keeping up-to-date, accurate accounts.

Computer-produced invoices, for example, show sales information more clearly compared with the handwritten equivalent. Additionally a sales invoicing system can hold standard information such as names, addresses, item descriptions, prices and VAT information. All of this can be used to reduce the time needed for producing invoices and completing VAT returns. Often sales invoicing systems can be linked into stock control and sales ledger systems for automatic customer and stock updating. Sales ledgers maintain balances and history for each customer account. Credit limits can be set with automatic indication of over-limit spend. Perhaps more importantly, computer-based sales ledgers give a small businessman the ability to identify easily aging debtors and/or large amounts outstanding. Purchase ledgers maintain a mirror image of the sales ledger information, here giving the small businessman the ability to manage better payments to suppliers.

Many small businesses, particularly manufacturing, use a job costing system to record costs, times, purchases, etc., against a particular customer order. This is a difficult task to perform manually but the information generated by computer can be used for accurate billing and subsequent tendering.

A stock control system allows small businesses to identify quickly the value of stock they hold, the balance against any item and any purchase orders outstanding. A manual system would also show clearly stock against a particular item, but the analysis of, say, five hundred or a thousand stock records to identify valuations, usage, trends, etc., would be a mammoth task manually and probably would not be undertaken.

For the larger small business, the speed and power of the computer can be used to calculate pay, produce payslips and produce, for example, a BACS analysis.

The advent of personal computers and software packages gave rise to software that was universally applicable. Anybody can take a spreadsheet and adapt it for their own use. Such software is known as horizontal. Producers of horizontal software hope to have enormous markets (the whole world) with large sales at lowish prices. Unfortunately there is lots of competition as competitors see the expanding markets for such packages as spreadsheets.

Whilst there is a large number of packages on the market, most of these (certainly the biggest selling packages) can be considered in four groups: word processing, spreadsheets, graphics and database systems.

Word processing packages on a personal computer provide a range of facilities such as easy error correction, multiple copies and other helpful features. Because most business communications sent and received are in written form such as memos, letters and reports, word processors are the most widespread computer application. Word processors allow documents to be proofread and edited on a screen rather than being typed and retyped. Furthermore, because all documents are stored but easily accessible, word processor packages can be used for retrieving and printing standard letters, official documents, etc.

Word processors are, perhaps, best known for their mailshot output. Using a database of names and addresses of potential customers, it is possible to merge marketing letters with names and addresses to send a unique letter to all prospects. Using a word processor in this way leads to the infamous '*Mr Smith* of *3 Railway Terrace*, you have been chosen from thousands of people to receive a satellite dish . . .'

Spreadsheets allow the user to handle data in tabular form such as rows and columns of numbers. It has been argued that every manager has at least one information processing task which could justify the use of a spreadsheet package. Such tasks will vary from manager to manager but include any task that involved columns of figures such as accounts, cash flows, budget projections, etc. More sophisticated uses include sets of linked spreadsheets which can form the basis of sophisticated financial modelling.

Manual models of cash flow, changes in prices or costs can be extremely time consuming and at times confusing. A spreadsheet allows small businessmen to review the impact of major changes in sales and purchases on the company's cash flow.

Columns of figures and tables of data are often difficult to understand. Their significance is more easily recognized through graphics and charts. This is particularly true when presenting data to others. Some personal computing packages can take in data as lists of numbers and prepare a variety of graphic displays as required. If the owner/manager needs to present information to a bank manager, customers, partners or creditors, computer-produced graphics can enhance the message.

Another method of improving presentation used by some small businesses is desk-top publishing (DTP). DTP can be used to produce good quality brochures or catalogues as well as publicity material.

Much of a small businesses' administration involves storing and retrieving information from files. The better organized the filing system, the easier it is to access information. It is therefore worthwhile investing time and effort in storing information to give easy access when needed. Manual filing systems have extremely limited access facilities. Personal computer data management systems give very flexible retrieval facilities. Data management systems, however, vary considerably from simple, easy to use, personal filing systems to powerful database system packages.

Information is the lifeblood of an organization. Rapid access to information is extremely important. Any collection of information can be put into a database, ranging from simple name and address files to complex sets of interrelated data such as stock files and suppliers files. A personal computer can support large sophisticated database systems with thousands of entries.

As mentioned above, when the contents of a database are combined with a word processed standard letter the effect is to give each prospective customer a letter with the right personal touch.

In an attempt to create a niche for their products, some producers go for industry markets with specialized software. An example of such software would be where a producer has used a database to create a booking system for a hotel. The producer hopes to sell the booking system to all hotels at a higher price than the original database.

Such software, often written using a spreadsheet or database, is geared to particular groups, for example packages for hotel management, estate agents, bakers, publicans, etc. As the competition for the general markets becomes more and more aggressive, so software suppliers are turning to vertical markets. It is likely that there exists vertical software to suit the business. If not yet available, it will be soon. Such packages are advertised in the trade press.

There has been a very rapid development of communications technology which use standard telephone lines. Many organizations and individuals make use of the PRESTEL information service which gives access to large amounts of information. Prestel is similar to TV's teletext but it is interactive allowing the user to make bookings, etc. Systems such as BT Gold and others give the benefits of electronic mail by subscription.

There are external databases which provide information for small businesses. These are set up and maintained by a variety of organizations such as universities, government departments and trade associations.

They allow access to world-wide information about prices, markets, etc., through the communications links mentioned above.

During the last few years computer hardware and software have become cheaper and more powerful. These changes have contributed significantly to the efficiency, effectiveness and profitability of small businesses as reviewed above. It is reasonable to assume that this trend will continue. Within the next few years personal computers will be built which will have vast increases in power and memory. This will allow enhanced graphics and much more on-screen help for the user. In addition personal computers will be networked, that is connected to large, central computers to give local power as well as access to large central databases. Changes in hardware will be reflected in improvements in software.

A SYSTEMATIC APPROACH TO IDENTIFYING POTENTIAL APPLICATIONS IN A SMALL BUSINESS.

In determining where information technology can have the most positive impact on a small business, a systematic, top-down approach should be adopted. In other words, any system should contribute to the overall objectives of the business.

Thus the first step when considering potential applications is to review the business objectives and the nature of the business environment. This analysis should include a review of market trends, the competition and any possible applications from developments in technology that may affect the business. The analysis may include business objectives and the business environment. The business objectives should be identified and explicitly stated. Table 22.1 gives some examples.

Table 22.1 Examples of business objectives

1.	**Growth**: to achieve £500 000 p.a. turnover in three years.
2.	**Profitability**: to achieve a profit of 10% on sales.
3.	**Job satisfaction**: to allow the owner/manager to increase the rewards and satisfaction from working.

The analysis of the business environment may show that competitors are beginning to introduce computing technology to improve their services to their customers. Table 22.2 gives some examples.

From the overall business objectives and the assessment of the business environment, the owner/manager should be able to develop a series of issues or business applications that are critical to the business achieving its objectives. Table 22.3 gives some examples.

Table 22.2 Some examples of the analysis of the business environment

1.   A rival printing business introduces computers and laser printers to rapidly produce personalized business cards, letter headings or leaflets for subsequent photocopying.
2.   In the property market a competitor estate agent may be using a computer system to match house attributes with purchaser requirements.
3.   A competitor dentist may be using a computer to hold patient records and to graphically display charts, as well as run the administration system.

Table 22.3 Critical issues for the achievement of business objectives

Objectives	Example of critical issues
Growth	Sell more of existing products to existing customers
	Sell more of existing products to different customers
	Improve the competitive position through improving service levels and customer satisfaction
	Improve presentation and image of the company.
Profitability	Reduce costs and administration
	Reduce stock levels
	Speed up invoicing, collection of bad debts
	Improve marketing information
	Improve information about profitability of certain products
	Difficulty of getting and keeping good staff.
Job satisfaction	To free time so that the owner/manager can do other things.

Following the review of the key issues facing the business it is appropriate to prioritize these issues so that the major ones are addressed first. Each business is different so the priorities will be different but it is essential to follow a top-down approach to ensure that the key areas are addressed first and are part of an integrated plan.

For each of these key issues alternative ways of achieving the objective should be considered, one of which may be a computer-based solution. For example, one electronic components supplier has broadened his market from essentially a local one to a national one. This was achieved by allowing other computer users to link over the telephone system into his computer-based sales order system reviewing electronically the catalogue and prices and placing orders directly into the system.

Having identified the key issues that are of most critical importance to the success of the business the next step is to develop a specification of needs for each area which are being considered for computerization. This stage requires a clear and detailed statement of precisely what the computer system should do. It may be that many different reports containing information will be required. It is important for the owner/

manager to be quite specific at this stage as to what the layout should be and the content of each report. If the system is to undertake a particular task, for example invoicing, the layout of the preferred invoice should be determined, ensuring it relates exactly to the services and products sold and the image of the business.

This yardstick or specification of needs is crucial as it will act as a basis for the evaluation of any hardware and software offerings. Without this specification it is difficult to judge critically. It is through this mechanism that a small businessman can manage an encounter with computer salespeople.

Developing the specification may involve other people outside the organization, such as other small businessmen using a similar system, or attending a course or seminar. Often these discussions will allow a clearer specification of needs in line with what is possible. Clearly defining the real requirements at this stage will reduce the likelihood of problems later on. At this stage it is important to begin to quantify the situation. It is necessary to identify and measure certain attributes of the system, for example how many customer accounts now and in the future, how many stock items, how many transactions are performed in a particular day, week or month, how much information is needed now or in the future. It is important to get some idea of the size of each record needed. Detailed analysis and measurement is vitally important as this will affect both the software and hardware required.

Contemplating the implementation of a computer system is a headache for even the largest company. For a smaller business, the decision may tie up the total capital expenditure for the next year or two. Clearly, there is a need to think through the pros and cons of implementing a system using the framework of cost-benefit analysis. First, consider the cost of running the current system: How many man hours are involved in running the current system? How much does it cost in terms of paper, equipment and so on? And what is the performance level from the current system? Secondly, consider the potential benefits such as direct saving (e.g. staff, equipment, reduction in stock, etc.), other benefits (e.g. improved service, increased sales, etc.). Try to quantify these benefits wherever possible. These measurements will give an indication of the potential benefits against which the costs of the system will need to be measured.

Having considered the various aspects of computers, it should be possible to evaluate the financial and business implications involved in the development of a computer system. Table 22.4 gives an indication of the headings to consider when completing a cost-benefit analysis.

The analysis of the business, its objectives and potential areas of computerization will form the basis of the decision whether or not to proceed with

Table 22.4 Some suggested costs and benefits

Costs
Capital costs, that is the costs involved in obtaining and implementing the complete system, and include:
   Hardware costs including cables
   Software costs
   Installation costs, including testing of equipment
   Special furniture or equipment costs
   Training costs
   File conversion costs

Running costs:
   Consumables, e.g. forms, disks, tapes, paper, ink, etc.
   Maintenance contracts both hardware and software
   Insurance premiums
   Any additional salaries

Benefits
Direct benefits which are possible:
   Staff costs savings
   Reduction in overtime
   Reduction in stock
   Reduction in paperwork

Indirect benefits which are less easy to quantify:
   Better information
   Improved morale
   Better customer service
   Improved products/marketing potential

---

the introduction of technology, at what pace and in which order to maximize the benefits to the business.

SUCCESSFULLY INCORPORATING INFORMATION TECHNOLOGY INTO A SMALL BUSINESS'S OPERATIONS

Having decided to introduce a system the small businessman needs to manage the incorporation of the new system to ensure there are no detrimental effects on the operation of the business. The owner/manager needs to consider the total impact of the systems on the business. This means that all aspects of the change associated with developing and running the computer system need to be managed effectively in order to ensure a smooth introduction. Too often some of these issues are left undone until it is too late because 'we thought someone else was doing it'.

Planning the change is a crucially important activity which is often under-resourced. Meticulous planning and attention to detail are at the heart of good system implementation. There are numerous tasks that may need to be coordinated, these tasks need to be managed and effort applied to monitor performance. Thorough planning of new computer systems is vital. Essentially the plan must address the following issues in detail: deciding what has to be done, when it should be done, where it is to be done, who is to do it and how it is to be done.

The owner/manager needs to underpin the above by retaining clearly in mind why the system is being introduced and subsequent benefits. This will not only help retain the focus but also remind staff as to why the change is needed.

The changeover is a crucial and again an under-resourced activity. Often vast amounts of new data need to be entered into the system. The workload involved in inputting data will appear high and paper records may be incomplete or out of date, often causing considerable checking in order to validate the data prior to entry. A computer system will highlight deficiencies in the existing system. Suspect controls in manual book-keeping, for example, may not always be serious, but in a computer-based system could be catastrophic. Finally, the interface between the new computer system and the remaining manual system needs to be clearly and explicitly defined.

Any organizational change will have an impact on staff. This is particularly true for the introduction of technology. The new system will require different skills than those necessarily currently used in the business. A small business may be the best in the world at providing service X or producing product Y, but it may have little knowledge of computers and their use. Several aspects are important. For example, jobs will change. It may be that no new jobs are created but the work content of, say, the invoice clerk will be radically different. This will be reflected in the job, job title and possibly the job description if one exists. To accompany these new tasks, training will have to be given. Such training is vital not only to the actual users but also to others in the business who may be affected. This usually means all employees need an introduction at least to the new systems. There also may not be the necessary skills or potential within the company. This leads to the major difficulty of recruitment of staff who are qualified in technology. Where are they? How do you measure their competence? How much should you pay them? The changeover to the new system will place a great strain on the business, diverting attention from its main business. Resourcing of this task, whether to use temporary staff, overtime or weekend working is a decision which should be taken as early as possible. Overall responsibility needs to be taken for maintaining motivation and morale during this often hectic and traumatic stage.

A decision to include security procedures in a system may involve a slight amount of effort, but once included, that procedure will then be used by the computer for the entire life of the system. If there is doubt as to the need for a particular procedure, always err on the side of caution and include it. The purpose of security is threefold: to ensure information availability, confidentiality and integrity.

Whatever procedures are incorporated into a system, it is not possible to ensure totally that information will be available when it is required. Buying ten computers to ensure that a computer is always available does not guarantee absolutely that at least one will be working when required. It is possible for them all to be malfunctioning at the same time. To be realistic, the best that can be achieved is a minimization of the unavailability of information.

For a whole system to be available, each element in that system must be similarly available. Therefore, each of the elements in Table 22.5 require consideration.

Table 22.5 Elements for information availability

The computer
Computer programs
The master data files
The input data
A knowledgeable operator
A power supply
Various sundry items (i.e. stationery)

The purpose of the procedures relating to confidentiality is to ensure that the availability of confidential information is restricted to authorized persons. Imagine the problems of a firm of chartered accountants which misplaced the account details of all its clients, or that of an insurance broker 'losing' the names, addresses and renewal dates for all its customers to another broker. Having compacted large amounts of data onto small disks, it is not difficult to copy or transfer the data to another computer. This susceptibility was recognized by the Council of Europe when it drew up its Convention for the protection of individuals with regard to automatic processing of personal data, that is the storage and handling of information about individuals using computers and other devices. The United Kingdom signed the Convention in 1981 and subsequently passed the Data Protection Act 1984. The Act covers all users of personal data, that is information about individuals. Users must ensure that the information they hold is correct and secure. Furthermore, users must register with the Data Protection Registry. If a computer is to process confidential information there should be procedures to safeguard the information using passwords, etc.

Sometimes constant availability is an issue and sometimes confidentiality is the main requirement. However, all businesses should be concerned with information integrity. The purpose of integrity procedures is to ensure that the information produced is correct and continues to be so throughout the life of the system. Integrity procedures can be subdivided into three groups: those devised with the purpose of minimizing a breach occurring; those devised with the purpose of detecting any breaches that have occurred; and lastly, those devised with the purpose of recovering from a breach. Measures to detect breaches also contribute towards minimizing the occurrence of an intentional breach, just as the existence of procedures to detect fraud may well discourage fraudulent behaviour.

No matter how many checks are built into a system to minimize the possibility of a breach of integrity, such breaches will occur and, hopefully, will be detected. It is therefore necessary to implement further measures to locate the breaches and create procedures to enable recovery from such situations. It must be possible to recreate files that have become corrupted in error. This can be achieved by keeping copies of old files and reprocessing as required.

Possibly the single most important aspect for recovery is to maintain up-to-date documentation for all aspects of the system. Documentation is all too often neglected in the panic to implement a system. Recovery is hampered tenfold by not knowing in detail how a system functions. Inconsiderate staff with the knowledge in their heads have been known to leave or die very suddenly!

The cost of including the majority of the procedures is very small, provided they are planned at an early stage in development. To add procedures later can be expensive. The exclusion of necessary procedures can lead to insolvency or business failure.

CONCLUSION

Whilst computers can make a significant contribution to any business, they can create problems by adding a new dimension to current activities. The introduction of technology into a small business must be managed effectively to ensure a positive impact on the business. More and more small businesses are buying systems to improve their efficiency and effectiveness.

The question for any small business is not if but when! The change will happen. It should be managed.

FURTHER READING

Azis, K. (1986). *So You Think Your Business Needs a Computer?* Kogan Page.

Edwards, C. and Bryant, N. (1987). *Developing Business Systems Applications: A Managerial Approach.* Prentice Hall.

Small Business Software Series. McGraw-Hill. (Six programs and accompanying books to explain different aspects of financial management.)

Townsend, K. (ed.) (1986). *Choosing and Using Business Micro Software.* Gower.

DISCUSSION QUESTIONS

1. Are you aware of any local small businesses that have introduced computers? What applications are they running and why do you think they have introduced those particular applications?
2. Identify the critical areas for success of a small business and discuss how computer technology can contribute to improving performance in these areas.
3. Discuss in your view who will be affected and how by the implementation of a computer system in a small business. Who should manage the implementation?
4. Computer security in all its aspects is vital to the running of a business operation. What arguments and practical advice would you give a small business person to ensure they maintain the disciplines necessary for a computer system which is supporting their business operation?

8 Special Topics

In a book of readings such as this the
overwhelming problem for the editors is not
what to include but what to leave out. In this
section four papers have been selected which
highlight areas of increasing interest to the
student of accounting. In the case of at least one
of the subject areas, auditing and computers,
there are very strong arguments for giving this
subject a section of its own. However, as some
authorities would say that the future of
accounting, and indeed all the professions, is
going to be heavily linked with the development
of artificial intelligence, the problem as already
stated is where to draw the line. The four subject
areas tackled are, however, more closely related
than may at first be obvious. The problem of
computer crime is receiving growing public
awareness and its containment may be facilitated
by three strategies that are examined here. These
are the development of auditing techniques, the
use of artificial intelligence, in other words using
computers to replace or augment human
judgement, and the general education of
accountants to operate in a computerized
environment.

This Part begins with a chapter by Nigel
Connell which gives a clear picture of the current

use of artificial intelligence techniques in accounting. In this paper he investigates the accountant's relationship with decision support software with special emphasis on expert systems. He also looks at the role of the accountant within a technological environment and the likely impact of artificial intelligence on the future of accounting.

The second chapter by Barry Spaul looks at the increasing problem in business of computer crime. The paper begins with an examination of the public perception of computer crime and then examines the execution of computer crimes that have been brought before the courts. The motivation and organizational position of known perpetrators of computer crime is described and also some of the practical difficulties in gaining evidence and therefore convictions in this area. The chapter concludes by suggesting possible developments in the field of forensics to meet the threat of computer crime.

The third chapter in this Part by John Court and Nicki Muggridge tackles the use of computers and auditing. This paper takes the view that IT should be recognized as strategically relevant to the development of both the auditing and accounting professions. The paper confirms the increasingly held view that IT can no longer be viewed as a narrow specialism or side issue in auditing. The point is made that there is a need for ever higher requirements in computing abilities for all auditors. If standards of competence are not maintained the paper foresees problems for the auditing profession and the society it serves.

The final chapter almost begins where the

previous chapter concludes, in discussing how the changing role of accountants in a technological environment is reflected in accounting courses. Ted Wildey's chapter considers the two opposing views in the literature that an accountant's response to computers might be either that of minimization or adaptation (i.e. accountants may be educated users or information systems professionals with a specialism in financial systems). The implications for accounting education are considered and this is transformed into suggestions for changes in accounting courses.

Chapter

23 Artificial intelligence and accounting
Nigel A. D. Connell

INTRODUCTION

This chapter embodies within it some challenging and contentious ideas. To model human intelligence and then to represent that model in a machine demands agreement concerning some important preconceptions. We need to know if it is possible to define intelligence, particularly that intelligence peculiar to the role of the practising accountant. We need to know the circumstances in which that intelligence is applied, and how it is applied by a skilled practitioner. We need to agree that the model we have built adequately represents the intelligence in question, and applies it appropriately. We need to consider how those who come into contact with the model, either as providers of the intelligence on which the model is built, or consumers of the intelligence within the model, will react to their contact with it, and how it will react to their contact. The scope of this chapter is therefore potentially very broad and realistically we cannot hope to address in detail all these issues. Fortunately, the chapter is not about intelligence in general, but about aspects of an accountant's intelligence. In some of the examples which are discussed in the following pages, the scope of the intelligence in question is narrowed still further, for example to auditing or particular audit judgements. Readers interested in the wider issues should look elsewhere for a more detailed discussion (see further readings at the end of this chapter).

Although the recent history of artificial intelligence goes back a number of years, at least to the mid-1930s, the application of this emerging

Specially commissioned for *IT and Accounting: The impact of information technology*.
Edited by Bernard C. Williams and Barry J. Spaul.
Published in 1991 by Chapman & Hall, London ISBN 0 412 39210 0.

technology to the accounting profession has a shorter, more focused, lifespan. This chapter examines the relationship between artificial intelligence (AI) and the accounting profession, in particular examining those situations in which the technology has actually been applied.

The structure of the chapter is as follows. It begins by very briefly describing the history of AI, identifying those aspects of the technology thought to be commercially promising rather than of purely research interest. It considers the environmental context of the late 1970s and early 1980s, in particular the receptiveness of the UK economy to AI, in order to explain why AI technology was thought to have any practical business (and more particularly accounting) application. The application of one aspect of AI, expert systems, is then studied in more detail. The role of expert systems within the UK business community is overviewed, before a more detailed analysis of some accounting expert systems is presented and discussed. Finally, some thoughts are offered on the likely direction of future research and development in the application of AI to accountancy.

WHAT IS ARTIFICIAL INTELLIGENCE?

Human skills are wide ranging. Much of our intelligence we take for granted – our ability to manipulate symbols either written or pictorial, to communicate our ideas, to negotiate physical obstacles. As a consequence, AI research has a long history across a broad spectrum of disciplines. The *Handbook of AI* (Barr and Feigenbaum, 1981) lists some of the aspects of intelligent behaviour that AI researchers are addressing, including problem-solving, logical reasoning, language manipulation, learning, robotics and vision, and expertise. Expertise, such as that manifest by an accountant, is a particular type of intelligence. Expertise is more focused and therefore specific to a particular domain. It may embody formal rules, rules of thumb and experience, in a way that differs from general intelligence and is therefore more interesting to the student of accountancy.

Early applications of AI had been in the manipulation of physical objects by program-controlled machines. Many of the earliest efforts were thought to have little short-term commercial or practical benefit. The evaluation of AI's contribution to scientific research, as expressed in the infamous Lighthill Report, had 'declared the work sadly wanting at best and bordering on charlatanism at worst' (Feigenbaum and McCorduck, 1983). However, in the early 1980s events occurred which led to a reappraisal of the role intelligent computer systems might play in the coming decade, in particular their likely commercial impact.

THE INFLUENCE OF THE JAPANESE FIFTH GENERATION PROJECT

At the beginning of the 1980s, the Japanese Ministry of International Trade and Industry announced their ambitious ten-year plan to develop the next generation of computer systems. This new, 'fifth' generation would have at its heart knowledge-based systems. In 1982 the first stage in the ten-year programme was marked by the establishment of the Institute for New Generation Computer Technology (ICOT). An important feature of the Japanese strategy was the close cooperation between academics and industrialists, thus ensuring the development of systems embodying leading-edge research ideas yet likely to be commercially relevant and immediately applicable.

The UK government's response to the Japanese initiative was, in mid-1982, to announce its own initiative. The Alvey Programme outlined a five-year strategy for government-supported collaboration between academics and industry under four broad research areas: software engineering (SE), very large-scale integration (VLSI), man-machine interfaces (MMI) and intelligent knowledge-based systems (IKBS). An important outcome of the programme would be the construction of a number of large systems, built to demonstrate the commercial viability of systems using results arising from the four research areas. In addition, a number of Alvey Community Clubs would be set up, to further research and development in specific areas of interest to, and determined by, Club members. A number of the larger accounting firms took an active role in these Clubs, particularly the ALFEX (ALvey Financial EXpert systems) and ARIES (Alvey Research into Insurance Expert Systems) Clubs.

A typical outcome of the Clubs' activities was the construction of prototype expert systems. For example, the ALFEX Club members agreed jointly to construct a system which would offer advice on the financial health of a company operating within the specific domain (for the pilot project) of high-technology retailing. A financial consultant could use such a system to assess the long-term viability of the retailer under examination and thus form a more 'expert' opinion of risks relating to loanworthiness. The prototype system offered advice as the consultation developed and at the end of the consultation gave advice in the form of sales projection figures, an opinion on the reasonableness of management projections with which it has been provided, and advice on 'company sensitivities', indicating those variables most likely to prove critical for this company's future. The system could therefore be seen to exhibit the sort of intelligence, in the sense of the definitions mentioned above, that an accountant might display in making an analysis of a situation similar to that presented to the computer system.

The membership of most Alvey clubs was drawn from competitors in the chosen field; in the case of the ALFEX Club members were from the larger banks and accounting firms. The focus of interest of the Clubs' membership was not confined to the systems built, but also to the lessons learnt during the construction process. In this way the participating firms hoped to construct systems, independently of the Club activities, which would provide the firm with a competitive edge.

The Alvey Programme did not receive further government funding following the initial five-year period, although a number of club members continued to participate in joint research within sub-groups of the original Clubs. European Community initiatives, notably ESPRIT, continued to foster work in some areas of AI, although there was little involvement from the accounting community. Accounting firms whose appetites had been whetted by the Alvey Programme continued to develop systems independently and some of these systems are described in a later part of this chapter. Such systems were usually based upon an accounting expert's (or more typically experts') knowledge.

EXPERT SYSTEMS

To remind ourselves, an expert system can be defined as:

A computer based system in which representations of expertise are stored and which allows a user to access this expertise in a way similar to that in which he might consult a human expert, with a similar result (Edwards and Connell, 1989).

The construction of expert systems typically involves two stages. First, the knowledge must be extracted from its source, which may be a single expert or number of experts. Once extracted, it must be represented in such a way that it can be examined by the expert(s) to confirm the validity of conclusions which the system might have reached, or by the user to shed light on how the decision was, or is being, reached. These two stages, knowledge acquisition and knowledge representation, are time-consuming and exacting, culminating in the production of the knowledge base. This production is usually iterative and can never be said to be capable of final completion, even in operational systems. In use, the expert system draws inferences and reaches conclusions based upon this knowledge, subject to additional information provided by the user via interaction during consultation with the system or via existing databases. Systems are typically built using development tools which contain a general purpose inferencing structure (or sometimes choice of structures) and knowledge representation scheme(s). The developer can therefore introduce knowledge pertinent to the domain into this 'empty' but receptive framework, usually referred to as an expert system shell. In this way it is claimed that non-technical specialists are able to develop expert systems, although as with any framework the price paid for such corner-cutting is sometimes the need to compromise in terms of flexibility, which may or may not affect the effectiveness of the final, operational product. For a more comprehensive non-technical discussion of the nature of expert systems readers are referred to Harmon and King (1985).

A number of successful systems have been built and used in a variety of domains. Often these systems operate in narrow, technical domains, rather than in the domains of main-stream business management or commerce. It is important to recognize that some application areas intrinsically lend themselves better to expert system application than others (Prerau, 1985). One of the reasons for this is that the nature of the expertise within these domains is well-structured, and can therefore be captured and represented with more ease than the expertise of ill-structured domains. A widely accepted view of the criteria which may be applied to ascertain the suitability of a domain for successful development of an expert system can be found in Duda and Gaschnig (1981), who suggest:

1. There must be at least one human expert who is generally acknowledged to perform the task well.
2. The primary source of the expert's exceptional performance must be special knowledge, judgement or experience.
3. The expert must be capable of explaining the special knowledge and experience and the methods used to apply them to particular problems.
4. The task must have a well-bounded domain of application.

A review of working expert systems carried out in 1986 (Buchanan, 1986) listed about sixty systems which were classified within twelve broad application domains, such as agriculture, medicine, etc. Only three systems were cited in the financial subdomain, and only one in what the review described as 'information management'. The most recent comprehensive survey of expert systems in the UK (DTI, 1990) found evidence of 90 installed expert systems. The survey categorized the systems by sectors, within which the application area most closely allied to accounting, 'Finance', yielded only five systems worthy of further investigation (DTI, 1990, p. 58).

THE PROFESSIONAL ACCOUNTANT AND EXPERT SYSTEMS

The profession cannot be accused of a total disregard of expert systems. Respondents to Collier's (1984) survey of 400 members of the Institute of Cost and Management Accountants working in the UK private sector had foreseen expert systems as a potential future development. The survey undertaken the following year by Clarke and Cooper (1985) recognized the likely potential of expert systems, with over eighty per cent of respondents believing that expert systems for tax, audit and other accounting areas would be commonplace by 1995.

The ICAEW recognized the potential of expert systems for the professional accountant and in 1986 sponsored a survey of expert systems use made by accountants in the UK, USA and Canada (Edwards and Connell, 1989). The survey was conducted in two phases. The first phase was designed to establish the level and extent of involvement of firms who were developing or using expert systems. The second phase was intended to seek a more detailed response from those firms who seemed to have a substantial involvement in expert system development. The first phase yielded 189 respondents. Only twelve respondents (out of 45 who had initially expressed a willingness) responded to the second, more detailed, phase.

The results of the first phase showed 60 systems to be under development by accountancy firms. Audit was the most common application area, with 23 systems cited. Of these, almost half were concerned with the design of the audit programme. A further nine systems were under development in taxation, nine in data processing functions, and seven systems in general business areas, which included categories such as business modelling, employment legislation, and personnel. The remaining twelve systems were in a variety of areas which were difficult to categorize, usually because of the vagueness of the system's title.

With approximately half the respondent firms stating that they were not involved in expert systems, the reasons given for lack of involvement are worth examining. Over sixty per cent of respondents thought that the benefits of the new technology were insufficiently clear. This figure was precisely replicated in the 1988 survey of the industrial and commercial sectors of UK industry (DTI, 1990), in which over sixty per cent of those respondents who had no current interest in expert systems cited lack of an economic case as the most important disincentive. In the ICAEW survey, over fifty per cent of respondents felt other commitments merited development in preference to expert systems, further reinforcing the view that tangible or immediate problems may not appear to be addressed by expert systems.

The second phase of the survey investigated not only the current level of activity among the more mature users of the new technology, but also solicited their opinions on their likely involvement in future activity, as well as their views on the potential impact such activity might have on the way in which the profession may operate. Most of the accounting firms who responded to this part of the survey had at least three years' experience in developing expert system applications in accounting. This degree of experience merits the inclusion here of some of their opinions and conclusions, despite the small sample size. They may well represent a useful indicator of how the profession as a whole might be reacting within the next decade, assuming the gradual acceptance of some aspects of expert system technology.

Perhaps the most outstanding feature of the use made of expert systems by this group of firms was that three of the twelve firms had already obtained a financial return on the development of their system(s) and that a further three expected a return within two to four years. It is clear from independently published sources that systems developed for tax planning (Shpilberg *et al.*, 1986), audit planning (Pattenden 1986) and tax advice (Susskind and Tindall, 1988; DTI, 1990) have proved financially successful. Respondents to the ICAEW survey considered the magnitude of the likely return on development costs to be made in the ratio 2:1. The application about which most financial data is currently available is VATIA. The system, which assists auditors to check their client's compliance to UK value added tax (VAT) legislation, was released in 1988 after 15 months' development effort costing £138 000. Ernst and Young believe the payback period on investment to have been less than three months (DTI, 1990, p. 13). ExperTax, the system developed by Coopers Deloitte in the USA to assist with tax planning during the audit process, almost certainly involved considerably higher development costs, but was distributed and used world-wide (in modified form) by the firm's audit offices.

A key feature of the more successful applications of expert system technology in non-accounting applications has been the choice of problem-led rather than solution-led applications (see, for example, McDermott, 1981). The developers of accounting applications recognized the value of this feature, although a number were prepared to admit that solution-led applications had some value in terms of introducing staff to the technology, for example in terms of providing the opportunity to examine development tools or allowing users to become familiar with interactive systems of this type. The most likely users of expert systems were ranked in the following order:

1. managers
2. supervisors

3. partners
4. trainees
5. newly qualified staff
6. clients.

Such a ranking is interesting, particularly when taken in conjunction with the view that expert systems are more likely to be used to help firms to perform existing tasks more efficiently rather than provide opportunity to undertake tasks not currently thought of as mainstream accountancy. This is not to say that firms will not use expert systems as a means of supplementing corporate skills which are perceived to be scarce. However, the emphasis of such use is on supplementing skills in short supply, rather than deskilling existing staff. This might go some way towards explaining the prominence of audit applications in expert systems currently under development, for it could be argued that it is in the audit function where the manager has the greatest responsibility for displaying judgement (which in this domain might be viewed as a reasonable surrogate for expertise). An equally plausible argument may be that auditing is the principle revenue source for most firms and as a consequence savings in this activity may be replicable elsewhere and are therefore likely to yield worthwhile financial returns.

EXPERT SYSTEMS RESEARCH IN ACCOUNTANCY

In parallel with the exploitation by accounting firms of expert system technology for immediate practical use within the practice, a number of firms have sponsored or encouraged research into AI and expert systems. In addition, a number of university and polytechnic departments within the UK and USA have also examined the relationships between expert systems and accountancy.

AI research is usually categorized within two broad approaches. The first is primarily a process model, concerned with modelling the way in which human experts address situations in which they apply their intelligence. The second is more concerned with the construction of problem-solving machines. The former may result in new knowledge, the latter in more efficient application of existing knowledge. The 'process model' approach is concerned with questions such as 'what constitutes expertise in this domain?' For example, what is auditing expertise? Why do we view this particular auditor as an expert? It has been proposed that the answer is because he or she exhibits certain behaviour which characterizes expertise (Meservy *et al.*, 1986). When confronted with a task, the expert will 'solve the problem, explain the result, learn, restructure knowledge, break rules, determine relevance and degrade gracefully.' A different view is taken by Johnson (1986) who distinguishes between expertise and expertness. According to Johnson, expertise is a body of knowledge used as a basis for the performance of certain functions and therefore providing a theory or rationale for action. Johnson argues that it is possible to use expertise, for instance in the performance of certain tasks to a level of proficiency, but not necessarily to the same level of those who designed the activities they have mastered. This Johnson refers to as expertness, which can be said to be displayed in the performance of the tasks. Such distinctions may seem unnecessarily pedantic, but they do expose the essential ingredient in the nature of expertise, particularly as it is applied to the accounting profession. It is the performance of a task or set of tasks to a certain level, by applying a set of identified knowledge carefully selected from a larger set of knowledge. If these important ingredients are to become features of an expert system, then an additional step, involving the verification of that selected set of knowledge, must be included. Indeed, such constant verification is a natural activity for the human expert, as well as the artificial one, if the expertise is to remain current in a changing environment.

Once the expertise has been defined, it must then be acquired from those who are acknowledged to exhibit it. Such acquisition need not necessarily involve the expert. Many accounting firms, for example, hold their corporate expertise in the form of manuals, handbooks or checklists and some researchers of accounting expertise have used these sources, at least as a preliminary technique (Grudnitski, 1986; Hansen and Messier, 1986; Steinbart, 1986). Where expertise needs to be extracted from a human expert, the technique of protocol analysis is often employed (Bailey *et al.*, 1985; Meservey *et al.*, 1986). This technique involves the expert describing to a non-expert the thought process he or she is making while performing a task. These verbal protocols are then analysed, a laborious and time-consuming activity. An alternative approach is suggested by Shpilberg *et al.* (1986) who arranged for a non-expert user to be placed in the same room as two experts, but separated from them by a curtain. The non-expert is then presented with a case study together with reference material and is permitted to consult with the experts verbally. This rather theatrical-sounding variation of protocol analysis produces a dialogue between non-expert (who may be said to represent a user of the potential expert system) and the experts. This dialogue is subsequently analysed and used as a foundation for the knowledge base. This method can also be very time-consuming; the system in which its use was pioneered consumed over a thousand hours of expert time in development costs.

The outcome of much of the above research has been published in a number of reviews of the expert systems literature in accounting (see, for example, Abdolmohammadi (1987) for a review of expert systems in auditing, and Connell (1987, 1988) for reviews of accountancy applications generally). Table 23.1, taken from Edwards and Connell (1989), summarizes the thrust of the expert systems research literature.

Table 23.1 Expert systems in accountancy

Sub domain	System name	Current status	Tools used	Reference
Auditing	EDP-EXPERT	Prototype	AL/X	Messier and Hansen (1984)
	TICOM	Working	PASCAL	Bailey et al. (1985)
	AUDITOR	Working	AL/X	Dungan et al. (1985)
	AUDITPLANNER	Research	EMYCIN	Steinbart (1986)
	CFILE	Prototype	NEXPERT	Willingham et al. (1986)
	CheckGaap	Working	C	Pattenden (1986)
	ICES	Prototype	EMYCIN	Grudnitski (1986)
Taxation	TAXMAN	Prototype	LISP	McCarty (1977)
	CORPTAX	Prototype	BASIC	Hellawell (1980)
	ACCI	Working	ADVISER	Roycroft and Loucopoulous (1984)
	TAXADVISOR	Working	EMYCIN	Michaelsen (1984)
	TA	Working	PROLOG	Schlobohm (1985)
	DIRECTORS-TRANSACTIONS	Prototype	CRYSTAL	Evens (1986)
	EXPATAX	Under development	APES	Cunningham (1986)
	ExperTAX	Working	LISP	Shpilberg and Graham (1986)
	PAYE	Prototype	PROLOG	Torsun (1986)
	VATIA	Working	C	Susskind and Tindall (1988)
Financial planning	CASHVALUE	Product	BASIC	Ash (1985)
	FINANCIAL ADVISOR	Product	LISP	Bernstein (1985)
	PLANPOWER	Product	LISP	APEX (1986)
Government grants	GRENSIDESE	Prototype	SHELLS	Gambling (1984)
	GGA	Prototype	TESS	Evens (1986)
Risk management	ALFEX	Under development	PROLOG	ALVEY Reps (1986)
	CIRAX	Prototype	CRYSTAL	Edwards (1986)

Source: Edwards and Connell (1989), Table 4.1.

As can be seen from the table, the systems cited represent a spectrum of developmental stages, ranging from academic prototypes to truly operational systems, some of which have already been referred to in the preceding sections. As with the earlier examples, the majority of research work has been focused on auditing and taxation applications. It is interesting to note that the earliest system was developed in 1977, representing one of the first examples of expert systems in any non-technology oriented domain.

FUTURE DEVELOPMENTS IN EXPERT SYSTEMS FOR THE ACCOUNTING PROFESSION

It is clear from the preceding sections that the current level of acceptance of AI in general and expert systems in particular has not been as high as some pundits in the early part of the 1980s were predicting. In common with other areas of application, the attitude of the accounting profession could probably best be summed up as 'interested, but not yet convinced'. The final section of this chapter is based upon the assumption that, after a hesitant start, expert systems *will* find an important niche in the profession. The reason for this optimistic assumption is based partly on the benefits intrinsic to expert systems which will prove valuable to the profession, partly on the removal of perceived obstacles which currently stand in the way of a more enthusiastic adoption of such systems and partly on contextual factors such as the growing maturity of the technology and of the market-place. The adoption of expert systems will affect the relationship of firms with their competitors and their clients, and affect their own internal structure.

The motivation for accountants to use expert systems in anything other than an experimental fashion will eventually be a business one. Expert systems will be used because they offer benefits which no other technology can give. They can:

1. store and synthesize knowledge and offer advice based upon such knowledge;
2. archive skills that are rarely used, or in danger of disappearing from the organization;
3. act as an interactive training medium for junior members of staff, particularly in the acquisition of technical skills;
4. act as an 'on the job' assistant for junior members of staff, particularly in the context of skills beyond their accustomed day-to-day use;
5. provide guidance through rule-based situations such as applicability of legislation, allowances, etc.

All of the above are valuable features. The principle concern is that these benefits may be difficult and costly to achieve. The wider dissemination of notable success stories such as VATIA and ExperTax is needed if the benefits are to be appreciated. An examination of the business benefits of successful systems in business and commercial domains other than accountancy, such as those currently being publicized by the UK Department of Trade and Industry, may also give the profession a reason for considering applications in accounting. Quantification of the benefits is not always straightforward, which further serves to complicate their accurate identification and measurement, and published reports sometimes have a tendency to exaggerate benefits for a variety of reasons. However, as many of the successful applications have demonstrated, a powerful motivator may well be the presence of an otherwise intractable business problem which is difficult or expensive to resolve in any other way, such as shortage of key expertise, variable quality of service provided to clients in a key area, lack of uniformity in approach to a particular situation, etc.

The development of expert systems represents an opportunity cost. The decision to make such an investment is still one which the majority of accounting firms seem unwilling to take. Obstacles to success may be viewed as strategic obstacles or operational obstacles.

At the strategic level, use of intelligent software will bring about changes in the way that traditional tasks are undertaken, in much the same way that audit practice, for example, has been changed by the use of file-interrogation software. Staff may need a higher minimum level of computer literacy, which may necessitate changes in recruitment and training policy. Amongst the smaller firms, there will be little incentive to risk the development of what may turn out to be unattractive or unprofitable systems. The larger firms, however, particularly those with a reputation among the profession (and more importantly their clients) for being at the forefront of IT developments, may see it as imperative to be seen to be developing systems to maintain their reputation. If systems become generally available which capture a particular aspect of an accountant's work, the smaller firms may take the opportunity to purchase a cheap and accessible desk-top 'expert', where previously they may have found it necessary to refuse the work on the grounds that it was beyond the scope of their regular expertise. This situation may be threatening to the larger firms. Ernst and Young has received, and declined, a number of offers to hire or buy the VATIA system.

At the operational level, the obstacles concern software, hardware and the people who will build and use the systems. Most firms and their clients have, for their larger systems at least, a considerable investment in the traditional DP languages. Unless a shell is used, these traditional languages suffer some drawbacks as tools for expert system development. AI languages include fundamentally different programming concepts (for example, Predicate Calculus with PROLOG, List Processing with LISP). There are problems associated with the familiarity of staff to these concepts, and the difficulty of integrating programs written in these languages with other more traditional software, e.g. COBOL, spreadsheet packages, etc. Neural networks may suffer similar disadvantages, as may the more costly expert system environments provided by products such as KEE, ART and ESE, which may in addition require dedicated hardware. Some expert system shells permit a degree of integration with other software, allowing data to be transferred between the shell and other packages such as Wordstar, Lotus 1-2-3, dBase III, etc. One way in which successful implementers of some accounting systems have bypassed this problem is by building their own, domain-specific, shell (see, for instance, Shpilberg *et al.*, 1986; Pattenden 1986).

The hardware problems associated with expert systems relate most acutely to compatibility with existing systems. Problems of compatibility relate not only to systems internal to a firm but also to client organizations' systems. Although software is available to provide a bridging facility between most manufacturers's hardware, future expectations might include integrated expert systems which, for instance, retrieve and inspect data from clients' own files.

The availability of appropriately trained staff presents short-term problems for any organization about to construct full-scale expert systems, although most of the larger firms engaging in expert system construction encouraged the growth of in-house expertise, which has the additional benefit that it can be sold on via consultancy activities.

CONCLUSIONS

This chapter set out to examine the role of AI in the accounting profession. The overall conclusion is that current activity is limited, but has potential. An important focus of the chapter has been the use made by the profession of expert systems. Two strands to expert systems application were identified, research and development. Conclusions arising from the first strand, research, concerned the nature of expertise and the structure of problem-solving. It seems clear that if the nature of accounting expertise can be defined, then the insight gained may assist organizations in assessing how they should select, train and develop staff in a way which maximizes human expertise. Expert systems can be developed which embody this expertise and therefore complement or assist users in solving problems specific to accounting. The expert can learn during the knowledge acquisition process exactly how he applies and makes use of his expertise in solving problems. This contemplation most typically takes place during knowledge acquisition, but may re-occur during system testing, and possibly even consultation. Extremely valuable insights into the decision process may be gained both by the system developer and the expert. Thus the process of building the system becomes more valuable than the system itself. Some accounting systems have even been developed with this aim in mind (Steinbart, 1986). At present, the areas of accounting which offer the most promise appear to be audit and taxation.

The second strand, development of expert systems, also shows only limited evidence of success to date. Accountancy represents a domain in which it is possible to find applications requiring judgemental expertise as well as more structured, rule-based applications. It is imperative to use expert systems only in appropriate circumstances; the pitfall of applying an inappropriate technology is as present with expert systems as with the other forms of information technology with which this book deals. It is unlikely that most serious developers will escape a share of failed systems, but there is the added need to resist the situation where the expert system becomes a 'solution looking for a problem', and the domain is scoured accordingly until such a 'problem' is found. There undoubtedly exists a niche in the accounting profession for expert system applications, particularly small systems. However, the overall view of the application of AI to accounting is of a community that is still in the early stages of learning how to exploit a new technology, particularly one in which the benefits seem unclear. Nonetheless, there has been some considerable effort on the part of one or two of the larger firms to use such systems to their commercial advantage. In these cases the efforts seem to have been rewarded, not only in financial terms but also in a deeper appreciation of the problems surrounding the technology and of the nature of the expertise upon which the accounting profession is based.

DISCUSSION QUESTIONS

1. Discuss the contention that accountancy represents the type of domain which does not, in general, lend itself to expert systems application.
2. A computer system can never replicate human expertise. Discuss this statement with regard to the role of the:
   (a) partner
   (b) audit senior
   (c) business services manager
   within a medium-sized accounting practice.

3. Discuss the likely developments in artificial intelligence in the next decade. How might these affect the accounting profession in terms of its:
   (a) internal structures?
   (b) relationships with its clients?
   (c) relationship with its competitors?

REFERENCES

Abdolmohammadi, M. J. (1987). Decision support and expert systems in auditing: a review and research directions', *Accounting and Business Research*, Vol. 17, No. 66, Spring, pp. 173–83.

APEX (1986). *PLANPOWER: technical overview and publicity material*, Applied Expert Systems, Five Cambridge Center, Cambs, MA 02142.

Arnold, M. E., Gambling, T. E. and Rush, D. G. (1985). 'Expert systems: as expert as accountants?', *Management Accounting*, October, pp. 20–22.

Ash, N. (1985). 'How cash value appraises capital projects', *The Accountant*, 2 October, pp. 18–9.

Bailey, A. D., Duke, G. L., Gerlach, J., Meservy, R. D. and Whinston, A. B. (1985). 'TICOM and the analysis of internal controls', *Accounting Review*, April, pp. 186–201.

Barr, A. and Feigenbaum, E. A. (1981) *Handbook of Artificial Intelligence*. Pitman, London.

Bernstein, A. (1985) 'Money Experts', *Business Computer Systems*, December.

Buchanan, B. G. (1986). 'Expert systems; working systems and the research literature, *Expert Systems*, Vol. 3, No. 1, pp. 32–51.

Clarke, F. and Cooper, J. (1985). *The Chartered Accountant in the Information Technology Age*. Coopers and Lybrand and ICAEW, London.

Collier, P. A. (1984) *The Impact of Information Technology on the Management Accountant*. ICMA, London.

Connell, N. (1987) 'Expert systems: a review of some recent accounting applications', *Accounting and Business Research*, Vol. 17, No. 67, Summer, pp. 221–33.

Connell, N. A. D. (1988). 'The current impact of expert systems on the accounting profession and some reasons for hesitancy in the adoption of such systems', *The Knowledge Engineering Review*, Vol. 2, No. 3, pp. 207–11.

Cunningham, J. (1986). Private correspondence. July.

Department of Trade and Industry (1990) *Expert System Opportunities*. HMSO, London.

Dungan, C. W. (1983). *A model of an audit judgement in the form of an Expert System*. PhD dissertation, Department of Accounting, University of Illinois at Urbana.

Dungan, C. W. and Chandler, J. S. (1985). 'AUDITOR: A micro computer-based expert system to support auditors in the field', *Expert Systems*, Vol. 2, No. 4, pp. 210–21.

Edwards, A. V. J. and Connell, N. A. D. (1989) *Expert Systems in Accounting*. Prentice Hall/ICAEW, London.

Evens, M. (1986). *Expert Systems in the Accountancy Profession*. Conference proceedings of London Expert Systems Conference, Mackintosh International.

Feigenbaum, E. A. and McCorduck, P., (1983) *The Fifth Generation* Michael Joseph, London.

'Financial expert systems from Apex', *Expert Systems*, Vol. 2, No. 4, p. 242, October 1985.

Gambling, T. E. (1984). *An expert system for government cost accounting standards*. Informal discussion paper, Department of Business Studies, Portsmouth Polytechnic.

Grudnitski, G. (1986). *Prototype of an Internal Control Expert System for the Sales/ Accounts Receivable application*. Working draft, University of Texas at Austin, January.

Hansen, J. V., Messier, W. F. and Johnson, P. E. (1986). 'A preliminary investigation of EDP-XPERT', *Auditing: A Journal of Practice and Theory*, Vol. 6, No. 1, pp. 109–23.

Harmon, P. and King, D. (1985). *Expert Systems: Artificial Intelligence in Business*. John Wiley and Son, New York.

Hellawell, R. (1980). 'A computer program for legal planning and analysis: taxation of stock redemptions', *Columbia Law Review*, Vol. 80, No. 7.

Johnson, P. (1986). *Cognitive Models of Expertise*. Symposium on Expert Systems and Audit Judgement, University of Southern California.

McCarty, L. T. (1977). 'Reflections on TAXMAN: an experiment in artificial intelligence and legal reasoning', *Harvard Law Review*, Vol. 90, No. 5, pp. 837–93.

McDermott, J. (1981). 'R1, the formative years', *Artificial Intelligence Magazine*, Summer, pp. 21–9.

Meservey, R. D., Bailey, A. D. and Johnson, P. E. (1986) 'Internal Control Evaluation: A Computational Model of the Review Process', *Auditing: A Journal of Practice and Theory*, Vol. 6, No. 1, pp. 44–74.

Michaelsen, R. H. (1984). 'An expert system for federal tax planning', *Expert Systems*, Vol. 1, No. 2, pp. 149–67.

Pasricha, N. and Evens, M. (1986). 'Building systems to do expert jobs', *Accountancy Age*, 13 February.

Pattenden, N. (1986). quoted in *Expert Systems User*, June 1986, p. 26.

Prerau, D. S. (1985). 'Selection of an appropriate domain for an expert system', *The Artificial Intelligence Magazine*, Summer, pp. 26–30.

Roycroft, A. E. and Loucopoulous, P. (1984). 'ACCI – an expert system for the apportionment of close companies' income'. In Bramer, M. A. (ed.), *Proceedings of Fourth Technical Conference of the British Computer Society Specialist Group on Expert Systems, University of Warwick, 1984*. Cambridge University Press, Cambridge, 1984, pp. 127–39.

Schlobohm, D. (1985). 'Tax advisor: a Prolog program analyzing income tax issues', *Dr. Dobbs Journal*, March, pp. 64–92.

Shpilberg, D. Lynford, E. and Schatz, G. H. (1986). 'ExperTAX: an expert system for corporate tax planning', *Expert Systems*, Vol. 3, No. 3, July, pp. 136–51.

Steinbart, P. J. (1986). 'The construction of a rule-based expert system as a method for studying materiality judgements', *The Accounting Review*, Vol. 62, No. 1, July, pp. 97–116.

Susskind, R. and Tindall, C. (1988). *VATIA: Ernst and Whinney's VAT Expert System*. Ernst and Whinney Working Paper, London.

Torsun, I. S. (1986). PAYE A Tax expert system. In Bramer, M. A. (ed.), *Proceedings of the Sixth Technical Conference of the British Computer Society Specialist Group on Expert Systems, Brighton, 1986*. Cambridge University Press, Cambridge, pp. 69–80.

Willingham, J. J., Kelly, K. P., Ribar, G. S. (1986). *Interim Report on the Development of an Expert System for the Auditor's Loan Loss Evaluation*. Paper presented at the 1986 Touche Ross/University of Kansas Auditing Symposium, May 1986.

Chapter
24 Computer crime
Barry J. Spaul

INTRODUCTION

The Law Commission in the summary of its Working Paper No. 10 defines computer crime as 'conduct which involves the manipulation of a computer, by whatever method, in order dishonestly to obtain money, property or some other advantage of value, or cause loss'.

Computer-based fraud, contrary to popular belief, is still largely an occupational crime; even though the average level of computer access controls in most businesses is very poor, they are capable of keeping out the casual intruder, if not the skilled hacker. However, most computer systems are to a large extent unprotected from the dishonest employee. In spite of the impression given by the media attention to the exceptions, most computer-based frauds are inside jobs – in fact they are not committed by Raffles-like outsiders hacking into the system from the other side of the world but by employees of the firm working with the computer system every day.

Sociologists and psychologists tell us that the born criminal is a very rare breed indeed; they hold that most criminals become such as a result of cultural and environmental influences. This proposition places great responsibility on the manager of a computer installation to create an environment where computer-based fraud is both technically difficult and socially unattractive. What can a system's manager do to create such an environment, and what sort of environment should make the auditor beware?

Specially commissioned for *IT and Accounting: The impact of information technology*.
Edited by Bernard C. Williams and Barry J. Spaul.
Published in 1991 by Chapman & Hall, London ISBN 0 412 39210 0.

In today's business environment computers even in the smallest organization are commonplace. The machines themselves are often small and inexpensive, and this tends to lead to a relaxed attitude to the general controls applied to them.

The environmental conditions that can foster a predilection for computer fraud can be found in both the internal organizational environment and the external world or market environment. The facts that can influence an individual to commit computer fraud can include the following:

1. The reward system of the organization both formal (salary) and informal (praise and recognition).
2. The level of management ethics in dealing with employees, customers, etc.
3. The level of performance-related stress (including the validity of measuring factors).
4. General working conditions.
5. The level of interpersonal trust and responsibility.
6. The level of internal controls.
7. The perceived danger of being caught.
8. In the event of being apprehended the nature of sanction applied.
9. Current mores and social values of society.

Even when a fraud is committed by an outsider, it is often with the help and assistance of an insider. Insider computer frauds are obviously the most difficult to guard against because of the betrayal of trust which is usually a part of the employer–employee relationship. Also it is often an employee's absolute familiarity with a system has led to the discovery of a weakness in the system controls that first inspires a fraud.

The reasons for this betrayal of trust are varied and may include persuasion on the part of a friend or acquaintance, extreme personal financial difficulties, a real or perceived grievance against the employer, just thrill-seeking, or sometimes even blackmail.

POLICE OR PRIVACY?

In recent years there have been a number of well-publicized frauds involving computers which have stimulated both public and government interest, but the suspicion of the police and many other bodies is that many computer frauds go unreported and therefore unpunished. In 1978 Stanford University abandoned its yearly recording of computer abuses in the USA for this reason. What are the reasons for this reluctance to report computer fraud? Any organization reporting a large computer fraud knows that it will immediately be focused on by the media – the larger the company, the greater the sum involved, the more the technical difficulties of the fraud, the greater the attention paid by the media.

Business sectors such as banking and investment rely heavily on public confidence in them. The cost of simply absorbing the loss of a fraud is often the preferred option. This may be the most practical solution for an individual organization if the method by which the computer was attacked is known, but if the method remains unknown then this is a very high-risk policy indeed. The cost of absorbing the loss is often chosen because it is much cheaper compared with the cost in terms of lost public confidence and how this is manifested, for example in the case of a bank by cash withdrawals. In a recent report in the USA it was noted that only 51% of all known fraud perpetrators were ever prosecuted; of those, while 98% were found guilty, only 31% were incarcerated, and 52% of those sentenced received less than two years.

The normal policy in this situation is to keep the fraudsman in the dark for as long as possible concerning the discovery of a fraud. They certainly do not actively encourage the attentions of the media. At this stage, before the fraud is made public, the police are in the best position to catch the perpetrator before he is aware of their attentions. Having stated it is not normal police policy to court publicity, because of their duty of public accountability they would only deny an investigation was taking place when it in fact was for exceptional operational reasons.

THE TECHNIQUES

Several writers in the area of computer crime have used the framework of dividing computer-based abuses into three types: input, processing and output. This categorization obviously matches the three traditional stages of data processing. While output abuses such as the theft of computer-generated reports may facilitate a fraud, they in themselves do not constitute a computer-based fraud. The occurrence of processing abuses such as salami slicing (rounding tiny amounts from, for example, payroll accounts to a false account which is later emptied by the perpetrator) are comparatively rare. However, before we draw too much comfort from this apparent fact, it should be considered that this form of computer-based fraud is probably the most difficult to detect.

The most common form of computer-based fraud is input related, that is the entry of false or fraudulent data that has been altered, forged or counterfeited into the computer to facilitate fraudulent disbursement of funds. This type of fraud is usually perpetrated by a data entry clerk either acting alone or in collusion with another insider, for example their supervisor. The result of this type of fraud results in a debit to one or several expense accounts and a credit to the cash account for the issuance of a cheque. The other type of input-related computer-based fraud that is usually perpetrated by senior level executives is the overstatement of profits. Management bonus schemes which have become so popular in our increasingly 'payment by results' oriented society have had the tendency to invite this type of offence.

COMPUTERS – WHAT ARE THE EXTRA WORRIES?

What are the characteristics of a computer environment that make it more susceptible to fraud?

The fact that computers concentrate data has done much to make the fraudsman's task easier. Computers using the modern database approach to information management only store an individual item of information once, for example a customer name. This results in a great saving in both storage space and effort in updating records, it also results in greater data consistency. The difficulty relating to computer-based frauds is that, unless access and the ability to make changes to a firm's database of information are strictly controlled by the use of passwords, etc. the fraudulent changing of data is much simpler than in a manual system where data items may be physically written in a number of ledgers located in offices under the scrutiny of a number of individuals.

Hiding one's tracks in computer-based fraud is comparatively easy. The volatility of the magnetic storage media means that by preprogrammed means the later interrogation of files likely to lead to the discovery of a fraud can automatically set in motion a program that will erase all the evidence of a fraud and in the process severely damage the organization's records. One technical answer to this problem now exists in the form of the Write Once Read Many times optical disk (WORM). This type of storage media uses lasers to 'etch' data permanently onto the surface of a disk. This type of disk can be used for a reasonable length of time because the capacity of these disks is such that updated records are simply positioned on an unused area and redundant records are marked as such but are still retained in a readable form. The fact that records in a computer-based system are not visible means that a non-specialist scanning through records for a normal operational purpose would not be likely to come across and comprehend a fraudulent entry by chance.

The huge systems that computerization has made possible in some cases process millions of transactions per week. There has been an increased use of international on-line systems and networks over the past decade. The combination of these and other factors have in many cases tended to obscure the audit trail of transactions, thus making the scope for detection of computer fraud somewhat limited.

A figure in a ledger crossed out and replaced usually leaves some trace of alteration, if not to the casual observer at least to the forensic scientist. This is not normally the case with computerized records where data can be replaced without any sign whatsoever.

The speed with which computers can alter one or many records is phenomenal, therefore the amount of time that the fraudsman spends 'in the act' of committing a fraud is very small, much smaller than in a manual system committing the same offence. Also the perpetrator while committing the crime may be sitting at a terminal where he or she has every right to be and therefore is less likely to be exposed.

The design of much computer hardware and software still used in business today did not specify security as a high priority. MS-DOS, arguably the most widely used operating system, for example does not allow the simple technique of password locking a file or program, and most PC's do not have keyboard locks. The latest designs, however, are taking this problem seriously and security is now designed into much computing equipment.

THE LATEST TRENDS IN FRAUD

A recent survey conducted by Albrecht, Howe and Romney (1984) that appears in their book *Deterring Fraud: The Internal Auditor's Perspective* casts some interesting light on the nature of commercial fraud in the USA. They were not examining computer fraud specifically but the little available evidence, although largely anecdotal, seems to indicate that trends in computer fraud are very similar.

Their findings regarding collusion were that 29% of frauds involved some degree, while 71% did not. An interesting finding that backs up the experience of many auditors is that management often failed to enforce existing controls and indeed deliberately overrode them in many cases. A fact which may well surprise those outside the accounting profession was that only 18% of frauds were detected by internal auditors while 33% were detected by anonymous tips. Because of the unacceptable level of costs for a full computer audit it might well be expected that the level of computer-based frauds discovered by external auditors would be very low indeed.

Of the actual fraudsmen themselves, 74% of them had an age range of 26 to 45 years of age, while 72% had been with the company they defrauded less than ten years. While 76% of 36 to 45 year-olds had committed fraud for more than $100 000, the tendency was the older and more educated the perpetrator the higher the amount taken. On the whole, fraudsmen started younger in banks and other financial institutions, a comforting thought! Women tended to be less ambitious in the amounts they took than men and tended to work on their own more often.

STRATEGIES TO FIGHT COMPUTER CRIME

The problem of computer-based fraud is compounded by the failure of the authorities to prosecute successfully perpetrators of computer crime. As the MP Michael Colvin stated on 9 February 1990 in the House of Commons debate on the Computer Misuse Bill:

> Unfortunately the perception is that there is a very low probability of successfully prosecuting computer misuse under present law. That leads to organizations being reluctant to admit unauthorized access because they see that as a bit of an embarrassment.

Any system of controls can be classified as either proactive or reactive. In relation to computer crime proactive controls are responsible for preventing criminal acts by reducing opportunities. This type of control is emphasized in computing and accounting literature. However, these controls alone have proved insufficient to stop the increase in computer misuse and reactive controls, such as the effective detection and prosecution of computer criminals, must supplement them. In an attempt to assist this process many countries have passed computer crime related legislation. However, legislation in isolation is inadequate to combat computer crime and any effort to control computer crime must include the provision of the means to enforce laws. A crucial element in achieving this will be the development of forensic perspectives on computing and computerized business information systems as an identifiable discipline.

DEFINITION OF FORENSICS

The word forensic is defined in the *Oxford English Dictionary* as an adjective meaning '... used in, or connected with a court of law', and the term forensic science as 'a science that deals with the relation and application of scientific facts to legal problems'. Traditionally forensic science has centred on the physical and applied sciences such as medicine, engineering, chemistry, ballistics, etc. However, more recently social sciences, such as psychology and accounting, have been added to the forensic science armoury. These social science extensions of forensic science have a dominant requirement for interpretive and judgemental skills, rather than the detection of physical evidence. This chapter advocates an extension of forensic science to cover crimes committed using computerized information systems. The extension is termed information systems forensics (IS forensics) and would cover the collection of IS forensic evidence for use in a court of law which places unique burdens on forensic scientists. For the IS forensic expert the problems are exacerbated by the obvious difficulties of explaining the complexity of criminal computer-based activities to a jury of twelve members of the public, and uncertainties in the UK on what constitutes admissible computer-generated evidence (see, for example, Chapter 14).

ROLE OF IS FORENSICS

The different areas in which IS forensics play a constructive role include:

1. *Civil matters.* There is an increasing need for expertise in the investigation and assessment of the integrity of computer systems in civil cases. The estimation of the size and nature of losses from negligence, invasions of privacy, industrial espionage and social nuisance (e.g. the release of computer viruses) are increasingly required in civil cases.
2. *Criminal matters.* Recently white collar crime has become increasingly computerized as criminals recognize the potential for crime given by the anonymity of computer systems and the development of electronic funds transfer systems and electronic data interchange systems.
3. *Insurance.* The preparation and assessment of insurance claims arising as a result of system failure or penetration on behalf of both insurers and the insured may well require the assistance of a forensic systems analyst.
4. *Government.* The forensic systems analyst can assist governments with regulatory compliance by ensuring that the appropriate legislation is being applied in private organizations, where applicable.

The growth in computer crime also requires that society ensures that those who are likely to prevent, detect or otherwise counter computer crime are properly trained. At a minimum training should cover:

1. *The police.* According to Cornwall (1988) out of 144 000 police officers only four or five officers concentrate on computer crime at any one

time, an unacceptable situation given the importance of securing evidence as soon as a crime is detected.
2. *The Crown Prosecution Service.* Prosecuting barristers specializing in computer crime are essential if the current prosecution success rate is to be improved.
3. *Senior management in public and private sector organizations.* Countering computer fraud requires that management in all organizations be aware of the threat and the importance of a systematic approach to its prevention, detection and prosecution.
4. *Security officers in public and private sector organizations.* Despite counter measures, computer crimes will occur in firms. An important deterrent is the 'on the spot' expert.

THE IS FORENSIC METHODOLOGY

It is possible to look at the investigation process from two standpoints:

1. *Internal investigations* carried out by the possible victim organization or their agents, in the case of a criminal matter, as a preliminary to involving public agencies, or until sufficient evidence is collected to pursue a civil case in the courts.
2. *External police investigations* either from the outset, utilizing a specialist team of experts, who deliberately distance themselves from employees of the victim organization, or following on from an internal investigation.

The skills implicit in an IS forensic approach to a computer crime investigation will probably be provided by a multi-disciplinary team of a similar constitution regardless of whether an internal or external investigation is taking place. However, the *modus operandi* of the two types of team would necessarily be quite different.

The members of a forensic team conducting an investigation will have the following skills:

1. *Investigative* – to supervise the conduct of the investigation and interview suspects and witnesses;
2. *Legal* – a knowledge of the laws which can be applied against computer-related offences and the laws of evidence;
3. *Court room presentation* – acting as a witness or expert witness; and
4. *Computing* – to uncover how the crime was committed, assist in reconstructing computer evidence and tracing proceeds of the crime.

Investigative, legal and court room presentation skills will be provided by the police, legal professionals or security advisers. Computing expertise could be obtained from EDP auditors or computer specialists. If the growth of computer crime continues, it is possible that IS forensics specialists with the complete range of skills listed above will emerge from consultancy firms or be provided by the police.

It is agreed by most pundits that the problem of computer crime is like an iceberg – nine-tenths of it lies hidden. If this is the case then in terms of cost-effective policing it is a problem area that is hugely under-resourced in most countries. This chapter argues that the moves by governments to legislate against the increased threat of computer crime and abuse will fail unless there is an extension of forensic science into the computing field. The term adopted for this new discipline is information systems or IS forensics, and four main skill areas have been identified. It remains to be seen whether this new discipline emerges in the next few years or whether it will take a further series of abandoned or failed major prosecutions before the subject is treated seriously.

CONCLUSIONS

The problem of computer fraud is not one of new crime adding to existing crime but existing crime being replaced by a new technological environment giving rise to different encouragement and opportunities for criminal behaviour. As existing business, accounting and retailing systems become automated to a greater extent, the scope for criminal behaviour will become more limited in the 'blue collar' smash and grab vein since the quantities of cash used by society will be replaced by electronic funds transfer systems. This of course means that there will be scope for a corresponding growth in 'white collar crime' such as computer-based fraud. The question that has to be asked is, what are we as a profession and a society doing about preparing for this eventuality?

Many commercial concerns are now taking the issue of computer security very seriously in the light of computer viruses. A few organizations of sufficient size like the Post Office are even taking preventative steps by training their own staff to investigate allegations of computer abuse. The government is clearly not sufficiently worried about the current situation relating to computer crime to pass any legislation – this is left to a few perceptive backbenchers. Also in other ways the government is demonstrating a worrying lack of action. In the recent reading of Michael Colvin's Bill in the Commons it was stated that there were only 45 police officers in the UK with the most rudimentary training in investigating computer crime, and only one police officer in the whole country who was fully experienced in this area. One of the factors that acts as a deterrent to committing crime is the fear of being caught. In the area of computer crime the fear of being caught would not be a very great factor in prevention if these statements are true.

Lastly, what of the computer fraudsmen? What or who is he? The evidence seems to say that he rather than she usually falls into one of two categories. The first type is often a disgruntled data entry clerk who has worked at his present job for a few years and is in his late twenties or early thirties, bored and disillusioned with little technical skill. The second type is higher in the company, at managerial level, worried about his performance in the company and trying to massage the figures to gain directly or indirectly. Neither seem to be natural successors to Raffles or Robin as they are often portrayed in the media.

DISCUSSION QUESTIONS

1. What issues must an organization take into account when reporting a computer crime?
2. In the light of the nature of computer crime, what measures might you as a chief constable take to set up and maintain a capability to investigate crimes in this area?
3. List in order of expense the most cost-effective ways an organization can protect itself against computer crime.
4. List ten adjectives which describe to you a computer criminal. Ask a friend who is not doing this course to do the same, then ask another friend to list ten adjectives that describe a computer 'hacker'.
5. Give as many reasons as you can to support the statement 'Computer crime is a problem of increasing importance to society'.

REFERENCES

Albrecht, W. S., Howe, K. R. and Romney, M. B. (1984) *Deterring Fraud: The Internal Auditor's Perspective*. The Institute of Internal Auditors Research Foundation, Altamonte Springs, Florida, USA.

Burger, R. (1985). *Computer Viruses: A High-Tech Disease*. Abacus, Grandrapids, USA.

Colvin, M, (1990). *Parliamentary Report on 2nd Reading of the Computer Misuse Bill*, Hansard, London, 9th February 1990.

Comer, M. J. (1985). *Corporate Fraud*, 2nd edn. McGraw-Hill, London.

Cornwall, H. (1988). Hacking away at computer law reform', *New Law Journal* **738** (6376), 30 September, pp. 702–3.

Hoffer, J. A. and Straub, D. W. Jr. (1989). 'The 9 to 5 underground: are you policing computer crimes', *Sloan Management Review*, Summer.

Hollinger, R. C. and Lanza-Kaduce, L. (1988). 'The process of criminalisation: the case of computer crime laws', *Criminology*, Vol. 26, No. 1, pp. 145–52.

Law Commission (1989). *Computer Misuse*. Law Com. No. 186, Cm. 819, HMSO, London.

Nasuti, F. W. (1986). Investigating computer crime, *Journal of Accounting and EDP*, Fall.

'Opinion, computer fraud, treasurer, March 1990.

Reed, C. *Computer Law*. Blackstone Press, London.

Simons, G. (1989). *Viruses, Bugs and Star Wars: The Hazards of Unsafe Computing*. NCC Blackwell, Oxford.

Tate, P. (1988). 'The third factor', *Datamation*, 15 April 1988, pp. 58–63.

25 Auditing and computers
John M. Court and Nicki J. Muggridge

INTRODUCTION

'Computer auditing' was a term coined in the days when none quite knew what it meant or what it ought to mean. For a long time the activity has been better described as 'auditing in a computer environment'. This is also the title of the UK auditing practices guideline which discusses the subject.

Auditing in a computer environment, since its inception in the early 1960s, has always included:

1. The use of programs (i.e. file interrogations) to assist auditors in analysing and confirming the accuracy of data.
2. The use of test data to confirm (or otherwise) the accuracy of programs.
3. The use of programs to confirm (or otherwise) the accuracy of other programs (i.e. comparison of an operational program with a master copy known to be correct).
4. The use of questionnaires and other procedures to help auditors to evaluate internal control within the organization or function being audited.

Item 1 above is an example of a 'substantive' audit procedure, i.e. a procedure, performed without reference to internal control procedures or norms, to determine whether the results of processing have given rise to accurate data. Items 2, 3 and 4 are examples of 'compliance' audit techniques, i.e. techniques applicable to testing whether internal control procedures and norms have been observed.

Specially commissioned for *IT and Accounting: The impact of information technology*. Edited by Bernard C. Williams and Barry J. Spaul. Published in 1991 by Chapman & Hall, London ISBN 0 412 39210 0.

More recently, the scope of auditing in a computer environment has widened. It now includes 'audit automation', such as the maintenance of audit records on computer files, the application of programmed quality control procedures and the use of automated questionnaires or expert systems covering aspects of an auditor's knowledge base.

Such procedures involve the use of the auditor's own computer systems to assist in the administration and recording of the audit procedures. This is an important development which should lead to significant improvements in auditing quality.

The third main aspect of 'computer auditing' is the review of the internal control procedures surrounding the application of computers. In this respect, the term 'computers' includes any computer, of whatever physical size, processing power or storage capacity, which is used to process important data. The control procedures may relate to the computer installations themselves, to the communications between them or to the systems which are processed on the installations. The procedures may be either programmed or clerical – almost always they are a combination of both.

Auditors' reviews of internal control procedures do not necessarily presuppose that auditors will subsequently place reliance on such procedures. The usual purpose of the reviews, however, is to gauge the extent to which the internal control procedures provide a sound basis for reliance on the results of processing.

At best, the auditors may decide that they have such a degree of reliance on the internal control procedures that there is no need to carry out periodical 'compliance tests' to ensure that the control procedures have in fact been observed. Typically, however, auditors will be inclined to do so, at least to a limited extent, in order to ensure that the control procedures operate in practice as well as in theory.

So the initial reviews of systems and subsequent compliance tests of their operation provide the basis for a 'compliance audit' in relation to the computer systems.

However, systems-based auditing is often a daunting exercise. Auditors relying on compliance with systems must be aware of the relevant control principles and thereby put themselves in a position to ensure that there are sufficient control techniques and procedures to protect the system against the threats of hacking and fraud, to facilitate the effective use of the system and to determine that its output is accurate. Systems auditors have to prove that they are competent in these respects and that their more old-fashioned audit skills are supported by a good technological understanding. Otherwise, mainstream computer professionals, without necessarily demonstrating a grasp of wider audit objectives, will advance their own claims of superior competence in the field of systems auditing. On that basis, other professionals will sometimes be invited to displace the auditors.

The ICAEW's recent report on *IT and the Future of the Audit* identified the following key issues in the development of audit theory, practice and administration.

1. High volume, rapid response computer systems need to be particularly well controlled. Users expect their auditors to understand such systems and to be able to provide critical comment on the requisite controls. External regulatory authorities, such as the DTI and the SIB, may also have such expectations in respect of the categories of audit which they regulate.
2. However, the trend in external auditing is away from compliance testing and towards substantive testing.

These issues constitute a dilemma for auditors. This dilemma is mainly caused by the following two factors:

1. Despite the expectations of clients, regulators and the general public that auditors ought to criticize the operation of internal control systems and to test compliance with them, it remains the case that substantive auditing is often more cost-effective (for internal auditors as well as external auditors) than compliance testing based on systems auditing.
2. Auditors may find it difficult to acquire for themselves, or to buy in from outside, the necessary skills to carry out effective reviews of internal controls, or compliance tests in respect of them.

The remainder of this chapter is intended to examine these issues and the implications for auditors. The examination of the issues leads to suggestions of audit methods which may help to resolve the dilemma and to enable auditors to meet the public expectations of them – subject always to their possession of prerequisite competence.

The question of competence is of the greatest importance, yet it is often overlooked or under-emphasized. As the ICAEW's report also pointed out, it is strategically important for chartered accountants, as auditors, to continue to demonstrate competence in dealing with information systems and technology. Chartered accountants must continue to develop functional expertise in dealing with advanced information processing systems such as those discussed in this chapter. The scale of the required expertise must match the complexity of the systems in relation to which the audits are being performed. That is why there is significant emphasis on technical overview in the consideration of the issues which follows.

HARDWARE-BASED DEVELOPMENTS

PCs AND WORKSTATIONS

Hardware capability in terms of processing power and storage capacity continues to be developed at a rapid rate. This is particularly evident at the PC end of the market. It is now possible to purchase PCs with the performance levels of minicomputers at a very low price. The move among corporate users away from mainframes towards high powered personal computers is an important trend for the industry. The chief reason for the migration is to allow users to take advantage of the power and sophistication of the latest software which combine graphical user interfaces, multi-tasking and three-dimensional reporting capabilities. Only PCs using high performance microprocessor chips such as Intel's 80/386 and 80/486 and Motorola's 68000 family are able to exploit such software.

Trends seem to indicate that the industry is moving towards graphical user interfaces as the common interface between user and machine. Graphical user interfaces have two components: the WIMPs interface (windows, icons, mouse and pull-down menus) and applications windowing. Versions of the WIMP interface were first adopted by Apple and have now been mimicked by a host of suppliers including Microsoft (Windows) and IBM (Presentation Manager).

The distinction between PCs and technical workstations is beginning to blur. Traditionally power, functionality and price were the dividing factors; however, the emergence of 32-bit chips from Intel and Motorola has made it possible to build machines with the performance of a workstation for the price of a PC.

Leading workstation manufacturers include Dec, Hewlett Packard and Sun Microcomputer. The workstation market is growing dramatically – in the USA alone sales rose from $150m in 1983 to $4.3bn in 1988.

In the ever-increasing battle between personal computer manufacturers for developing faster machines at lower prices, reduced instruction set computing (RISC) will be one of the techniques used to improve performance. The technology is based upon the principle that the instructions used by a computer 80% of the time were simple ones, while complex instructions which were time-consuming for the computer to process were used only 20% of the time. New computer architecture, developed as a response to this principle, involves only a small number of simple instructions each of which can be processed at high speed. Complex instructions can be built up in software from a series of simple ones using 'optimizing compilers'. This has meant, however, that simplicity in the instruction set has been traded off against software complexity.

MAINFRAME COMPUTING

ICL have recently launched a new high-performance mainframe processor which they claim is 25% more powerful than any other uniprocessor currently available. The processor has a power rating of 80 MIPS and ICL plan to introduce further variants delivering up to 300 MIPS as the need arises. Despite this activity the total market for mainframes is growing at a much smaller rate (4–10% annually) than that for personal computers and workstations and some analysts have used the dinosaur metaphor when predicting market activity.

The 'distributed computing' model may, however, create a new role for the mainframe. Instead of carrying out the actual processing the mainframe will become a repository for huge quantities of data which can then be manipulated on the PCs and workstations. In support of this view, leading US mainframe manufacturers are developing software and networking technology that integrate mainframes into heterogeneous computer networks and provide ways for workstations, personal computers and minicomputers to communicate with mainframes.

SUPERCOMPUTERS

In 1988 the supercomputers market was dominated by two US companies: Cray Research and Control Data. The market is now fragmenting into a series of niche markets, each distinguished by a particular technology and a particular level of price/performance.

The rise of the mini-supercomputer has made supercomputing accessible to a much wider range of businesses. The tasks which require near supercomputing power include technical, scientific and numeric-intensive computing, an area which it is estimated will represent approximately 23% of the $240bn world market for data processing in 1993. Technical computing is currently growing at 18% per year world-wide and 23% in Europe.

Since 1981 the six leading Japanese computer companies have been involved in a $100m government-funded project to develop supercomputers 1000 times faster than those available at the start of the project. The two principle research areas are densely integrated, high-speed logic and memory chips using gallium arsenide and advanced circuitry and high-speed parallel processing techniques.

IMAGE PROCESSING

An early illusion held within the IT industry was that computers would result in, if not a 'paperless office', then certainly a paper-reduced office;

documents would all be stored on computers making hard-copy redundant. Unfortunately many business documents are not in a format readily acceptable by a computer, e.g. photographs, drawings, handwritten forms, etc. The first image-processing systems overcame the limitations of input into computers by using optical scanning technology. However they were based upon minicomputers and therefore expensive. Until recently such a system would have cost over £300 000 but the combination of PCs, networks, optical storage technology ('opto-electronics') and advanced software has created systems which may be purchased for as little as £20 000. Once again the major factor in the growth in such systems is the increased power available within PCs.

The fall in cost has made the technology more widely available and market research suggests that the market is about to enter a period of rapid growth. (Reports vary between world market estimates of from £1.7bn by 1992 to £6.9bn by 1991.)

RE-WRITABLE OPTICAL DISKS

The take-up of optical disk technology has been hampered by two technical limitations. Until recently it has not been possible to erase or change information on the disk and data retrieval is, by magnetic standards, extremely slow. For archiving purposes and applications which require a strict audit trail the inability to rewrite the storage medium can be a positive advantage, but for many users it is an unacceptable limitation on the way in which they use computers. By combining optical technology with magnetic methods some companies have developed rewritable, magnetic neto-optical disks. However, these devices share some of the instability problems associated with magnetic disks making them unsuitable for critical back-up storage. Later this year both Philips and Panasonic intend to launch rewritable disks that use no magnetic technology at all and which will be able to read the write-once read-many disks already on the market.

SMART CARDS

The main advantage of smart cards (cards which store information on microprocessors rather than magnetic stripes and so possess memory and intelligence) is their ability to counter fraud.

It is the possibility of preventing fraud losses which has led to opinion within the retail financial services market (particularly in mainland Europe) being broadly in favour of the cards. Smart cards may provide an alternative to both PINs and signatures. Customers would provide bio-metric data which would be stored on their card and then used to identify them at a terminal when making a purchase or cash withdrawal.

A simpler use of smart cards is as precharged and rechargeable carriers of funds, e.g. akin to travellers' cheques etc. Problems with this type of usage include the expense of the terminals to read the card and the ease with which a lost or stolen card can be used.

THE EFFECTS OF HARDWARE-BASED DEVELOPMENTS ON THE AUDITOR

As computer storage capacities increase, more data can be processed. As more systems become computerized, more statistics and reports therefore tend to be produced. As storage costs diminish, the concept of permanent archiving becomes feasible.

Developments in networks have increased interconnectivity. It is easier for organizations to access and use information which is being held outside the organization. Greater quantities of new information are publicly available in the form of databases which can be interrogated.

Organizations may experience difficulty in converting data into information, analysing information, discriminating between more useful and less useful information and making decisions based on the best information available.

User-friendly software may enable non-specialist personnel to gain access to the information but they may not have the skills to discriminate between the quality of different pieces of information or to evaluate them. In time, expert systems may be developed sufficiently to differentiate between the wheat and the chaff, but in the meantime analysis of information and recommendations based upon that analysis will come within the role of the auditor irrespective of whether the information is confined to financial areas.

The auditor's role will become increasingly concerned with performance indicators. Analysis of finance is only an aspect of overall performance and the techniques that are the forte of the accountant can be applied to other issues within the organization. The auditor will use the information systems as a knowledge base or information collator and concentrate on the interpretation and relevance of the information.

It is already commonplace to find organizations reporting internally on a monthly or even weekly basis. Formal reporting of financial information is also likely to be on a much more continuous basis in future. Businesses are already regularly reporting quarterly and half yearly figures. It may be only a matter of time before such figures are available monthly or even weekly.

Market and/or regulatory trends may force on-line reporting in real time to become the norm. It would then be the auditor's role not only to confirm the accuracy of such information but also to interpret its relevance to the continuing operating of the organizations being audited.

INTELLIGENT KNOWLEDGE-BASED SYSTEMS

ROBOTICS

Robotics are used in many manufacturing organizations. At present they take the form either of unsophisticated manual manipulators worked by human beings or quasi-intelligent robots with sensory perception which can perform simple tasks and can determine changes in the working environment and act accordingly, making minor adjustments where necessary. At present, adaptable and multi-purpose robots do not widely exist. However, technological development will increase the capabilities of these machines, enabling machine tools to carry out varied functions. It is already the case that straightforward machine tools are capable of monitoring themselves and by integrating with the organization's financial system will be able automatically to generate analysed production and cost information.

EXPERT SYSTEMS

A robot may be considered intelligent in that it can perform actions. An expert system attempts to simulate intelligence at the level of thought rather than action.

The IT industry in general has tended to foster unrealistic expectations of expert systems. However, from early attempts at building perhaps too ambitious systems, certain areas of expertise have been targeted as being appropriate domains where expert systems might contribute to the efficiency and profitability of an organization.

The implementation of a system is most successful where there is an acceptance that there is an essential knowledge base which is a prerequisite for carrying out tasks within the domain. Systems are being used successfully for design, diagnosis and monitoring in a range of professions and industries. In areas where the expertise is limited and very specialized an expert system can be an effective training tool.

Expert systems are being introduced into areas that have historically, and in some instances legally, been under the control of accountants and auditors. Expert systems are being used as tools by the larger practising firms in the field of auditing and the provision of tax advice. Industry is beginning to include expert systems in the design of computer applications to support and assist decision-making, strategic business planning and production control. Expert system shells are widely and increasingly available. Provided that auditors have a conceptual understanding of the technology (even if they do not necessarily have detailed technical expertise), use of the shells will enable them to build their own knowledge bases and expert systems.

Many IT products and services have not achieved effective market penetration. This has largely been a result of the IT industry paying insufficient attention to the interface between the high technology and the user – the system is not 'user-friendly' and is perceived by the average user as being too difficult to learn to use effectively. Advanced programming languages, including fourth and fifth generation languages, have made some progress towards improving the user interface between computer and network and computer and computer. Current developments will result in a system being able to respond to a particular user and only that user in a specific way, a development that will increase the inherent security within a system.

Eventually, expert systems will be able to respond to the user by way of speech recognition and image processing and will directly link expert systems with robot-operated processes. This will eliminate the requirement for some current control procedures. It will, however, require auditors and financial controllers to be more technologically literate in order to perceive the circumstances under which the system might be abused. This responsibility will be shared with software and hardware suppliers, DP managers and systems support staff.

VIRTUAL REALITY

The manipulation of three-dimensional images of real objects on computer screens, with the opportunity to provide tactile as well as visual input, has become a possible means of defining processes of manufacture, construction or service, as well as carrying out research and development.

The facility constitutes a 'virtual' world within the computer system which can represent the real world and offer a test-bed for real operations. This permits experimentation without danger or waste of materials. It also permits a high level of precision in the programming of a robotic operation.

THE EFFECTS OF KNOWLEDGE-BASED SYSTEMS ON THE AUDITOR

As the use of robotics and expert systems becomes more commonplace in the production and manufacturing environment, the integration of an organization's manufacturing and fnancial systems will become typical. This will eliminate much of the traditional routine work of the cost and management accountant. It will, however, still be necessary for the auditor to advise on the implementation of sufficient controls over the system to ensure the validity and accuracy of the data used for management decision-making.

Good expert systems that increase the efficiency of audit procedures and the maintenance of audit records are likely to be of definite commercial advantage to auditors.

Expert systems will increasingly be used as decision support systems. In terms of auditing, fear of litigation could force professionals to use their own expertise and knowledge and corroborate it by the use of an expert system, or vice versa, rather than one or the other. Generally, such systems are perceived more as a corporate technology asset to aid human judgement than as an investment in labour replacement, although an audit team using such systems might well need fewer qualified personnel.

A reduction in the numbers of staff required, or even the amount of hours of overtime worked, would significantly lower the total costs of the audit process.

Much of the routine work might be carried out by technicians aided by the expert systems.

COMMUNICATIONS AND NETWORKING

GENERAL ISSUES

The 1990s seem likely to bring about increasing deregulation Europe-wide. In December 1989 European ministers agreed two important Directives: the first was to open up the market in telecommunication services, and the second to agree technical rules for free access to networks. The compromise reached in December bridged a gap between the opposed attitudes of member states. France, Belgium, Italy and Greece are reticent about free competition in telecommunications; West Germany, the UK and Holland have already liberalized their own markets to varying degrees and are anxious to see free competition in Europe.

If the Directive does go through, competition will be introduced into all areas except simple voice telephony. Private companies will be able to offer value-added services in competition with monopolies in the EC. Even though voice accounts for 90% of telephone companies' business, it is the remaining areas that are the most profitable and which are growing most quickly. The market will be opened up in stages with PTT (providers of public telecommunications services) monopolies given until the end of 1992 before being forced to give up their control over all basic data communications.

The second Directive, the 'Open Network Provision', is aimed at harmonizing rather than liberalizing the market.

Overall, the aim is to wipe out the inefficiencies that come from running twelve district telecommunications markets, and to make Europe more competitive against the USA and Japan. Perhaps one of the most important EC measures is the inclusion of telecommunications within the Commission's new procurement rules.

The political and economic developments taking place within Eastern Europe will also impact upon communications generally. The opening up of Eastern Europe will of necessity require rapid expansion of the telecommunications systems currently present in those areas. Poland, Hungary, Russia and East Germany are all looking at alternative strategies for developing improved telecommunication systems so as to facilitate international trade.

CELLULAR TELEPHONES

The market for cellular telephones in leading Western countries is continuing to expand at a rapid rate. In the UK the number of cellular subscribers should reach around 1 million by the middle of 1990; the US market has just reached 4 million according to latest estimates. Growth within this market will be fuelled by the launch in 1991 of the first digital cellular network which will conform to a common European standard. This will mean that subscribers will be able to use the same telephone across most of Europe. It will also mean that equipment manufacturers will be able to address a single market of 350 million people.

VALUE-ADDED SERVICES

Value-added services (VAS) may be defined as digital telecommunications over network telephone lines where information, usually in computer data form, is manipulated in some way. The biggest segment of VAS is on-line information services – approximately two-thirds of the $3bn European market last year. Messaging services (including EDI) represent around a fifth of the market and the third segment comprises of processing services such as airline reservation systems, EFT, etc.

Analysts have agreed that the market is finally beginning to develop and have projected the total European market to be worth ECU 12.55bn by 1994. Factors influencing this growth projection include the increasing demand of customers representing a wide range of industries for access to sophisticated data communications networks and 'paperless trading' technologies in order to cut costs, improve efficiency and compete more effectively domestically and internationally.

ELECTRONIC DATA INTERCHANGE

Electronic data interchange (EDI) is a generic term for cooperative systems whereby several organizations transfer data between them in an agreed format and in accordance with predetermined standards of control and authentication. Examples include the 'SWIFT' world-wide inter-bank system and, among UK trading companies, the 'TRADACOMS' system. EDI is currently moving through the initial stages of technological evolution. It is gradually building up a user base but has yet to reach the stage where 'everyone must join in'.

Expansion is occurring, however, not least because those companies that use it are being provided with a competitive edge in terms of efficiency, lower costs and therefore cheaper prices. The main impediments to this gradual growth at present are a profusion of incompatible standards, unfamiliarity with the technology and a lack of critical mass in the industry.

Standards are gradually moving over to the UN Edifact standard which aims to create an internationally agreed electronic syntax and data dictionary for use in composing messages. Familiarity with the technology is increasing through the encouragement given to third-party suppliers to enter into the market. Critical mass is gradually evolving on an industry-by-industry basis, often with a powerful player within a specific industry making electronic trading a prerequisite of any supplier relationship.

The advent of 1992 will put pressure on telecommunications suppliers and users to modernize their approach to pan-European business. On the supply side this will mean reducing the cost of leased lines and simplifying the bureaucratic procedures for running services across national boundaries. A lot of the infrastructure is in place in the international telecommunications network and the Edifact standards are being accepted world-wide but the industry needs to prove to users that it can run EDI operations internationally.

THE EFFECTS OF IMPROVED NETWORKS AND EDI ON THE AUDITOR

As the use of networking and interactive systems throughout organizations becomes commonplace, control becomes increasingly vital. The auditor will need to understand control theory, to analyse the risks and to evaluate preventative measures and to be aware of the requirements of network security and the risks of unauthorized access such as line tapping or interception. Secrecy and authentication can be controlled by using encryption and authentication programs. Systems auditors must ensure that they understand these concepts and that they are in a position to advise on their implementation.

The use of passwords is the minimum control for ensuring only authorized access to the network, and for particularly sensitive systems it may be necessary for the systems auditor, together with technical specialists, to become involved in providing advice on more extensive security procedures for the company's or its client's systems.

As more organizations move towards automatic bill payment through services such as BACS, intelligent systems could handle the interactive operations across the networks between the organizations. It may become necessary for legislation to dictate to the systems the time that the bills could remain unsettled so that systems do not vie with each other for 'cash control' and effect the liquidity of an organization. Computer law is a growth area in the USA and, increasingly, in the UK and other parts of Europe. It is likely to be the responsibility of financial controllers, together with internal auditors and company lawyers, to ensure that an organization's system complies with such legislation.

As more organizations take advantage of improved networking technology, the paperless or at least paper-reduced system will become increasingly common. Control of such systems needs to be thought through from the development and implementation stage. Once the auditors have satisfied themselves that the outputs of a system are guaranteed (i.e. that it does what it is required to do) they must then review the controls incorporated within the system to ensure its accuracy and validity.

Such reviews may need to include audit tests of the validity of the operating system and associated software such as the teleprocessing monitor program or the database management system. All this requires extensive (and expensive, because rare) technical expertise.

CONCLUSIONS

The economy has become information-based. It is possible for businesses to succeed or fail as a result of how effectively they use data and convert data into useful information.

Strategic management systems, providing accurate corporate information, are a prerequisite of successful strategic management. Such systems may help to provide the necessary competitive edge to increase an organization's market share. At the very least, a well-specified and well-implemented system with adequate controls is likely to ensure that the organization's market position is maintained.

A major effect of information technology on the role of auditors will therefore be a requirement for them to diversify. The large accountancy firms have already recognized this fact and have developed specialist areas of expertise, particularly in the implementation of IT strategies and in systems control and security.

The Institute's report on *IT and the Future of the Audit* draws a number of conclusions about the need for wider recognition of computer auditing qualifications. These are currently under discussion. The need for specific qualifications is particularly necessary in relation to systems-based auditing. The Institute's report remarks that, while the systems-based audit approach is best applied to those businesses in which the internal control systems are crucial to the protection of the assets, there needs to be further debate about the relative value of systems-based auditing and substantive auditing, respectively, under different circumstances and in different types of business and administrative activity.

Whatever the results of that debate, the technological developments mentioned earlier in this article make it almost certain that auditors will spend a significant proportion of their time in activities directed towards the review of systems. Such reviews will require expertise in the functions of operating systems, telecommunications and network software and database technology, as well as the application of computer systems to specific commercial, industrial or administrative processes.

There certainly therefore ought to be emphasis, in the training of an auditor, on numeracy skills and on technical skills in systems engineering, advanced control methodology and security techniques. Because of the need to communicate equally well with both technical and non-technical personnel, there should also be significant emphasis on creative and inter-personal skills and on presentational techniques (relating to such mundane activities as report writing). Many auditors will hold a variety of professional qualifications. Auditors' education and training will need to be updated frequently and regularly: the business schools almost certainly have a continuing role to play in this respect.

Above all, however, the implications of IT should be recognized as strategically relevant to the development of the auditing profession (and also, more widely, of the accountancy profession). There has been a tendency over the past twenty years to regard IT either as an interesting but non-strategic side-issue or as a relatively narrow specialism. There is also a tendency to think that an average amount of technological know-how ('computer literacy', meaning the ability to use a screen, a keyboard and maybe a mouse; possibly also the ability to use audit interrogation software) somehow makes an ordinary auditor into a 'computer auditor'. Both these tendencies are dangerous. The former fails to take account of the extent to which IT pervades all aspects of business life and considerations. The latter is simply Panglossian. These tendencies have not gone away just because we are in the 1990s.

As illustrated above, the technological water can get very deep very quickly. Failure to recognize the strategic importance of information technology, and to understand its potential and its limitations, will be very dangerous for the profession and for the future of the valuable service which it provides to management and to the economic welfare of society.

FURTHER READING

Computer Industry, Financial Times Survey, April 1990.

Ferrands, C. (1988). 'Users of information technology: software in financial services', *European Trends*, No. 1. Economic Intelligence Unit.

Information Technology in Finance, Financial Times Survey, November 1989.

International Telecommunications, Financial Times Survey, April 1990.

Lynch, G. (1989). 'It's time to put on the running shoes', *ICL Today*, October.

Martin, J. (1988). 'What the future holds for technology', *PC Week*, November.

Using expert systems by accounting and auditors, NIVRA Conference, 1988.

Using computers in business and industry, Financial Times Survey, November 1989.

DISCUSSION QUESTIONS

1. What are the relative merits of systems-based auditing and substantive auditing? Are there any circumstances under which one is to be greatly preferred to the other?
2. How can a major system be properly audited? How can the complexities be fully taken into consideration? How can its modifications and variations over time, both programmed and manual, be fully reflected in the audit approach?
3. Is there a contradiction between a systems-based approach (based on

the fiction that the system is static) and the fact of the matter (that the system, both programmed and manual, changes over time)?

4. What technological developments are likely to have the most far-reaching effects on (a) business; (b) management information; (c) the accountancy/auditing profession?
5. What are the dangers for the accountancy/auditing profession in the application of advanced IT? Which aspects of IT present the greatest dangers?
6. Can the accounting/auditing profession, as traditionally understood, survive the application of advanced IT? How is the profession changing? How will it continue to change?
7. What are the opportunities for the accountancy/auditing profession in the application of advanced IT? Which aspects of IT present the greatest opportunities?
9. To what extent can audit expertise be reflected in expert systems?
10. What should be the basic level of IT knowledge and expertise of a qualified professional auditor? How best should this be taught and examined?
11. Which aspects of auditing best lend themselves to automation?
12. Which aspects of audit automation present the greatest promise and what is the nature of that promise?

26 Computers in accounting and education: how the changing role of accountants could be reflected in courses
Edwin M. Wildey

INTRODUCTION

This chapter considers how the developing role of computers in all but the smallest business is changing the role of accountants and how this could be reflected in the teaching of accounting. It is an attempt to take forward the approach suggested in Kaye (1985) that the accountant's response to computers could either be that of 'minimization', i.e. that the accountant is primarily a user, or of 'adaptation', whereby the accountant becomes almost indistinguishable from the computer professionals. It concludes that current ideas and developments justify a new strategy for teaching somewhere between Kaye's two approaches.

The chapter is organized as follows. The next section is a brief historical review of the use of computers in accounting education. It concludes that the introduction of computers has caused no fundamental change in the way that accounting is taught. The following section examines the business and technological environment in which accounting is practised and suggests that changes are taking place in both the role and priorities of the accounting function. The implications for accounting education are then considered and a number of topics are discussed which the earlier analysis suggests should be given greater emphasis in accounting courses. The next

Source: *CIMA Research Studies – Computing in Accounting Education: Theory and Practice*
Edited by G. Curtis.
© 1990 CIMA

section provides an approach to the design of a full-time accounting degree course which meets the points raised previously. The approach is also considered as appropriate, *mutatis mutandis*, for all HND and degree courses where accounting is taught. It is then argued that students will require access to software that provides an integrated view of an information system and describes a research project designed to provide it.

The chapter is based on four years' experience of using computers in accounting classes (including computer-based examinations and assignments), a year's research into the use of relational databases in accounting education, observation of how a number of other institutions handle the problem, discussions at conferences and, of course, the literature.

It should be pointed out that although an increasing amount of relevant literature originating in the UK has been appearing in recent years, little is in the form of refereed publications. It is therefore necessary to refer frequently to unpublished conference papers, working papers, articles in professional journals and professional institute publications, etc., including those from America where available, for an indication of relevant ideas and developments. In view of the rate of technological change this is probably inevitable.

There are of course many more refereed articles in American journals. However, they are generally not relevant to the UK in general and this chapter in particular (Zeff, 1988; Shaoul, 1988).

In order to restrict the chapter to a length appropriate to its purpose the following assumptions will be made:

1. computers need to be 'integrated' into courses;
2. accounting lecturers should control the use of computers in accounting courses;
3. current approaches will continue to be appropriate for some courses;
4. re-orientation of staff and courses will take some time;
5. these proposals can be discussed without consideration of the teaching/ learning theories involved;
6. accountants need to be computer literate.
7. CAI (Computer-Aided Instruction) (Bhaskar, 1982) is not a strategic issue.

HISTORICAL DEVELOPMENT

In 1970 the American Accounting Association (AAA) gave three reasons for the introduction of computers into accounting education (AAA, 1970). They can be summarized as follows:

1. *Vocational* – as students will need to understand and use computers when they are working as accountants they must be introduced to them in their studies.
2. *Pedagogic* – computers allow students more meaningful activity in the areas of analytical techniques and problem-solving using algorithms.
3. *Technological* – because the computer has fundamentally altered the way in which accounting data is processed it is no longer adequate to teach in a manner which is processing independent.

It is clearly possible to disagree with the final reason (see Pratt (1987) for discussion of the issues). This chapter accepts the view that whilst the computer has not caused any changes to accounting concepts it has so changed the environment of accounting in practice that there must be a fundamental change in the way accounting is taught if these aims are to be met. This is discussed later.

A review of the literature since 1970 (Wildey, 1987a) suggests that little fundamental change has taken place. The progress that has been made involves the integration of the computer into the course. Early attempts were not integrated. They were wasteful of time in that they involved learning the topic first and then applying the knowledge to an application. Subsequently, integration has been introduced in the sense that the computer is used as part of the learning process of a topic. This can be thought of as 'one dimensional' integration and is the predominant mode at present. The interactive environment of the spreadsheet made this transition easier.

Few accounting lecturers (but see Kaye (1987)) appear to have considered a second dimension of integration, i.e. a natural connection and progression between applications, thus integrating the study of individual procedures and concepts. Even fewer have considered further dimensions incorporating other disciplines and an information systems view. In view of technological advances a multi-dimensional approach is now technically possible and is consistent with both business developments and the AAA view. This is in fact the basis for the proposals made in this chapter.

Another change that has taken place involves the introduction of a new subject within some accounting courses known as 'Accounting Information Systems' (AIS) on the grounds that accountants need to understand how both large and small AISs work (Seddon, 1987). This follows from an AAA recommendation in 1977 (AAA, 1977). Unfortunately it is generally regarded as a subject in its own right which is usually taught only in the final year of accounting degrees. The opportunity is rarely taken to use it for all accounting and related studies within a multi-dimensional framework.

There has also been some use of accounting packages outside the AIS courses. In general they have been found unhelpful in the learning of double entry and, in the absence of the AIS context (Seddon, 1987), only marginally useful because of the extra burden their management requires.

One imaginative, if over-ambitious, project is the Salford Nelson Project (Neal, 1987). It proposes to load 'real' data concerning a particular industry and specific firms into a database. It envisages accounting, economics and quantitative methods classes using the data and thus produce an integrated approach to study. It is not clear whether the data will be at the transaction level or at some level of aggregation (summary), nor is it clear whether it is intended to be modifiable. It does, however, represent a step forward, although whether the advantages of 'real' data outweigh the disadvantages remains to be seen. Using 'real' data at various levels of aggregation is an important experience for students but it seldom shows clearly the features the lecturer wants to emphasize and in the author's experience prepared data is more useful and manageable.

Another development is the Beanstore Project from Thames Polytechnic which is now available commercially. They have created a model company which operates a chain of department stores. It would appear to have the potential to offer a multi-dimensional framework but may lack the flexibility as discussed in a later section and, in any event, its restriction to department stores means that it cannot offer a sufficiently wide range of experiences for an accounting course.

In conclusion it can be said that there is now widespread use of spreadsheets to teach discrete aspects of syllabuses, which presumably follows the tendency to teach accounting generally as though it is a series of techniques (Robinson, Davis and Alderman, 1982; Scapens, 1983; Laughlin and Gray, 1988a) rather than a coherent whole. However, with the exception of the Beanstore example above, there is little evidence of attempts to simulate the way computers are used in business (other than the use of spreadsheets) or to indicate explicitly to students that accounting data represents a sub-set of a wider information system which is itself a reflection of its organizational context.

THE BUSINESS AND TECHNOLOGICAL ENVIRONMENT

As previously established, an important objective of using computers in accounting education is to prepare students for when they leave education.

When we look at the organizations in which accountants work we find that all but the smallest (Robinson et al., 1982; Franks, 1987) are moving rapidly to the situation where:

1. The computer is central to the process of data capture, analysis, storage and reporting (Carr, 1988a).
2. The monopoly that accountants once enjoyed (Godfrey, 1983) over centrally controlled business information is weakened by the advent of centralized storage of functional (marketing, personnel, operational) data in addition to the traditional financial data, i.e. the AIS is becoming seen as an (albeit major) sub-set of a business-wide management information system (MIS) (Mepham, 1988).
3. Information is regarded as a resource to be managed (Carr, 1988b). It is seen as being held within a system which consists of a series of interrelated subsystems. The design of modern integrated computer systems to handle the information starts from this assumption.
4. Modern software developments enable 'end-users' to access the data themselves and to determine the form and timing of their information requirements. This will reduce the reliance on the traditional reporting system and makes possible the development of an effective decision support system (DSS) for both routine and *ad hoc* queries (Clark and Cooper, 1985).

Before considering the effect of these changes on the role of the accountant it is appropriate to consider the data modelling techniques and software that make them possible.

An effective DSS requires, *inter alia*, the capability of bringing together data from a variety of sources within the MIS which were not specified in advance (Sorter, 1969). It must be technically possible to do so within an acceptable timescale and end-users must find the software sufficiently user-friendly to be able to conduct their own enquiries.

The software most likely to be able to meet these requirements on a consistent basis is the database, and in particular the relational database (RDB) (Mepham, 1988). These have always provided the querying facilities but have been criticized in the past because their transaction processing speeds were far inferior to other databases, etc. A professional view of this is given in Faden (1987). The numerous academic criticisms of this aspect of the RDB are not available at the time of writing. RDBs were therefore considered inadequate for the MIS approach where large volumes of transactions usually need to be captured. However, at the July 1988 meeting of the Oracle RDB Users Group, a representative of Mercury PLC presented a summary of the results of their testing of Oracle's recently introduced transaction processing system showing its performance was comparable to the more established methods.

The data modelling approach used is known as the entity-relationship model (E-R) (McCarthy, 1979). This involves capturing data in a manner which ignores double entry, cuts across traditional functional boundaries when necessary and stores the data in a disaggregated form, i.e. no aggregation or summarizing takes place as is common in the traditional accounting model (Sorter, 1969).

In an RDB the physical storage of the data does not determine or restrict the form and complexity of querying or reporting. The qualities of the RDB and E-R modelling mean that both the designer and the user can think of the data as existing in a logical form (known as the 'conceptual schema') which corresponds to how it might be prepared manually. Each user department, including accounting, can then use the various querying facilities and report generators (4 G/L Tools) to create desired 'views' (or 'sub-schemas').

These developments alter the environment in which accountants operate (Arnold, 1986). It is not simply that computers have supplanted manual or mechanical methods but that there is ceasing to be a clear distinction between the recording of financial information and functional information (List, 1986). Perhaps of even more significance for the future role of accountants is that non-accountants are not only taking the leading role in the design of systems but are controlling their operations. To give an example, at meetings of the Oracle RDB Users Group discussion of accounting matters, including controls, takes place without mention of accounting or accountants. The assumption is that it is simply a subset of information for which the computer professionals are responsible and of which accounting staff are users.

IMPLICATIONS FOR ACCOUNTING EDUCATION

The changes will affect the work of all accountants in the future to a greater or lesser extent. As accounting teaching should reflect accounting practice (taking care to discriminate between training and education) (Bhaskar and Kaye, 1985) accounting lecturers must soon decide whether all or what proportion of students should be introduced to the issues which are now so important but which are ignored or mentioned only in passing in many current courses. They must also decide whether these issues can be satisfactorily introduced within the current course structures. These points will be considered after a discussion of the emerging issues themselves, as follows.

SYSTEMS ANALYSIS AND DESIGN

Accountants must be involved in the analysis and design of information systems if integrity is to be maintained (Robinson *et al.*, 1982). In order to be able to communicate adequately with the computer professionals during this process, and indeed in the development and operation of systems, the accountant must have some knowledge of information systems theory, systems analysis and data modelling techniques, organizational hierarchies, software appropriate for an information system and 4 G/L Tools. It is also desirable that they have had experience of applying this knowledge in a practical situation. At present both the knowledge and the experience are largely acquired 'on the job'. This chapter argues that the developing situation means that this is no longer a viable option and accounting students, or at least a significant proportion of them, must have been introduced to accounting systems project work during their studies.

CLASSIFICATION AND CODING

The classification and coding of data are at the heart of an information system yet few accounting textbooks give anything but a cursory treatment to the subject (Fox, 1986; Cole, 1988). Indeed, academic and standard setters in this country have shown little interest in accounts codes (Garbutt, 1979) which are seldom mentioned at all. Financial accounting books usually perpetuate the traditional classification, i.e. at the level of accounts and the major subdivisions of the final accounts, without comment. In cost accounting books the process is taken further but is always constrained by a recognition that information analysis abilities are limited.

In the database (and in particular the RDB) environment these constraints largely disappear and it can reasonably be assumed that decision-makers will demand more sophisticated analysis as they become aware of the possibilities (Bhaskar, 1983). This will involve a more detailed analysis of reporting requirements and the organizational structure of the business prior to the design of an information system. It will also require knowledge of the factors involved in designing and operating efficient coding schemes.

In the computer environment accountants are unlikely to have the prime responsibility for either the classification or coding schemes but in order to be able to ensure that accounting requirements are met by the system will need to be aware of these issues. Once again it is argued that they should be introduced during study rather than learned on the job. In any event they are an inescapable part of the project work previously mentioned and allow for the demonstration of creative analysis on the part of the student.

CONTROLS – MANUAL AND COMPUTER

Accountants have always been concerned with internal control. The increasing use of computers has not reduced this concern in any way but has introduced a new element – the control of computer operations (Bentley, 1986). Any study of accounting applications must have a heavy emphasis on controls (Gelinas and Verreault, 1984).

EVALUATION OF ACCOUNTING AND RELATED SOFTWARE PACKAGES

There are many packages on the market and a lack of generally accepted standards for their evaluation (Franks, 1987). In order to be able to make the right choice the accountant must be aware of the factors to take into account. A study of the principles involved is a legitimate area of study and the application of them to a number of packages during an accounting course will lay the groundwork for the development of these skills (Cerullo *et al.*, 1984).

FINANCIAL MODELLING

Spreadsheets and modelling packages, which require an ability to think algorithmically (Ijiri, 1983), are being used increasingly for modelling purposes (Clark and Cooper, 1985). It is essential that there is widespread awareness of their weaknesses as well as strengths (Carr, 1988b) and an important aspect of this is the development of construction and design standards for models and templates (Carr, 1988b; Holt, 1987).

EVALUATION OF NEW TECHNOLOGY-BASED SYSTEMS

Even though they may not have the prime responsibility for either the design or the operation of information systems, the accountant will still be required to play a major role in the determination of strategy and the evaluation of their efficiency and effectiveness (Williams, 1987).

This will require the learning of new skills and the application of existing techniques to new situations. For example, the traditional approach to investment appraisal and treatment in the accounts must be reviewed to ensure that it is appropriate for circumstances in which:

1. replacement costs are reducing and capabilities are increasing;
2. development costs, which are a significant proportion of the total, tend to be treated as expenses rather than capitalized;
3. many benefits are not quantifiable. See Finnie (1988) for discussion of this topic.

Accountants can also take a lead in ensuring a system is seen as essentially human activity-based and not limited to the hardware and software. This will involve study of texts such as Hirschheim (1985) and Checkland (1981).

DATA PROTECTION ACT

The Act is now a significant factor to be considered in both the design and operation of information systems (List, 1986).

PRESENTATION AND REPORTING SKILLS

As the day-to-day control of the reporting process passes to the end-user there will be increased need for skills in the use of productivity tools (Kaye, 1985) such as networks and graphics/statistics packages. These may be 4G/L 'add-ons' to the database or micro packages capable of accessing and manipulating the database prior to presentation of the information.

In addition to the ability to use the software and to appreciate how they can be used to produce information it will be necessary to consider the quality of the resultant report in order to achieve the greatest impact.

The above topics are indicative of the growing gap between accounting practice and accounting education (AAA, 1986). What is required is a major re-orientation of accounting education to reflect accounting's role as an information development and distribution function for economic decison-making (AAA, 1986). This cannot be done while the teaching (unconsciously?) assumes that accounting is still a paper-based process with the computer intruding as a peripheral topic (Carr, 1985; Garbutt, 1980).

It will also be necessary for the status of double entry to be examined. Some writers suggest that it is in some senses obsolete (List, 1986; Mepham, 1988) because the computer does not require a transaction to be entered twice. It is, however, not simply a matter of ceasing to teach the subject. In an earlier publication Mepham (1980) distinguished between the 'financial accounting model' and 'double entry', which was described as a systematic method of collecting and processing data for use in an underlying financial accounting model. The transaction may not need to be recorded twice but 'dual aspect analysis' (Garbutt, 1980) is still fundamental to reporting under the financial accounting model. Accountants, and therefore accounting students, must understand what underlies the process even if there is no need for data entry staff to do so.

One recently made suggestion concerning an approach to the teaching of the accounting which may prove appropriate is the 'Organizational Systems Model' (Laughlin and Gray, 1988a) because it places the accounting procedures clearly within the organizational and systems framework. A textbook (Laughlin and Gray, 1988b) will be published this year.

As the computer becomes more central to the teaching of accounting procedures the matrix could offer a suitable framework (Mepham, 1988) but at the practical level it may prove more satisfactory to introduce the three column (debit, credit, balance) form to students from the start and ignore the 'T' account, on the grounds that it is more consistent with computer presentation. However, textbook treatment will probably prove a constraint and the value of this suggestion remains to be seen.

The introduction of the new material discussed above raises the question of how to find time to teach it. It may be that the time taken by students to learn many of the traditional procedures will be reduced because of the systems framework within which the learning takes place. This may mean that less pruning may be necessary than might be imagined. Staff at Bentley College in the United States came to the conclusion that the subject matter of their AIS course was more important than some advanced accounting topics (Gelinas and Verreault, 1984). This chapter accepts that view of priorities if it becomes necessary.

The analysis to date does seem to indicate that a change of strategy is required. Kaye (1985) suggests that those courses that have made a serious attempt to incorporate computers have adopted the 'minimization' strategy, i.e. the accountant is primarily a user of information systems but is also responsible for ensuring that controls are adequate for audit purposes. The picture that emerges is that an intermediate solution is required without adopting the full 'adaptation' strategy of the accountant being responsible for the design, management and use of the system and almost indistinguishable from the computer professionals.

It appears that the accountant will need to be a 'super-user'. This will require skills in the use of the technology and an understanding of information beyond the traditional accounting view. More importantly, especially as promotion is achieved, it will require an understanding of the implications and potential of both. It will then be possible to specify the requirements and be involved in the design and management of the system without usurping the role of the computer professionals or losing the predominant position in the control, analysis and dissemination of information within and without the organization.

The next section puts forward an outline of a course designed to produce students capable of developing naturally in this direction.

A PROPOSED COURSE OUTLINE

There is clearly a strong argument for deriving and presenting a series of principles to underly the course design. However, the purpose of this chapter, having set out the issues involved is, to suggest one way forward: there has been sufficient discussion of strategy, let us now consider tactics as part of an iterative process that may highlight the principles and refine the tactics.

Table 26.1 is an outline for a three-year degree in 'Systems Accounting' which has been informally discussed at the Dorset Institute of HE. It is designed to provide students with the knowledge and skills discussed earlier in this chapter and also to meet the objectives of both the universities and CNAA.

Table 26.1 Proposed course outline

The Business Environment	Accounting	Technological Environment
	Year 1	
Economics/Statistics	Accounting Process	Information System Theory
Organizational Studies	(double weighting)	IT and Computers
Business Law		Software Skills
	Year 2	
Business Functions	Financial Accounting	Systems Analysis and Design
	Management Accounting	MIS/DSS
	Auditing/Controls	Software Skills
	Project	
	Year 3	
Business Strategy	Advanced Accounting	IT Strategy
	Financial Modelling	
	Project	

The table shows how the accounting studies are supported and supplemented by studies of the business and technological environment. No indicative content is given; the subject headings should be regarded only as descriptive of the study material. It will be noted that no sandwich year is included in view of the proposed project work.

No detailed consideration has been given at this stage to the ICAEW consultative paper (ICAEW, 1987) or some of the subsequent correspondence (CHAP, 1988; ICAEW, 1988) but these proposals would appear to offer the possibility of being structured to obtain 'specially relevant degree' status.

The first year conforms to the standard three-term format except that

Software Skills will last for only two terms and not be specifically examined. The year is intended to provide both a foundation and a direction for the course. The Accounting Process will concentrate on transaction processing, both manual and computerized, within the context of the financial accounting model and incorporate only sufficient of the concepts, financing and interpretation to explain the processing in a general way. Software Skills is intended to introduce students to the productivity tools in a formal way so that they are aware of their main functions and potential. It will also have the effect of reducing the occasions when students are having trouble with an activity and it is not clear whether the difficulty is caused by problems with the software or the subject matter.

In years two and three of the proposed outline in Table 26.1 there are two features not apparent:

1. subjects other than the project will be examined after two terms;
2. the summer terms are given over to project work.

During year two students should be introduced to research methods and the approach to project work and reports. It is envisaged that year two projects will be on an individual basis and year three a team effort preferably in a live situation.

This may appear to involve too radical a departure from the norm for polytechnics/colleges but the format has received CNAA approval for the final year of a BSc(Hons) degree course in Information Technology at Huddersfield Polytechnic (CNAA, 1988).

A course of this nature is intended to demonstrate the integrated nature of business and of its information system from an accounting perspective. It will require a greater than usual integration between the various elements and disciplines within the course. This will apply both to the presentation of subject matter during the year and from one year to the next. In addition, experience has shown that when computers are an integral part of a course and are used to a significant extent in assessment then the assessment schemes are best determined before the schemes of work are designed.

It is also argued that the course will be more effective if it is structured around a business application that enables the integrated nature of an information system to be demonstrated and explored. Before considering this, however, it is necessary to point out that:

1. students also require access to a wide range of software as previously discussed, i.e. productivity tools and accounting packages;
2. all software is ultimately only a tool which can be used effectively for

certain aspects of a syllabus (Watson, 1987). Pen, paper and calculator will still be absolutely essential tools in learning (Ijiri, 1983; Seddon, 1987).

The next section suggests what might be the aims of the proposed business application and the criteria by which it should be judged. It then describes the preliminary work that has taken place on a research project designed to produce an application. In order to avoid confusion over terminology the whole model is called a 'suite' with sub-sets known as applications.

AN INTEGRATED SOFTWARE SUITE

The overall aim of the suite will be to provide an environment for all disciplines which reflects the integration of the subject matter and the technology at the strategic level such that the structure, content and the process of teaching utilize the technology naturally within both single and multi-disciplinary activities (adapted from Kaye (1985)).

To this end the information system of a business will be simulated using a commercially available integrated application written in a relational database. Data will be prepared and entered for one year's activities. This will provide an environment in which students can learn, where appropriate, the traditional topics and also meet and explore the emerging issues as described in the earlier section on implications for accounting education. Aspects of the suite design and use are now discussed.

CRITERIA REQUIRED OF SUITE

In order to achieve its aims and ensure its use by all (most?) lecturers on a course, the suite should meet the following criteria (Wildey, 1987a):

1. Provide (the potential for) a full information system for a medium/large company which incorporates historical data and has been adapted for teaching purposes. This would include such features as a multi-user capability and the possibility of 'Help' messages.
2. Be capable, if required, of adaptation to a wide range of learning strategies to suit the particular situation. There are two main aspects of the teaching/learning process that must be addressed:
   (a) the procedures themselves and the concepts underlying them, and
   (b) using the resulting output for analytical and conjectural purposes.
   Lecturers use different approaches to assist their students in these

processes, ranging from the barely mentionable 'drilling' to open-ended, wide-ranging case studies. Each have their place and the suite should be able to accommodate them.

3. Be adaptable, within a reasonable timescale, by individuals or groups of lecturers, to achieve their changing teaching objectives or personal preferences without completely rewriting the program and without demanding a programming background from lecturers. The essence of this criterion is adaptability within the control of the lecturer. Software that cannot be modified without professional help is not attractive because it seldom does what is wanted in the way that is wanted. Formats and data must be able to be created and/or standard ones modified by the lecturer.

THE RELATIONAL DATABASE SOLUTION

The section above on the business and technological environment indicated that there is a growing recognition that the RDB provided the most suitable environment for an MIS. It would therefore seem logical to utilize the same software because the suite will be simulating the same functions and at the same time be required to be more adaptable to accommodate the changing requirements of individual lecturers.

Preliminary work has been carried out on the development of such a suite (Wildey, 1987b) using the Oracle RDB. Other software solutions were considered and discarded on the grounds of cost and/or lack of flexibility. Oracle was chosen because it is available on site but was particularly attractive because Oracle UK Ltd market a range of application modules known collectively as the 'Business Patterns'. They cover the major subsystems other than, for the present, stock control and fixed assets. Work on the suite has been delayed until the latest version becomes available on site (hopefully by September, 1991). Use of the Patterns will ensure professional quality, avoid 're-inventing the wheel' and allow available development time to be directed at the design and uses of the suite rather than building it from scratch. Also available with the database are a series of fourth generation development tools, a graphics module and a Lotus 1-2-3 'add-on' which enables the spreadsheet to be used for data entry and manipulation via a PC. Oracle itself can run on a PC but the 'Patterns' require a mini given present PC capacities.

COMPANY SIMULATION AS BASIS FOR MIS

It is intended to simulate the information system of a manufacturing company as this is considered to allow the widest range of activities. The company will be manufacturing high value products in order to produce realistic monetary values with relatively few transactions. Where specialized activities are required they will be accommodated within a subsidiary company.

Owing to the nature of a relational database it is not necessary to set limits to the size of the various aspects of the company but the following give an indication of the intended initial overall size:

Shareholders	50	Customers	200
Factories	1	Suppliers	50
Warehouses	2	Stock items –RM	1 000
Sales regions	4	–WIP	50
Production departments	3	–FG	20
Prod. service depts	3	Employees	200
Non-prod. service depts	6		

An opening position will be established for all relevant items but no prior history given except the previous year's Cost of Production and Revenue Statements. One year's transactions will be prepared and entered as permanent data. A significant number of transactions will be entered in order to provide a sufficient base for analysis but they will be coded to allow views of only a limited number where that is required.

USING THE SUITE

There will be two main approaches:

1. *Company simulation* – where the model (or part of it) is used as designed. The permanent data will be used or added to in one of the following ways:
   (a) as static data, e.g. for analysis;
   (b) dynamically, i.e. students are allowed a view of some transactions and required to enter (or predict) the succeeding ones. As these entries are already part of the permanent data they will only be stored until the student has completed the work and then deleted. The effect of this is that every student can be given the same starting point and carry out the same process.
   (c) after agreement between lecturers, new transactions can be added to create an extended database, e.g. a second year's permanent data.
2. *Spin-offs* – where the model and/or data (or part of them) are copied and then adapted by one or more lecturers to be used to achieve a specific objective. No changes occur to the model or permanent data.

Either approach can be used to create applications for demonstration, student practice, coursework or examinations. Individual sets of data can be generated quite simply using random numbers applied to the permanent data with student's work individually identified and stored. With a little effort it would be possible to produce answers in appropriate situations.

Three types of application have been identified which are applicable to individual disciplines or for multi-disciplinary work, although naturally the emphasis may be different:

1. *Process learning* – concerned with individual topics within a syllabus. These are frequently the subject of computer applications at present and under this proposal would be achieved using the 'spin-off' approach or written in Oracle as stand-alone applications.
2. *Data capture, processing and reporting* – the routine recording and reporting, initially using the 'spin-off' or stand-alone approaches but when students are considered competent they will add to the permanent data.
3. *Case studies* – using the model as designed and reports derived either from the permanent data or specially prepared.

All three types can adopt the traditional approach but when used on the proposed course would incorporate a substantial systems emphasis. A number of examples, from a range of disciplines, have been identified which demonstrate how the model may offer opportunities which are not conveniently available at present (Wildey, 1987b).

ACADEMIC SUPERVISION

When operational, an academic member of staff will be required to coordinate the use of the suite by staff and students, assisted probably by research assistant(s). Functions identified to date are:

1. controlling access to the suite and supervising relevant instruction;
2. ensuring 'good housekeeping', e.g. that unwanted data etc. are deleted frequently;
3. controlling the accumulation or modification of permanent data.

STAFF TRAINING

In order to make the most of the model it will be necessary for staff to receive some training but it must be made clear that although the changes may be significant in teaching terms they will be trivial in database systems design terms. It was originally assumed that end-users could develop their own applications with 4 G/L products but this is now discounted because considerable design skills are required to design successful systems (Butler, 1988).

There is, however, no reason why lecturers, whose computer experience does not extend beyond using a spreadsheet, should not be capable of adapting and/or using the model for their own purposes. Based on the author's experience it is anticipated that twenty hours of training and practice will be needed for inexperienced lecturers to be able to use the model and make simple modifications, a further twenty hours to learn to use the query language, SQL, which is necessary for more complicated work.

Not all lecturers will wish to become fully trained and will choose to rely on Computer Centre assistance to some extent, but some formal classes will be essential – especially at the beginning – for everyone and for learning SQL if required.

RESOURCING DEVELOPMENT

Models such as this have been proposed before but the one original aspect of this proposal is that it should be built using a relational database and have attributes of an authoring system. If it is to be successful it will need to be done in a professional manner. At the very least it requires a small team of systems oriented accountants and computer lecturers who are given significant teaching reduction for at least the first year together with research assistants and technical assistance from the Computer Centre.

This could be a locally based project but if done properly could have a wide appeal and it may be that collaboration should not simply be between disciplines at the Dorset Institute but between institutions.

CONCLUSION

This chapter has suggested that a re-orientation of accounting education is necessary to ensure that accountants maintain their position in the business world. There is no suggestion that accounting concepts have changed. However, the environment in which accounting is practised has changed radically as a result of the introduction of the computer and a range of issues have arisen which are scarcely mentioned in most accounting courses. It is suggested that the accountant's traditional knowledge and skills must be supplemented to the point of being an advanced, even expert, user of the computer in order to be able to communicate with, and maintain equality with, the computer professionals without usurping their role.

It has been suggested that current course structures may not be suitable for the inclusion of the new orientation. An outline has been proposed which attempts to provide a course which will prepare students for professional life by meeting the AAA (1970) aims:

1. *Vocational* – students will have been introduced to a wide range of computer software and associated techniques in addition to the traditional skills and knowledge
2. *Pedagogic* – the course and the use of the computer makes possible more activities which develop both an understanding of the underlying concepts and the ability to apply them in a modern context
3. *Technological* – without abandoning the commitment to teaching the traditional skills in the preparation and reporting of accounting information (AAA, 1985) the course introduces students to current practice and prepares them for informed participation in future developments.

It is also proposed that a simulated information system for a manufacturing organization should be designed, possibly on a collaborative basis, in order to provide an environment most appropriate for the development of the above aims and suggests that the relational database provides us, for the first time, with software suitable for the purpose.

Academic staff will naturally retain control of course design and operation: they must also ensure that lecturers with the necessary imagination and energy take and keep control of the simulation in order to ensure that academic direction and priorities are maintained. When a proven, working model is available that is relevant, easy to use and non time-consuming no lecturers will have an excuse for standing aside. Then higher education will offer accounting students the environment they need to develop the knowledge and skills required in the future.

REFERENCES

American Accounting Association (1970). 'Report of the 1968–69 Committee on the Role of the Computer in Accounting Education', *The Accounting Review* **45** Supplement, pp. 29–43.

American Accounting Association (1977). 'Report of the Committee for New Courses for Professional Accounting Programs', *The Accounting Review* **52**.

American Accounting Association (1986). 'Future Accounting Education: Preparing for the Expanding Profession', *Issues in Accounting Education* pp. 168–95.

Arnold, J. (1986). *The Education of Accountants: At the Crossroads*. The Fourth Armitage & Norton Lecture, Huddersfield Polytechnic.

Bentley, T. J. (1986). *Control in the Computing Environment*. Management Information Systems Series, ICMA.

Bhaskar, K. N. (1982). 'Use of computers in accountancy courses', *Accounting and Business Research*, **13** (49) Winter, pp. 3–10.

Bhaskar, K. N. (1983). 'Computers and the choice of accountancy syllabuses', *Accounting and Business Research*, **13** (50) Spring, pp. 83–93.

Bhaskar, K. N. and Kaye, G. R. (1985). 'Computers and accounting courses: a reply to Collins', *Accounting and Business Research*, **15** (59) Summer, pp. 239–40.

Butler, M. (1988). 'Why the data dictionary holds great IT promise', *DEC User*, August.

Carr, J. G. (1985). *Information Technology and the Accountant*. Gower. Aldershot.

Carr, J. G. (1988a). 'IT on line for target', *Certified Accountant*, January, pp. 15–16.

Carr, J. G. (1988b). 'Meeting a competitive challenge', *Certified Accountant*, July, pp. 30–31.

Cerullo, M. J., Garsombke, H. P. and Klein, L. A. (1984). 'Using microcomputers in the accounting curriculum', *Information Systems & Management Consulting*, **7** (2) Winter, pp. 22–6.

CHAP (Committee of Heads of Accounting in Polytechnics) (1988). *Response to ICAEW consultative paper*. Chairman, R. Nunns, January.

Checkland, P. (1981). *Systems Thinking, Systems Practice*. Wiley, Chichester.

Clark, F. and Cooper, J. (1985). *The Chartered Accountant in the Information Technology Age*. Coopers & Lybrand/ICAEW.

CNAA (Council for National Academic Awards) (1988). *Information Services Digest*, May.

Cole, M. (1988). 'Choosing the right nominal ledger', *Accountancy*, **101** (1137) May, pp. 74–86.

Faden, M. (1987). 'Relational systems are answering the critics', *DEC User*, January.

Finnie, J. (1988). 'The role of financial appraisal in decisions to acquire advanced manufacturing technology', *Accounting and Business Research*, **18** (70) Spring, pp. 133–9.

Fox, R. P. (1986). *The Classification and Coding of Accounting Information*. ICMA.

Franks, R. V. (1987). *Choosing Accounting Software*. Management Information Systems Series, ICMA.

Garbutt, D. (1979). *Problems in Teaching the Foundations of Accounting – a Background Paper*. Paper at the annual conference of the Association of Lecturers in Accountancy (ALIA).

Garbutt, D. (1980). 'Teaching the foundations of accounting', *ALIA Bulletin*, October.

Gelinas, U. J. and Verreault, D. A. (1984). 'Structuring the accounting information systems course', *Information Systems & Management Consulting*, **7** (2) Winter, pp. 11–21.

Godfrey, R. (1983). *CAL for Computer-Based Accounting Systems*. Paper at CAL in Tertiary Education Conference, Brisbane, October.

Hirschheim, R. A. (1985). *Office automation: A Social & Organisational Perspective*. Addison-Wesley, Wokingham.

Holt, P. J. (1987). *Spreadsheet design standards*. Internal working paper/class handout available from the author.

ICAEW (1987). 'Training the business professional', a consultative paper, November.

ICAEW (1988). Letter to responders to consultative paper, June.

Ijiri, Y. (1983). 'New dimensions in accounting education: computers and algorithms', *Issues in Accounting Education*, pp. 168–73.

Kaye, G. R. (1985). 'Teaching strategies in computers in accounting', *British Accounting Review*, **17** (1) Spring, pp. 22–36.

Kaye, G. R. (1987). 'Conceptual design of an accounting skills workshop'. In Kaye, G. R. (ed.), *Proceedings of Computers in Accounting Education Workshop*. ICMA, pp. 63–88.

Laughlin, R. C. and Gray, R. H. (1988a). *A model of organisational systems: a pedagogic note on bookkeeping and accounting theory*. Paper at British Accounting Association annual conference.

Laughlin, R. C. and Gray, R. H. (1988b). *Financial Accounting: Method and Meaning*. Van Nostrand Reinhold International, London.

List, W. (1986). 'Exit double entry?', *The Accountant's Magazine*, **90** (962) September, pp. 44–5.

McCarthy, W. E. (1979). 'An entity-relationship view of accounting models', *The Accounting Review*, **54** (4) October, pp. 667–86.

Mepham, M. J. (1980). *Accounting Models*. Polytech Publishers.

Mepham, M. J. (1988). *A conceptual model for data base accounting*. Paper at the European Accounting Congress.

Neal, F. A. (1987). *Computer-Assisted Integrated First Year Teaching Programme*. Paper to Computers in Teaching Accountancy, Economics, Business and Management Conference in Stirling, September.

Pratt, N. (1987). 'Summary of discussion group on "Accounting Courses"'. In Kaye, G. R. (ed.) *Proceedings of Computers in Accounting Education Workshop*. ICMA, pp. 49–52.

Robinson, L. A., Davis, J. R. and Alderman, C. W. (1982). *Accounting Information Systems: A Cycle Approach*. Harper & Row, New York: London.

Scapens, R. W. (1983). 'Closing the gap between theory and practice', *Management Accounting*, **61** (1) January, pp. 34–6.

Seddon, P. (1987). 'Yet another view on the role of computing in the undergraduate accounting curriculum'. In Kaye, G. R. (ed.), *Proceedings of Computers in Accounting Education Workshop*. ICMA, pp. 97–110.

Shaoul, J. (1988). *The Impact of New Technology on The Curriculum and Teaching Methods in Accounting*. Paper at British Accounting Association annual conference.

Sorter, G. H. (1969). 'An "events" approach to basic accounting theory', *The Accounting Review*, **44** (1) January, pp. 11–19.

Watson, D. (1987). *A CAL development team in the process of change*. Abstract of paper to CAL 87 conference in Glasgow.

Wildey, E. M. (1987a). *An exploration of a prototype accounting teaching system based on a relational database*. MSc dissertation submitted to School of Information Systems, University of East Anglia.

Wildey, E. M. (1987b). *Proposed Institute company simulation and MIS for teaching*. Internal steering committee report, Dorset Institute of HE, available from the author.

Williams, B. C. (1987). 'Summary of discussion group on "IT Courses"'. In Kay, G. R. (ed.), *Proceedings of Computers in Accounting Education Workshop*. ICMA, pp. 53–62.

Zeff, S. (1988). *Some trends in accounting education and research in the USA*. Paper at British Accounting Association annual conference.

Index

A Statement of Basic Accounting
  Theory 149, 155
Absorption costing 198
Account based procedures 140
Accountant as modeller 325
Accounting
  curriculum
    and computers 2
    integrating computers 4
  entity 131
  identity 318
  information
    supply 33
    systems (AIS) 2, 5, 13, 160, 170,
      447
    systems case study approach 3
  practices 30, 33
  principals 169
  profession 402
  reports 139
  surrogates 169
  theory 143, 173
Accounting Universe of Discourse 180
Acquisition methodologies 260
Ad hoc methods 133
Adaptability 458
Adaption strategy 454
Admissibility 249
  of computer output 236, 238
  of hearsay 238
Agency theory 45
Agent of change, computing 5
Agents 172
Aggregated values 151
Aggregating financial data 160
Aiming to miss 257
ALFEX 403
Algebraic
  models 220
  operations 133
  relationships 229

Alvey programme 403
Analytical economic models 33
Anonymous tips 422
Anthropology 322
Application templates 212
ARIEL 84
ARIES 403
Artemis 284
Artificial intelligence 8, 11, 91, 217
  shells 13
Assessment of Schedule D (CODA)
  278
ATM 240
  services 114
  see also Autoteller machines
Audit 13, 406, 414
  automation 430
  function 408
  techniques 213
  trail 422, 434
Authoring system 461
Automatic
  monitoring systems 240
  recording systems 240
Automation 25
Autonomy 291
Autoteller machines (ATMs) 100, 111,
  113

B vector 138
Back-office 377
  activities 376
BACS 441
Balance sheet 153
  construction 154
Batch
  processing 278
  system 107
Baye's rule 62
Beanstore Project 448
Behavioural

dimensions 321
factors 5
Benefits
  based planning 96
  bottom-line 92
  from IT investment 8
BEST (Kleinwort Benson) 87
Best-execution rule 86
Betrayal of trust 419
Big Bang 81
Black box 320
Branch terminals 107
Breakeven chart 318
Bridges 163
Budgetary
  control 195
  systems 206
Budgeting 8, 206
Business
  advantages 385
  applications 384
  benefits 412
  case for investment 96
  communications 237, 241
  environment 419, 455
  goals 96, 98
  needs 271
  organization and policy 7
  performance measures 98
  transformation 94

C2/D/E social categories 106
CAI 13
CAL 13
  packages
    earnings per share 2
    financial accounting 2
CALCSTAR 323
Capital
  flows 369
  investment analysis model 191
Cardinality constraints 165
Case studies 375, 460
Cash flow
  accounting 8
  forecasting 327
Cellular telephones 439
Central EDP departments 360
Centralization of power 283
Centre 1 272, 281

Chain of reasoning 258
CHAPS 100
Chart of accounts 160, 170
Chinese walls 86
Choice
  of model form 320
  of technology 117
Civil Evidence Act 1968 (CEA) 235
Classes of events 156
Classification and coding of data 451
Closing entries 139
Co-ordination tasks 369
Cognitive
  mapping 310, 329
  structures 259
Commercial
  advantage 438
  sensitivity 50
Communications
  networks 217
  systems 96
Community charge 9
Company
  simulation 459
  strategies 367
Compatibility
  issues 112
  problems 413
Competition 114
Competitive
  advantage 11, 98, 117, 370, 372
  analysis 198
  edge 404, 440
  environment 351
  factors 106
  markets 368
  pressures 353
Complete markets efficiency 80
Completion of markets 42
Compliance audit techniques 429
Computer Science Corporation (CSC)
  285, 281
Computer
  abuses 420
  auditing 11, 429
  crime 418
  evidence 236, 242, 239
    admissibility 245, 248
  incompatibility 107
  meaning of 245

Computer *contd*
  networks 366, 369
  numerical control (CNC) 355
  readable records 235
  record reliability 244
  science 13, 220
  system security 247
  terminal 108
  viruses 424
Computer-aided design 91
Computerization
  impetus 272
  of existing procedures 10
Computers in accountancy framework 13
Conceptual
  data model 142
  model 133, 142
  schema 160, 177, 450
    specification 162
  structures 256, 264
    of knowledge 254
Conditions for admissibility 242
Confidential information 393
Confidentiality 342
Conflicting evidence 241
CONNEX EFT package 114
Constraints 164
Consultant and staff integration 291
Consultants 286
  use of 282
Contexual factors 41
Continuous Net Settlement Service 83
Contract existence 240
Contractual limitations of liability 255
Control 360
  situations 211
  technology 26
Conventions in society 74
Cooperative venture 71
COP Steering Group 284
Corporate skills 408
Cost
  accountants' work 438
  accounting 357
  considerations 114
  drivers 192, 198
  estimation 8
  pressures 353
  structure 193
Cost-benefit analysis 390

Costs and benefits 94
Counter transactions 115
Creative analysis 451
Critical
  awareness 340
  operating events 155
Customer
  relations 110
  servicing 104
  transactions 82
Customer/supplier linkages 372

Data
  with intrinsic value 9
  model 142
  modelling 451
    techniques 449
  processing, traditional 91
Data oriented DSS 221
Database
  accounting 179
  events accounting system 140
  management system (DBMS) 140
  systems 386
  theory 170
Datastream 85
DBMS
  query generating facilities 141
  report generating facilities 141
Decentralization of organizations 208
Decentralized system 272
Decision
  conferencing 312
  horizon 197
  models 151
  support systems 9, 220, 304
Decision-makers 451
Decision-making 191, 208, 211, 218,
    227, 256, 312, 362, 367, 384, 437
  centralized 352, 358
  delegated 358
  non-instrumental 61
  strategic 223
  unstructured 263
Defeasible principles 261
Defendable penumbra 257, 263
Desk-top
  publishing 387
  workstations 116
Deskilling 408

Devolution of power 283
Disaggregated
    data 140, 181, 321
    form 151
Dissipative signalling equilibrium 47
Distributed computing 433
Documentation 212
Double-entry 160, 170, 179, 453
    system 128
DP era 94
Drilling 458
DSDM 285
DSS 227, 271
    definition 221
Dual
    capacity 81
    transaction 173
Duality
    principle 129
    relationships 173
DVLC 271

East Kilbride 281
Eastern Europe 439
Economic
    processes 22
    value 21
Economics 7
Economics of scale 371
EDI 237
    messages 236, 243
    see also Electronic data interchange
EDP 227
Educational 13
Effect of the transaction 131
Effectiveness 372, 388
Efficiency 274, 372, 388
EIS 228
    see also Executive information
        systems
Electronic
    communications 383
    data interchange 9, 189, 372, 424, 440
        processing 216
    mail 225, 375
    office 224
    point-of-sale (EPOS) 190, 354
    signatures 247
Elements 130
End-user 216, 292, 353, 449, 453, 460

computing 2, 4, 91, 94, 208, 230
    tools 13
Engineering modelling 33
Enterprise-wide perspective 162
Entity relationship model 160
Environment 328
Environmental
    changes 382
    factors 104, 246
EPIC 85
Epistemological error 338
Equal probabilities assignment formula
    64
Equilibrium concepts 34
Ergonomics 220
Error rates 275
ESPRIT 404
Estriel Series 280
Ethical factors 54
European Community 29
Events 172
    accounting 8, 160
    system 143
    approach 149
    theory 150
    of accounting 140
Evidence Act of 1979 (S. Aust.) 248
Evidence 235
Evidence, Uniform Rules 248
EXCEL 127
Executive
    information systems 9, 223
    support systems 225
Expectation formation 68
Expected utility 36
Expert system
    definition 404
    system shell 405
Expert systems 9, 226, 229, 252, 406,
        435, 436
    and accountancy 408
    literature 410
    as managerial tools 303
ExperTax 407
Expertise 409
    accounting 409
    corporate 409
Expertness 409
External environmental influences
    210

False data entry 421
Familiar technology 289
Feasibility study 274
Fibre optic cables 113
File management systems 13
Finance 7
Financial
  accounting 7, 143
  model 453
    requirements 194
  modelling 142, 317
  reporting 32, 49
Financial-legal domain 252
Fineness theorem 37
Fixed costs 190, 207
Flexibility 354
Flexible manufacturing systems 356
Forensic team 425
Forensics 423
Form of life 337
Formal
  rules 402
  structure 352
Fraud 11, 246, 394, 434
  commercial 422
  computer-based 418, 420
Fraudsmen 423
Fraudulent data entry 421
Functional
  decomposition 285
  efficiency 79
  structure 368
Funds statement 155
Fuzzy
  data 199
  logic 9, 226, 229

Game of perfect information 69
General software 384
Graphical
  constructs for schema 163
  user interfaces 432
Graphics 386
  integrated 324
Group
  decision support systems 222, 308
  workshops 311
Growth 389

Hardware failure 243

Hearsay 237
  admissibility 241
Hermeneutical reflection 338
Heuristics 226, 229, 257
Hierarchial models 291, 160
Hierarchies 357
Home banking 112, 117
Hotline 85
Human
  activity 452
  dimension 335
  effects 116
  intelligence 401
  semantic systems 334
  skills 402
Hume 73
Hypermedia/hypertext 13

ICT 367, 374
Ideas 163
Impact of IT 7, 28
Implementation
  of technology 313
  strategy 277
Improper
  operations 245
  use 246
Income
  measurement 49
  statement 154
  valuation model 151
Individual
  rationality 54
  utility functions 152
Individualism 363
Industrial organization 368
Industry-specific software 384
Informal systems 198
Information
  asymmetry 44
  for contract enforcement 48
  cost 24
  economics 32, 52
    models 35
  economy 29
  efficiency 80
  integrity 394
  measurement 25, 30
  overload 34, 72
  perfect 61

post-decision 40
pre-decision 40
processing 26
production 28
public 38
quality 198
related activities 29
sector 28
social value 38, 39
storage 241
structure diagram (ISD) 175
systems 48, 96
    spending 91
    strategy 227
    theory 451
Inland Revenue 270
Innovation champion 118
Insider dealing 87
Institutional Net Settlement system
    (NIS) 83
Instrumental rationality 62, 65
Integrated
    information system 456
    software 205
computers 447
Intellectual work 26
Intelligent
    machines 263
    terminals 374
Inter-corporate networking 379
Inter-dealer-broker (IDB) 84
Inter-organizational networking 371
Interactive
    computing power 306
    system 305
Interconnectivity 435
Internal
    control procedures 430
    environmental influences 210
Interpersonal relationships 110
Intra-market transactions 82
Investment
    appraisal 452
    centre 197
    decisions 44
    levels 98
Irregular share dealing 86
IS forensics 424
ISD notation 168
ISE 81

Islands of automation 188
ISRO 81
Issue analysis 376
IT
    and the future of the audit 431, 442
    investment evaluation 24
    skills 27
    strategies 442
    training 288

Japanese fifth generation project 403
Job
    re-definition 288
    satisfaction 105, 389
Just-in-time (JIT) 9, 189, 194

Kant 73
Key characteristics of small firms 11
Key-word-in-context 334
Knowledge
    base 229
    defensively orientated 263
    engineer 259
    of financial environment 254
    of governing laws 254
    heuristic 260
    informal 290
    representation 405
    tacit 362

Labour flows 369
Learning by doing 27
Least-cost producer 378
Legal implications of errors in ES 253
Leisure 43
Linear relationships 319
Literary analysis 341
Loss of information 153
LOT 163
LOTUS 1-2-3 127

Macro issues of liability 253
Management
    accountants' work 438
    accounting 7, 190
        definition 187
        strategic 187, 193, 198
    effectiveness 98
    hierarchies 351, 368
    information systems 9, 24, 219

Management *contd*
  intelligence systems 222
  organization 355
  of process 375
  science 10, 220
  strategies 368
  of structure 375
  structures 358, 361
    matrix 359
  of territory 375
Manager as modeller 325
Manager's role 110
Managerial
  accounting 143
  see also Management accounting
  control 354
  ethos 359
  goals 356
  problems 301
Manpower planning 308
Manufacturing resource planning 189
Many-to-many relationship 166
Macro languages 212
Marginal benefit 62
Market forces 111
Market-makers 82
Marketing 104, 110
Mastery over the computer 209
Mathematical convention 130
Matrices 127, 157, 195, 352, 454
Matrix
  accounting 8, 132
    system 133
  algebra 128
  formulation 132, 142
  payoff 41
Means of production scholarly 342
Mechanization 25
Messy problems 313
Methods 13
Microchip revolution 26
Middleware 285
Miniaturized electronic circuitry 351
Minicomputers 217
Minimization stragety 454
Minimum standard of skills 258
MIS 222, 227, 458
  see also Management information
    systems
Mixed strategy equilibrium 69

Model building
  methodology 317
  nature of 325
Model structures 326, 329
Model-oriented DSS 221
Modelling 8
  activity 326
  exercise quality 328
  packages 452
  techniques 317
Morale 287, 393
Motivation 287, 393
Motivational benefits 358
MRP 198
Multi-column reporting 157
Multi-dimensional
  accounting 143
  framework 448
Multi-entry accounting 8
MULTIPLAN 127, 205
Multiple criteria decision analysis
  (MCDA) 309

Nash equilibrium 67
National Development Centre 281
National Tracing System (NTS) 278, 284
Natural
  language
    expression 168
    interface 163
  science paradigm 68
  world 66
NDPCAL 1
Neoclassical
  approach 194
  economics 60
Network models 160
Networked firm 366
Networking 277
Networks 311, 438
Neural networks 413
New Technology Agreement (NTA)
  288
NIAM model 162
NOLOT 163
Non-dissipative signalling equilibrium
  47
Non-financial
  indicators 187, 195
  performance indicators 198

Non-hearsay 239
Non-instrumental factors 5
Non-technological factors 104
Notional peer review 257
NPV techniques 192

Occurrence template 175
Off-board trading 84
Office
  automation 24, 224
  information systems 224
OLRT 106
On-line
  batch systems 103
  links 275
  technology 273
One-to-many relationship 166
One-to-one correspondence 165
Opacity 261, 321
Operational
  control 227, 353
  efficiency 289
  information 23
  level 412
  research 10
    Community Unit 301
    and computing 303
    definition 301
    future 302
    history 303
    techniques 303
Optical
  character reading (OCR) 340
  disk technology 434
Optimal estimation technique 330
Optimization 302
  models 221
Optimizing tax planning 9
ORACLE 458
Organisation
  management changes 351
  structures matrix 352
  of work 363
Organizational
  benefits 371
  change 109, 117, 271, 377, 392
  context 448
  continuity 277
  design 53
  game 328

hierarchies 451
innovations 370
structure 367
theory 53
Output 43
  requirements 134

PACTEL 281, 284
Page Report 102, 110
Paper-based systems 247
Paperless
  office 433
  systems 441
Parameter estimates 330
Pareto 40, 47
Payback periods 191
PAYE computerization 270
Payoff/utilities 72
Payroll systems 383
Pedagogic 13, 447
Perfect
  information game 67
  market 79
Performance measures 98
Personal computers 383, 432, 353
PIN 240
PIPE 89
Planning 211
  and control 218
  for decisions 8
PLATO 1
Point-of-sale 100
Police and Criminal Evidence Act 1984
    (PACEA) 235
Political dimensions 321
Portable computers 341
Power concentration 290
Principal-agent 45
Prior subjective probabilities 36
Priors of belief 63
Problem
  definition 5, 328
  solving 302, 312, 402, 408, 414
    characteristics 105
Process
  learning 460
  model 408
  transformation 94
Product
  innovation 115

liability 255
Production 22
  control 437
  decisions 44
  planning 308
  scheduling 188, 308, 357
  tasks 369
Productivity 22
  gains 370
  forecasting 327
  overstatement 421
Profitability 388
Project control mechanisms 291
PROMPT 284
Protocol analysis 409
Psychological trap 342
Public accountability 420

Qualitative
  computing 341
  data 10, 198, 311
  factors 211
  goals 257, 258, 263
  research 322
    methods 333
Quality 354
  assurance 252
  of Market Reports 87
Quantitative
  methods 7, 10
  studies 333
  techniques 301
Quill pens 159

Rapid proto-typing 308
Rational
  agents 69
  belief 60
  expectations hypothesis 66
  reconstruction of reasoning 259
Rationality assumption 34
REA
  accounting model 162, 170, 171, 180
  extended example 175
  framework 160
  transaction template 174
Real evidence 239
Real-time 105, 374
  banking 108
  technology 103

Real-world 169
  behaviour 328
Reality 164
Reasonable care 261
Reasonableness 256
Reasoning
  analytical probabilistic 264
  authentic 260
  contingent 264
  deterministic 264
  errors of 252
  logical 402
  paradigmatic 259
  process of professionals 256
Reduced instruction set computing
    (RISC) 432
Referential integrity 177
Regulation 51
Relational
  database managers 340
  systems 140
  databases 128, 375, 446, 449, 461
  models 128, 160
  table 141
Representation
  of real world 169
  of reality 164
Research
  data 343
  and development 23, 413
  methods 456
Residual probability 64
Resource management system 377
Resources 172
Reuters 85
Reverse product cycle 276
Reversing entries 139
Risk
  analysis 8
  sharing 42, 195
Rite of passage 342
Robotics 436
Role of
  accountants 445
  computers 445
  technology 22, 99
  the OR analyst 304
  workers 356
Rolling settlement system 89
Rule-based 275

Rules of thumb 402

SAEF (SEAQ Automatic Execution
    Facility) 87
Salami slicing 420
Salford Nelson Project 448
Scientific facts 336
Screening models 46
SEAQ (Stock Exchange Automated
    Quotations) 85
Search techniques 334
Securities and Investment Board 81
Security 11, 422
Semantic
    method 160
    modelling 170
Semi-structured
    decisions 227
    problems 306
    task 304
Sensitivity analysis 206
Sensor technology 26
SEPON 83
Service 276
    provider 361
Short-term emphasis 195
Shortage of specialists 283
Shorter product life-cycles 195
Signalling models 46
Simple model economy 39
Simulation 221
Single entry 129
Skills transfer 287
Small business 382
Smart cards 434
Social
    behaviour 322
    choice 336
    factors 5, 54
    world 66
Sociological factors 106
SODA 309
Software
    horizontal 386
    specialized 387
    vertical 387
    'bugs' 243
Spans of control 358
Spatial
    differentiation 376

restructuring 379
Specification of needs 390
Specifying the model 326
Speedlink 117
Spreadsheet
    auditing tools 212
    construction 211
    convention 130
    debugging tools 212
    modelling approach 207
    packages 340
Spreadsheets 5, 9, 13, 203, 323, 375,
    386, 448, 452
    large 211
SPSS 333
SQL 461
    forms 179
    statements 179
Staff
    satisfaction 276
    savings 110, 113
Staffing requirements 282
Standard costing 194
States of the world 35, 36
Statistical estimation 319
Stewardship 48
Stock
    level control 188
    market 79
Stock Exchange 80
    crash 7
Strategic
    business planning 437
    information 24
    investment 97
    level 412
    management 371, 441
    planning 96, 218
Strategy 288
Structural
    change 378
    changes in tax 276
    coherence 339
Substantive audit procedure
    429
Suggestion models 221
Super-user 454
SUPERCALC 205, 323
Supercomputers 433
SWIFT 100

System
  failure 246
  implementation 392
  security 244
Systematic errors 65
Systems 159
  accounting degree 455
  analysis 451
  auditors 441
  control and security 442
  design 13
Systems-based auditing 430

T matrix 134
Table structures 128
Tacit social assumptions 337
TALISMAN 83
Task
  automation 94
  contingencies 359
TAURUS 88
Tax
  and law 7
  credit scheme 273
Taxation 414
Teaching of accounting 445
Technical
  change 71, 99, 117
  information 23
  jargon 24
  payoff 97
  skills 271
Technocracy dangers of 5
Technological
  choice 103
  determinism 335, 337
  environment 455
  innovation 25
  knowledge 117
  somnambulism 335
Technology
  choice 109
  committees 384
  and the economy 25
  as facilitator 5
  social dimension 335
Telecommunications 21, 225, 353, 438
Text authority of 339
Thirst for new technology 115
Tolerance for ambiguity 363
Tools 13
TOPIC 85
Totality role constraint 166

TRADE (Barclay de Zoete Wedd) 87
Traditional accounting model 450
Training and development 110
Transaction
  matrix 129, 141
  messages 238
Transactions of a firm 369
Transfer of skills 290
Trial balance 138
True income figure 152
Trustre Savings Bank 99
TSB Computer Project 104
Two-column reporting 156

UK auditing practices guideline 429
UN Edifact standard 440
Uniqueness constraint 166
Universe of Discourse 162, 177
Unstructured decisions 227
UoD modelling 171
User
  creativity 208
  ownership of the problem 321
  requirements 286

Validation problem 320
Valuation efficiency 80, 90
Value
  approach 149
  theory 150
Value-added services 439
Valueline 85
Variable costs 190, 207
VATIA 407
View-based system 140
Virtual reality 437
VISICALC 204, 323
VISION 307
Visual interactive modelling 306
Vocational 447

What-if 320, 323, 328
  analyses 225
  scenarios 204
White collar crime 426
Word
  frequency analysis 334
  processing 115, 338, 354, 375, 386
Worksheets 203
Workstations 190, 432
WORM 421